INTRODUCING CRITICISM
AT THE 21st CENTURY

INTRODUCING
CRITICISM AT THE 21st CENTURY

Julian Wolfreys

EDINBURGH UNIVERSITY PRESS

© The chapters their several authors, 2002

Edinburgh University Press Ltd
22 George Square, Edinburgh

Typeset in Sabon and Gill
by Hewer Text Ltd, Edinburgh, and
printed and bound in Great Britain by
MPG Books Ltd, Bodmin, Cornwall

A CIP record for this book is
available from the British Library

ISBN 0 7486 1575 X (paperback)

The right of the contibutors to be
identified as authors of this work
has been asserted in accordance with the
Copyright, Designs and Patents Act 1988.

Michelle Boisseau's poem, 'Parchment', is
reprinted in Chapter 7 by kind permission
of the author, and the editors of *Poetry*,
where it first appeared in January 2000.

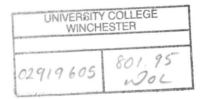

CONTENTS

MATERIALITY AND THE IMMATERIAL

ACKNOWLEDGEMENTS

I would like to thank the contributors to the present volume; I would also like to thank, both personally and on behalf of those contributors, all of our students, undergraduate and graduate, who have been asked to engage in debate over the issues which inform both our research and our teaching. Certain students and other interlocutors also deserve acknowledgement and appreciation: Alissa Fessell, Emily Garcia, Afshin Hafizi, Lessley Kynes, Jonathan Hall, Nicole LaRose, Karina Mendoza, John Ronan, Jonathan Ruiz, Naomi Weiss.

Particular colleagues in the Department of English at the University of Florida (other than those who have contributed essays to this volume) have made contributions also; thank you to Donald Ault, Pamela Gilbert, Terry Harpold, Susan Hegeman, Brandon Kershner, John Leavey, Judith Page, Stephanie Smith, Chris Snodgrass, Maureen Turim, Greg Ulmer.

Beyond these immediate circles, I would also like to thank Mark Currie, Thomas Docherty, Jonathan Dollimore, Peggy Kamuf, Sam Kimball, Jim Kincaid, Martin McQuillan, Peter Manning, J. Hillis Miller, Tom Pepper, Arkady Plotnitsky, Jean-Michel Rabaté, Ruth Robbins and Jane Stabler.

Finally, I would like to thank Jackie Jones for her continued support at EUP, as well as James Dale and Carol Macdonald.

INTRODUCTION: DEVELOPMENTS, DEBATES, DEPARTURES, DIFFERENCES, DIRECTIONS

Julian Wolfreys

INTRODUCTION? WHAT INTRODUCTION?

Any volume announcing itself as 'introducing criticism at the twenty-first century', whether directly or indirectly, immediately falls foul of its own, perhaps hubristic, project. After all, in the most basic sense the century in question can hardly be said in purely chronological terms to have got underway, let alone be near its conclusion (there might be philosophical arguments otherwise, but I cannot address those here, as interesting as these might be). The implications of a volume such as this would appear, therefore, to generate certain questions: Can the shape of criticism to come be predicted? Who would be so foolhardy? Does not the act of prediction suppose the eventual arrival of a particular form? Will there be criticism, either as such, or as we know it? Will there be universities and institutions of higher education in one hundred years' time? If there are, will there still be Departments of English and Cultural Studies or, more generally, studies in what we call the humanities? As much as such questions might sound like idle sophistry, there are very real concerns behind them. Even a cursory knowledge of the history of the development of literary studies, studies having to do with vernacular rather than 'classical' literature, will indicate a life of just over one hundred years, with cultural studies being much younger.

It has to be remarked, then, from the outset or, if at all possible, slightly before beginning, that *Introducing Criticism at the 21st Century* does not endeavour to be predictive. The present collection of essays does not attempt any form of proleptic gesture. Rather the reverse is the case, in fact, each of the essays here being in some measure, if not retrospective exactly (they are not in any straightforward sense surveys of 'where we are', or 'how we got to be here'), then *interruptive*: the various chapters of the present volume situate themselves within current aspects of critical discourse, gathering the discourses which come to inform the positions and interests under discussion as so many incisions or, to think this another way, intensities – instants of a provisional gathering of flows and forces. Each essay addresses the fluidity of various 'states of criticism' at the beginning of the century, taking into account how the different, yet occasionally overlapping critical discourses have come to assume their present identities. At the same time, however, of the thirteen essays presented here, not one is content simply to offer a disinterested survey. These are not, to use the language of speech-act theorists, extended constative utterances. Having something of the performative of them, they not only traverse their respective fields, they also transform. And more than this, the essays of this collection not only engage in discrete ways with the particular critical 'lines of flight' that come to inform their own singular articulations, they also overflow any arbitrarily imposed boundaries of a particular field of interest, in many cases touching upon implicitly or otherwise more directly addressing concerns and issues raised by other essays in this volume.

INTRODUCING INTRODUCTIONS

Consider the following definitions of 'introduction', taken from the *Oxford English Dictionary*:

1. **a.** The action of introducing; a leading or bringing in; a bringing into use or practice, bringing in in speech or writing, insertion, etc.
   b. Something introduced; a practice or thing newly brought in, etc.
   c. An inference. *Obs. rare.*
2. The action or process of leading to or preparing the way for something; that which leads on to some result; a preliminary or initiatory step or stage. *Obs.*
3. Initiation in the knowledge of a subject; instruction in rudiments, elementary teaching. *Obs.*
4. That which leads to the knowledge or understanding of something. **a.** In early use, that which initiates in a subject, a first lesson; in *pl.*, rudiments, elements (*obs.*).
   b. A preliminary explanation prefixed to or included in a book or other writing; the part of a book which leads up to the subject treated, or explains the author's design or purpose. Also, the corresponding part of a speech, lecture, etc.
   c. A text-book or treatise intended as a manual for beginners, or explaining the elementary principles of a subject.
   d. A course of study preliminary and preparatory to some special

study; matter introductory to the special study of some subject, e.g. of a book or document of the Bible.

5. **a.** The action of introducing or making known personally; *esp.* the formal presentation of one person to another, or of persons to each other, with communication of names, titles, etc.

   c. The process of becoming acquainted, or that makes one acquainted, with a thing.

6. *Mus.* A preparatory passage or movement at the beginning of a piece of music.

There is, clearly, more than one 'introduction'. We appear to have a family of introductions, allowing for the moment the figure of the family as the appropriate collective noun for introductions, while still allowing for the fact that difference, as much as any resemblance, is vital in the production of any identity or meaning. Each shares elements in common, while some are more familiar than others; certain of these definitions alert us to a fall into disuse. In what ways do these determinations of the notion of introduction and the introductory apply to *Introducing Criticism at the 21st Century?* In what manner, if at all, are they 'appropriate'? Can they be appropriated, is it proper to do so? Or is it improper to assume that an 'introduction' can ever truly be so, whether in some propaedeutic or apodictic fashion?

There are six principal definitions for introduction, and, in each of these, further subdivisions for the purpose of determination. Introduction is introduced, but never simply for the first time. There is something excessive at work in the very idea of the introductory, so much so in fact, that the dictionary feels the need to keep reintroducing it, as though it somehow knew that the very work of introduction will always and in some fashion overflow its own boundaries, that it will disseminate itself in excess of the very contours assumed for the so-called concept that goes by the name of introduction. Introduction exceeds its parameters in the very act of speaking of itself. Despite the desire to remain constant in its constative constitution – there's that speech-act theory creeping in again – there appears to be some kind of disruptive performative at work here. Every time introduction is introduced, something different, some sign of difference incommensurable with or irreducible to the confines of the introductory, takes place in the very gesture of preamble or overture. This, I would contend, is precisely what takes place, again and again, in each of the chapters presented here. Each chapter is supposedly 'introductory' in its own right, and yet each disrupts the introductory in its critical interventions, its epistemological interests. In doing so, the propaedeutic function of the 'introduction' is left in ruins.

Or, rather, say that criticism which is transformative does not so much point out, desire or attempt to bring about the ruination of any pedagogical work grounded in the belief of preliminary work, often, in the case of criticism, having to do with methods or theories which, once learnt, can then be put into practice;

instead, the kind of criticism envisioned in this volume makes it possible to understand how the imperative towards knowing the fundamentals that is implied in both the general conceptualization of 'introduction' and in the specific institutional drive to separate the introductory from the supposedly more 'advanced' work is always, in its very processes, already in ruins. Like the phenomenon which becomes available to our view through a consideration of the nature of multiple definitions concerning 'introduction', *Introducing Criticism at the 21st Century* stresses the impossibility of any simple introduction; it keeps 'introducing' and, in doing so, keeps on exceeding introduction, recognizing as it does that the notion of introduction is fallacious, to the extent that no entry onto a subject can ever be *for the first time*. No beginning gesture ever takes place which does not imply or otherwise orientate itself with regard to other forms of knowledge. Even a 'rudimentary teaching' operates through the possibility of relation and orientation, the principle being that something new can be shown only because the 'new' can be explained with reference to something not new. Every introduction fails, therefore, inasmuch as it is impossible to state first principles, and this failure is the sign not so much of what is lacking as it is of that excess within the introductory of which I have already spoken.

ORIENTATIONS

Introducing Criticism at the 21st Century is organized around five themes or motifs: *identities, dialogues, space and place, critical voices, materiality and the immaterial.* As will be understood immediately, none of these 'orientations' of the act of criticism implies methodologies, approaches, schools of thought. Instead, each operates, in a more or less oblique way, by naming certain interests of criticism having emerged in recent years, and which continue to provide different epistemological foci in the humanities, largely as a result of the increasingly interdisciplinary nature of critical and cultural studies.

The first three chapters address the question of how our identities are understood, how they are constructed, and how they are projected, both by ourselves and by others. Each of the chapters stresses how manifestations of identity, often imposed from without, either strive to determine particular social and cultural groups, frequently in negative or limiting ways, or alternatively, in being engaged from within those groups in a self-reflexive fashion, come to affirm alternative ideologies of identity. Acts of criticism and critical articulation offer ways of reading such alternative affirmations.

Sudesh Mishra explores how diaspora criticism, a genre of theoretical writing, marks itself off as a distinct domain by positing, circumscribing and specifying an object called 'diaspora'. Using the experiences of classical diasporic groups (Jews and Armenians) as a point of departure, diasporists, Mishra argues, attempt to account for the mass dispersal of various ethnic collectivities in the time of (late) modernity. The assumption is that transnational capital generates hypermobile populations that can be clearly distinguished from other types of social formations. Emphasis is placed on hybrid identity formations, multiple identifications and double consciousness – in short, forms of subjectivity and subject constitution that define and describe such translocated clusters. Diasporic art, music, film, literature, architecture, clothing and cuisine are seen to furnish symptoms of this peculiar way of being and belonging.

Sarah Gamble's chapter looks at the rapidly expanding field of gender and transgender studies, beginning with Judith Butler's assertion that gender is not innate but 'performed' upon the surface of the body. It then moves on to the writings of transgender theorists such as Kate Bornstein and Ricki Ann Wilchins, who base their arguments on the idea that gender is a radically unstable category dependent upon personal experience. The chapter ends with an analysis of Angela Carter's novel *The Passion of New Eve*, a futuristic fable in which no gendered body is ever what it appears to be.

In their chapter, Tace Hedrick and Debra Walker King emphasize the work of women of color who seek to use the notion of love, and of mutual care, as epistemological frameworks designed to produce a 'knowledge' from which both a critical oeuvre and an activism can emerge. The chapter offers critiques of the value of current critical and analytical work produced by Black, Latina and Chicana feminist critics, and discusses the cultural activism of performers like Lil' Kim and Jennifer Lopez, aided by the critical work of writers such as bell hooks. Hedrick and King's purpose is to address current trends in pop culture in an attempt to reinvest representational analysis with notions of self-love and mutual care. The authors suggest that current manipulations of sexuality fail to do the work of recuperation and redefinition that they are intended to achieve. They suggest, instead, that the liberating movements of sexual healing enacted as loving confrontations with the self, the other and the past, provide a place for current constructions of social, personal and private realities to be successfully reformulated.

The second part of this volume concerns itself with dialogues – dialogues between literary and cultural criticism and other discourses and disciplines. Particularly, scientific, philosophical and psychoanalytic discourses are witnessed in communication with literary and cultural studies, as critics seek to explore what literature and textuality in general have always addressed, but which has remained relatively unexplored until recently. The question of dialogue is engaged, therefore, from the perspective of the critical act, in order to open the work of reading beyond its traditional confines.

Stuart Sim's chapter outlines the major features of chaos and complexity, scientific theories which challenge some of our most deeply held notions about the nature of reality. In particular, chaos and complexity problematize the notion of identity, a pressing concern of recent critical and cultural theory, as well as a major theme of authors from the early days of the novel to the present. Laurence Sterne's *Tristram Shandy* and Jeanette Winterson's *Gut Symmetries*, both narratives which self-consciously engage with the problem of identity in terms of the scientific theories of their time, are then analysed, to demonstrate that chaos and complexity inform both narrative and critical practice.

Questions about ethics continue to exert a significant influence upon the direction of contemporary literary criticism, as Kenneth Womack's contribution makes clear. In addition to addressing particularly striking aspects in continental philosophy's interest in matters of ethics alongside North American manifestations of ethical criticism, Womack examines the revealing differences that exist between each paradigm's approach to the ethical nature of human interrelationships. Drawing upon exemplary readings of George Eliot's *Silas Marner* and Spike Jonze's *Being John Malkovich*, this chapter illustrates each movement's modes of ethical critique.

Julian Wolfreys' chapter also speaks to ethical concerns in relation to the question of reading, but it does so specifically to reflect on an ethics of reading in the wake of what a number of critics define as an age of trauma: the twentieth century. The chapter begins by asking what the responsibility of critical reading is, and what might be understood as the relation between literature and acts of bearing witness in response to traumatic events and its aftershocks. Engaging in dialogues with psychoanalysis, philosophically inflected debates concerning responsibility and testimony, the representation of history, and the question of the efficacy of history as a narrative discourse in the face of traumatic and catastrophic events, the chapter considers the necessity and the obligation of reading to exceed any formal calculation or programme of analysis, in order to respond appropriately to the idea that all literature is an act of bearing witness.

The chapters gathered under the motif of *space and place* all concern themselves with the development of critical interventions concerned with the identities of the locations we inhabit, and which, in turn, determine who we think we are.

Kate Rigby considers the burgeoning new area of 'ecocriticism' as entailing a remembering and revaluing of the earth in the context of global ecological imperilment. She argues that ecocriticism emphasizes the indebtedness of human culture to the more-than-human natural world, while also exploring critically the constructions of 'nature' that are frequently embedded in literary, philosophical and religious texts and traditions, noting that these views of 'nature' have implications for the treatment of subordinate humans as well as for the earth. She then proceeds to show how ecocriticism challenges earlier human-centred methods of literary and cultural analysis, practices of canon-formation, and understandings of language and textuality, before concluding with a model reading of Wordsworth's *Home at Grasmere*.

Phillip Wegner's chapter maps out what he terms the spatial turn in contemporary literary and cultural criticism. Beginning in the latter part of the 1960s and the early 1970s, thinkers from a number of different disciplines began to call into question dominant assumptions about space and spatiality that had come to prevail in the histories of western modernity. Against such presuppositions, the work of these diverse thinkers shows in a stunning variety of ways how space itself is both a production, shaped through a diverse range of social processes and human interventions, and a force that, in turn, influences, directs and delimits possibilities of action and ways of human being in the world. This new attention to the productions of space has entered into literary studies from a number of different directions: from Marxism and critical theory, colonial and postcolonial studies, feminism and gender studies, popular culture and genre studies, and a rich and growing conversation with work being done in a broad range of other disciplines. At the same time, such a spatial turn calls into question the very constitution of the literary canon, as it helps the reader become more sensitive to the different kinds of work that is performed by various literary genres, modes and other forms of textuality. Finally, Wegner suggests that the examination of space and spatiality more generally converges with the burgeoning interest in the issue of 'globalization': for it is here that we can develop the tools that will enable us to 'think' a new kind of global cultural and social reality, as well as our place within it. Wegner concludes the chapter with an exploration of the spatial issues raised by Joseph Conrad's novel, *Lord Jim*.

Stacy Gillis' chapter provides a broad exploration of the auspices of the cybersubject and the nascent field of cybercriticism. Informed by a history of the computer, a study of cyberfiction and the problematics of the posthuman 'body' (again, a consideration of how one's identity is constituted today), it emphasizes the relevance of such terms as hypertext, technopoly and cybercritic to an analysis of contemporary culture. In doing so, it offers a critique of the formation of identity which has to become rewritten and reread, given the transformation of the politics of subjectivity brought about by the shift from the topoi of the land and the urban, as considered in the previous two essays, to the utopos of both virtual space and the 'place without place' of hypertextuality.

The fourth section of *Introducing Criticism at the 21st Century, critical voices*, concerns analytical reorientations having to do with dialogues between criticism and philosophy. While this extends in part the explorations of Chapters 4, 5 and 6, in the second part of the book, *dialogues*, the emphasis in the chapters by Colebrook and Young is on the engagement between critical language and the work of two philosophers in particular, Gilles Deleuze and Emmanuel Levinas. While literary and cultural criticism has been responding directly for some years now to a number of voices outside the discipline of literary and cultural study, it is arguably the case that Deleuze and Levinas offer what are among the most radical epistemological challenges presented to thought.

Claire Colebrook looks at the criticism of the whole notion of theory, through the work of Gilles Deleuze. Deleuze's philosophy was not committed to providing a metaperspective from which we might judge literature, Colebrook argues. Rather, he thought of philosophy as a different and distinct power which might encounter other powers, such as literature. The result of such an encounter, this chapter contends, would not be a 'reading' or 'interpretation' but an act of thought and a way of seeing the text and the world anew.

In 'Levinas and Criticism' Fredrick Young suggests that the crucial problem to be addressed after Levinas is that of relation. Traditional criticism is (unwittingly?) predicated on ontological and philosophical notions of representation (mimesis). Young sees Levinas's ethical project, based on a performative disruption of philosophy and ontology, as a radical way of refiguring literary criticism – in a broad sense, concerns which Levinas shares with thinkers such as Blanchot, Derrida and Cixous. What is at stake, after Levinas, is the question of how to think about the 'literary' when there is no literary object per se. In other words, as the chapters argues, the very relation that would set up a literary object (book) is already part and parcel of philosophical duality or a binary system of subject/object. This problematizing notion is worked out by Young in a sketched reading of Tarkovsky's film *The Sacrifice*.

The final two chapters in the collection continue the insistence on transforming the ways in which we think about matters of reading and criticism, and the epistemological bases of such acts. Organized around the instability of the conceptualization of materiality and immateriality, the chapters by David Punter and Tom Cohen challenge any normative critical modality reliant on intertwined notions of 'literature', 'materialism' and 'history'.

In 'Spectral Criticism', David Punter addresses the increasingly prominent critical issues of spectrality and the phantom. He assesses the paradoxical presence of these features in the thought and writing of Freud, Derrida and Abraham and Torok, and suggests that much contemporary criticism is now explicitly or implicitly based on the spectrality of literature, on the curious mix of presence and absence of which the literary is composed. He explores some aspects of Hamlet in a spectral light, while demonstrating that in the end, for spectral criticism, even the notion of the text itself is phantasmal, fading and shading away as it does into its own afterlife, its own echoes, its own ambiguous status as memory and recapitulation.

In his chapters, Tom Cohen explores the value and legacy, today, of what has been termed 'materialistic' criticism in the past, and finds that the post-humanist digital age requires a dematerialization – a 'spectralization' perhaps in the light of David Punter's essay – or dispersal among networks of signification, for any rescue of the term in the coming horizons. Rather than the promise of a referential ground, the term today, incorporating its others and opposites, can be accessed through inscription, the trace, and a performative and discontinuous concept of the historical event.

All good reading should be critical; not suspicious of its subject, but engaged and responsible. No reading can ever truly be called such unless it manifests both an openness to that which is to be read and a respect for the singularity of that other. At the same time, it has to be said that, coming to terms with openness and obligation, reading also has to recognize its own role as being defined through continual reorientation and readjustment of its procedures, without allowing those procedures to ossify into protocols, mere programmed excuses for limiting the act of reading, or, worse still, not reading at all and avoiding reading in the name of methodology, ideology or institutionalized demand. In the end, as the chapters in this collection demonstrate, all criticism comes down to reading. But that 'in the end' is no ending at all, only the endless demand placed on reading. There can be no introduction to reading, but all reading can do is to reintroduce itself to the ways in which reading must take place, if it is to take place at all. If *Introducing Criticism at the 21st Century* can be said to introduce anything at all (and even now, at the end of this introduction, I remain uncertain as to what to think about this), it is to introduce the ends of criticism as the beginning – again – of reading.

IDENTITIES

CHAPTER

I

DIASPORA CRITICISM

Sudesh Mishra

LOCATING DIASPORAS

In attempting to set itself up as 'a genre of theoretical writing' (Frow, 1997, 15), diaspora criticism takes as its object a thing called 'diaspora'. The viability of the critical genre, it follows, rests on defining and delimiting the object of its inquiry. This act of positing a new critical site through the inscribing of parameters is, paradoxically, at odds with the site-violating implications of its primary signifier or object, since *diaspeir* is Greek for 'scattering' *(speir)* and was originally employed to explain the botanical phenomenon of seed dispersal. In any event, this chapter is concerned with diaspora criticism's attempt to mark itself off as a new theoretical domain by targeting an object called 'diaspora', an enterprise in which the present writer is wryly implicated. What it says or avoids saying about this object creates (after Foucault) the condition for the emergence, delimitation and specification of the domain itself. So, to begin with the obvious question, what is this thing called 'diaspora'?

One of the founding editors of the multidisciplinary journal *Diaspora* (inaugural issue, 1991), Khachig Tölölyan uses the term to designate specific 'social formations' that are 'exemplary communities of the transnational moment' (Tölölyan, 1991, 5). By limiting himself to the transnational temporality, Tölölyan means to draw a distinction between the pre-modern or classical 'ethnodiasporas' – Jews, Greeks and Armenians – and the large-scale dispersal of significant ethnic clusters, or what Arjun Appadurai terms 'ethnoscapes' (Appadurai, cit. Roberts, 1992, 234), witnessed in the time of advanced capital. While murmurs of protest have been raised in various quarters concerning the modern application of an ancient category,[1] scholars in the field have largely endorsed this annexation. Iain Chambers, for instance, claims that the 'chronicles of diasporas – those of the black Atlantic, of metropolitan Jewry, of mass rural displacement – constitute the ground swell of modernity' (Chambers, 1994, 16). While this assertion correctly reinserts Jews into the narrative of modern diasporas, Chambers' timescale is too sweeping for any meaningful discussion of the specific historical causality of such social formations. Vijay Mishra, on the other hand, conceives of diasporic formations as 'the exemplary condition of late modernity' (Mishra, 1996, 426), although his account of the labour migrants of indenture directs us to an earlier modernity driven by colonially administered plantation capital. Mishra argues that the practice of issuing emigration passes facilitated the peasant labourers' entry into 'the regulative history of the Empire' (Mishra, 1996, 429), but, somewhat oddly, declines to dwell on the supplementary function of the variant modernity articulated by the same subjects in their formulation of *girmit,* a term collectively assigned to the atemporal ontology of suffering, hardship and deceit in the plantations. The history of modernity as rendered by the *girmityas,* that is to say by those who endured *girmit,* departs significantly from the archives of officialdom. Several years before Mishra, Paul Gilroy had written a groundbreaking study on a different diasporic formation of classical modernity in his book, *The Black Atlantic: Double Consciousness and Modernity.* In this study, Gilroy chronicles the subaltern history of the 'black Atlantic' – a phrase he coins to describe the intersecting threads (of politics, music and memory, for instance) linking the deterritorialized descendants of plantation slavery – that discontinuously haunts and radically infects *as well as* inflects the unfinished project of modernity. Gilroy's main assertion is that 'commercially deported'[2] blacks and their descendants were not only victims of modernity, but also producers of the post-middle passage dimensions of Euro-American culture and history (Gilroy, 1993). Sorting through the general confusion regarding periodization, it seems that there are three distinct historical moments corresponding to the emergence of diasporic social formations: the classical or pre-modern, the (early) modern and the late (post) modern.

While diasporists have stressed the last of these moments to record the types of socio-economic pressures that have led to the emergence of diasporas of late modernity, the mapping of this different historical vector has occurred in relation to schema drawn from earlier diasporic social formations motivated by their specific historical circumstances. Mishra's account of the 'new' border diaspora in his Indian example is made possible, for instance, by his articulation of the differential/definitional relations between it and the 'old' exclusivist diasporas of indentured labour that 'share many of the characteristics of the so-called ideal type of the Jewish diaspora' (Mishra, 1996, 427). Although one can see the historical disjuncture that sustains Mishra's distinction, the exact kinship between the exclusivist diaspora and plantation capital as a subspecies of political economy, or the connection between the border diaspora and late modernity, remains partially developed. The attempt by diasporists to tease out the complications that pervade the relationships between diasporic social formations on the historical horizon, that is to say the diachronic horizon in which the various diasporas come into being, and the synchronic links (or discontinuities) perceived in the triadic interaction among *social formations,* their *cultural production* and the *brute socio-economic processes* that underpin them, often culminates in theoretical confusion. Furthermore, there is a trend among diasporists to adopt a happy reflective model when discussing the above three items as they jostle on the synchronic scale. Here the assumption is that transnational economics encourages the transnationalization of certain social formations *and* their cultural productions. Opposed to this is Appadurai's identification of 'the fundamental disjunctures between economy, culture and politics' (Appadurai, cit. Roberts, 1992, 233) in the global system, although this too is problematic if it licenses popular diasporists to engage with one of the categories in comfortable isolation from the rest. An added pitfall is that very few diasporists undertake to investigate the actual workings of transnational or what economist Samir Amin calls 'delinked capital' (1997, 1). Are we really in the middle of a metamorphic stage in the history of capital? Has post-Fordist speculative capital based on market predictions and exchange rates mechanisms – the spectral economy – finally replaced the humdrum systems of surplus value production and accumulation? Is it true that floating capital no longer relies on classically anchored modes of production for its daily proliferation? Has the information age indeed brought with it a new mode of production or does it generate (technological) effects or 'mediascapes' (after Appadurai) that conceal the old dialectic of value production?[3] Clearly the domains of material production are no longer nationally based (German cars manufactured in India, Australian electric lamps made in China), but should this new arrangement be taken to intimate a seismic shift in capital's structure or just an operational one? Is transnational or global capital, in other words, merely another way of describing a new strategy for the old game of surplus value acquisition, with the difference that *selected* groups from the ex-colonies have penetrated, possibly for the first time in the scheme of modernity, *at all levels but in different degrees* the hierarchy of social relations set up by the bourgeois political economy? When was capital, in any event, not transnational if value is found, in one form or another, in every society?

When not dodging such base-level questions, most diasporists prefer to go along with the idea that 'the transnationalization of capitalism' involves 'the breakdown of national economies, and the creation of a more interconnected world economic system' (Jusdanis, 1996, 141), but the statistical data needed to support this claim is typically absent. It could be argued, for instance, that workers from Kerala who flock to the Gulf States are lured there by auxiliary industries that rely on a relatively primitive mode of production (although the 'means' employed are certainly advanced), namely the extraction of crude mineral oil from the bowels of the earth; it could also be argued that the 80,000 Indo-Fijians who left Fiji after the events of 1987 and 2000 did so as the scapegoats of a belated indigenous nationalism rather than as willing subjects of a hypermobile capital; and, finally, as Milton J. Esman shows, 'large-scale labor migration', whether documented or undocumented, may be directly induced by vulgar demographics inasmuch as '[h]igh-income and growing economies', due to low birthrates, 'have a compelling need for labor' whereas '[l]ow-income economies with high rates of population growth generate large and chronic labor surpluses' (Esman, 1992, 3). All too hastily, then, the transnational moment is invoked by diasporists as a mantra to prepare the ground for the engendering of 'models' that identify the characteristics of one or another diasporic social formation or for expatiating on the hybrid texture of diasporic aesthetic productions. This lack of rigorous engagement with the inner workings of late capital is what makes diaspora criticism a genre of theoretical writing rather than an economically informed analysis of such social formations. In short, then, diaspora criticism is concerned with the social and aesthetic effects of transnational or global capital which it assumes as a condition of late modernity when it might be a condition of late capitalist ideology *about* economics. The point is that by treating the global economy as a 'given' rather than as a site for in-depth investigation, the implied links between diasporic social formations and the transnational moment are based on, at best, appearance and, at worst, conjecture. Having said that, it is necessary to assess the 'coming into being' of diaspora criticism in relation to the discursive (literary, sociological, historical, philosophical, psychological and so on) apparatuses it deploys around what it conceives of as unique types of social formations engendering specific kinds of cultural and aesthetic products.

A common strategy among diasporists is to classify diasporic social formations by (1) identifying new structures of *being* (identity) of an uprooted ethnic collectivity as it oscillates between homeland (the absent *topos*) and hostland (the present *topos*), (2) by tabulating a set of defining *characteristics* of this collectivity and (3) by alluding to some kind of departure manifested on the plane of *consciousness,* as reified in memory. Diasporists also tend to draw on the cultural productions (aesthetic, musical, electronic, etc.) of such social formations to back up their assertions. Sometimes, as I've pointed out earlier, this leads to an oversimplification of the entangled relationship that actually exists between a social formation and its cultural productions. Of all the models proposed by diasporists, William Safran's enumeration of six characteristics for defining and delimiting a diasporic formation has stimulated the most debate on the subject. Concerned that 'diaspora' is used too freely 'as a metaphoric designation for several categories of people – expatriates, expellees, political refugees, alien residents, immigrants, and ethnic and racial minorities *tout court*', Safran suggests pinning it down '[l]est the term lose all meaning' (Safran, 1991, 83). Citing Walker Connor's broad-brush definition of diaspora as 'that segment of a people living outside the homeland', Safran adds that members of this 'expatriate minority community' must share 'the following characteristics':

> 1) they, or their ancestors, have been dispersed from a specific original 'center' to two or more 'peripheral', or foreign, regions; 2) they retain a

collective memory, vision, or myth about their original homeland – its physical location, history, and achievements; 3) they believe that they are not – and perhaps cannot be – fully accepted by their host society and therefore feel partly alienated and insulated from it; 4) they regard their ancestral homeland as their true, ideal home and as the place to which they or their descendants would (or should) eventually return – when conditions are appropriate; 5) they believe that they should, collectively, be committed to the maintenance or restoration of their original homeland and to its safety and prosperity; and 6) they continue to relate, personally or vicariously, to that homeland in one way or another, and their ethnocommunal consciousness and solidarity are importantly defined by the existence of such a relationship. (Safran, 1991, 83–4)

Scholars have reacted diversely to this schema, but all responses have served to promote, in one form or another, the accretion of discursive matter around the term 'diaspora'. Robin Cohen, for one, contends that Safran needlessly belabours the issue of a diaspora's relationship to the homeland, thereby downplaying 'the nature of the diasporic group in its countries of exile'. He also feels the need to supplement Safran's list by adding the following items (and here I adduce the pivotal ones): (1) 'the memory of a single traumatic event' that sustains the diaspora in the aftermath of dispersal; (2) the dream harboured by some diasporas to actively *create* a spatial homeland out of an imagined one, as is the case with Sikhs and Kurds; and (3) the inclusion of those diasporas 'that scatter for aggressive or voluntarist reasons', such as colonial settlers and traders, distinguishable from the 'victim' diasporas of slavery and genocide and the 'labour' diasporas of colonial plantation economy (Cohen, 1997, 22–5). Curiously, neither Safran nor Cohen feel the need to critically reflect on the dangers of representing model diasporas as class-neutral, gender-neutral and generation-neutral ethnic collectivities that uncritically project homelands and hostlands as homogeneous territorial entities. Too much emphasis is also placed on the diaspora's collective agency vis-à-vis homeland and hostland. In ascribing to the diaspora this will-to-self-definition ('they retain', 'they believe', 'they regard', 'they . . . relate'), Safran gives short shrift to a whole host of external factors, both 'here' (hostland) and 'there' (homeland), which may nurture the necessary conditions for the type of interpellation he describes. Discussing the fate of Turkish guest workers in Germany, Esman affords us one example of these 'external factors' that powerfully impress on, and to a large measure determine, the psychological constitution of such (quasi)-diasporic formations:

In an exercise of calculated self-deception, the political elites of Germany have cultivated the myth of return, the comforting illusion that resident foreign workers and their families will one day return to their country of origin. The myth asserts that, having benefited economically from their presence, Germany will one day again be ethnically pure . . . The Turkish government has been an ally in perpetuating this myth, because it clings to the policy of *ius sanguinis,* that all persons of Turkish blood must remain forever Turkish, and rejects categorically the notion that Turks in Germany should be offered the option of German citizenship. A venal reenforcement of such Turkish nationalism is its government's recognition that more than half of Turkey's foreign exchange is earned by remittances from its nationals working abroad. (Esman, 1992, 20–1)

Here the German and Turkish nation-states insert quasi-diasporic worker-subjects into ideologies of provisional residence and eventual return for mutually self-serving reasons; it is reasonable to suppose that the agency of the worker-subject is partially determined by such extra-subjective processes of interpellation.

In his influential article entitled 'Diasporas', James Clifford takes issue with the topographic certitudes regarding the homeland that inform Safran's conception of the social and psychological attributes that define diasporic identity and consciousness. Declaring that 'there is little room in . . . [Safran's] definition for the principled *ambivalence* about physical return and attachment to land which has characterized much Jewish diasporic experience', Clifford makes the point that 'multi-locale diasporas are not necessarily defined by a specific geopolitical boundary' (Clifford, 1994, 304–5). Arguing against teleologies of origin and return, he refers to Gilroy's formulation of an Afro-Caribbean–British–American or black Atlantic network where Africa is no longer the primary referent and to S. D. Gotein's account of the medieval *geniza* world (linking the Mediterranean countries, North Africa, Arabia and coastal India) in which commerce, travel, familial, cultural and communication networks are determined by the 'lateral axes' of dissemination rather than by bipolar concepts of origin and return, symbolic or otherwise (Clifford, 1994, 315–27). Although Clifford does not put it in such terms, his remarks on the *geniza* world end up describing the extensive 'affiliational structures' (Shapiro, 2000, 80) that governed ancient concepts of citizenship. In any case, his central argument seems to be that, as border communities, diasporas are not necessarily attached to or detached from macrocosmic centres of homeland and hostland; they may, as is illustrated by his *geniza* world example, create microcosmic alliances by attending to 'cultural forms, kinship relations [and] business circuits' or by attaching themselves to religious institutions and cities (Clifford, 1994, 305).

Admittedly there is much merit in Clifford's resistance to Safran's emphasis on solid and symbolic bipolar topographies and his encouragement of the border (decentred, lateral) dimensions to the diaspora experience (though one could justifiably argue that the border itself is a centring motif in his scheme);[4] even so, his paradigm departs only marginally from Safran's in its persistent focus on identity formations, identifications, defining features and distinctive consciousness, in short, subjectivity and subject constitution. Clifford refers more than once to 'transregional identities' when discussing Roger Rouse's observations about spatially disaggregated Aguilillans who maintain filiations through 'telephone circuits'; he talks at length about 'diaspora consciousness' as it is negatively and positively constituted – negatively, he asserts, 'through discrimination and exclusion' and 'positively through identifications with world historical cultural/political forces such as "Africa" or "China" ' (Clifford, 1994, 311–12). One suspects that the category of 'world historical cultural/political forces' is not altogether dissimilar to Safran's notion of symbolic homelands that are, whether one admits it or not, politically and culturally constituted mythic points of reference. Clifford remarks that identifications when hitched to 'a negative experience of racial and economic marginalization can . . . lead to new coalitions: one thinks of Maghrebi diasporic consciousness uniting Algerians, Moroccans, and Tunisians living in France, where a common history of colonial and neocolonial exploitation contributes to new solidarities' (Clifford, 1994, 312). Such coalitional solidarity based on short-term identifications may – to give another example of this type of empathetic transference – periodically unite the Australia-based descendants of Indo-Fijian 'coolies' with the progeny of indentured or blackbirded 'Kanaks' shipped to the sugarcane plantations of Queensland in the nineteenth century. In essence, then, Clifford does not depart substantively from the practice of accounting for group subjectivities of diasporic social formations, albeit he does make a significant intervention by breaking away from territorially and ethnically based 'models'. Instead, he commends (after Gilroy) the anti-teleological 'history of displacement, suffering, adaptation, or resistance' (Clifford, 1994, 306) as the target *topos* for the inscription of definitional possibilities about diasporic peoples. What this means in practice is that the geopolitical entities of homeland and hostland fade as referential points in the analysis of diasporic formations. In brief, the conceptual framework need not extend beyond the dynamic situational narratives of dispersal itself. So it turns out that a history of roots predicated on purist cartographies of the homeland is jettisoned in favour of a history of routes, predicated on itineraries of travel, hybrid exchanges and shifting localities. And while the border paradigm may at times resemble a postmodern hyphen adrift from its prefix and its suffix, it has the virtue of stimulating debate on the unstable relationship between classically autocentred and ideologically homogenized nation-states and ethnocommunities whose affiliations and allegiances may be territorially as well as culturally disaggregated.

In fact, the question of the bourgeois nation-state[5] and its troubled relations with diasporic groups and practices, frequently seen as symptomatic of global capital, has preoccupied many diasporists. The debate seems to focus on the *perceived* divergence between the ideology that undergirds the nation-state and the ideology disabusing – and this need not be, and seldom is, a deliberate act – presence and practices of diasporic subjects and formations.[6] So what is this ideology propping up the bourgeois nation-state? Drawing on the work of Jürgen Habermas, Michael Shapiro writes that '[t]he primary understanding of the modern "nation" segment of the nation-state is that a nation embodies a coherent culture, united on the basis of shared descent or, at least, incorporating a "people" with a historically stable coherence'. Since this is so transparently a myth, 'the symbolic maintenance of the nation-state requires a management of historical narratives as well as territorial space' (Shapiro, 2000, 81). It is this activity of symbolic maintenance that renders the nation-state an 'imagined political community' (Anderson, 1991, 6). Indeed citizen-subjects receive a 'double coding' in that 'citizenship is located both in a legal, territorial entity, which is associated with the privileges of sovereignty and the rights of individuals, and in a cultural community where it is associated with a history of shared ethnic and social characteristics' (Shapiro, 2000, 81). Diasporic groups are inserted schizophrenically into this ideological scheme, by integrationist as well as pluralist nation-states. As documented citizen-subjects of the nation-state, diasporic clusters may enjoy the abstract rights and privileges of citizenship manifested in a juridical or constitutional sense. Since, however, they may not share a common cultural ground with the hegemonic community whose particular values and goals are, at least in an ideological way, mediated by the nation-state and subtly incorporated into its laws, the right to culture-specific practices may be denied them. Even a pluralist nation-state will tolerate only those practices that do not directly collide with the universal rights abstracted from the belief systems, historical struggles, discursive practices and economic ambitions of the foundational community. If a British-Pakistani subject were to wed more than one wife as is possible under Islamic practices, his action would be in direct violation of British marriage laws based on the monogamous structures of its 'mythic' foundational community. It would also be claimed that the practice of polygamy is an anachronism in the time of modernity and violates the individual rights of women.

If they are documented resident-subjects (not citizens) of the nation-state, diasporic constituents may find certain rights and privileges withheld from them. Although required by law to pay taxes that make the business of governing possible, they may not be allowed by this same law, as is clearly evident in the Australian case, to participate in national elections or, if newly arrived, to qualify for social welfare benefits. Of course diasporic subjects may exercise the option of declining the right to citizenship (as is the case with a significant number of North Africans living in France),[7] thereby foregoing the entitlements extended to them by the hostland for the (symbolic, spiritual, nostalgic or plainly material) entitlements of the homeland. Falling outside the purview of legally sanctioned subjects of the nation-state, undocumented diasporic subjects are the least happy of the three categories delineated above. Even when they succeed in surmounting the deadly obstacles involved in crossing borders (only in 2000 several Chinese 'illegals' suffocated to death in the hold of a truck that had crossed the English Channel on a ferry bound for Dover), the great majority live 'underground' lives in the bourgeois nation-state and earn low (unofficial) wages in manual work or service (including sex) industries. Holston and Appadurai claim that this is the result of a trade-off between nation-states that are out to attract resources and global economic institutions that are on the lookout for scab labour. This pact is manifested in new legal regimes designed to render 'significant segments of the transnational low-income labor force illegal by using the system of national boundaries to criminalize the immigrants . . . [that the nation-state] attracts for low-wage work' (Holston and Appadurai, 1996, 199). Illegality, according to this perspective, is a tactic used by the nation-state in complicity with itinerant capital to produce a docile, non-unionized labour force that may be exploited through renewed threats of deportation. Not able to impose direct taxes on this underground labour force, the nation-state will frequently levy consumer taxes (VAT and GST) on goods essential for its subsistence.

Contemplating the tricky issue of the 'nexus-cum-rupture' between 'incompletely nationalized' (Appadurai, cit. Chuh, 1996, 93) diasporic populations and nation-states, Vijay Mishra attempts to come up with a theory of diasporic subjectivity (although he restricts his analysis to the citizen-subject type) by attending to what he calls 'the semantics of the hyphen' (Mishra, 1996, 433). He builds his theory on the understanding that the subject's unresolved positionality in relation to the homeland and hostland creates a severed/sutured identity that may be conceived of as 'the third time-space' (Lavie and Swedenburg, 1996, 16):

> Within a nation-state citizens are always unhyphenated, that is, if we are to believe what our passports say about us. In actual practice the pure, unhyphenated generic category is only applicable to those citizens whose bodies signify an unproblematic identity of selves with nations. For those of us who are outside of this identity politics, whose corporealities fissure the logic of unproblematic identification, plural/multicultural societies have constructed the impure genre of the hyphenated subject. (Mishra, 1996, 433)

Mishra cites Slavoj Žižek to justify his remark about the 'unproblematic identification' of citizens who require 'no particular verification of this "Thing" called "Nation". For this group the "nation" simply *is* (beyond any kind of symbolization)' (Mishra, 1996, 423). This Lacanian loss of selfhood through absorption into the imaginary realm of the nation is a condition available only to those citizens that perceive themselves as belonging to the foundational community ruled by the 'idea of "homogeneous, empty time"' (Anderson, 1991, 24) and not to those groups that bear in body (clothing, speech, culinary habits, etc.) and in mind (corporeally 'here' but neurologically 'elsewhere') the markers of difference, creating the symbolic fracture. A theoretical difficulty arises from the above argument. How is it possible for the foundational citizen to achieve an imaginary identification with the nation thing in the space of the diasporic other without experiencing a rupture from the homogeneous, empty time of the imaginary? To put it differently: if the other is here in the same 'imaginary' space that I inhabit, then where am I? (The very act of posing this question signals a loss of the imaginary order.) Am I then outside the imaginary space and so in the space of the heterogeneous, brimming time of the symbolic? Surely this is the abiding contradiction of nationalistic avowals of racial homogeneity – that it must be predicated on its loss. Stumbling upon the Patels at their dinner in the family-run motel, the narrator of Bharati Mukherjee's 'Loose Ends', a hitman yearning for a mythically pure America, maliciously admits to the loss of this imaginary order: 'They look at me. A bunch of aliens and they stare like I'm the freak' (Mukherjee, 1988, 52).

One of the persistent dilemmas confronting diaspora criticism is how to configure diasporic subjectivity as hybrid, liminal, border and hyphenated without recourse to the strategy of consigning non-diasporic groups to imaginary domains of non-liminality, non-hybridity, non-heterogeneity and so on. Then again, if non-diasporic subjects are capable of the type of diasporization I have described, then where does this leave the diasporic subject or, for that matter, the whole enterprise of diaspora criticism? By ascribing to the diaspora a third time-space, that is 'the borderzone between identity-as-essence and identity-as-conjuncture' (Lavie and Swedenburg, 1996, 17), diasporists withhold from non-diasporic subjects the experience of similar on-the-verge critical subjectivities in contextually driven moments of epiphany. If we take the threshold of diasporic enclave spaces (restaurants, video outlets, cinemas, religious institutions, etc.) within the bourgeois nation-state as inscribing the hyphenated third time-space, then *any* subject inhabiting that zone would be susceptible to the experience of the border flux that constitutes identity-as-essence on the one hand and identity-as-conjuncture/disjuncture on the other. To their credit, diasporists are aware that while the border zone encourages democratic porosity and fusion, it also facilitates reactionary identity formations, identifications, dangerous disavowals of otherness (the anti-hybrid values of the Muslim patriarch married to an English woman, as depicted in the film *East is East*, comes to mind) and nostalgias for racially pure domains.[8] Drawing on Amit S. Rai's research on the virtual web, Mishra points to six site 'postings [that] indicate a desire to construct India in purist [Hindu] terms' (Mishra, 1996, 424). Thinking along the same lines, Stephen Vertovec asserts that 'right-wing religious organizations in the homeland are known to gain much support from overseas populations: most notably Hindus, through the Vishwa Hindu Parishad (and, by extension, the Bharatiya Janata Party or BJP) in India, and Muslims, through Jamaat-i-Islami, a prominent Islamicist political party in Pakistan' (Vertovec, 1997, 280). What these examples indicate is the danger of ignoring the principle of *cognitive* congealment in identity-talk whereby the subject or collectivity may get off at the identity-as-essence station before the hybrid train can chug along to identity-as-conjuncture.[9]

Perhaps in an arcane and implicit way I have professed that the focus on ethnic identity formations allows diasporists to pay lip service to or to flagrantly disregard disjunctures as well as conjunctures that occur *because of but also in spite of* identifications based on class, gender, sexuality, kinship, generation, profession and ideology.[10] While digging for specificities may admittedly lead to the discovery of further layers of such specificities (or a rosary of pieties about them) in an endless series, thus rendering impossible the task of theorizing, it is the business of theory to develop rigorous paradigms that subsume most parts of any given complexity. For this reason, the primacy afforded by diasporists to deterritorialized *ethnic* identity formations over other types of identity constitution and identifications may be theoretically suspect. With some justification, they can be accused of reproducing an ideological manoeuvre when they ought to be interrogating it.[11] Targeting racial identity formations among South Asians in the United States, Kamala Visweswaran, makes this point bluntly:

> Without more attention . . . to how class determines the differential nature and experience of racial formations, there is a danger . . . that 'popular diaspora theory' of neoliberals like Joel Kotkin or conservatives like Thomas Sowell will substitute uncontested stories of culture for accounts of capital, contributing to the deployment of culturalist arguments against economic 'failures' of inner-city minorities. (Visweswaran 1997, 5)

Later, she goes on to pose a most penetrating question: '. . . what does it mean when culture increasingly grounds the language of capital?' (Visweswaran, 1997, 11). The classical answer from the left would be that instead of being the secondary effect of the relations of production, it means that culture now acts as its primary agent. It is no longer the discursive domain where the social contradictions get played out, either subversively or symptomatically, but an autonomous value system that determines the success or failure of the capitalist enterprise. Culture has some degree of autonomy and agency certainly, but the increasing tendency among cultural theorists to treat it as somehow anterior to or detached from surplus accumulation, and yet capable of impinging on it negatively or positively, is cause for worry. Visweswaran observes that popular diasporists explain 'the economic failures of inner-city blacks' as opposed to 'the success of particular Asian immigrant groups; not by accounting for how Asians organize capital, but by positing the existence of essential cultural traits which blacks are seen to lack' (Visweswaran, 1997, 7). Any paradigm that equalizes the different degrees of causal intensity associated with such terms as culture, race, gender and class or assigns surplus causal value to the wrong category (to culture instead of economics, race instead of class) is bound to come up with highly dubious conclusions.

Rather than ride rough shod over them, diasporists would do well to attend more closely to those elements of identity formation and identification that fissure the imagined ethnic collectivity and bring to light the social relations that underpin it. Discussing the contemporary fate of what Hamza Alavi calls the subcontinental 'salariat', a comprador middle class that stood in a subordinate relationship to the British colonizer but was the dominant class in its own cultural environment, Visweswaran, summarizing Alavi, observes how 'increased competition for a limited number of positions' at home coupled with the acquisition of an 'English education' led to the global mobilization of 'large sections of this community' but also contributed to its fragmentation 'along ethnic or communal lines', consequently 'preventing the consolidation of class interests' (Visweswaran, 1997, 11). Presumably this type of fragmentation along ethnic or communal lines is followed by strategic class/ethnic/gender alliances with non-subcontinental social formations in the hostland. Class divisions across the *same* ethnic formation are also obviously vital to inter-rogate. For instance, if we were to consider the Chinese diaspora in its multi-locations, we would need to sort out, among other things, the temporal, social and psychological agreements and disagreements between the 'coolie' sojourners of nineteenth-century Malaya, the service and garment industry workers 'temporalized' in various global metropolitan centres and the *taikongren* or 'astronaut' professionals that leave their families in safe havens and 'commute . . . between Australia and New Zealand and the booming cities of Asia: Hong Kong, Singapore, Taipei, Guagzhou, [and] Shanghai' (Giese, 1997, 5). Moreover, we would have to include in this diagram those diasporic subjects who hold 'flexible citizenship'[12] as well as 'diasporic entrepreneurs' who, according to Lever-Tracy, Ip and Tracy (1996), draw on the *'guanxi* (personal relationships)' system to invest in the homeland with the result that 'they have contributed over three-quarters of foreign investment in China' in terms of 'investment and export generation' (Bolt, 1997, 216). An examination of *guanxi* would also mean exploring how such personal networks encourage a social psychology based on obligations that lead to periodic transclass coali-tions, which no doubt account for the tremendous inroads made by diaspora capital in this particular home territory.

Of the other factors I mentioned earlier, generation and gender are perhaps the pivotal ones for diaspora criticism. Generational changes can and do affect the nature of diasporic formations and sometimes their very existence. Some diasporas do vanish into the homogenizing ideology of the nation-state (one need only think of the Irish diaspora in Australia) while others go on to create their own nation-states, such as the Chinese diaspora in Singapore, thereby shedding the minority expatriate status that is a defining feature of such formations. Gender, it goes without saying, is a common factor in determining the nature of a diasporic group. The most striking example of this is afforded by the statistics available on Filipino migrant workers in Europe. Of the 500,000 workers that were, legally and illegally, residing in Europe (Italy, Britain, Spain, Greece, Germany, France, Austria and the Netherlands) in 1995, a vast majority (95 per cent in some countries) were women hired as private domestic helpers or employed in the service sector (restaurants and hotels), while a significant percentage that made up the diaspora in Austria and the Netherlands worked as nurses.[13] What is the impact of this type of gender imbalance combined with low-status employment on this diasporic formation? Is it a diasporic formation? Is gender imbalance simply determined by the sexual division of labour or are other factors involved? Do migrant Filipino women define themselves as a displaced collectivity, exhibiting the characteristics enumerated by Safran? How are Filipino women interpellated in the ideologies of these nation-states, prior to and after their arrival in Europe? Such gender-oriented questions may open up vistas into Europe's relationship to Asia, the links between patriarchy and capitalism, and women as highly valuable transferable commodities in a resource-impoverished Third World. Loretta Ann Rosales points out 'that official bank remittance receipts of 1997 from the [Filipino] migrant labor market amounted to $6.2 billion'.[14] Another example of gender playing an important historical role is within the old labour diasporas of indenture. The gender breakdown for the 'coolies' shipped to Fiji between 1879 and 1916 was 'forty women for every hundred men'. Even at that historical juncture, it was admitted by the recruiting company 'that the sex ratio was an important cause of murder, suicide, and labour trouble . . .' (Gillion, 1962, 56). Clearly gender disproportion played a less than negligible 'sexual' role in the psychopathology of indentured men and women that made up the Indian diaspora in Fiji; however, more archival work needs to be carried out to determine the precise links between gender, violence and the *girmit* (indenture) consciousness.

When they move away from the slippery area of transnational capital and the development of general models for dispersed social formations to analysing the symptomatic presence of the above elements in specific cultural products and productions, diasporists tend to be at their most persuasive. They can also be at their most infuriatingly simplistic. Discussing bhangra music, for instance, Gayatri Gopinath writes that 'the diasporic web of "affiliation and affect"' (Gilroy, 1993, 16) that bhangra calls into being within and across various national contexts displaces the '"home" country from its privileged position as an originary site and redeploys it as but one of many diasporic locations'. She continues:

> Similarly, bhangra's incorporation into the nation in its transformed and transformative state refigures, to a certain extent, the very terms by which the nation is constituted. In this sense, an analysis of bhangra demands not only that diaspora be seen as part of the nation but that the nation be rethought as part of the diaspora as well. (Gopinath, 1995, 304)

One can see how the transnational dissemination of bhangra can reshape its form/content, whereby the originary country becomes, *for the genre,* another location in a network of diasporic locations and no longer a primary geocultural defining point, but it is very difficult to see how, in its metamorphosed condition, bhangra can be thought to engender new terms and conditions for the nation's constitution. Surely a minority song and dance form, *seemingly* sundered from economic and political motivations, cannot possibly have the kind of nation-redefining impact Gopinath has in mind. A more persuasive account of diasporic cultural flows and formations is afforded by Martin Roberts. Investigating the emergent world music 'as a new kind of commodity in the global marketplace of the popular music industry' (Roberts 1992, 232–3), Roberts refutes the seductive argument that mass culture simply territorializes vernacular cultural forms by pointing to 'a complex process of *indigenization,* whereby the interaction of global mass culture with local cultures produces hybrid cultural forms which render simple oppositions between core and periphery problematic' (Roberts, 1992, 230). He goes on to demonstrate how western musical forms have been assimilated into or vernacularized by 'non-western musical cultures'. To his credit, Roberts rarely loses sight of the commodity function of world music and refers to the 'six transnational recording companies (RCA, CBS, Time Warner, EMI, Polygram, MCA) and their subsidiary labels' that control the 'global music finanscape' (Roberts, 1992, 236). Furnishing relevant data, he also shows how multinational and transnational corporations, whose modus operandi is governed by shifting localities, disrupt nationally based economies where the raw material (music) gets disengaged from its cultural terrain (community, nation-state, region) in the process of its reproduction (overseas recording studios) and consumption (First World markets). Roberts refuses, however, to see world music simply in terms of its commodity function; he acknowledges the ambiguous energy in cultural artefacts that can turn power against itself:

> On the one hand . . . the ideoscapes that world music articulates are co-opted as just another marketing strategy. Recognizing a booming sector of the market, record companics and musicians alike have in recent years been jumping in the world-music bandwagon. The very idea of alternative, globally aware politics has been commodified: consumers are *sold* the idea that they are responsible, even participating in a form of cultural resistance, by the very system they are supposedly resisting . . . On the other hand, the implication of world music in the system of global capitalism allows for the possibility of turning that system against itself by using world music's mass cultural status as a kind of Trojan horse for disrupting the system from within, as sales from records, concerts, and tour merchandise are put to work, funding progressive political agendas, causes, and movements. (Roberts, 1992, 239)

While the last assertion may be mildly utopian considering the actual might of the corporate system the 'progressives' are battling, the general point about the way a cultural product can function antagonistically in spite of its co-optation tells us a lot about the elusive, anarchic character of the sign, whether it is sign musical, sign filmic or sign literary. This may, in turn, have a great deal to do with the aesthetics of affect that, in the final count, evades the commodity function but acts enigmatically on the consuming subject. It is on this threshold of inquiry that Roberts, unfortunately, terminates his stimulating account.

NOTES TOWARDS READINGS OF *SAUTU* AND *JASMINE*

Taking 'Sautu' and 'Jasmine' as examples of diasporic cultural productions and applying the analytical tools and procedures developed by diasporists, the rest of this chapter critically evaluates two short stories that consider the life-worlds of subjects belonging to the Indian diaspora. The first story is by the Indo-Fijian writer and academic Subramani, while the second is by Bharati Mukherjee, an American writer of Indian background. Set among the 'sugar' or 'exclusivist' diaspora in Fiji, 'Sautu' departs from the usual First World/Third World dimensions of diasporic temporality, but not simply in order to establish a 'nexus-cum-rupture' between the two ex-colonies of Britain, Fiji and India, the respective hostland and homeland of the Indo-Fijian diaspora. On no occasion does the story's protagonist, Dhanpat, experience the spectral translocation via the mechanism of memory that seems to be a feature of the diasporic consciousness as defined by Safran. Despite the fact that it is his birthplace, India does not seem to be a topographic point of reference/transference for Dhanpat; it is mentioned once in the context of a broken dholak, but what is being targeted here is the drum's non-functionality in its present milieu rather than its links to a past cultural geography. When we encounter it, the dholak has lost the acoustic and symbolic functions it presumably had at an earlier point in Dhanpat's life in Sautu village, ironized to represent the antithesis of the semantic values of 'peace, prosperity and abundance' associated with its name. Through his central character, Subramani explores the diaspora's self-traumatizing dissociation not so much from a geopolitical entity situated 'here' or over 'there', but from the assortment of 'milieu effects' (Wise, 2000, 296) on which its sense of territory-as-habitat is predicated. (In this sense, Subramani's conception of diaspora is closer to Gilroy's than to Safran's.) Milieu effects are any markers that convert a terrain into habitable/hospitable territory. In the story's context, these effects are anything from family members and *jahajibhais* (indentured shipmates) to old photographs and devotional icons/practices. First, however, we need to explore the connection between the foundational history of the village and the milieu effects that afford territorial cohesion to the community.

Sautu is founded on land leased/gifted from the *taukei* (indigenous landowner) by a group of ex-*girmityas* (indentured labourers) who mean to continue on the island as free farmers:

> There were no rivers and the sea was thirty miles away. The village was hemmed in by an irregular stretch of unprosperous sugar cane fields in the south, and, in the north, by partly barren soapstone hills bearing occasional guava bushes and stunted rain trees and reeds. (Subramani, 1988, 2)

What is captured in this brief textual cartography is the allegoric link between a closed-in physical terrain and the cultural enclavism of its inhabitants. We discover that Sautu has 'turned its back on the world beyond'; that the villagers worked 'the obstinate earth' only because 'there was nowhere else to go'; and that 'they were no longer moved by a momentum of their own'. Rather:

> Habit and custom held them fettered to the place. Ultimately, Sautu, like its inhabitants, became an aberration, a contortion of history on the landscape. (Subramani, 1988, 2–3)

The key to the story is contained in the implied juxtaposition between 'habit and custom' and the assertion that the village and its denizens are historical anomalies on the landscape, the suggestion being that the cultural time of the village is out of synch with the spatiality of the host territory. Since there is a social aspect to this spatiality inasmuch as it is associated with the cultural time of the indigenous population or the *taukei*, the 'historical aberration' of the villagers is seen in relation to their dislocation from the indigenous cultural time. But the dislocation can also be construed in other terms – as the enclave turning its back on the historical march of modernity in the aftermath of indenture. The social factors contributing to this dislocation are 'habit and custom' – both associated with static, repetitive milieu effects – that serve to reinforce the observation that the villagers are no longer driven by a dynamic group-generated energy.

Of the various figures that people the story, it is Dhanpat who comes to realize that the 'unchanging life of village' is based on static milieu effects that transform the village into an enclave territory, insulated from different temporalities, signs and cultures. This enclave territory reproduces 'the symbolic spatial structure of India' (Ghosh, 1989, 76), although India here is no longer a dynamic referent, across a terrain that is linked to the symbolic structure of another culture. Treated uncritically, ritualistically, milieu effects lose their semantic function, becoming fetish objects that inertly affirm an archaic order of things. When treated critically, however, they are flexible dispute-generating signs encouraging a continuous refiguring of territory in relation to contiguous signs, temporalities and cultures. Subramani avails himself of defamiliarizing or 'making strange' strategies to express Dhanpat's growing disenchantment with milieu effects that sustain the communal enclave. A number of unrelated incidents act to engender a rift in his sensibility whereby the milieu effects, instead of inscribing a sense of territory that forms the brimming ground for cultural practices, provokes feelings of emptiness and estrangement associated with the loss of territorial coordinates. With the death of his wife in sinister circumstances and the departure of his children, especially the youngest son, Somu, Dhanpat's corporeality is cut off from familial milieu effects that endow it with motives and moorings in the new territory. To make matters worse, his *girmitya* friend, Kanga, dies without faith or self-assurance, having failed to resolve many an existentialist doubt. It is Kanga's anxious question about the affinity between memory and death that triggers Dhanpat's trauma in the first instance. For Dhanpat, Kanga operates as a milieu effect connecting him to the time-space of indenture, but the period 'seemed like a labyrinth full of shadows and memories' (Subramani, 1988, 1). Two milieu effects that are external to the enclave catalyse his final, irrevocable breakdown: Somu's letters from abroad that bring to bear on his mind a wholly alien epistemological territory and Tomasi's ambivalent indigenous presence, which, while affording him the pleasures of intellectual combat, reminds Dhanpat that his territory is mapped on a terrain that belongs to someone else. At one point in the story, after contemplating the shabby milieu effects of 'his earthly belongings' that furnished 'signs of a past order', Dhanpat picks up a mirror and examines himself. This deliberate act of self-identification merely confirms his acute existential cleavage from the web of material and human effects that constitute the different points of identification in his framing of territory:

> Dhanpat had always considered himself inviolate. That was why he moved through life with such splendid reassurance. Now, sitting in front of the temple, he saw how the protective armor had gradually disintegrated. (Subramani, 1988, 7)

After this, 'the tenuous bonds that existed among the disparate items of his daily life' (Subramani, 1988, 7) start to break up. Seen as something of a free thinker by the rest of the community, Dhanpat finally sees the enclave territory (and its attendant practices) for what it really is – an insulated fragment that stifles the becoming of its inhabitants, whether individually or collectively, by keeping the world out. In other words, milieu effects are dynamic when bound up with an existential or an ontological momentum that allows for the admission of milieu effects exterior to the territory. Since they are linked to other ways of knowing, being and doing, these exterior effects work to reconfigure the contours of a given territory, thereby saving it from stultification and self-referentiality. Such an epiphany comes to Dhanpat too late in his life, and the new knowledge drives him mad. 'Sautu' can be read as a brooding parable on the dark side of hybridity and hyphenated subjectivity.

Due to their lack of an organic cross-referentiality, the milieu effects in 'Sautu' produce the ideological conditions for the nurturing of a delusional enclave mentality. There is another type of ideology that slots Third World subjects into the material myths of the First World, even in the face of a counter-reality, leading to the wholesale rejection and denigration of the 'home' territory. Here the notion of a 'double consciousness' takes on an entirely negative tenor in that the perception derived from one set of milieu effects works against itself as the subject yearns to be part of another territory and its milieu effects. Something of this sort occurs in 'Jasmine', a story that tracks the history of a double dissemination. The descendant of plantation labourers shipped from India to the Caribbean, Jasmine gives up her bank-teller's job in Trinidad for the 'good life' of an illegal alien in North America. Clifford's concept of the lateral axes of diasporic flows is borne out by Jasmine's rhizomic itinerary which – if I may provisionally treat her as a transgenerational historical subject – takes her from India (home territory) to Trinidad (first host territory-cum-home territory) to Canada (transit territory) to the United States (second host territory). While on the face of it, every change in territory marks the diaspora's upward mobility in general economic terms, Jasmine's personal economic status in relation to this movement tells a different story. Whereas the shift from India to Trinidad is socio-economically progressive (her father is a doctor of some description while Jasmine is employed by a bank), the move from Trinidad to North America, when seen along the same lines, is decidedly regressive. In Detroit, she is a live-in unwaged cleaner/book-keeper/match-maker for the Daboos, an Indo-Trinidadian family who run the suggestively named Plantations Motel. Her impulsive decision to move to Ann Arbor as the Moffitts' live-in housemaid/au pair, while apparently improving Jasmine's financial status, actually worsens her social situation, since she ends up losing her sexual surplus to Bill Moffitt.

Jasmine's transformation from bank-teller to domestic prostitute, 'with no visa, no papers, and no birth certificate' (Mukherjee, 1988, 135), is terrifying because it reveals the 'irrational' ideological factor that determines certain types of diasporic flow. This ideological factor has two sides to it, both based on the movement of desire and denial. The first concerns Jasmine's representation of the imaginary 'positive' relations she keeps with North America to her real, 'servile' conditions of existence 'here', while the second involves the representation of the imaginary 'negative' relations she has with Trinidad to her real, 'semi-independent' conditions of existence 'there'.[15] Throughout the story, the milieu items associated with the host country turn into euphoric signs affirming her interpellation as the fortunate subject of the American dream. Similarly, the milieu items that summon images of the home country turn into negative signs of the objectionable territory from which she has escaped. So it turns out that Trinidadian money is 'pretty, like a picture' while American dollars are 'businesslike, serious', hence 'real' (Mukherjee, 1988, 124). While Jasmine's comments may be accurate in the context of the relative monetary worth of the two currencies, she is really referring to their comparative *aesthetic* value. Jasmine then takes this aesthetic value as evidence of *reality* in the one and of *pseudo-reality* in the other. Despite having worked in a bank, she has little idea that money, whether American or Trinidadian, has no *reality* value per se; it simply facilitates the actual or potential exchange of commodities. The aesthetic factor (appearance, proportion, colour, novelty, etc.) is a central feature in the imaginary relations she keeps with the actual conditions of her existence in the hostland (North America) and homeland (Trinidad). In Jasmine's eyes, Trinidad is negligible because 'tiny'; the Daboos, despite their economic successes, are 'nobodies' since Mr Daboo is 'a pumpkin-shaped man with very black skin' while Mrs Daboo is 'a bumpkin too; short, fat, flapping around in house slippers'; the Daboo daughters, however, having shed all traces of Trinidad, 'seemed very American' in their 'leather boots and leotards' and 'didn't seem to know that they were nobodies'. Taken to her 'grand' room, she notices that it has 'a double bed, a TV, a pink sink and matching bathtub' (Mukherjee, 1988, 124–5). After the move to Ann Arbor, she describes the university catalogue as 'bigger than the phonebook for all Trinidad'; Bill Moffitt in his 'blue jeans and thick sweater' is unlike 'Dr. Parveen back home' whose 'cotton jacket' is 'ratty at the cuffs and lapel edges' (Mukherjee, 1988, 129–30).

Ideology maintains its grip on the subject through instigating acts of repetition and renewal that consolidate the interpellation. These acts are carried out willingly, if subconsciously, by the subject of ideology. Jasmine draws on the aesthetic factor to perform acts of ideological reaffirmation as well as reinforcement, whereby the real conditions of her Trinidadian life are distorted by an imaginary discourse that belittles nearly all aspects of the island and its culture. At the same time, the imaginary representation of First World affluence, grandness, cleanliness, superiority and romance permits her to conceal from herself the real conditions of an illegal migrant's life in North America. On the rare occasion the ideology nearly shows itself. One such moment is when Mr Daboo, after giving Jasmine 'a miniature sleigh loaded down with snowed-on mistletoe', remarks that it is the 'year for dreams coming true':

> Jasmine started to cry, too. There was nothing wrong, but Mr. Daboo, Mrs. Daboo, she, everybody was crying.
> What for? This is where she wanted to be. (Mukherjee, 1988, 132)

Between the affect and the question, there is an important link that the answer negates rhetorically. The answer bolsters the imaginary relations Jasmine maintains with North America, whereas the question is inviting her to account for an emotion that seems at first unaccountable but is really an affective symptom of the real conditions she has chosen to repress. Even her seducer and employer, Bill Moffitt, is little more than an ideological/patriarchal agent in Jasmine's desperate bid to maintain her imaginary relations with the host country:

> She never felt this good on the island where men did this all the time, and girls went along with it always for favors. You couldn't feel really good in a nothing place. She was thinking this as they made love on the Turkish carpet in front of the fire . . . (Mukherjee, 1988, 135)

That she is 'thinking' comparatively as they make love tells us something about the split ideological field that allows Jasmine to forget 'the dreariness of her new life' (Mukherjee, 1988, 135), albeit this last act of forgetting actually returns the repressed in a provisional, non-epiphanic way. As the subject of an imaginary field that codes Third and First Worlds in terms that distort the real conditions of the *individual's* existence in one place or another, Jasmine is ideologically fated to relinquish her exotic sexual surplus to a man who meets appearances and to a *consciousness* that is nothing but appearance.

CONCLUSION

As an interdisciplinary genre of theoretical writing devoted to issues relating to identity politics, migratory subjectivity, identifications, group taxonomy and double consciousness, diaspora criticism is at its strongest when investigating varieties of continuity and discontinuity that exist (1) within and across the different diasporic formations, (2) within and across their various cultural and aesthetic productions and (3) between one social formation and its cultural and aesthetic effects. It is at its weakest as a conceptual field when dealing with hard economic issues that variously impinge on diasporic social formations and their cultural productions, since it relies exceedingly on a set of popular assumptions in so far as it takes for granted the view that there has been a momentous structural shift in the nature of capital. It also overemphasizes the *direct* causal force of transnational economics in matters of global dispersion and migration. This critical genre's best work has yet to be done and will stand to benefit from a more rigorous encounter with the economic part of the scheme. It will also gain from developing models that view the triadic relations between economic forces, social formations and cultural productions as grotesque, symptomatic and refractive rather than verisimilar, unencumbered and mimetic. By its very nature a symptomatic sign – whether textual, social or economic – discloses the presence of a trauma by disguising its proper name and territory. Criticism is obliged to lay bare the ruse.

QUESTIONS FOR FURTHER CONSIDERATION

1. Nostalgia may be defined as the desire for an absent *topos*. With this in mind, discuss the role played by nostalgic affects in the constitution of diasporic subjectivity.
2. By overvaluing ethnic constellations, diasporists ignore many other types of identity formations, identifications and affiliations. The up-shot of this is that we are given a partial, if not distorted, account of how individual subjectivity is articulated within a community and across different communities. Whether you agree or not, comment on this statement.
3. Discuss the contention that diasporic spaces – such as restaurants, religious sites, community centres and video outlets – function as familiar temporalities in the unfamiliar temporality of the host terri-tory.
4. Provisional identity, hybrid effects, liminal or border zones – these are notions frequently found in postcolonial and postmodern criticism. Is diaspora criticism, then, little more than a para-site? Discuss.
5. There is a tendency to think of diasporic formations as somehow existing para-nationally, that is to say, beyond the confines of a single geopolitical entity, and that this has wide-ranging implications for the future of the classically defined nation-state. Do you agree with this view? Discuss with examples.
6. In a symptomatic way, diasporic texts chronicle a global crisis in social relations as manifested in the time of (late) modernity. Comment with examples.

ANNOTATED BIBLIOGRAPHY

Clifford, James. 'Diasporas', *Cultural Anthropology*, 9, 3, 1994, 302–38. Clifford provides an excellent overview of the field and crucially privileges the border paradigm over earlier territory-centred models.

Esman, Milton J. 'The Political Fallout of International Migration', *Diaspora*, 2, 1, 1992, 25. Esman furnishes a statistically informed account of the relationship between global demographics, economic imperatives and diasporic labour flows.

Gilroy, Paul. *The Black Atlantic: Double Consciousness and Modernity*. Cambridge, MA: Harvard University Press, 1993. In this highly influential or even foundational text, Gilroy argues against history writing based on 'nationalist or ethnically absolute approaches', preferring to emphasize the lateral networks of dispersal – namely, that of the black Atlantic – to account for the *productive* cultural, social and political place of the African diaspora in European modernity.

Mishra, Vijay. 'The Diasporic Imaginary: Theorizing the Indian Diaspora', *Textual Practice*, 10, 3, 1996, 421–47. By addressing a specific diasporic cluster, this essay avoids the definitional pitfalls encountered by the more generalist paradigms. It makes a notable intervention by bringing to light historically motivated differences within the Indian diasporic formation.

Roberts, Martin. '"World Music" and the Global Cultural Economy', *Diaspora*, 2, 2, 1992, 229–42. A fine account of how the category of world music has been invented, classified, marketed and distributed by itinerant recording corporations.

Safran, William. 'Diasporas in Modern Societies: Myths of Homeland and Return', *Diaspora*, 1, 1, 1991, 83–99. While it has met with mixed success in its attempts to come up with a general model for describing diasporas, the real strength of this seminal essay lies in the range of debate it has stimulated subsequent to its publication.

Tölölyan, Khachig. 'Rethinking Diaspora(s): Stateless Power in the Transnational Moment', *Diaspora*, 5, 1, 1996, 3–35. A critically aware reflection on the field by one of the founders of the influential journal, *Diaspora,* this essay sets the trend for thinking of diasporas as communities formed in the transnational moment of late modernity.

Visweswaran, Kamala. 'Diaspora by Design: Flexible Citizenship and South Asians in U.S. Racial Formations', *Diaspora*, 6, 1, 1997, 19. Not only does Visweswaran examine the altering nature of racial identifications and taxonomies among South Asians in North America, but she also points to a vital flaw in popular diaspora criticism's strategy of privileging ethnic identifications and formations over and beyond class divisions and affiliations.

SUPPLEMENTARY BIBLIOGRAPHY

Althusser, Louis. *Lenin and Philosophy and Other Essays*, trans. Ben Brewster. London: New Books, 1977.

Amin, Samir. *Capitalism in the Age of Globalization: The Management of Contemporary Society*. London: Zed Books, 1997.

Anderson, Benedict. *Imagined Communities: Reflections on the Origin and Spread of Nationalism*. London: Verso, 1991.

Appadurai, Arjun, and Carol Breckenridge. 'On Moving Targets', *Public Culture*, 2, 1989, i–iv.

Baumann, Martin. 'Shangri-La in Exile: Portraying Tibetan Diaspora Studies and Reconsidering Diaspora(s)', *Diaspora*, 6, 3, 1997, 377–404.

Bolt, Paul. 'Chinese Diaspora Entrepreneurship, Development, and the World Capitalist System', *Diaspora*, 6, 2, 1997, 215–25.

Brah, Avtar. *Cartographies of Diaspora*. London: Routledge, 1996.

Chambers, Iain. *Migrancy. Culture and Identity*. London: Routledge, 1994.

Chuh, Kandice. 'Transnationalism and its Pasts', *Public Culture*, 9, 1996, 93–112.

Cohen, Robin. *Global Diasporas*. London: UCL Press, 1997.

Edwards, Brent Hayes. 'The Uses of Diaspora', *Social Text*, 66, 19, 1, 2001, 45–73.

Frow, John. *Time and Commodity Culture: Essays in Cultural Theory and Postmodernity*. Oxford: Clarendon Press, 1997.

Ghosh, Amitav. 'The Diaspora in Indian Culture', *Public Culture*, 2, 1, 1989, 73–8.

Giese, Diana. *Astronauts, Lost Souls and Dragons*. Queensland: University of Queensland Press, 1997.

Gillion, K. L. *Fiji's Indian Migrants*. Melbourne: Oxford University Press, 1962.

Gopinath, Gayatri. ' "Bombay, U.K., Yuba City": Bhangra Music and the Engendering of Diaspora', *Diaspora*, 4, 3, 1995, 303–21.

Hall, Stuart. 'Cultural Identity and Diaspora'. In *Identity, Community, Culture, Difference*, ed. Jonathan Rutherford. London: Lawrence & Wishart, 1990, 222–37.

Holston, James, and Arjun Appadurai. 'Cities and Citizenship', *Public Culture*, 8, 1996, 187–204.

Howell, Sally. 'Cultural Interventions: Arab American Aesthetics between the Transnational and the Ethnic', *Diaspora*, 9, 1, 2000, 59–82.

Jusdanis, Gregory. 'Culture, Culture Everywhere: The Swell of Globalization Theory', *Diaspora*, 5, 1, 1996, 141–61.

Lavie, Smadar, and Ted Swedenburg (eds). *Displacement, Diaspora, and Geographies of Identity*. Durham, NC: Duke University Press, 1996.

Lever-Tracy, Constance, David Ip and Noel Tracy. *The Chinese Diaspora and Mainland China: An Emerging Economic Synergy*. London: Macmillan Press, 1996.

Marx, John. 'Capitalism after Globalization', *Diaspora*, 6, 2, 1997, 253–71.

Mercer, Kobena. 'Diaspora Culture and the Dialogic Imagination'. In *Blackframes: Celebration of Black Cinema*, eds Mbye Cham and Claire Andrade-Watkins, Cambridge, MA: MIT Press, 1988.

Mishra, Sudesh. 'Estranged and Estranging Bodies: Gazing on Caliban, or An Essay against Hybridity', *UTS Review*, 2, 1996b, 108–28.

Mishra, Vijay. 'Bordering Naipaul: Indenture History and Diasporic Poetics', *Diaspora*, 5, 2, 1996, 189–237.

Mukherjee, Bharati. *The Middleman and Other Stories*. New York: Fawcett Crest, 1988.

Ong, Aiwha. 'On the Edge of Empires: Flexible Citizenship among Chinese in Diaspora', *Positions*, 1, 3, 1993, 745–78.

Rouse, Roger. 'Mexican Migration and the Social Space of Postmodernism', *Diaspora*, 1, 1, 1991, 8–23.

Shapiro, Michael J. 'National Times and Other Times: Re-thinking Citizenship', *Cultural Studies*, 14, 1, 2000, 79–98.

Smith, Paul. *Millennial Dreams: Contemporary Culture and Capital in the North*. London: Verso, 1997.

Subramani. *The Fantasy Eaters: Stories from Fiji*. Washington, DC: Three Continents Press, 1988.

Tölölyan, Khachig. 'The Nation State and its Others: In Lieu of a Preface', *Diaspora*, 1, 1, 1991, 3–7.

Vertovec, Stephen. 'Three Meanings of "Diaspora", Exemplified among South Asian Religions', *Diaspora*, 6, 3, 1997, 277–99.

Wise, J. Macgregor. 'Home: Territory and Identity', *Cultural Studies*, 14, 2, 2000, 295–310.

NOTES

1. Citing James Clifford's advice to scholars not to foreclose definitional possibilities by taking the Jewish diaspora as the 'ideal type', Martin Baumann claims that this licenses 'scholars not to bother at all about the origin and coinage of the term. Thus, a rather free, arbitrary and often plainly metaphorical use of 'diaspora' has emerged in recent years, 'decomposing' in exactly the early Greek philosophical meaning the

term's ability to encompass properly certain situations and relations ... The currently predominant emphasis on the mournful experiences of exile, flight, and expulsion tells only half the story of the diaspora concept' (see Baumann, 1997, 395).

2. A phrase attributed to George Lamming by Kobena Mercer (1988, 56).
3. Paul Smith provides a persuasive account of the way apologists of capitalism have deployed discourses of global economy to distract from its age-old dependence on surplus value appropriation (Smith, 1997). See also John Marx's intelligent review of the book (1997, 253–71).
4. Since borders and decentres figure crucially in the conceptual framework of post-modernism, Clifford can be charged with simply transferring the items that make up one conceptual framework to another, masking the obvious equivalences between the two domains through the enunciative force of nomenclature.
5. Since they work in western academies and since modern diasporic formations are endemic to bourgeois nation-states of the North, diasporists tend to neglect other types of nation and state formations in their commentary.
6. As I write this chapter in Melbourne, the lead article in *The Weekend Australian* fuels the immigration paranoia/hysteria with the caption 'Our Open-door Borders: Fortress Australia Under Attack'. Losing even the semblance of journalistic dispassion, the article goes on to discuss 'how guns, drugs and people are swamping the nation's barely protected coastline'. Asylum seekers are not desperate people fleeing terrible regimes in Afghanistan or Iraq or poverty in South East Asia, but ruthless gunrunners and drug smugglers who violate 'the sanctity of our borders'. Needless to say, these people are out to destroy the actual rather than the *imagined* fabric of Australian society. See *The Weekend Australian*, 25–26 August 2001, 1. A few days after I entered this note, the Norwegian freighter, *Tampa*, with its 'human cargo' of 438 asylum seekers (mostly Muslims fleeing the Taliban regime) rescued from a dilapidated ferry, has been refused docking rights at Christmas Island by John Howard, the Prime Minister of Australia. Military personnel are currently on board the vessel and the government is threatening to force the ship out of Australian waters. A mixture of racial panic and callous electioneering seems to be behind this attitude. Defending the severity of his stance, Mr Howard says: 'We appear to be losing control of the flow of people coming into this country . . . we have to take a stand'. See *The Australian*, 29 August 2001, 1.
7. Esman claims that North African Muslims decline to accept French citizenship since it involves the renunciation of 'their former allegiance, as France does not sanction the practice of dual citizenship. Some are reluctant to displease their parents; others sense that accepting French citizenship implies the embrace of an alien Christian culture and the symbolic repudiation of their Arabic and Muslim roots' (1992, 25).
8. Mishra, for instance, claims that '[u]nder a gaze that threatens their already precarious sense of the "familiar temporariness", diasporas lose their enlightened ethos and retreat into discourses of ethnic purity that are always the "imaginary" underside of their own constructions of the homeland' (1996, 421).
9. For an extended analysis of the cognitive difficulties of hybridity, as theorized by Homi Bhabha, see Sudesh Mishra (1996, 108–28).
10. Sally Howell, for instance, explains how the 'overrepresentation in Detroit of Arab minorities and politically disenfranchised populations . . . makes it difficult for Detroit's Arabs to imagine themselves as a single "Arab community". In most situations, smaller, more localized identities hold sway. Family, village, church, mosque, nation: each category entails its own sense of community and creates overlapping sets of inclusion and exclusion. These smaller communities are often at odds with each other. They are unevenly committed to the maintenance of transnational networks, and they resist or encourage new identifications with American culture in different ways' (2000, 63).

11. Khachig Tölölyan seems aware of one aspect of this problem when he alludes to the 'inadvertent discursive complicity between diasporists and the transnational project' (1996, 4).
12. Visweswaran attributes the coinage to Aiwha Wong, who uses it to denote the capacity of Asian diasporas to 'facilitate their strategies of flexible accumulation and their attempts to evade the political costs and debits of minority entrepreneurs in Western countries' (Visweswaran, 1997, 19).
13. See 'Filipino Migration to Europe: Country Profiles' on the website http://www.phil-sol.nl/of/country-profiles.htm.
14. See Loretta Ann P. Rosales, 'Empowering Seven Million Migrant Filipinos for the Next Millennium' on the website http://www.philsol.nl/F-Rosales-may99.htm.
15. I am drawing here on Louis Althusser's assertion that 'ideology represents the imaginary relationships of individuals to their real conditions of existence' (Althusser, 1977, 122).

CHAPTER 2

GENDER AND TRANSGENDER CRITICISM

Sarah Gamble

In the introduction to their book *Genders,* David Glover and Cora Kaplan make the observation that: '*gender* is a much contested concept, as slippery as it is indispensable, but a site of unease rather than agreement' (Glover and Kaplan, 2000, ix). As a neologism founded upon an already disputed term, therefore, 'transgender' is doubly problematic. Describing the etymology of the word, Jay Prosser observes that 'transgender' has both a specific and a general function, describing an individual who 'crossed the lines of gender but not of sex', as well as

> function[ing] as a container term, one that refers not only to transgen-
> derists but to those subjects from whom it was originally invented to
> distinguish transgenderists: transsexuals and drag queens, transvestites
> and cross-dressers, along with butches and intersexuals and any subject to
> 'trans-es' sex or gender boundaries. (Prosser, 1998, 176)

Furthermore, it is difficult to define exactly the ground covered by either term, since both tend to elide into theoretical territories identified by other names. Indeed, it could be argued that it is only recently that gender and transgender theory have emerged as categories in their own right, as both have tended to have been developed through debates within, for example, feminist theory, queer theory, masculinity theory, postcolonial theory, philosophy, and gay and lesbian studies. Both words also 'double up' in another way, too, for they are as much political as they are theoretical, interacting with the material world that exists beyond the intellectual realm of the academy, and are thus descriptive of movements within politics and sociology as well as ideas to do with culture and representation.

One of the founding thinkers concerning gender was the psychoanalyst Robert Stoller, who in 1968 published *Sex and Gender: On the Development of Masculinity and Femininity*, in which he drew a distinction between sex and gender which has proved invaluable to subsequent theorists. Regarding gender as 'culturally determined' (Stoller, 1968, ix), he argued that an individual's gender identity may not necessarily correspond to their biological sexual characteristics:

> [O]ne can speak of the male sex or the female sex, but one can also talk about masculinity and femininity and not necessarily be implying anything about anatomy or physiology. Thus, while sex and gender seem to common sense to be practically synonymous, and in everyday life to be inextricably bound together, one purpose of this study will be to confirm the fact that the two realms (sex and gender) are not at all inevitably bound in anything like a one-to-one relationship, but each may go in its quite independent way. (Stoller, 1968, xiii)

From this perspective, therefore, gender can be viewed as a *behaviour*, a learned or conditioned response to a society's view of how men and women should act. The motivation behind much of the twentieth-century feminist movement stems from such a view: the belief that, while men's and women's biological difference is an inescapable fact, inequalities between them stem from culturally generated biases concerning the gendered categories of 'masculinity' and 'femininity'. The idea that gender is culturally constructed was invaluable to feminists of the second wave, such as Kate Millett, who in *Sexual Politics* (1970) drew on Robert Stoller's work in order to argue that women's oppression is rooted in social conceptions of 'femininity'. Gayle Rubin's 1975 essay, 'The Traffic in Women: Notes on the "Political Economy" of Sex', made a very similar point. She defines what she calls a 'sex/gender system' as 'the set of arrangements by which a society transforms biological sexuality into products of human activity' (Humm, 1992, 257).

By the late 1980s, however, such feminist arguments were coming under attack from theorists steeped in postmodernist theory, for whom the assumption that all women are oppressed within a cross-cultural gender system appears dangerously simplistic. In 'The Technology of Gender', published in 1987, Teresa de Lauretis claims that 'the notion of gender as sexual difference' has 'now become a limitation, something of a liability to feminist thought' (de Lauretis 1987, 1). In its insistence on placing 'male' and 'female' in opposition, the feminist definition of gender 'keeps feminist thinking bound to the terms of Western patriarchy itself, contained within the frame of a conceptual opposition' (de Lauretis, 1987, 1). In order to escape from this dialectic, which does not enable differences between 'women' as a category to be articulated, 'we need a notion of gender that is not so bound up with sexual difference as to be virtually coterminous with it' (de Lauretis, 1987, 2). For de Lauretis, the answer lies in approaching gender as a *representation*, 'a symbolic system or system of meanings, that correlates sex to cultural contents according to social values and hierarchies' (de Lauretis, 1987, 5), and investigating how the gendered subject is produced through a variety of discourses and technologies. As a film theorist, her primary concern is with cinema, which functions as a 'technology of gender' (de Lauretis, 1987, 13) in the way in which it constructs sexualized images of women through a range of cinematic techniques (camera angles, lighting and so on), and codes (the positioning of the viewing subject in relation to the image viewed). The consequence of such an anatomization of gender as a system is that it will enable the feminist theorist to occupy (however briefly) a space *outside* the gender system in an 'ongoing effort to create new spaces of discourse, to rewrite cultural narratives, and to define the terms of another perspective – a view from "elsewhere" ' (de Lauretis, 1987, 25). Such a perspective, however, is always contingent, in a permanent process of oscillation within and without gender ideologies: what de Lauretis terms 'a movement between the (represented) discursive space of the positions made available by hegemonic discourses and the space-off, the elsewhere, of those discourses' (de Lauretis, 1987, 26).

De Lauretis's argument, therefore, abandons simplistic sex/gender distinctions in order to argue for gender as a complex discursive construction. The theorist Judith Butler, however, whose book *Gender Trouble*, published in 1990, has exercised an enormous influence upon modern gender theory, goes even further. Like de Lauretis, Butler takes issue with feminist conceptions of gender, which, she says, 'has assumed that there is some existing identity, understood through the category of women, who not only initiates feminist interests and goals within discourse, but constitutes the subject for whom political representation is pursued' (Butler, 1990, 1). While de Lauretis, however, retains an adherence to the notion of a subjectivity which is implicated in a process of 'continuous engagement in social reality' (de Lauretis, 1987, 18), Butler is concerned with a more radical deconstruction of the subject. Her argument proceeds from the assumption that a universal concept of 'woman' is a signifier which has become divorced from humanist conceptions of subjectivity, and thus 'is no longer understood in stable or abiding terms' (Butler, 1990, 1) – it is 'a troublesome term, a site of contest, a cause for anxiety' (Butler, 1990, 3).

For Butler, the distinction between sex and gender is one way in which simplistic notions of 'woman' are troubled, for '[t]he unity of the subject is thus already potentially contested by the distinction that permits of gender as a multiple interpretation of sex' (Butler, 1990, 6). Following the path of her logic to the extreme, she proceeds to argue that:

> If gender is the cultural meanings that the sexed body assumes, then a gender cannot be said to follow from a sex in any one way. Taken to its logical limit, the sex/gender distinction suggests a radical discontinuity between sexed bodies and culturally constructed genders. Assuming for the moment the stability of binary sex, it does not follow that the

construction of 'men' will accrue exclusively to the bodies of males or that 'women' will interpret only female bodies. Further, even if the sexes appear to be unproblematically binary in their morphology and constitution (which will become a question), there is no reason to assume that genders ought also to remain as two. The presumption of a binary gender system implicitly retains the belief in a mimetic relation of gender to sex whereby gender mirrors sex or is otherwise restricted by it. When the constructed status of gender is theorized as radically independent of sex, gender itself becomes a free-floating artifice, with the consequence that *man* and *masculine* might just as easily signify a female body as a male one, and *woman* and *feminine* a male body as easily as a female one.

This radical splitting of the gendered subject poses yet another set of problems. Can we refer to a 'given' sex or a 'given' gender without first inquiring into how sex and/or gender is given, through what means? And what is 'sex' anyway? Is it natural, anatomical, chromosomal, or hormonal, and how is a feminist critic to assess the scientific discourses which purport to establish such 'facts' for us? . . . If the immutable character of sex is contested, perhaps this construct called 'sex' was as culturally constructed as gender; indeed, perhaps it was always already gender, with the consequence that the distinction between sex and gender turns out to be no distinction at all. (Butler, 1990, 6–7)

This statement constitutes a radical leap beyond the sphere of debate established by de Lauretis, for what Butler effectively does in this passage is to turn the 'sex versus gender' argument on its head. Not only does she point out the radical consequences of cutting gender free from sex, the signifier from the body being signified, she also begins to interrogate the very means by which the concept of 'sex' itself is produced. In this context, 'sex' has as little to do with biology as gender: '[g]ender ought not be conceived merely as the cultural inscription of meaning on a pregiven sex . . . ; gender must also designate the very apparatus of production whereby the sexes themselves are established' (Butler, 1990, 7).

The implications of this argument are far-reaching, since it comes to affect the very concept of identity. As Butler asks, '[h]ow do the regulatory practices that govern gender also govern culturally intelligible notions of identity?' (Butler, 1990, 16–17). The subject, therefore, is not granted *a priori* existence in Butler's argument, but is in the constant process of being constituted and maintained through a network of discourses: it is always, to use her words, a 'fictive production' (Butler, 1990, 24).

In this sense, *gender* is not a noun, but neither is it a set of free-floating attributes, for we have seen that the substantive effect of gender is performatively produced and compelled by the regulatory practices of gender coherence. Hence, within the inherited discourse of the metaphysics of substance, gender proves to be performative – that is, constituting the identity it is purported to be. In this sense, gender is always a doing, though not a doing by a subject who might be said to preexist the deed. (Butler, 1990, 24–5)

Although this process is rendered invisible within the context of the cultural 'norm' of heterosexuality, subversive sexual practices and bodily performances call it into question by threatening to establish identities outside of the confines of the masculine/feminine paradigm. In *Gender Trouble*, Butler looks at practices such as cross-dressing and drag, arguing that, in their parodic imitation of gender norms, they highlight the performativity which is an essential element of *all* gendered behaviour.

> As much as drag creates a unified picture of 'woman' (what its critics often oppose), it also reveals the distinctness of those aspects of gendered experience which are falsely naturalized as a unity through the regulatory fiction of heterosexual coherence. *In imitating gender, drag implicitly reveals the imitative structure of gender itself – as well as its contingency.* (Butler, 1990, 137)

If no appeal can be made, therefore, to a 'true' or 'authentic' identity based on gender or on sex, heterosexual binarism gives way to an infinite range of gendered identities and practices: and it is from this line of reasoning that transgender theory springs.

It has already been noted that gender theorists such as Judith Butler seek to destabilize universal notions of 'woman': an endeavour which argues against centuries of certainty concerning the meaning of that term. 'Transgender', on the other hand, is a word which has no history, and no basis in a stable epistemology – it is, axiomatically, a volatile and much-disputed term. As transsexual activist Riki Anne Wilchins says, the meaning of 'transgender' is fluid, and under constant qualification:

> *Transgender* began its life as a name for those folks who identified neither as crossdressers nor as transsexuals – primarily people who changed their gender but not their genitals . . .
>
> The term gradually mutated to include any genderqueers who didn't actually change their genitals: crossdressers, transgenders, stone butches, hermaphrodites and drag people. Finally, tossing in the towel on the noun-list approach, people began using it to refer to transsexuals as well, which was fine with some transsexuals, but made others feel they were being erased. (Wilchins, 1997, 15–16)

In her book *Gender Outlaw*, Kate Bornstein displays a similar struggle with definition, arguing for the use of 'transgendered' as a collective noun capable of encompassing the infinite variety of subversive gender identities in order to bind them together into a cohesive site upon which to base a politics of activism.

> So let's reclaim the word 'transgendered' so as to be more inclusive. Let's let it mean 'transgressively gendered'. Then, we have a group of people

who break the rules, codes, and shackles of gender. Then we have a healthy-sized contingent! It's the transgendered who need to embrace the lesbians and gays, because it's the transgendered who are in fact the more inclusive category. (Bornstein, 1994, 234–5)

Many texts in transgender studies do not make use of the term at all, as evinced by Sandy Stone's essay 'The *Empire* Strikes Back: a Posttranssexual Manifesto', published in 1992. This essay outlines the key features of this area of theory, arguing that, for transsexuals themselves, the transsexed body does not necessarily represent the potential for gender subversion envisaged by theorists such as Butler. Instead, Stone asserts that transsexuals, who desire surgical intervention in order to literally become a member of the opposite gender, have very stereotyped ideas concerning gender identity. 'Sex and gender', she argues, 'are quite separate issues, but transsexuals commonly blur the distinction by confusing the performative character of gender with the physical "fact" of sex, referring to their perceptions of their situation as being in the "wrong" body' (Stone 1992, 281–2). In fact, the medical discourse surrounding gender reassignment surgery demands that no differentiation be made between gender and sex, since 'candidates for surgery were evaluated on the basis of their *performance* in the gender of choice. The criteria constituted a fully acculturated, consensual definition of gender' (Stone, 1992, 291). This is reflected in the narratives of sex change found in transsexual autobiographies, in which 'the authors . . . reinforce a binary, oppositional mode of gender identification. They go from being unambiguous men, albeit unhappy men, to unambiguous women. There is no territory between' (Stone, 1992, 286).

Stone's essay is an appeal to the transsexual community to formulate different stories of gender identity, instead of colluding with medical discourses that entrap them within the male/female binarism. She portrays the transsexual body as a 'battlefield . . . a hotly contested site of cultural inscription, a meaning machine for the production of ideal type' (Stone, 1992, 294), and argues for the necessity of a counterdiscourse which would originate from within transsexualism itself. Such a refusal to be reabsorbed into society's views of what constitutes 'normal' or 'natural' gender would result, according to Stone, in the construction of a historical narrative of transsexualism which would throw into high relief the constructedness of *all* gender identities:

In the transsexual as text we may find the potential to map the refigured body onto conventional gender discourse and thereby disrupt it, to take advantage of the dissonances created by such a juxtaposition to fragment and reconstitute the elements of gender in new and unexpected geometries. (Stone, 1992, 296)

Transsexuals must, therefore, resist the imperative to 'pass', creating identities for themselves which correspond absolutely to dominant ideological expectations concerning gender. Instead, they should seek for ways to represent 'the intertextual possibilities of the transsexual body' (Stone, 1992, 297), grounding their histories in the gaps and interstices between gender categories. Stone ends her essay by imagining the implications of such an act. In articulating their difference and variety, Stone envisages a situation in which

> [t]he disruptions of the old patterns of desire that the multiple dissonances of the transsexual body imply produce not an irreducible alterity but a myriad of alterities, whose unanticipated juxtapositions hold what Donna Haraway has called the promises of monsters – physicalities of constantly shifting figure and ground that exceed the frame of any possible representation. (Stone, 1992, 299)

Stone's mention of Donna Haraway in the extract quoted above indicates the importance of her work as an intertext for her essay. Indeed, Stone's choice of title – 'The *Empire* Strikes Back: A Posttranssexual Manifesto' – itself constitutes a linguistic gesture towards Haraway's influential piece 'A Cyborg Manifesto: Science, Technology, and Socialist-Feminism in the Late Twentieth Century', originally published in *Socialist Review* in 1985. Although Haraway is not a transgender theorist *per se*, in that she does not herself write from a position within the transgender community, Stone's referencing of Haraway indicates the usefulness of many of her ideas to the ongoing task of formulating a transgendered discourse.

The figure which occupies an iconic position in Haraway's argument in this essay is the cyborg, which she describes as 'a hybrid of machine and organism, a creature of social reality as well as a creature of fiction' (Haraway, 1991, 149). Although the cyborg is an imaginary creation drawn from science fiction, for Haraway it functions as a potent symbol of the contradictions encountered by female subjects in a twentieth-century technocracy, in which they are aligned with a 'natural' condition which is increasingly being called into question by the expansion of industrial capitalism. Although Haraway's concern is with women, as Stone discerns, her statements concerning the cyborg translate well into a transgender context. For a start, Haraway is emphatic in her claim that '[t]he cyborg is a creature in a post-gender world; it has no truck with bisexuality, pre-oedipal symbiosis, unalienated labour, or other seductions to organic wholeness through a final appropriation of all the powers of the parts into a higher unity' (Haraway, 1991, 150). The cyborg, therefore, like the transgendered subject, disrupts gender binaries purely by the fact of its existence. Because its genesis lies outside the boundaries of gender, it has no myth of origin, and thus no history: it 'would not recognise the Garden of Eden' (Haraway, 1991, 151). Instead, the body of the cyborg springs from a complex of alliances formed between technology, capitalism and science, just as does the surgically transformed transgendered body in Stone's analysis. But although both the cyborg and the transgendered individual are generated from within such materialistic practices, they also call them into question through the very fact of their hybridity. As Haraway says:

A cyborg world might be about lived social and bodily realities in which people are not afraid of their joint kinship with animals and machines, not afraid of permanently partial identities and contradictory standpoints. The political struggle is to see from both perspectives at once because each reveals both dominations and possibilities unimaginable from the other vantage point. Single vision produces worse illusions than double vision or many-headed monsters. Cyborg unities are monstrous and illegitimate; in our present political circumstances, we could hardly hope for more potent myths for resistance and recoupling. (Haraway, 1991, 154)

Compare this with Judith Butler's assertion in *Gender Trouble* that 'the very notion of "the person" is called into question by the cultural emergence of those "incoherent" or "discontinuous" gendered beings who appear to be persons but who fail to conform to the gendered norms of cultural intelligibility by which persons are defined' (Butler, 1990, 17). Both cyborgs and the transgendered subject are figures who disrupt determinist ideologies and standpoints, breaching categories and signalling new, often contradictory, possibilities for alliances across boundaries. Moreover, both call the concept of subjectivity itself into question, for neither can be codified and contained within discourses which appeal to essentialist conceptions of what constitutes the 'natural'. The cyborg, says Haraway, 'is a kind of disassembled and reassembled, postmodern collective and personal self', and a cyborg politics would foreground the belief that 'the body . . . can be dispersed and interfaced in nearly infinite, polymorphous ways' (Harway, 1991, 163). Indeed, by the end of her essay, Haraway, while still ostensibly addressing a feminist audience, certainly gestures towards the possibility of the cyborg's functioning as a transgendered symbol.

Our bodies, ourselves; bodies are maps of power and identity. Cyborgs are no exception. A cyborg body is not innocent; it was not born in a garden; it does not seek unitary identity and so generate antagonistic dualisms without end (or until the world ends); it takes irony for granted. One is too few, and two is only one possibility . . . Cyborgs might consider more seriously the partial, fluid, sometimes aspect of sex and sexual embodiment. Gender might not be global identity after all, even if it has profound historical breadth and depth. (Haraway, 1991, 180)

In her wish to cut the transgendered body lose from essentialist myths of origin, and her assertion that its '[e]mergent polyvocalities of lived experience' (Stone, 1992, 293) will lay stress on gender identity as something attained rather than something inborn, Sandy Stone develops the possibilities Haraway's cyborg presents to transgender theory. Moreover, Stone does not merely extend the content of Haraway's argument: importantly, she also appropriates its rhetorical tone. The first section of 'A Cyborg Manifesto', subheaded 'An *Ironic* Dream of a Common Language for Women in the Integrated Circuit' (Haraway, 1991, 149, italics mine) signals the importance of irony as a key tactic in Haraway's debate:

> Irony is about contradictions that do not resolve into larger wholes, even dialectically, about the tension of holding incompatible things together because both or all are necessary and true. Irony is about humour and serious play. It is also a rhetorical strategy and a political method. (Haraway, 1991, 149)

It can be argued that irony forms the dominant mode of representation, too, within many transgendered narratives which, like Sandy Stone's, tend to mingle the personal with the political and lived experience with theory. Stone's essay draws attention to the importance of autobiography in transgender writing, texts which conventionally chart the process of surgical gender reassignment. The first fully autobiographical work by a transsexual, *I Changed My Sex!*, was published by Hedy Jo Star in the mid-1950s, and it has been followed by many other transgender accounts, including *A Personal Biography* by Christine Jorgensen (1967) and *Conundrum: An Extraordinary Narrative of Transsexualism* by the journalist Jan Morris (1974).

The autobiographical mode, however, gave way in the 1990s to a new form of transgender writing which has clearly been influenced by the rise of gender theory, but which also retains, albeit in an ironic form, much of the autobiographical drive towards self-disclosure. In 'The *Empire* Strikes Back', Sandy Stone comments that 'many transsexuals keep something they call by the argot term "O.T.F.": The Obligatory Transsexual File. This usually contains newspaper articles and bits of forbidden diary entries about "inappropriate" gender behaviour' (Stone, 1992, 285), and this notion of a transgendered identity assembled, postmodern style, out of fragments collated from a variety of sources, becomes a concept central to theoretical writing produced by the transgendered themselves.

One of the texts in this area which has achieved the most prominence is *Gender Outlaw: On Men, Women and the Rest of Us* by the male-to-female transsexual Kate Bornstein. The critic Jay Prosser has observed that this text constitutes '[o]ur first "postmodern" transsexual (thus posttranssexual) autobiography' which 'fragments continuous and connective narrative into deliberately disjointed vignettes. Bornstein doesn't so much narrativize her transsexual life as (a performance artist) she performs it, acting out – without integrating into a singular stable gendered identity – its parts' (Prosser, 1998, 174). Bornstein herself claims the book is an attempt to develop 'a transgendered style' which is 'based on collage. You know – a little bit from here, a little bit from there? Sort of a cut-and-paste thing' (Bornstein, 1994, 3). The typography of her text emphasizes this, its mosaic of different typefaces and layouts echoing Bornstein's vacillation between personal disclosure and theorizing. At the heart of it all, however, is a serious debate about identity, both personal and collective. But as far as Bornstein is concerned, as a heterosexual man transformed into a lesbian woman, gender identity is a polymorphous, infinitely mutable, concept:

> I love the idea of being without an identity, it gives me a lot of room to play around; but it makes me dizzy, having nowhere to hang my hat. When I get too tired of not having an identity, I take one on: it doesn't really matter what identity I take on, as long as it's recognizable. I can be a writer, a lover, a confidante, a femme, a top, or a woman. (Bornstein, 1994, 39)

Bornstein is a true posttransexual in the sense of Stone's use of the word, in that she argues against the transsexual desire for gender conformity, for the attainment of 'true' masculinity or femininity. And while she clearly believes in the necessity of the acquisition of a gender identity, which, she says, 'answers the question "who am I?"' (Bornstein, 1994, 24), that identity is neither innate nor fixed:

> What **does** a man feel like?
> What does a woman feel like?
> Do **you** feel 'like a man?'
> Do you feel 'like a woman?'
> I'd really like to know that from people.
>   (Bornstein, 1994, 24)

Instead, she argues for a fluid concept of gender, which 'is the refusal to remain one gender or another. Gender fluidity is the ability to freely and knowingly become one or many of a limitless number of genders, for any length of time, at any rate of change' (Bornstein, 1994, 52). To this end, Bornstein proposes the concept of the 'third', 'the concept of the outlaw, who subscribes to a dynamic of change, outside any given dichotomy' (Bornstein, 1994, 97).

Bornstein's approach, if not quite her upbeat tone, is echoed in a text published three years later: *Read My Lips: Sexual Subversion and the End of Gender* by Riki Anne Wilchins. Like Bornstein, Wilchins' book is a mixture of theorization (Michel Foucault and Judith Butler are among the references cited) and personal exploration, presented in an assemblage of styles and typography. Wilchins, another male-to-female transsexual, similarly argues against the sex/gender distinction:

> Gender is not what culture creates out of my body's sex; rather, sex is what culture makes when it genders my body. The cultural system of gender looks at my body, creates a narrative of binary difference, and says, 'Honest, it was here when I arrived. It's all Mother Nature's doing.' The story of a natural sex that justifies gender evaporates, and we see sex standing revealed as an effect of gender, not its cause. Sex, the bodily feature most completely in-the-raw, turns out to be thoroughly cooked, and our comforting distinction between sex and gender collapses. We are left staring once again at the Perpetual Motion Machine of gender as it

spins endlessly on and on, creating difference at every turn. (Wilchins, 1997, 51)

However, the tone of the extract cited above is an indicator that Wilchins regards the creation of a 'third' space as a more problematic project than does Bornstein. As she says: 'Perhaps sex is not a noun at all. Perhaps it is really a verb, a cultural imperative – as in "Sex yourself!" – in the face of which none of us has a choice' (Wilchins, 1997, 57). Whereas Bornstein portrays the trans-gendered as totemic shaman figures who, in the exhibition of their own ambiguous bodies, open the way to new conceptualizations of gender, Wilchins envisages an escape from the constrictions of the sex/gender system as a more complicated and tortuous process. In her analysis, a transgendered identity is defined much more by reference to separation from others, and what links are established between transgendered subjects are both tenuous and provisional:

> Loneliness, and the inability to find partners, is one of the best-kept secrets in the transcommunity. It's something many of us carry around like a private shame, a secret wound we hide from view. This is because we are convinced the isolation only confirms our deepest fears – that we are somehow deficient. It should remind us, instead, once again, that the personal is political.
>
> The gender system, which marks many kinds of bodies as either nonerotic or erotically problematic, is at work in the most intimate spaces of our lives. We fall off the grid of erotic intelligibility which sections the body into known, recognizable parts. Transbodies are the cracks in the gender sidewalk. When we find partners, they must be willing to negotiate the ambiguity of the terrain. (Wilchins, 1997, 120)

Wilchins's reiteration of the feminist slogan 'the personal is political' is significant here. *Gender Outlaw* ends with a monologue entitled 'The Seven Year Itch', which concludes with a vision of the transsexual subject sloughing off a succession of identities in order to become 'the one the dictionary has trouble naming':

> Get your last looks now, 'cause I'm changing already
> And by the time the next seven years have come and gone
> I'm gonna be new all over again.
> (Bornstein, 1994, 238)

Bornstein's concern here is with cultural classification, metamorphosis and performance: in contrast, *Read My Lips* concludes with a 'selected chronology' of significant events in the history of transsexual activism. In these very different conclusions are foregrounded both the differences and similarities between Bornstein and Wilchins. Bornstein is a performer, her text grounded in the *acting out* of a transgendered identity which does not seek to reconcile its disparate parts into a unified whole, and which lays far more stress on the 'personal' side of 'the personal is political' equation. Wilchins's intentions, however, are more explicitly political, as one would expect from one of the founders of the activist organizations Transexual Menace and GenderPAC, a conclusion backed up by her claim that 'everything I've been saying has an explicit political agenda to it: I am absolutely trying to use language and knowledge to subvert certain ideas about bodies, gender and desire' (Wilchins, 1997, 194).

In her text, Wilchins seems torn between the desire to formulate some kind of cohesive identity for trans people – arguing, for example, that 'if you're engaged in an activist struggle, you'd better look very closely at the identity you're choosing to mobilize around' (Wilchins, 1997, 186) – and an awareness that it is both impossible and inadvisable to do so. Indeed, her vision of 'a third force, another kind of politics', which is not grounded in an appeal to a unified identity, is distinctly reminiscent of Bornstein's concept of the 'third space'.

> Will a movement without identities be messy? Yes, as messy and multi-layered as we actually are. Won't a political movement lacking a unified subject have contradictions and discord? Of course. But as Judith Butler suggested, maybe it's time to stop sacrificing the complexity of our lives at the altar of unified identity, to acknowledge our contradictions and take political action with all of them intact. Unity is a product of encouraging diversity, not of reinforcing its absence.
>
> Our contradictions and differences are more than political obstacles: they are reminders of our boundlessness, confirmations that we can never be fully captured or circumscribed, that no label or movement can ever hope to encompass all we are or hope to be. And that diversity is our strength in the face of the familiar, tyrannical Western project to impose the monolithic, all-enveloping truths that marginalized, suppressed, and erased us in the first place. (Wilchins, 1997, 199)

The contradictions within Wilchins's argument – with which she is very consciously struggling throughout her text – is indicative of both the problems and the possibilities presented by the attempt to formulate a transgender identity. After all, 'transgender' itself is an amorphous term, and any body of theory has to define the kind of 'body' from which it arises: a difficult task, given the multiplicity of different possibilities and permutations which arise from the overturning of dualistic conceptions of gender. The view that the 'contradictions and differences' of transgendered identity are envisaged at once as 'political obstacles' and as utopian 'reminders of our boundlessness' may be a neat paradox, but it's unclear exactly how – in spite of Wilchins's assertion that 'a unified national movement to end gender-based oppression is right before us (Wilchins, 1997, 200) – such a conundrum can be resolved.

It is this which many feminists see as an insurmountable problem to an acceptance of a transgender politics: in particular, an essentialist feminism associated particularly with the second wave which is concerned with establishing a firm definition of 'woman' on which to base an activist politics. From such a standpoint, 'gender' does not unproblematically elide into 'transgender'. On the contrary, from such a perspective any ideology which blurs gender boundaries is profoundly threatening, and therefore it is perhaps not surprising that one of the common themes linking all three of the transgender texts discussed here is the voicing of the authors' concern regarding their relationship with feminism. Sandy Stone's reference to 'Empire' in 'The *Empire* Strikes Back' is to Janice G. Raymond's contentious work *The Transsexual Empire: The Making of the She-Male*, which not only exemplifies the hard-line feminist reaction to transgenderism, but also included a personal attack upon Stone herself. Raymond's book was originally published in 1979, and is outright in its condemnation of male-to-female transsexuals who wish to identify themselves with feminist aims and objectives. Raymond argues that 'the transsexually constructed lesbian-feminist may have renounced femininity but not masculinity and masculinist behaviour (despite deceptive appearances)' (Raymond, 1994, 101). In other words, once a man, always a man, regardless of surgery or any sense of identity which argues to the contrary: instead, 'the transsexually constructed lesbian-feminist is the man who indeed gets to be "the man" in an exclusive women's club to which he would otherwise have no access' (Raymond, 1994, 111).

A revised edition of *The Transsexual Empire*, published in 1994, demonstrated Raymond standing by the ideas she had first posed fifteen years before. In a new introduction, she reiterates her view that transsexualism is 'largely a male phenomenon' (Raymond, 1994, xiii), 'the invention of men initially developed for men' (Raymond, 1994, xiv). In seeking to transform themselves through surgery, male-to-female transsexuals merely perpetuate the patriarchal assumption that women's bodies can be owned and controlled. Raymond has little patience with postmodernist theories regarding performativity, arguing that, far from revealing gender as being acted out upon the body, surgically constructed transsexuals 'are not simply acting, nor are they text, or genre . . . They purport to be the real thing' (Raymond, 1994, xxiii). Moreover, transgenderism is condemned for 'encourag[ing] a *style rather than a politics of resistance*, in which an expressive individualism has taken the place of collective political challenges to power . . . men and women mixing and matching but not moving beyond both' (Raymond, 1994, xxxiv–xxxv).

Nor is Raymond alone in her opinion that the transsexual identification with feminism is problematic. Giving the lie to Sandy Stone's assertion that *The Transsexual Empire* represented 'a specific moment in feminist analysis' (Stone, 1992, 283), as recently as 1999 Germaine Greer published *The Whole Woman*, in which, in a chapter provocatively entitled 'Pantomime Dames', she attacks the transsexual phenomenon in terms which echo Raymond's. She regards transsexualism as symbolizing an insidious attempt to infiltrate the feminist movement, appropriating it from within. Her conclusion is that, when the transsexual 'forces his way into the few private spaces women may enjoy and shouts down their objections, and bombards the women who will not accept him with threats and hate mail, he does as rapists have always done' (Greer, 1999, 74).

One of the most common narrative tropes of transgender narratives, therefore, is the experience of exclusion from feminist – particularly lesbian-feminist – networks. Indeed, Bernstein comes to the conclusion that

> [a]ny revolution in deconstructing gender should look for no support among communities of people whose identities depend on the existence of . . . [a] bi-polar gender system. This would include, but most certainly is not limited to, the fundamentalist right wing, purists in the lesbian and gay male communities who believe in the ultimate goal of assimilation into the dominant culture, and some cultural or radical feminists. (Bernstein, 1994, 132)

Riki Anne Wilchins relates the story of attempting to infiltrate the Michigan Womyn's Music Festival, which had instituted 'a policy of "womyn-born womyn only"' (Wilchins, 1997, 109). Although this episode ends in triumph, with the women at the festival voicing support for the transgender cause, Wilchins nevertheless gives bitter voice to an extended policy of exclusion on the part of the lesbian feminist movement

> I knew the name for what I was, and I knew I belonged with other lesbians. But the women's community greeted us less like prodigal sisters returned to the fold than like the unchanged kitty litter. Following a decade of fruitless efforts to claim my place in the lesbian movement and sick of being harassed at parties, in bars, and in groups, I left for good. (Wilchins 1997, 111)

Such wavering between isolation and collectivism is, it seems, a common characteristic of transgendered texts, which struggle to construct a cohesive identity outside the common frame of reference provided by heterosexuality. However, perhaps the plight of the transsexual can be regarded as paradigmatic of the dilemma of the twenty-first-century subject, in which identity is no longer necessarily codeterminate on gender.

NOTES TOWARDS A READING OF ANGELA CARTER'S *THE PASSION OF NEW EVE*

The Passion of New Eve was published in 1977, hence predating the advent of the gender and transgender theories outlined in the chapter above. However, it is extraordinarily amenable to readings which draw on such theories, since the narrating subject is itself transgendered, relating a story of metamorphosis from male to female achieved through surgical intervention. Evelyn begins his narrative as male, but, caught up in a futuristic civil war in America, he is kidnapped by a militant feminist group and surgically transformed into New Eve, 'a perfect specimen of womanhood' (Carter, 1982, 68). The rest of the novel centres around Eve's adventures in a post-apocalyptic world, in which she experiences the difference of life as a woman. 'The technological Eve in person' (Carter, 1982, 146), she can also, of course, be regarded as a literal incarnation of Donna Haraway's cyborg.

Although Angela Carter herself never cited transsexual autobiography as a referent for this text, *The Passion of New Eve* nevertheless follows a trajectory which is reminiscent of such narratives, reproducing the split consciousness which Jay Prosser regards as a foundational characteristic of autobiographical texts written by transsexuals: 'the split between the "I" of the *bios* and the "I" of the *graph*, the past self written and the present self writing, [which] is heightened by the story of sex change' (Prosser 1998, 102). Read in such a context, Eve/lyn's narration in *The Passion of New Eve* is itself revealed as transgendered, for although the narrative voice with which the novel begins is apparently gendered male, it is refracted through the female consciousness of Eve, who is telling her story in retrospect.

However, while *The Passion of New Eve* may employ, whether knowingly or not, many of the tropes and conventions of transsexual autobiography, it does not, ultimately, sustain them. In 'The *Empire* Strikes Back', Sandy Stone – as has already been described – is critical of the way in which such narratives record the male subject's attainment of an unambiguous, essentialist femininity, ' "woman" as male fetish . . . replicating a socially enforced role' (Stone, 1992, 285). Carter's novel is crucially different, in that it is based around a character who makes the transaction from male to female unwillingly. Therefore, whereas the narratives described by Stone and others relate the experience of transition from the 'wrong' body to the 'right' one, Carter's evokes a subject who in the wake of surgery is left struggling with the very sense of bodily estrangement the transsexual has left behind:

> [W]hen I looked in the mirror, I saw Eve; I did not see myself. I saw a young woman who, though she was I, I could in no way acknowledge as myself, for this one was only a lyrical abstraction of femininity to me, a tinted arrangement of curved lines. (Carter, 1982, 74)

Such a dislocation between the gendered subject and the gendered body opens the novel out to interpretations based upon Judith Butler's conception of the performativity of gender. Indeed, Eve/lyn's dilemma can be read as a literalization of Butler's point that 'the inner truth of gender is a fabrication and . . . a true gender is a fantasy instituted and inscribed on the surface of bodies' (Butler, 1990, 136). The transformation of Eve/lyn's body may make her biologically female, but that is not enough – the attainment of 'true' femininity also demands the conscious acquisition of a whole range of different behaviours. This experience, however, leads her to the belief that all feminine behaviour is essentially performative: 'although I was a woman, I was also passing for a woman, but then, many women born spend their whole lives in just such imitations' (Carter, 1982, 101).

There is another figure in *The Passion of New Eve*, however, who can be read as reinforcing the notion that gender identity is constructed rather than natural. Embedded in the narrative of an 'enforced' transsexual is the tragic story of an 'authentic' transsexual, Tristessa de St Ange. Denied the opportunity to 'match his function to his form' (Carter, 1982, 173), Tristessa instead becomes 'the greatest female impersonator of his generation' (Carter, 1982, 144) by transforming him/herself into a Hollywood movie star and an icon of femininity which is all the more powerful for its ultimate artificiality:

> He had made himself the shrine of his own desires, had made of himself the only woman he could have loved! If a woman is indeed beautiful only in so far as she incarnates most completely the secret aspirations of man, no wonder Tristessa had been able to become the most beautiful woman in the world, an unbegotten woman who made no concessions to humanity.
>
> Tristessa, the sensuous fabrication of the mythology of the flea-pits. How could a real woman ever have been so much a woman as you? (Carter, 1982, 128–9)

The ironic tone in which that question is posed again recalls Stone's critique of transsexual depictions of women. Although undeniably tragic, Tristessa is not, in many ways, supposed to be seen as an admirable figure, for in her screen roles she perpetuates an image of femininity which defines it through repeated references to suffering and passivity – as Eve/lyn observes, '[h]ow much he must have loved and hated women, to let Tristessa be so beautiful and make her suffer so!' (Carter, 1982, 144).

Indeed, *The Passion of New Eve* can be read as a satire upon transsexuality which retraces some of the same ideas as those evoked by essentialist feminists such as Janice Raymond and Germaine Greer – that transsexualism perpetuates a male conception of what femininity is. Eve/lyn later learns that Tristessa was refused surgery by the radical feminist Mother because 'she was struck by the awfully ineradicable quality of his maleness' (Carter, 1982, 173). That idea can only be taken so far, however, for Carter's other target in this novel is essentialist feminism itself. Mother performs surgery upon herself, not to change her gender, but to align herself more firmly with mythic archetypes of femininity: she is 'the hand-carved figurehead of her own, self-constructed theology' (Carter, 1982, 58), and 'her own mythological artefact' (Carter, 1982, 60). But in the final analysis Mother is not meant to be taken any more seriously than Tristessa, for like Tristessa, Mother's transformation is a performance which is ultimately incapable of being sustained. By the end of the novel, Mother has deteriorated into a mad old drunk singing on a Californian beach, having failed in her attempt to convert the world into a place where her mythic symbolism will have meaning and power.

Stone, Bornstein and Wilchins all envisage an ideology which has escaped the prison-house of gender dualism – be it a 'third space' (Bornstein), a 'third force' (Wilchins) or 'a myriad of alterities' (Stone). *The Passion of New Eve* can be approached as a novel which encourages a supportive reading of such theories. It critiques dualistic conceptions of gender by presenting its reader with grotesque parodies of extreme masculinity and femininity, while at the same time centring its narrative in a voice which encompasses the experience of both. When Eve/lyn – once a man and now a woman – and Tristessa – the man who has lived his entire life as a woman – have sex in the middle of the desert, it is portrayed as an act which so confounds customary ways of conceptualizing gender that the system founders in confusion:

> Masculine and feminine are correlatives which involve one another. I am sure of that – the quality and its negation are locked in necessity. But what the nature of masculine and feminine might be, whether they involve male and female, if they have anything to do with Tristessa's so long neglected apparatus or my own factory fresh incision and engine-turned breasts, that I do not know. Though I have been both man and woman, still I do not know the answer to these questions. Still they bewilder me. (Carter, 1982, 149–50)

At the end of the novel, Evelyn, who may or may not be pregnant with Tristessa's child, sails off into an unknown and unimaginable future. Such an inconclusive conclusion is indicative, it could be argued, of the difficulties involved in challenging dominant ideologies of gender, which shape our patterns of thought at the deepest level. As Sandy Stone says of the attempt to formulate a position from which a transsexual discourse could be enunciated:

> For a transsexual, *as a transsexual*, to generate a true, effective and representational counterdiscourse is to speak from outside the boundaries of gender, beyond the constructed oppositional nodes which have been predefined as the only positions from which discourse is possible. How, then, can the transsexual speak? If the transsexual were to speak, what would s/he say? (Stone, 1992, 295)

It is significant that Carter's chosen mode is science fiction, while Stone makes extensive use of science fiction referents in her essay (after all, 'The *Empire* Strikes Back' is not only a sideswipe at Raymond, but also echoes the title of George Lucas's cinematic science fiction epic). For both Carter and Stone, the individual who is no longer bound within gender dualisms is a cyborg subject, their half-natural, half-technological origins placing them in the futuristic realm of the posthuman. From this perspective, the transgendered subject represents the culmination of all our thinking about gender, becoming the symbol of future, as yet half-imagined, possibilities.

QUESTIONS FOR FURTHER CONSIDERATION

1. In *The Second Sex* (1949), Simone de Beauvoir asserts that 'One is not born, but rather becomes, a woman'. Debate the relevance of this statement to contemporary gender theory.

2. Is feminism necessarily dependent upon the maintenance of a stable definition of 'woman'?

3. Consider the role of the autobiographic mode in transgender theory.

4. How does gender identity affect narrative identity in *The Passion of New Eve*?

5. Does Eve/lyn symbolize emancipation from the confines of gender, or does s/he simply move from one sex to the other?

6. Does the ending of the book indicate the possibility of a future for the transgendered subject?

ANNOTATED BIBLIOGRAPHY

Bornstein, Kate. *Gender Outlaw: On Men, Women and the Rest of Us*. London and New York: Routledge, 1994. Bornstein's book is an example of postmodernist transsexual writing, which combines autobiographical material with a more general theorization concerning the place of the transsexual in culture and discourse. It is written in a distinctive, informal and often humorous style, which makes it an accessible introduction to the issues which preoccupy the transgender community. Bornstein posits a view of the transsexual as opening the way to a multiple conception of gender, and of possible sexual roles, thus eliminating the oppression of any individual – whether transsexual or not – who seeks to assume roles not sanctioned within a culture based upon the dualism of male and female.

Butler, Judith. *Gender Trouble: Feminism and the Subversion of Identity*. London: Routledge, 1990. Judith Butler's work has been enormously influential within gender and transgender studies. *Gender Trouble* is her most frequently cited text, in which she challenges feminist theory's assumption that 'woman' is an unproblematic category upon which a collective identity is capable of being based. Drawing on the work of French feminists such as Luce Irigaray and Monique Wittig, as well as Foucault's theories concerning the relationship between sex and power, Butler argues that the subject achieves a sense of internal coherence precisely by conforming to socially approved sex/gender roles. Neither sex nor gender are therefore innate, but roles people perform: a conclusion which opens out the seductive possibility of a multiplicity of gender identities rather than the 'either/or' polarity of male and female. The subject, therefore, is no longer localized and self-sufficient, but circulates within networks of interlinking discourses, paving the way for a feminist politics which seeks to contest the naturalization of heterosexist ideologies.

Stone, Sandy. 'The *Empire* Strikes Back: A Posttranssexual Manifesto'. In *Body Guards: The Cultural Politics of Gender Ambiguity*, eds Julia Epstein and Kristina Straub. London: Taylor & Francis Books, Routledge, 1992: 280–304. Stone's 'Posttranssexual Manifesto' is a seminal work within theoretical transsexual debates. Stone traces a history of male-to-female transsexual autobiographical writing dating from 1933, and argues that it conventionally traces a process of surgical metamorphosis which has the assumption of an extremely conventional feminine identity as its ultimate aim. It is a tendency encouraged by a medical establishment, which requires the 'mtf' transsexual to demonstrate their suitability for surgery by demonstrating that they can fit into socially approved gender categories. Therefore the transsexual is denied any position in discourse which lies outside the male/female paradigm: he/she must always speak 'as' a man or a woman. Stone proposes that transsexuals will only be able to formulate an effective counterdiscourse when they abandon the attempt to 'pass', and begin to articulate their multiple, often incompatible, experiences of gender ambiguity.

Tripp, Anna (ed.). *Gender*. Basingstoke: Palgrave Press, 2000. An excellent anthology of writings on gender, this book is valuable for its illustration of the broad spectrum of debate that can fall under the rubric of 'gender theory', demonstrating the way in which gender issues intersect with feminist theory, queer theory, masculinity theory, post-colonialism, postmodernism and psychoanalysis. The writers included are all well-known authorities within their specialisms, and include Judith Butler, Virginia Woolf and Chandra Talpade Mohanty. None of the extracts are very long, but detailed bibliographies simplify the process of following up the debates presented in more detail. Anna Tripp's introduction also gives a clear introduction to the many applications of gender theory. This book is a good starting point for students wishing to investigate gender, acting as a stepping stone to the complex theoretical debates it has initiated.

Whittle, Stephen. *The Transgender Debate: The Crisis Surrounding Gender Identities*. Reading: Garnet, 2000. This recently published text is a brief but extremely accessible introduction to the current state of transgender studies. Whittle, himself a female-to-male transsexual, outlines the history of theorizing about gender and transgender, as well as the medical theories surrounding the phenomenon and the surgical process involved in gender reassignment for both men and women. He also includes short introductions to key texts in transgender theory and autobiography, a list of significant dates charting the development of the transgender movement, and a useful glossary of key terms in transgender studies.

Wilchins, Ricki Anne. *Read My Lips: Sexual Subversion and the End of Gender*. Ithaca, NY: Firebrand Books, 1997. Ricki Anne Wilchins is a founder member of the most visible activist group in the United States, Transsexual Menace. Her book, a volatile mix of autobiography, trans history, theorization and vehemently argued personal opinion, is an appeal for an end to oppression on the grounds of gender. Wilchins records a history of persecution of transgendered individuals, arguing that behind such high-profile cases as the rape and murder of female-to-male transsexual Brandon Teena in 1993 lie an almost universal experience of abuse and social isolation. Wilchins draws on personal experience of exclusion from lesbian-feminist organizations in order to make a point that this oppression originates from all sectors of society, since society is founded on preserving an 'either/or' distinction between male and female. Instead, she argues for the acceptance of difference, and celebrates the multiple sexual and political possibilities that such tolerance would bring.

SUPPLEMENTARY BIBLIOGRAPHY

Bornstein, Kate. *My Gender Workbook: How to Become a Real Man, a Real Woman, the Real You, or Something Else Entirely*. London: Routledge, 1997.

Butler, Judith. *Bodies That Matter: On the Discursive Limits of 'Sex'*. London: Routledge, 1993.

Califia, Pat. *Sex Changes: The Politics of Transgenderism*. San Francisco, CA: Cleis Press, 1997.

Carter, Angela. *The Passion of New Eve*. London: Virago Press, 1982.

Cixous, Hélène. 'Sorties'. In Hélène Cixous and Catherine Clément. *The Newly-Born Woman*. Manchester: Manchester University Press, 1986, 63–132.

Cromwell, Jason. *Transmen and Ftms: Identities, Bodies, Genders and Sexualities*. Chicago, IL: University of Illinois Press, 1999.

Devor, Holly. *Gender Blending: Confronting the Limits of Duality*. Bloomington, IN: Indiana University Press, 1989.

Fausto-Sterling, Anne. *Sexing the Body: Gender Politics and the Construction of Sexuality*. NY: Basic Books, 2000.

Feinberg, Leslie. *Stone Butch Blues*. Ithaca, New York: Firebrand Books, 1993.

Feinberg, Leslie. *Transgender Warriors: Making History from Joan of Arc to Dennis Rodman*. Boston, MA: Beacon Press 1997.

Feinberg, Leslie. *Trans Liberation: Beyond Pink or Blue*. Boston, MA: Beacon Press, 1999.

Foucault, Michel. *The History of Sexuality Volume 1: An Introduction*. London: Penguin Books, 1990.

Fuss, Diana. *Essentially Speaking: Feminism, Nature and Difference*. New York: Routledge, 1989.

Glover, David and Cora Kaplan (eds). *Genders*. London and New York: Routledge, 2000.

Greer, Germaine. *The Whole Woman*. London: Doubleday, 1999.

Haraway, Donna J. 'A Cyborg Manifesto: Science, Technology, and Socialist-Feminism in the Late Twentieth Century'. In *Simians, Cyborgs, and Women: The Reinvention of Nature*. London: Free Association Books, 1991, 149–81.

Humm, Maggie (ed.). *Feminisms: A Reader*. Hemel Hempstead: Harvester Wheatsheaf, 1992.

Kessler, Suzanne J. *Lessons from the Intersexed*. New Brunswick, NJ: Rutgers University Press, 1998.

Kotz, Liz. 'The Body You Want: An Interview with Judith Butler', *Artforum International*, 31, 3, 1992, 82–9.

Lauretis, Teresa de. *Technologies of Gender: Essays on Theory, Film, and Fiction*. London: Macmillan, 1987.

Millett, Kate. *Sexual Politics*. London: Virago Press, 1977.

More, Kate and Stephen Whittle (eds). *Reclaiming Genders: Transsexual Grammars at the Fin de Siècle*. London: Cassell, 1999.

Prosser, Jay. *Second Skins: The Body Narratives of Transsexuality*. New York: Columbia University Press, 1998.

Raymond, Janice. *The Transsexual Empire: the Making of the She-Male*. New York: Teachers College Press, 1994.

Riviere, Joan. 'Womanliness as a Masquerade'. In *Formations of Fantasy*, eds Victor Burgin, James Donald and Cora Kaplan. London: Methuen, 1986. 35–44.

Rubin, Gayle. 'The Traffic in Women: Notes on the "Political Economy" of Sex'. In *Toward an Anthropology of Women*, ed. Rayna R. Reites. New York: Monthly Review Press, 1975.

Sedgwick, Eve Kosofsky. *The Epistemology of the Closet*. Berkeley, CA: University of California Press, 1992.

Sedgwick, Eve Kosofsky and Andrew Parker (eds). *Performance and Performativity*. London: Routledge, 1994.

Stoller, Robert J. *Sex and Gender: On the Development of Masculinity and Femininity*. London: Hogarth Press, 1968.

Whittle, Stephen (ed.). *Journal of Gender Studies, Special Issue: Transgendering*, 7, 3.

CHAPTER 3

WOMEN OF COLOR AND FEMINIST CRITICISM: THEORIZING LOVE

Tace Hedrick and Debra Walker King

INTRODUCTION

Since the United States civil rights movements of the 1960s and 1970s, women of color have discovered it is as much love (self-love and love for those who share the jeopardy of race) that must be theorized, as it is the conjunctions of race and gender. Over against traditional academic critical work, which oftentimes disconnects itself from such a seemingly radical subjectivity, in this chapter we emphasize the work of women of color who seek to use the notion of love, and of mutual care, as epistemological frameworks designed to produce a 'knowledge' from which both a critical oeuvre and an activism can emerge. Thus, paradoxically enough, we begin our discussion of twenty-first-century feminists of color by briefly revisiting the late 1960s and early 1970s.

With so-called love-ins like the one held in Los Angeles on 29 April 1968, which drew up to 4,000 participants, one might argue that the late 1960s were indeed a time when 'love' seemed to be in the air. Love-ins, be-ins and happenings were staged across the nation; 1968 saw the Summer of Love announced in San Francisco's Haight-Ashbury district, an event which drew thousands of participants and tourists alike, and which was avidly reported on by the media with equal mixtures of fascination and horror. The 7 July issue of *Time*, for instance, had as its front-cover story 'The Hippies: The Philosophy of a Subculture', and on 22 August CBS aired a news special with Harry Reasoner entitled 'The Hippie Temptation' (*Colin's Haight-Ashbury Archives*, 1998). For young women, such media scrutiny meant that not only love but also change was in the air. The 'Summer of Love' and all its variations signalled the arrival of a degree of sexual freedom for women, who were only then beginning to have access to a reliable birth control pill and, in some places, access to safe and legal abortion on demand (*American Cultural History*). However, this was a freedom which seemed to benefit mostly young, white, middle-class women and the white men who accompanied them on their journeys of self-discovery.

Oftentimes, instead of attending love-ins and participating in sexual revolutions, women of color were contemplating their role and visibility in politically inspired sit-ins and social revolutions. They were privileged to either experience or observe some of the most intense moments of socio-cultural confrontation and political upheaval in twentieth-century American history. On one front of the decade's multifarious revolutionary rebirth stood the Nation of Islam, the Black Panthers and the student Nonviolent Coordinating Committee (SNCC) – each organized around the cause of Black liberation. On another was an emerging woman's movement, focused most intimately on the cause of white women's domestic and economic liberation. On a third front were organizations eager to redress the societal and economic inequalities facing America's Chicana/o and Latina/o populations. Under the banner of the United Farm Workers Union, Chicano/a migrant workers struck for better wages and living conditions, and in the Young Lords Party, Nuyoricans[1] and Afro-Nuyoricans organized around socialist ideas and issues of race. Each of these was founded upon different social, political, domestic and creative concerns. In fact, difference was central to the life of each group mentioned above – what some have called 'identity politics'. Ultimately, the value of difference became pivotal to intra-group dynamics. These ruptures exposed a phenomenon of exclusion arising within group dynamics that was not easily ignored by women of color, as the title of Gloria T. Hull, Patricia Bell Scott and Barbara Smith's 1982 *All the Women Are White, All the Blacks are Men, But Some of Us Are Brave* attests. Women of color, understanding that their needs differed from those of their male compatriots, were forced to shift their position from passive followers to active participants, demanding their own voices both within and outside civil rights movements. As a result, their gendered, and often classed, concerns presented moments of rupture within each group's hope of unity.

White feminism and women's studies, fighting their own battles to enter the nation's political and educational institutions, were less interested in the claims of race liberation. Women of color who were interested in feminism were told by race conscious 'brothers' that they were traitors to their race, dividing their loyalties and undermining the struggle. The late 1960s and early 1970s' Black and Chicano movements' emphasis on nationalism meant that liberation was first and foremost a masculine freedom to enter the public arena, as Aída Hurtado has pointed out in *The Color of Privilege*. Men of color dedicated to making their voices heard in public institutions emphasized that the fight belonged to the *carnales*, the blood brothers, while women stayed home and cared for the family – *la familia* – giving birth to soldiers for the revolution. According to Stokley Carmichel, woman's place in this revolution was 'prone', and, for the most part, literary productions of cultural nationalism supported his view. 'Colored' women interested in liberation, both sexual and civil, were told that the grand dame of such freedoms, feminism, was a 'white' thing, or even more potentially alienating, that feminism was a 'lesbian thing'.

Like the leaders of the radical movements from whence they often emerged, leading poets and creative figures of cultural nationalism, particularly during the Black Arts Movement, the Chicano Renaissance and the Nuyorican poets' movement, supported male empowerment while theorizing racially motivated rage, revolution and war. For Black women, questions of whether it was appropriate to step beyond the confines of race politics and into gender liberation politics abounded during the civil rights era. These questions culminated in a collection of essays edited by Toni Cade Bambara (*The Black Woman*) in 1970. Beyond Bambara's collection, however, only a few non-white female participants in the middle era of civil rights movements – the 1960s – addressed women's issues. Even poets like Nikki Giovani or Elaine Brown and Kathleen Cleaver (of the Black Panthers) expressed strong support of Black male empowerment and masculinist imagery in their writing, leaving the cause of female liberation hidden within the margins and symbolic undertones of their work.

Not until women writers began focusing on their own issues did the notion of female liberation become an issue for cultural nationalism. Such writers included Sarah Wright (*This Child's Gonna Live*, 1969), Toni Morrison (*The Bluest Eye*, 1970), Ntozake Shange (*For Colored Girls Who Have Considered Suicide When the Rainbow is Enuf*, 1976), Martita Morales, Lorna Dee Cervantes ('You Cramp My Style, Baby' and 'Para un Revolucionaro', 1975), and Berenice Zamora (*Restless Serpents*, 1976). By the early 1980s, feminists of color had begun to seriously rethink the masculine-oriented demands of cultural nationalism and race loyalty under whose terms they had come to political consciousness. In addition, the importance of thinking about the 'difference within' feminism – differences of race, class, sexual orientation – had become central to theorizing of racism and classism in feminist thought. One theme running through much of the writing done by women of color during this transitional period is pain: not only the pain of racism and sexism, but the pain of being pulled in too many directions by the requirements of loving one's race, loving men of the race and loving oneself as a brown- or dark-skinned woman.

For the past twenty years, feminists of color like the writers who first gave voice to their struggles have focused on the revolutionary power of love and self-care in order to, as bell hooks has it, create 'a revolutionary feminist movement that can speak directly to the pain that is within folks, and offer them healing words, healing strategies, healing theory' (hooks, 1994, 33). Recognizing the power of their voice and vision, women of color enter the twenty-first century mobilized against silence, lack and absence. Through acts of 'loving' and what this chapter will call 'sexual healing' (sexual expression that is both regenerating and self-affirming), they reclaim their past, reconstitute their present and justify their claim to human liberty, social autonomy and economic equality.

THEORETICAL CONSIDERATIONS

Women of color were rarely the subject of academic discourse (save for the rare sociological treatise) until the 1970s when Toni Cade edited *The Black Woman* (1970) and Marta Cotera published her ground-breaking 1976 *Diosa y Hembra: The History and Heritage of Chicanas in the U.S.* Not until the early 1980s did scholarly essays, published in scattered journals, begin to recuperate a history and tradition of Black, Chicana and Latina feminists and pre-feminists. To do this, it was necessary to cross borders as well as centuries. Latina feminists have been engaged in the task of re-discovering the work of Latin American as well as Hispanic American women, dating as far back as the figure of Sor Juana Inés de la Cruz (1651–95), a New Spain nun who was one of the most brilliant poets, theologians, composers and thinkers of her day. Different from the early interest surrounding black writers and lecturers like Maria Stewart and Zora Neale Hurston, the archaeology recuperating US Latina and Chicana writers (dating from the mid-nineteenth century up through the 1950s) has had to wait until recent years, with work such as Tey Diana Rebolledo's *Women Singing in the Snow* (1995).

Even as the academy began to realize the importance of this work to a thorough understanding of various cultural and literary histories, the issues, themes and social politics raised in this rediscovered and newly written literature were either ignored or undervalued by everyone except those struggling to do the work of reclamation and recuperation. Through their efforts most literary and cultural critics eventually offered a nod at race, class and gender oppression, but few acknowledged the impact all three have on the lives of women of color. Even more disturbing was the tendency of critics to rely upon literature's textual components for meaning with little or no consideration of context.

Scholars who rejected the 'author is dead' philosophy of fashionable literary criticism attempted to correct this oversight. African-American women, for instance, risked claims of essentialism while insisting any analyses ignoring the contextual (and, of course, the intertextual) dimensions of Black women's fiction distort meaning and invalidates the lives such literature represent.[2] Their calls for analyses grounded in contextual legitimacy were interpreted to mean no one but Black women could analyse Black women's literature authentically. Thus, Black feminist criticism entered a necessary, although regrettably alienating, phase – a move that raised another, even more problematic, concern. Does imposing alien (meaning, phallocentric or Eurocentric) values and ideologies on a work reflecting the 'oppressions, the insanities, the loyalties, and triumphs' (Walker, 1983, 250) of African-American women's lives somehow work to destroy or, in some way, corrupt that literature? Was it reductive – that is, did it reduce the importance of the work – for example, to read Hurston's *Their Eyes*

Were Watching God through a white feminist version of Freudian psycho-analysis? Was it even possible?

By the mid-1980s, these concerns forced discussions about what kind of criticism can best ensure the 'survival whole' of Black women and their creative voices. What kind of criticism can interpret the linguistic, cultural, physical, metaphysical, ideological and psychological complexities presented within African-American women's fiction without distortion or reduction? For many the answer was womanism, a sometimes nationalistic and deftly subjective approach to literary and cultural studies celebrating African-American women's culture and 'ways of knowing' while acknowledging the impact non-Black social structures and belief systems have on that knowledge.[3]

Womanists challenge racial, sexual and class oppression by exposing the effects of their intersectionality and reclaiming the experiences of literary characters as testimony of how our world influences Black women's development as people and as individuals.[4] As Barbara Smith notes, criticism validates the existence of literature and its realness (1982, 159). To validate the intellectual and creative work of African-American women, womanist critics, like the writers they study, focus on 'connection rather than separation, transforming silence into speech, and giving back power to the culturally disenfranchised' (Pryse, 1985, 5). Thus, the womanist critic is always mindful of sexual politics and cultural context, the intertextual development of language, myth, myth-making and the necessities of loving.

Similarly, Chicana and Latina feminists seek connections between themselves and context, particularly the contextual and intertextual development of language and the necessities of loving. For instance, language – specifically, code-switching, or mixing Spanish and English together – is important for Chicana and Latina writers. In particular, Chicana artists such as lesbian playwright, poet, and essayist Cherríe Moraga and the lesbian poet and essayist Gloria Anzaldúa have come to realize that their own language, sexuality, and their own sense of their bodies, is part and parcel of their sense of who they are as Chicanas.[5] Listening to Black feminist poet Ntozake Shange read in an auditorium in Berkeley, Moraga 'realized to the core of me that for years I had disowned the language I knew best. I had ignored the words and rhythms that were the closest to me: the sounds of my mother and aunts gossiping – half in English, half in Spanish, while drinking *cerveza* in the kitchen' (Moraga, 2000, 47). For Moraga, relearning Spanish meant returning to a love she had been turned away from: love for her working-class origins, for her mother and for women of color. 'In returning to the love of my *raza*, I must confront the fact that not only has the mother been taken from me, but her tongue, my mother-tongue' (2000, 131). Love in this context means accepting the fact that when she speaks in either language, that speech literally is a 'woman coming out of her mouth' (133) – a phrase which puns on the various contemporary meanings of 'coming out' and at the same time calls attention both in physical image and in metaphor to Moraga's idea that women's speech is intimately connected with her sense of what it is, socially, physically and sexually, to be Chicana.

The first task of recuperating the voices of women of color – for the academy and the public alike – consisted in locating connections that embody, reform and conjure (as Marjorie Pryse suggests) a linguistic and literary history lost or devalued due to neglect, ignorance and distortion. For Black women this work, done most effectively in *Conjuring* (1985), edited by Hortense Spillers and Marjorie Pryse, and in Cheryl A. Wall's edited collection *Changing Our Own Words* (1989), began with *All the Women Are White, All the Blacks Are Men, But Some of Us Are Brave* (1982) and Barbara Smith's edited anthology *Home Girls* (1983). Both of these texts work to reinstate Black women (and Black lesbians) into social, cultural and literary history as well as into academic studies – particularly women's studies. Both texts make connections with a past silenced in obscurity and hate, linguistic models of cultural authenticity devalued by distortion. Both validate the need for Black women's continued scholarship, restoration, reclamation and social activism.

Critical work seeking to reposition feminist thought from the standpoint of Chicana and Latina feminists also continued in 1983 with the cross-cultural, landmark collection *This Bridge Called My Back: Writing By Radical Women of Color*, edited by Anzaldúa and Moraga, and with a foreword by Toni Cade (Bambara) and essays by black poets Audre Lorde and hattie gossett as well as Chinese poet Nellie Wong (among others). This was, indeed, the first collection of essays speaking to needs, desires and loves claimed by women of color. Speaking more exclusively to Chicana feminist issues were essays such as Yvonne Yarbro-Bejarno's 'Chicana Literature from a Chicana Feminist Perspective' in Maria Herrera-Sobek and Helena Maria Viramontes' 1988 collection *Chicana Creativity and Criticism: Charting New Frontiers in American Literature*. And at the beginning of the 1990s, *Making Face, Making Soul/ Haciendo Caras*, edited by Gloria Anzaldúa (1990), brought together some of the most important work done over the last decade. The feminist consciousness of Cuban American women was highlighted via playwright Dolores Prida's *Beautiful Señoritas & Other Plays*, collected and published by the Arte Público Press in 1991, while work connecting women Cuban and Cuban-American poets came just a few years later with Ruth Behar's ground-breaking 1995 *Puentes a Cuba: Bridges to Cuba*.

Moraga is one of Chicana feminism's most important voices; in 1981, after editing the anthology *This Bridge Called My Back*, she helped to found, along with Black feminists Audre Lorde and Barbara Smith, the Kitchen Table/ Women of Color Press in New York, one of the first presses committed to publishing works by women of color. Even more importantly, Moraga's own plays, poetry and essays, which she has been publishing since 1983, have consistently centred on questioning Chicana and Latina relations with each other through a close examination of her own identity as a Chicana lesbian. Like the work of Black lesbian authors Lorde and Smith, Moraga's strong feminist voice keeps the issue of loving women of color front and centre in our feminist consciousness. 'Passion', a term rarely heard in academic feminist discourse, became a central concern of Moraga's. Using the tropes of hunger and sexual love-making to think through what loving other women of color might really mean, in *Loving in the War Years* she asks, 'But what of passion? I hunger to ask. There's got to be more than hand-to-mouth survival' (1983, 136).[6]

Through the cultural continuities and oral traditions celebrated in literary form, African-American women writers give voice to passion and a desire for survival. It is a literature that reconstitutes human value and gives back to Black women that which was stolen, denied, ignored and deemed worthless – the truth of their womanhood and the peace found only in knowing and loving – having a passion for – what that means. Black women writers align their work closely with the realities of African-American women's lives by exposing the barriers thrown up by patriarchy and racism to self-knowledge, self-love and individual wholeness. They investigate the effects such barriers impose upon the development of characters like Pecola in *The Bluest Eye* by Toni Morrison, Mem Copeland in *The Third Life of Grange Copeland* by Alice Walker, and Silla in *Brown Girl, Brownstones* by Paule Marshal. In many ways, then, their fiction and poetry are instruments of sociocultural archaeology as well as examples of some of the best American art has to offer.

In *The Third Life of Grange Copeland* and *The Color Purple*, for instance, the fragmented lives of Margaret, Mem and Celie epitomize the historically brutal realities of patriarchal control through which African-American women have survived. Breaking a cultural silence, a taboo if you will, about black on black abuse, these texts ask us to examine the ways Black women and men struggle against each other. Grange Copeland, Brownsfield and Albert represent men who fight to control, not to love, the bodies and minds of the women in their lives. Like their real-world counterparts, they share a self-betrayal consummated and endorsed by a white patriarchal system that has already circumscribed the boundaries of their lives. Subsequently, their behaviour nullifies the possibility for their wives and children to experience wholeness.

To illustrate this point, Walker draws each of these men as a murderer of one kind or another. Grange causes Margaret's suicide through deprivation of love, understanding and companionship. Brownsfield literally kills Mem by shooting her in a moment of enraged jealousy and Albert kills Celie's spirit by mentally abusing her and depriving her of the love she needs to develop positive self-esteem. These three women, Margaret, Mem (whose name means 'the same') and Celie, represent the many like themselves whose bodies are torn and mutilated, whose minds are bent and branded, and whose spirits are ripped away or hidden behind walls of violence and oppression. Each of them relinquishes a vital part of themselves to defeat. Ironically, it is this abandoned self, an emotionally and spiritually intact self, which they need in order to survive whole. With the assistance of a woman, Shug, whose care and love builds personal strength, one of them, Celie, is able to reclaim her right to life's vitality; and, by doing so, Celie achieves the type of wholeness necessary for loving and healing one's self.

Alice Walker, Toni Morrison and Paule Marshal are only three women of color who venture through the bowels of stereotypical propaganda, racism and male domination to tell of lives twisted, altered and suffocated by the harsh realities of living found there. Their characters are not beauties clad in silk; neither are they cherished and heroically protected from barbarism and disrespect. Instead, they are brutalized, abused and scarred, both mentally and physically. They are rendered invisible and mute beneath the weight of prejudices that threaten their existence and complicate their ability to love themselves purely, that is loving without rage and doubt. Those who survive the sting of their oppression successfully learn to understand and value 'something that precedes love, follows love, informs love, shapes it, and to which love is subservient' (Morrison, 1998, 7). They learn 'necessity' – the 'necessity' of living Black and female in a system that denies their basic right to human dignity, justice and equality.

For African-American women scholars and intellectuals, understanding today's 'necessity' involves theorizing the experiences of affection, physical and spiritual awareness, collective memory, myth and loving through which women like themselves have survived for over two centuries. It means focusing on the rhythms and needs of our bodies, minds and hearts. It means defining the boundaries of mutual care as women's capacity to give and experience love become more immediate, more intimate, more necessary.

Loving in the War Years, begun in 1976 though not published until 1983, investigates similar themes of mutual care and survival as Moraga contemplates various aspects of her life and its relationship to love's necessity. Comprising journal and dream entries, poems, and essays, Moraga writes about her relationship with color, with other women and with her mother. In the first pages of *Loving*, she makes clear what it is she will be searching for as she writes: '[w]e need a new language, better words that can more closely describe women's fear of, and resistance to, one another, words that will not always come out sounding like dogma' (46). As she says, it is 'women who agitate my consciousness' (131); through poetry, dreams and narrative, Moraga expresses both her anger towards and love for women of 'color'.

The daughter of an Anglo[7] and a Chicana, Moraga is light-skinned enough to pass for white. Yet she feels, as she writes, that such passing is always a front: as she makes clear in 'Pesadilla' (Nightmare), a short narrative about Cecilia, a light-skinned lesbian Chicana who moves in with her Black lover, Deborah: 'There came the day when Cecilia began to think about color . . . Soon her body began to change with this way of seeing . . . Always, the shell of this skin, leading her around . . . Then one day, color moved in with her' (30). As the story progresses, Cecilia realizes that she had learned to be a 'white' lesbian, depending if only unconsciously on the fact that whiteness – her own and that of her lovers – connected her to 'safety' (34). Now, however, that she has 'moved in with color', that safety net is gone; and as she and her lover Deborah try to cope with naked and unalloyed racism and homophobia, Cecilia remembers a particular fear that she has always had, since she was a child: that '[h]er loving couldn't change a thing'. That is to say, that love – her love for her mother, her love for Deborah (for women of color, in other words) – would not be able to break the 'circle of pain her mother drew like hot liquid from [her] body' (35).

In the first edition of *Loving*, covering the years 1976–83, Moraga has much to say about the loyalty and the pain which surround the mother–daughter relationship, especially for those Latinas and Chicanas who have grown up within a religious system which makes suffering a virtual requirement in order to be a 'good' woman. What Moraga's character Cecilia summons up is an image which becomes a sort of touchstone for the entire book: the image of a cycle of pain, loyalty, (mutual care) and rejection which was all the relationship the patriarchal world – of her white father, of her mother's Catholic religion – would allow women to have with one another. 'When she discovered the first woman wouldn't change', thinks Cecilia, 'it had sort of wrapped things up for the rest of them. Still she'd go through the changes of asking . . . *como su abuelita* [like her grandmother] during the english mass mouthing spanish a million miles an hour, kissing the crucifix of the rosary . . . Nothing to disturb her order of things' (37). And yet, as she has walked away from that order of things, 'right out of that kitchen and family-way of passing on daughter-daughter misery', Cecilia realizes that she must also let Deborah 'in'; to do this, she must go beyond words: 'Cecilia pressed her nose into Dee's hair . . . In the intake of breath, there was more familiarity, more loss of resistance, more sense of landing *somewhere* than any naming she had tried to do with words inside her head' (37).

Moraga is well-known for her insistence that if her own (biological and/or cultural) Chicana family will not accept her as a Chicana and as a lesbian, she will 'make *familia* from scratch':

> 'I'm still my mother's daughter. Keep thinking, *it's the daughters*. It's the daughters who remain loyal to the mother. She is the only woman we stand by. It is not always reciprocated. To be free means on some level to cut that painful loyalty when it begins to punish us. Stop the chain of events . . . Free the daughter to love her own daughter.' (ii, vii)

She has continued this line of thinking into the twenty-first century, as she does in 'Looking for the Insatiable Woman', where she recovers the traditional Mexican myth of *La Llorona*, the Wailing Woman (a story of a woman who kills her children and is condemned to wander the earth crying for them). Moraga rereads this popular myth in light of her feminist, and Chicana, sensibility. Here, *La Llorona* is the woman who looks for her lost daughters, and her own lost daughter, Moraga herself, says: '*Te busco a ti tambien, madre/ hermana/hija*' (I'm looking for you too, mother/sister/daughter) (147).

As a term growing out of a history of Black mother–daughter intimacies, losses and connections *womanism* expresses the same search Moraga expounds in her reading of *La Llorona*. Black feminists begin the new century here, ordering love, pain, the body and spiritual awakening in ways that make life and its losses make sense. For them, 'I'm looking for you too, mother/sister/ daughter' means seeking wholeness, love's necessity and the riches of life's joy. This search calls for a way to analyse the social means by which institutionalized patriarchy and racism can work to oppress people – that is, it calls for 'theory'. This call for theory is foreshadowed in Alice Walker's third definition of womanism, which states that a womanist 'Loves music. Loves dance. Loves the moon. Loves the Spirit. Loves love and food and roundness. Loves struggle. Loves the Folk. Loves herself. Regardless' (Walker, 1983, xii). Clearly, love is central to womanist ideology and to building a womanist critical discourse. This is a discourse inclusive of all women of color for womanists are 'feminist[s] of color – like a flower garden, with every color flower represented' (xi).

It is from this perspective that we should read bell hooks' most recent contributions to Black feminist (or womanist) intellectual thought. *In All About Love* (2000) and *Salvation* (2001), hooks examines various dimensions of love, its construction, cultural and national value, and twenty-first-century practicality. For hooks, love's viability leads from an understanding, an awareness, of one's self and one's relationship with the spirit and others as necessity. 'A culture that is dead to love can only be resurrected by spiritual awakening,' she claims. 'Our national spiritual hunger springs from a keen awareness of emotional lack in our lives. It is a response to lovelessness' (hooks, 2000, 71–2). For many Black women writers, love and its accompanying spiritual awakening are the only chances our communities and our nation have for true salvation. It is the ability to move from lovelessness into lovingness that women of color as cultural critics and as writers have been cultivating the past thirty years. It is now time for harvest.

While focusing on the body and our responses to the politics of various bodily 'necessities', women of color are asking what love is and how one loves oneself or cares for others amidst the cascading effects of trying to understand past oppressions and manoeuvre present obstacles. Perhaps the answer to these questions lies in being proud of our bodies, loving them and allowing ourselves to express that love publicly as well as privately (a subject we will take up later in this chapter).

DIVAS AND HOS: JENNIFER LOPEZ AND LIL' KIM

Just as Moraga uses literature to contemplate her relationship to loving women of color, we, as a society, should reconsider our relationships with women of color. Mass culture, for example, offers prime examples of how we express and explore 'loving' women of color. It is, as bell hooks reminds us, 'the contemporary location that both publicly declares and perpetuates the idea that there is pleasure to be found in the acknowledgment and enjoyment of racial difference' (hooks, 1992, 21). Ethnicity, and color, have become the 'spice' in contemporary mass culture, and especially in the public arena women's physicality is even now assumed to be much more a part of who they 'are' than it is for men (21). Thus it should not be surprising that, as is quite clear to any casual observer of the contemporary music scene – from MTV to CDs to magazines to the Internet – it is women's bodies in particular which have become the favoured resource for getting a bit of that spice (Figure 1).

Figure 1   Lopez in the earlier days of her film career,
as the dark-skinned, dark-haired Selena.

Since rap star Lil' Kim and movie star and singer Jennifer Lopez became success stories, therefore, media accounts have often centred explicitly on aspects of their bodies. For Lopez, this has been a focus on her behind and its relative size; thanks to this publicity, Lopez' butt has become something of a trademark for her. Likewise, rap sensation Lil' Kim, known as 'hell kitten, Queen Bee, hip-hop's nasty girl, sex symbol, glamour baby, diva ho and disgrace to Black womanhood' (Britton, 2000, 112), has risen to icon status by sexing up and decorating her body for public consumption.

Although Lil' Kim is Black and Jennifer Lopez Nuyorican, and their careers seem far apart in almost every conceivable way, there are in fact raced and gendered connections between the two. Puerto Rican critic Juan Flores points out in his *From Bomba to Hip-Hop* that one of the productive meeting grounds for racial and ethnic crossings such as that found in the black racial heritages of Afro-Cubans, Afro-Puerto Ricans and Nuyoricans has been the world of rap, hip-hop and 'Latin soul'. Pointing out the profusion of Latin American and US Latino musicians who are or were either Afro-Latin and/or influenced by African-American musical styles, Flores argues that a long cultural heritage of African styles and rhythms from the music of the Spanish-speaking Caribbean finds its most welcoming home in the cultural heritage of (urban) African Americans and their music (Flores, 2000, 110–11).[8] In fact, Jennifer Lopez, who was born of Puerto Rican parents and grew up in the Castle Hill section of the Bronx, has paired herself musically and personally with a largely African-American hip-hop, pop and rap scene. Getting her show business start as a Fly Girl – that is, a dancer on *In Living Color*, itself a comedy show featuring an almost entirely black cast – Lopez was also a back-up dancer for Janet Jackson. Most recently and most famously, she dated her black producer, Sean 'Puffy' Combs, who has also produced Lil' Kim (Lil' Kim herself was a protégée of the now deceased East coast rap headliner Notorious B.I.G., another rapper produced by Combs).

When we turn to Lopez' and Lil' Kim's images, a careful look makes it clear that here, too, there are connections to be made. For example, both women have undergone radical changes in their body structure, skin and hair color, and even, in the case of Lil' Kim, facial structure. Lil' Kim (a self-proclaimed feminist) is almost always scantily clothed, sporting platinum blonde hair and blue contacts (see Figures 2 and 3).

In fact, her image has been lightened to the point that, ironically enough, she conjures 'images of dearly departed blond bombshells Marilyn Monroe and Mae West' (Bernard, 2001, 23). Womanist critics have pointed out that it is necessary to redescribe or redefine female bodies outside those kinds of stereotypes that render Black women nothing more than sex-craved animals; despite Lil' Kim's self-proclamation as a feminist, her lightened, sexually 'wild' persona is the opposite of womanist ideas of bodily recuperation, sexual healing and love.

In fact, Lil' Kim has many Black women critics, and some of her most adversarial describe her presentation as evidence of a lost self-esteem, teetering somewhere between a disgraceful display of sex and a confused cry for help. But she and other pop stars have in fact publicly characterized the transformation of their images as the result of a far deeper loss: that of self-love. Singer Foxy Brown, for example, has been surprisingly candid about the fact that she finds it difficult to love herself as a Black woman. Foxy Brown's 2001 album, *Broken Silence*, according to *Vibe* magazine, shows that 'Brown [is] coming to terms with her dark-chocolate complexion, something that she has long struggled with. On the first single . . . the woman whose skin was lightened so much on early publicity photos that she looked ready to do Kabuki, is now referring to herself as "the dark-skinned/Christian Dior poster girl"' (Seymour, 2001, 130). Similarly, Lil' Kim claims her public persona is an attempt to overcome past rejections as a Black woman. 'When I was younger', Kim explains, 'all the men liked the same women: those light-skinned European-looking girls. Being the rapper Lil' Kim has helped me to deal with it a little better because I get to dress up in expensive clothes and look like a movie star. All the people responding to me [have] helped. Because I still don't see what they see' (Britton, 2000, 115).

Figure 2   With her shoulders slumped and with her body held firmly by designer Giorgio Armani, this photo speaks volumes about who controls the image and the 'posture' of the blonde, blue-eyed Lil' Kim. Unlike in other photographs, the rapper is not posed as self-confident and in control but appears over-shadowed, even dominated, by the bodies of men.

Figure 3   This photograph was part of an ad campaign promoting Lil' Kim's most recent album, 'Notorious K.I.M.'

Given Lopez' Bronx roots and the fact that she associates herself with the Black entertainment world, and finally given the combination of African-American and Afro-Latin influences found especially on her first album, it would be tempting to imagine that Lopez has moved towards a certain kind of Black- or even Brown-identified subjectivity which might provide room for a radical, or at the least transgressive, 'Latina' identity. Given that Lil' Kim is an

African-American rap star (a profession which is often presented as being almost 'inherently' Black), it would also be tempting to assume that she, too, has a strong Black-identified subjectivity – especially with other Black women.[9] Further, Lil' Kim's and Lopez' success seems to belie claims of ongoing racism in the United States, else why would Black stars Lil' Kim and Janet Jackson, to name only two, be so popular – and why would an acknowledged Latina be one of the biggest box-office draws of the moment? It would seem that our 'romance' with Lopez and Lil' Kim (and Mariah Carey, and Whitney Houston, and Christina Aguilera, etc.) proves that 'love' once again is in the air, and this time it's not just for white people.

But a feminist analysis would maintain that these women's images are, in the final analysis, ones which, while purporting to be supportive of 'diversity', in fact underwrite a popular gaze which is most often constructed as both white *and* masculine. What we mean is this: first, what Thomas Beller calls the 'sugar-glossed' image – of the 'G-string divas, the Britneys and Christinas and Destiny's Childs for whom self-empowerment and self-exposure are completely entwined' – is consciously oriented to appeal primarily to the majority consumer – white folks, that is (Beller, 2000, 109). For example, looking at the trajectory of Lopez' images traced from her 1995 *La Familia* to the 2001 *The Wedding Planner* to her album *On the 6*, we can see that Lopez has had her naturally dark hair bleached, straightened and thinned, and her normally curvaceous body has been trained out to produce a physically fit and lean body with the famous butt well under control (unlike Lil' Kim, however, she has never publicly discussed her own feelings about the transformations her image has undergone). Despite feminist critic Negrón-Muntaner's insistence that the (relative) largeness of Lopez' butt is the obvious sign of her racially-mixed Puerto Rican heritage, in the year 2001 the only contemporary signs of Lopez' 'ethnicity' are her high cheekbones, her slightly slanted eyes and her carefully managed, smooth light tan (Negrón-Muntaner, 1997, 188). Second, such images also consciously appeal to the ways in which most United States men (white, Black, and Latino) have *learned* to enjoy, and consume, representations of women. The fact that many women would undoubtedly love to look like Lil' Kim or Lopez underscores rather than negates this point.

That 'self-empowerment' is supposed to come with 'self-exposure', as Beller has it, is also a common idea in a time when the media increasingly saturates all aspects of our lives. This notion is never more true than for 'divas' like Lil' Kim, Foxy Brown or Lopez herself: these women, famously dressing in revealing clothes, have been presented as twenty-first-century women, in charge of their own sexuality, their own 'look' and their own careers. In this sense, the words to Lopez' hit song 'It's Not That Serious' seem at first glance reminiscent of earlier pro-woman raps: 'How could you tell me that you love me/When I know you were just trying to play me/but you're the fool/'Cause I know how to switch the game on you'. However, feminists of color would point out that instead of a pro-woman attitude which seeks to change the terms by which women have had to live their lives, the idea of a woman's autonomy and empowerment – her right to live for herself rather than by the dictates of *patriarchy*, for example – has morphed into a more familiar tune: that autonomy, money and power amount to the same thing, and that shocking folks is the same thing as being subversive of 'the system'.[10] Manipulation of the system is quite different from changing the system, and as Cherríe Moraga notes, '[s]ex turned manipulation, control . . . ravages the psyche, rather than satisfies the yearning body and heart' (Moraga, 2000, 137). Moreover, as Akissi Britton explains in a public letter to Lil' Kim published in *Essence* magazine:

> Sex equals money equals power is not a feminist principle. Power was being a female hip-hop fan ten years ago, back when we were singing songs like Latifah's 'Ladies First.' Sistah Souljah stood right up there with Public Enemy and shouted 'We Are at War.' Back then we wore the armor of self-love, self-respect and self-actualization, standing together with our men while we all did what it took to 'Fight the Power.' Word, that felt like power. Like love. (2000, 186)

To be up front and in people's faces with how it is to be a woman in a masculine world can feel liberating; but as more female rappers and hip-hop groups have entered the door opened by the success of rappers like Queen Latifah, the message has changed in important ways. The 'don't play me' attitude of hip-hop groups like TLC and rapper Missy 'Misdemeanor' Elliot began to interpret empowerment to mean just that: 'having power' over men, through the money the largely masculine-oriented entertainment world is willing to give them provided they behave in appropriately sexual ways. This means, however, that Lil' Kim and Jennifer Lopez have made their reputation as divas by offering their body's intimacies (and for Lil' Kim this includes sexual intimacies shared for a price), bereft of feminist notions about self-love and mutual care. Yet, such offerings are very attractive, precisely because the way we *consume* these women as products – buying their images, gazing at their images, listening to their music – appears to be free from sacrifice. 'Eating the other', as bell hooks terms it, seems to hold forth an escape from the threats of disappointment and pain that often loom along love's path, by replacing those threats with a call to personal power and a focus on 'getting paid'.

But let's not, as they say, throw out the baby with the bathwater. The use of eroticism and sex as tools of aggressive identity politics is not new, and neither is the success of such tools as vehicles for developing self-love unattainable. Moraga consciously constructs a notion of Chicana sexuality which refuses to disconnect sensual loving from a resistant voice: '[m]y mouth . . . will flap in the wind like legs in sex . . . It's as if *la boca* [the mouth] had lodged itself *en el centro del corazón* [in the centre of the heart] . . . The same place where the vagina beats' (2000, 133). And again, one of the primary ways Celie, in *The Color Purple*, relocates the self she loses beneath Albert's domination is by developing an informed relationship with her physical and sexual self. Only after she discovers virginal beauty and clitoral pleasure does she begin her journey towards self-love:

> I lie back on the bed and haul up my dress. Yank down my bloomers. Stick the looking glass tween my legs. Ugh. All that hair. Then my pussy lips be black. Then inside look like a wet rose. It a lot prettier than you thought, ain't it? [Shug] say from the door. It mine, I say. Where the button? Right up near the top, she say. The part that stick out a little. I look at her and touch it with my finger. A little shiver go through me. Nothing much. But just enough to tell me this the right button to mash. Maybe. (Walker, 1983, 82)

Unlike Celie and Shug, who, through acceptance of sexual exploration and a feminine erotic gaze, share the intimacy of personal beauty and mutual care successfully, Lil' Kim's offer of eroticism fails the feminist principles she claims to embody. Instead of teaching a lesson of liberation from patriarchy's demands on women, her 'mo' money, mo' money, mo' money' sexuality mutates from self-awareness and exploration into a straight-up gift of her self and sexuality, the consumption of her image becoming just another privilege that whiteness and masculinity continue to inherit.

Lopez' careful career of courting just the right amount of color and 'Latinidad', and Lil' Kim's (and other stars, like Foxy Brown's) attempts to lighten up indicate that in fact the careful editing of these stars' images has about as much to do with a transgressive or subversive Latina or Black woman's style as the Power Puff girls. To make themselves suitably 'spicy' yet also suitably 'beautiful' enough to be offered for consumption, feminists would note that Lil' Kim and Foxy Brown and Jennifer Lopez have had to deny what Moraga calls their 'common skin'. In the process, their success encourages other women of color to do the same. Thus although many women of color undoubtedly enjoy 'consuming' Lil' Kim's raps and videos and Lopez' music and films, the overt sexuality of these stars' image is not oriented towards the kind of intimate, and not always pretty, loving self-examination that we see, for example, with Celie and Shug, or that Moraga presents us with.

For Black and Latina feminists, the pop culture success of Lil' Kim and Jennifer Lopez' misfired sexual energy is reason enough for theorizing the relationship of spirit, love and sexual healing for women living in the twenty-first century. Is it as the Queen Bee proclaims? Is a philosophy of 'sex equals money equals power' substance enough to bring Black women into a deeper understanding of self-love and awareness or does it take something more corrective, something more ethically and morally acceptable? Does it take a new kind of spiritual awakening – one that leads not only to mutual care but also sexual healing?

Rather than love women's blackness, or brownness, in the revolutionary sense hooks suggests, these stars have chosen to participate in the manufacturing of a racially gendered sensibility which has more to do with erasing skin color, slimming down noses and butts, and bringing 'bad hair' under control, making women of color fit for consumption by toning down what might seem threatening or too different (see Figure 4).

Figure 4   Slimmed down, and lightened up:
Lopez' image for the cover of her second album, *J. Lo*, released in 2001.

Feminists such as bell hooks, however, insist on rejecting the notion that the 'emphasis on sameness is the key to racial harmony', maintaining instead that 'positive recognition and acceptance of difference is a necessary starting point as we work to eradicate white supremacy' (hooks, 1992, 13). We have seen that Moraga attempts to think through what this might mean: what does a 'positive recognition' of difference mean? How does one, as a woman, 'move in with color'? The healing involved in women of color's embrace of one another, we suggest in our section 'Notes towards readings' below, demands what Black and Latina feminists have long maintained: that healing follows the hard job of revaluing bodies and tasks long devalued in ways that seem a far cry from the easy, not to say pleasurable, job of consuming the 'sugar-glossed' images of divas like Lil' Kim and Jennifer Lopez.

NOTES TOWARDS READINGS OF
DREAMING IN CUBAN AND *THE AGÜERO SISTERS*

Cuban-born author Cristina García's *Dreaming in Cuban* (1992) and *The Agüero Sisters* (1997) trace the ways in which women's relationships with each other – mothers, daughters, sisters, half-sisters – are part of the entwining of United States and Cuban histories. Rather than being the stuff of heroics and grand gestures, however, the thesis of García's novels is that the history of these two nations is in fact writ 'small' in the domestic gestures and concerns of women's everyday lives. In something of the same way, Denise Chávez' 1994 *Face of An Angel* renders the life of the fictional small New Mexico town Agua Oscura in all its everyday ordinariness; although, in doing so, the book does not turn away from the dreariness and ugliness of poverty, racism and sexism, it does so with a sense of humour which leavens the work with a constant air of hope.

In the spirit of Latin American 'Boom' novels of the 1950s through the 1970s (such as Colombian author Gabriel García Márquez' famous 1970 *Cien años de soledad*, translated in English as *100 Years of Solitude*), Chávez' novel traces a sweeping and complex lineage of mothers, sisters, daughters and women-friends. Unlike the Latin American novels from which it derives its frame, however, Chávez' novel lovingly details the ordinary ways women live within two cultures: the Anglo and the 'Mexican-American', or Chicano. We follow the main character, Soveida Dosamantes, through her childhood and into adulthood in a small New Mexico town, from her immersion in Catholicism and the self-abnegation of her mother, aunts and their friends, through several marriages, through her 'consciousness-raising' as a Chicana via the tutelage of a boyfriend and of a professor of Chicano Studies, and through her career as a waitress at a local Mexican restaurant, El Farol (The Lantern).

It is via her life of waitressing at El Farol, in fact, that Chávez' character comes to understand what she feels to be the central fact of the relationship of working-class women of color with each other and with their world. Along the way, she acquaints the reader with the varying forms of internalized racism, or 'colorism', she meets among her co-workers and friends. Consuelo Larragoite, who owns El Farol, wants her son Larry to marry someone 'nice', meaning someone Anglo: Consuelo thinks of herself as a '*mexican mexican*, a once-middle, now upper class American . . . proud of her Mexican roots, just make sure they're clean and don't shove them in my face' (146). Larry, her son, manages the restaurant; he speaks no Spanish and calls himself a 'Spanish white man' (148). Soveida herself comes from a family who were once wealthy, 'still regal' and who still manage to live on the right side of town; her first boyfriend, Jester, a 'low-rider *pachuco*', is too Indian-looking – dark and hairy – to warrant her family's approval.

But it is not her boyfriend's dark skin which Soveida learns finally to distrust; after Soveida has her first sexual experience with him and he leaves her, she comes to realize that he had 'prepared' her for being used sexually and then abandoned. Thus Soveida begins to understand the great price she pays for her 'love' for the men in her life, and the lessons they teach her about who she is. She learns, for example, to 'be' a Chicana with Ivan, her first husband: 'I had never met anyone before who called himself Chicano. I didn't know what the word Chicano meant then. I knew I was a Mexican-American . . . I knew vaguely that my family's roots were in México . . . But in the course of that first evening with Ivan I became a Chicana. In between frenzied, passionate dances, I learned about the people I was supposed to be connected with and yet barely knew' (130–1). But Ivan only understands her to be an extension of his own image, that of a brown-beret wearing Chicano: he begins to tell her what to do and what to wear, refusing for example to allow her to wear white peasant blouses and multicoloured skirts because they are 'too Mexican' (144). Soveida also learns along the way that even women of color can oppress each other in an economic system which racializes and genders certain kinds of labour. Soveida's friend Chata, a 'domestic', tells Soveida that Mexican-American women who hire her to clean their houses think less of her because of the work she does: '[t]hey start on how you're a mexicana and nobody from México can do anything right and how *mexicanas* can't be trusted . . . And they forget they're *mexicanas*, too' (214). When Soveida decides to take a 'Chicano Culture' class at the local college, her brother Hector tells her, 'I know enough about my own culture already: Fiesta, party, *salud, amor y pesetas*' (*salud*, meaning 'health', is also a toast; *amor y pesetas* means 'love and money') (284). And when Soveida has to take a 'Chicano Culture Quiz' from her professor (and, incidentally, fiancé) Dr Velásquez, she begins to understand that there is more to 'culture' than what any of these men – her 'teachers' – have tried to tell her: 'dammit . . . Dr. Velásquez, you want to know about the Chicano culture: Well, here I am, smelling of hard work' (287).

In fact, it is less through the concept of race and more through a class-identified concept of women's (hard) work that Soveida learns what it means to be a 'Chicana'. As she writes in her term paper for her Chicano Culture class, the men of her culture oppress women, but the women continue the oppression:

> Who wrote the words that would betray all women? Men. And who allowed that betrayal? Women. Who perpetuated that betrayal? Mothers . . . My ex-husband was angry because one day he had to help me clean the house, saying later, that he hadn't done anything that day . . . Where, then, is the validity of women's work? Daily, uneventful, mono-tonous, universal work? . . . Now, on the eve of woman's great awaken-ing, we turn to each other and to those who would take our hands, and hold them. (317–19)

Such hands belong to Chata, who helps Soveida clean her house every Monday: 'Chata's hands are like Picasso's. They are thick, no-nonsense hands adept at any task. They are hands unafraid and willing to reach out. They are hands that can as easily comfort a child as pull long, tangled clumps of dark hair out of a clogged bathroom drain . . . They are hands that never recoil at soft, sick flesh, or untidy corners full of dark brown roach droppings' (211). Where she ultimately learns to value, respect and love herself and other women, in fact, it is not through the lessons in suffering Soveida has learned from men, or even from her mother, 'harnessed' by the demands of her family and her husband. Soveida learns the beginnings of respect for her self and for her labour, and even, it might be argued, begins to learn sexual healing, through the lives, day-to-day work and especially the oral tradition of 'women's wisdom' passed on to her by older, working women such as Chata: 'Chata has taught me what work is and how every woman should continue to work . . . There is peace on Chata's Monday. All is ordered. Calm. Correct. As any polite Mexican will say with great courtesy befitting something that is natural, apt, appropriate, "Es pro-pio". It's as it should be' (216).

Such a revaluation connects the '[d]aily, uneventful, monotonous, universal work' everyone must do to a capacity for love, for, as Chata tells Soveida, '"girl, let me tell you, loving is work!" ' (217). Just as Moraga learns to revalue women of color, Chávez's character Soveida learns to re-value, not the high-gloss impossibility of passing in a world of white masculine privilege, but, as Moraga puts it, the 'used body' of ordinary women:

I remember this common skin, mamá
oiled by work and worry.
Hers is a used body like yours
one that carries the same scent
of silence I call it home.

(140)

NOTES TOWARDS A READING OF *BELOVED*

In Toni Morrison's 1987 novel *Beloved*, Baby Suggs' exhortations to her congregation make it clear that the road to self-love and sexual healing begins, as Soveida learns from Chata, with love for one's own flesh. Just as Soveida celebrates Chata's hands, 'hands unafraid and willing to reach out', so too does Baby Suggs Holy call to her people to 'love your hands! Love them. Raise them up and kiss them. Touch others with them, pat them together, stroke them on your face . . . This is flesh I'm talking about here. Flesh that needs to be loved' (88). Even the novel's title suggests a desire, if not also a need, for loving and being loved. Yet, it is this theme that Morrison, as a critic of her own work, wishes to minimize or at least put into perspective. She comments that the next to last word in the novel, the word *kiss*, 'works at a level a bit too shallow. It searches for and locates a quality or element of the novel that was not, and is not, its primary feature'. Much like Lil' Kim's nudity and sex-for-hire propaganda, the word 'kiss' reduces the 'necessity' of the novel to physical desire, turning attention away from the novel's driving force, which Morrison claims is 'for connection, acknowledgement, a paying-out of homage still due' (Morrison, 1998, 7). The novel is not about physical desire, at least not as a primary focus. If we are to follow the author's lead, then, what kind of loving does *Beloved* and its 'necessity' ask us to seek, to taste, to enjoy and, ultimately, to theorize?

Certainly race is a central element for consideration – equally so are the intersections of gender and class. Morrison claims that in *Beloved* she wanted to 'explore the revelatory possibilities of historical narration when the body–mind, subject–object, past–present oppositions, viewed through the lens of race, collapse' (Morrison, 1998, 9). So, what revelations do we find beneath the rubble of this collapse? We find libratory movements of love – more specifically, self-love, loving mutual care and, yes, the gentle warmth and respect found in intentional moments of sexual healing.

Morrison presents several types of love in this novel: love of a son for his mother, a man for a woman, a mother for her child, and love of black people for themselves. The love most speculated about in critiques of the novel is the intense love Sethe expresses for her children, a love so powerful, so severe, so enraged it is deadly. Paul D, a man from Sethe's past and her present lover, says her 'love is too-thick' (164). Sethe regards it as 'true love' for she believes 'thin love ain't love at all' (251, 164) and Stamp Paid, another man from Sethe's past, describes it as mother's love 'trying to outhurt the hurter' (234). No matter how it is described, this love is the substance of tragedy and infanticide. As Euripides' Medea admits before killing her own children, Sethe knows 'what [she] intends to do is wrong, but the rage of [her] love is stronger than [her] reason' (64).

As wrong as it is, this love is the only love available to Sethe since she does not know how to free herself from its rage and thereby cannot love anything purely – including herself. This lack ultimately leads the character into expressions of anger and sexual submission that are neither self-affirming nor healing. Unlike Celie, Sethe has not experienced a 'mirror stage'. She does not see her body as separate from those she loves. She is her children; she is Beloved and Denver, Howard and Buglar. Through them slavery threatens her flesh, her heart, 'her beautiful, magical best thing – the part of her that was clean' (251). To protect this 'self' from the abuses it is sure to find in slavery, Sethe kills Beloved and tries to kill her other children. She then gives her body, sexually, to a stone carver in exchange for his carving the word *Beloved* on a headstone.

Enraged love accompanied by an inflamed and selfish, although understand-able, possessiveness destroys life while prostitution empties the soul of mean-ingful human connections and solace. The narrator tells us that for Sethe '[r]utting among the stones under the eyes of the engraver's son was not enough, those ten minutes she spent pressed up against dawn-colored stone studded with star chips, her knees wide open as the grave, were longer than life, more alive more pulsating than the baby blood that soaked her fingers like oil' (5). Sethe cannot escape the shame of those ten minutes; she cannot clean it from memory or limit its reach through time. The engraving earned through sexual exploitation is thereby emptied of worth. It has no redeeming attributes and offers no escape from the 'necessity' of her child's murder.

Making love with Paul D, on the other hand, defines a path to self-worth that adds a small measure of peace to a life stripped of it by a system of brutality and fear. He becomes her mirror. Through his eyes, Sethe sees her scarred body as worthy of love. She gives herself to the care of this man and is relieved briefly of rage and the responsibility for shouldering its weight (symbolized here as breasts):

> He saw the sculpture her back had become, like the decorative work of an ironsmith too passionate for display, he would tolerate no peace until he had touched every ridge and leaf of it with his mouth, the responsibility for her breasts, at last, was in somebody else's hands, naked from shoulder blade to waist, relieved of the weight of her breasts. Maybe this one time

she could stop dead still and feel the hurt her back ought to. Trust things and remember things because the last of the Sweet Home men was there to catch her if she sank. (18–19)

By novel's end Paul D offers Sethe something she needs more than anything – release from lost love, anger, guilt and emptiness. He gives her permission be an individual and soothe the rage of her love with the salve of self-acceptance: 'You your best thing, Sethe. You are' (273). From this moment we see the possibilities for Sethe's future. We can envision her finally understanding how to heal and accepting all she has left to love. We know she can follow Baby Suggs Holy's advice to her people – her instructions for soul's revival, spiritual healing and mutual care:

[s]he did not tell them to clean up their lives or to go and sin no more. She did not tell them they were the blessed of the earth, its inheriting meek or its glorybound pure. She told them that the only grace they could have was the grace they could imagine. That if they could not see it, they would not have it. 'Here', she said, 'in this here place, we flesh; flesh that weeps, laughs; flesh that dances on bare feet in grass. Love it. Love it hard, love your hands! Love them. Raise them up and kiss them. Touch others with them, pat them together, stroke them on your face. You got to love it, you! This is flesh I'm talking about here. Flesh that needs to be loved. Feet that need to rest and to dance; backs that need support, shoulders that need arms, strong arms I'm tell you . . . and the beat and beating heart, love that too. More than your life-holding womb and your life-giving private parts, hear me now, love your heart. For this is the prize. Saying no more she stood up then and danced, others opened their mouths and gave her the music. Long notes held until the four-part harmony was perfect for their deeply loved flesh. (88–9)

Unselfish love. Appreciating the flesh, accepting and giving mutual care while dancing in the spirit's magically healing embrace, Baby Suggs describes the 'necessity' of loving (loving the self and loving others). According to Carol Schmuddle, Baby Suggs 'teaches those whose bodies and spirits have been broken by slavery that they have the power to lay down the anger and pain associated with the past – they can learn to love themselves and begin again' (1993, 122).

Like Sethe and the community of women who sing away the spirit haunting 124 Bluestone Road, as scholars and intellectuals, we too must learn not to be condemned by love's rage or be afraid to accept and theorize its necessity – its relationship to successful living. This is the cry of Black, Latina and Chicana women writers, 'building voice upon voice' until there is 'no clamor for a kiss' (Morrison, 1987, 261). This is the challenge for women of color in the twenty-first century, a legacy of hope and the charge of Beloved's liberating love, Baby Suggs' consecrated faith, Sethe's newfound peace, and the lessons Soveida finds in Chata's work-worn hands, her 'common skin', as Moraga puts it, which 'smells like home'.

QUESTIONS FOR FURTHER CONSIDERATION

1. Feminists of color often emphasize working-class women's experience and concerns. Do you think that middle- and upper-class women would have a place in feminist discourses of this type? How?
2. If you are white (and/or male), how do you think you might be able to 'relate' or 'love' women of color? What does it mean to love blackness? brownness?
3. How might women put into practice the ideas about love, and self-love, that Morrison, Walker, Moraga and Chávez advocate?
4. Look up the work of other feminists of color (see our bibliography below). What other issues are of central concern to these women?
5. Do you think that non-Latinas or non-Blacks can have a place in Latina feminism or womanism? If so, how? If not, why not?

ANNOTATED BIBLIOGRAPHY

Alarcón, Norma. 'The Theoretical Subjects of *This Bridge Called My Back* and Anglo-American Feminism'. In *Making Face/Making Soul: Haciendo Caras. Creative and Critical Perspectives by Feminists of Color*, ed. Gloria Anzaldúa. San Francisco, CA: Aunt Lute Books, 1990. Gloria Anzaldúa's collection of important pieces from almost fifteen years of feminist thought (1977–90), annotated below, includes Norma Alarcón's oft-anthologized essay. Norma Alarcón, associate professor of Chicano/ethnic studies at UC Berkeley, examines the impact particularly on white feminist thought of *This Bridge Called My Back*. As Black and Latina feminists have often discovered, Alarcón posits that the gap between white, or 'Anglo-American', feminism and that of women of color remains, in fact, without much of a bridge – either way. As she reads *This Bridge* in conjunction with white feminist writing from the 1980s, Alarcón proposes a theoretical framework for thinking about this gap. For her, the differences between 'subjects of consciousness' need to be foregrounded in terms of the intersections of gender with cultural, economic and political considerations. Again, this essay constitutes an important call for decentring, though by no means leaving behind, an emphasis on 'gender' in feminist thought.

Anzaldúa, Gloria. *Making Face/Making Soul: Haciendo Caras. Creative and Critical Perspectives by Feminists of Color*, ed. Gloria Anzaldúa. San Francisco, CA: Aunt Lute Books, 1990. In *Making Face/Making Soul*, editor Gloria Anzaldúa collected some of the most influential and important writings from the mid-1970s through 1990, fifteen years of some of the most intensive work of the twentieth century by Latina, Black and Chicana feminists. As Anzaldúa notes, '*haciendo caras*' means to 'make faces'. Here, she uses the term in a political sense: to mean presenting a defiant or subversive face to the world. The lessons learned earlier with the publication of *This Bridge Called My Back* apply here: that differences in geography, immigration patterns, patterns of economic oppression and class mean that a white-skinned Puerto Rican feminist may see things quite differently to a dark-skinned, *mestiza* Chicana from Texas, and both of them may value different ways of coming to feminism than a middle-class African-American feminist. Thus, Anzaldúa wishes to emphasize the divergences, even the discrepancies, in the ways women write, think, and theorize feminism, warning us in her Introduction that the reader will have to work to fit this anthology's 'pieces' together.

Feminists of color, in particular, often insist that the sometimes invidious distinctions between 'academic' and 'non-academic' writing be questioned both in form as well as in content and venue; thus, this collection spans a range of forms, from poet Bernice Zamora's famous poem 'Notes from a Chicana "Coed"', first printed in 1977 in a small Chicana journal called *Caracol*, to critical pieces written by noted academic feminist/activists like Barbara Smith, bell hooks, Audre Lord, Norma Alarcón and María Lugones.

Bennett, Michael and Vanessa D. Dickerson (eds). *Recovering the Black Female Body: Self-Representations by African American Women*. New Brunswick, NJ: Rutgers University Press, 2000. Bennett, an associate professor of English at Long Island University, and Dickerson, associate professor of English at DePaul University, offer a collection of essays here which are dynamic in scope and complexity. This is a major critical text focusing on Black women's subjectivity, forms of individual and group agency and recovery. Contributors reconstruct the body of Black womanhood without becoming absorbed in discussions of the 'oppressive gaze' imposed by others. In this way the collection successfully highlights counter-hegemonic processes of taking back the self and stands as a marker for twenty-first-century Black feminist thought. Like Patricia Hill Collins' *Black Feminist Thought*, which preceded it in publication, this is a must-read. It is exciting to find Black women at the centre of Black women's cultural and literary studies in ways that decentre the priorities and concerns of their 'oppressors'. It is an accessible text and one clearly on target for understanding Black feminism and its focus in this new century.

Collins, Patricia Hill. *Black Feminist Thought: Knowledge, Consciousness, and the Politics of Empowerment*. New York: HarperCollins, [1990] 2000. Sociologist Patricia Collins sets the boundaries of Black feminism in a book that, from its publication, has been considered a landmark text in Black feminist thought. Collins outlines the history of Black women's lives and intellectual presence in America while offering a solid map for understanding the necessity, goals and politics of Black feminism. She defines an Afrocentric epistemology that moves through and beyond Black nationalism, settling in a place where Black women have voice and political impact. She describes and explores Black women's mothering, communal and national activism, sexual politics and identity politics. This is a must-read for anyone interested in Black feminism. It is an essential text for undergraduate and graduate feminist theory classes.

García, Alma M. (ed.). *Chicana Feminist Thought: The Basic Historical Writings*. New York: Routledge, 1997. In the first collection to ever bring together many of the most important, and most neglected, writings of Chicana feminism, this book reveals the intensity of feeling especially in the early years – around the beginning of the 1970s – when women in *el movimiento*, the Chicano civil rights movement, began to call for attention to their civil rights as Chicanas *and* as women. Through original sources – writings and poems from small journals and newspapers, primarily, although the last section includes pieces published in academic journals also – Alma García, associate professor of Sociology and Ethnic Studies at Santa Clara University, works to foreground the debates among Chicanas themselves and with their Chicano compatriots over issues of race loyalty, the importance of the family, birth control, abortion and the division of labour.

The collection documents Chicana feminist thought from the early 1970s through the mid-1990s. Dividing the book into three parts and subdividing it into sections within each part, García provides a concise and informative introduction to each, such as 'Analyzing the Dynamics of Chicana Oppression', 'Mapping a Chicana Feminist Agenda' or 'Chicana Feminism: An Evolving Future'. This book is an indispensable tool for teachers and professors of feminism, women's studies and ethnic studies, and a good resource for anyone curious about the origins, and ongoing issues, of Chicana feminism.

hooks, bell. *Ain't I a Woman? Black Women and Feminism*. Boston, MA: South End Press, 1981. In one of the first books of its type, the prolific cultural critic and feminist bell hooks explores the many ways African-American women have been oppressed, isolated and dehumanized. She wrote this book after sitting in women's studies classes where her history, her life-story, was never told. This text tells that story beginning with commentary on the history and treatment of slave women. Her ultimate objective is to charge all women with the responsibility for building a 'true' feminist bond – one absent of the racism demonstrated in the past. Although the text is quite repetitive, it is insightful. hook's position on the subjects of matriarchal families, the African-American male acceptance of patriarchy and the basic lack of concern for Black women's liberation is one of the first of its kind. She addresses herself to an audience who (at the time) either denied the sexist victimization of Black women or ignored the reality of it and presents a multitude of ways race and gender oppression affect the lives of African-American women.

hooks, bell. *Feminist Theory: From Margin to Center*. Boston, MA: South End Press, 1984. In her second book, bell hooks identifies capitalism as the primary culprit in Black women's oppression. She explains the theories behind the apparent abuse and betrayal of the African-American woman who has been pushed into the margins of the feminist movement's sisterhood and critical thought. Although she never uses the term *socialism*, hooks' book definitely points towards a socialist vision of equality. Her theories outline why the overthrow of a capitalist system is the pivotal point in obtaining freedom from sexism, classism and racism in America. She positions these issues as strongholds within the women's movement and asks for their elimination. This book outlines how the pedestal of elitism at the centre of our society is supported by capitalism and how its dominance overshadows the concerns of the oppressed who occupy the margins. The author addresses herself to anyone who is concerned about the survival of Black women's voices with modern feminist critical thought.

Hull, Gloria T. and Barbara Smith. *All The Women Are White, All The Blacks Are Men, But Some of Us Are Brave*. New York: Feminist Press, 1982. In this ground-breaking collection of essays, Gloria Hull, associate professor of English at the University of Delaware, and Barbara Smith, Black feminist writer and activist, approach the subject of African-American women's studies from a political perspective. These scholars and their contributors reject what they call 'intellectual passing' while acknowledging the dangers of overtly revolutionary expression in African-American Women's Studies. Women's Studies, from their view point, needs to hear from women of color who are not afraid to speak of themselves and of their world-views. Like bell hooks' position in her book *Ain't I a Woman*, Hull and Smith advocate a feminist politics for African-American women in which the abolition of elitist, racist and misogynistic attitudes is central and the causes of racism are exposed. Unlike hooks, however, their main concern is the academy and the development of an academic platform for change. The fiery 'call to arms' offered in the book provides thought-provoking information that will spark the interest of scholars as well as educated adults. The book includes several suggestions for developing courses in Black Women's Studies.

Hurtado, Aída. *The Color of Privilege: Three Blasphemies on Race and Feminism*. Ann Arbor, MI: University of Michigan Press, 1996. In the beginning pages of this book, Hurtado, associate professor of psychology at the University of California Santa Cruz, underscores what she considers to be one of the major differences between white women and women of color: white women's relationships with white men, giving them what Phyllis Marynick Palmer calls an economic (and we would add, psychological and social) 'cushion'. Her work centres on the inequalities attached to specific 'social identities', that is the parts of the self that are related to significant group memberships – groups constituting a social sense of race, gender, socioeconomic status and even sexuality. Rather than posit, as many feminists tend implicitly to do, a hierarchical framework of oppressions, Hurtado draws a picture of a web of inequities which are *relational*: it is the relations, and the nearness to or distance from, centres of power which dictate individual as well as group access to resources, relative power and autonomy.

Equally important is Hurtado's insistence on including Black women's experiences and histories along with that of Latinas and Chicanas. This is one of the few, if not the only, books to discuss, for example, the civil rights movements of all three groups together. Important parallels, as well as important differences, are to be drawn between these groups.

McDowell, Deborah E. 'New Directions for Black Feminist Criticism'. In *The New Feminist Criticism: Essays on Women, Literature, and Theory*, ed. Elaine Showalter. New York: Pantheon Books, 1985. Although this is an essay, it is essential to understanding early Black feminist discourse and its development. In this essay, McDowell, then assistant professor of English at Colby College, evaluates critical approaches to African-American fiction and proposes the development of a theoretical basis for future studies. She examines the work of Barbara Smith in 'Towards a Black feminist Criticism' and finds Smith's theories lacking in many areas. McDowell agrees that a contextual theoretical approach grounded in Black history and culture is necessary for a thorough analysis of African-American women's fiction. She also insists, however, that a rigorous textual analysis is necessary. African-American feminists, suggests McDowell, should investigate common themes and the use of female language in Black literature. McDowell addresses herself to the Black feminist critic in an essay void of rhetoric and empty claims. Her clarity allows for no confusion and her suggested direction for Black feminist criticism is clearly focused on methodological and theoretical development. Critics like Claudia Tate, in her 1998 *Psychoanalysis and Black Novels: Desire and the Protocols of Race*, answer this call to theory with book-length studies not only of Black women's fiction but also of language and body politics.

Moraga, Cherríe and Gloria Anzaldúa (eds). *This Bridge Called My Back: Writing by Radical Women of Color*. New York: Kitchen Table/Women of Color Press, [1983], 2000. An important essay collection edited by Cherríe Moraga, currently Artist-in-Residence at Stanford University, and Gloria Anzaldúa, Chicana feminist and activist, and with a Foreword by Black writer Toni Cade Bambera. Moraga and Anzaldúa bring together the writings of 'women of color' – including Black and Asian-American women, Latinas and Chicanas, as well as many other women considered 'of color', 'ethnic' or 'third world' in the United States. Because the editors wanted a collection which would reflect the thoughts of women excluded by their 'radical' views from academic and feminist institutions, the many entries take many forms: poems, essays, letters, 'rants'. Necessarily, then, the essays take many points of view.

Altogether, the collection helps show the differences within that undifferentiated mass, 'feminists of color'. This anthology was put together in an effort to make these women's voices heard twice over: first among women of color, and again among white feminists; in fact, as the 1983 Introduction plainly states, the volume began as a 'reaction to the racism of white feminists' (xxiii). At the same time, the volume became a 'commitment of women of color to our *own* feminism' (xxiii). What may seem hostile, or even separatist, about these statements, however, stands both as a witness to the distance to be travelled between white women and women of color in 1983, and also as a call, to all feminists, to engage in the hard work of shifting the grounds upon which they make claims about 'women'.

SUPPLEMENTARY BIBLIOGRAPHY

Alcoff, Linda (ed.). *Feminist Epistemologies*. New York: Routledge, 1993.

All Music Guide. AEC One Stop Group, Inc., 19 July 2001, http://allmusic.com/cg/amg.dll.

All Music Guide. Harris, Craig. 'La India', 19 July 2001.

American Cultural History 1960–1969, ed. Becky Bradley and Susan Goodwin. Kingwood College Library, Texas. http://www.nhmccd.cc.tx.us/contracts/lrc/kc/decade60.html#events.

Anaya, Rudolfo and Francisco Lomelí (eds). *Aztlán: Essays on the Chicano Homeland*. Albuquerque, NM: Academia/El Norte Publications, 1989.
Anzaldúa, Gloria. *Borderlands/La Frontera: The New Mestiza*. San Francisco, CA: Aunt Lute Books, 1987.
Behar, Ruth. *Puentes a Cuba: Bridges to Cuba*. Ann Arbor, MI: University of Michigan Press, 1995.
Beller, Thomas. 'Believe: The New M.C', *Elle*, July 2001, 106+.
Bernard, Audrey J. 'The Notorious K.I.M. – The "Queen Bee" Is Back'. In *The New York Beacon*. V. 7 (August 2001): n. 31, 23.
Britton, Akissi. 'Deconstructing Lil' Kim', *Essence*, October 2000, 112–15, 186.
Carby, Hazel. *Race Men*. Cambridge, MA: Harvard University Press, 1998.
Chávez, Denise. *Face of an Angel*. New York: Farrar, Straus & Giroux, 1994.
Christian, Barbara. *Black Feminist Criticism*. New York: Pergamon Press, 1985.
Colin's Haight-Ashbury Archives, ed. Colin Pringle. 'The Haight-Ashbury 30 Years Ago: A Timeline', 19 August 1998, http://colinp1.home.mindspring.com/archives.htm.
Crawford, Vicki L., Jacqueline Anne Rouse and Barbara Woods. *Women in the Civil Rights Movement: Trailblazers and Torchbearers, 1941–1965*. Bloomington, IN: Indiana University Press, 1993.
Crenshaw, Kimberle et al (eds). *Critical Race Theory: The Key Writings that Formed the Movement*. New York: New Press, 1995.
DuCille, Ann. *The Coupling Convention: Sex, Text, and Tradition in Black Women's Fiction*. New York: Oxford University Press, 1993.
Euripides. *Medea*. London: Oberon Books, 1992.
Flores, Juan. *From Bomba to Hip-Hop: Puerto Rican Culture and Latino Identity*. New York: Columbia University Press, 2000.
García, Cristina. *Dreaming in Cuban*. New York: Knopf, 1992.
García, Cristina. *The Agüero Sisters*. New York: Knopf, 1997.
Harding, Sandra. *Is Scienc3 Multicultural? Postcolonialism, Feminisms, and Epistemologies*. Bloomington, IN: Indiana University Press, 1992.
Herrera-Sobek, María and Helena María Viramontes (eds). *Chicana Creativity and Criticism: Charting New Frontiers in American Literature*. Irvine, CA: Mexico/Chicano Program, University of California, 1988
Hill Collins, Patricia. *Fighting Words*. Minneapolis, MN: University of Minnesota Press, 1998.
hooks, bell. *Black Looks: Race and Representation*. Boston, MA: South End Press, 1992.
hooks, bell. 'Theory as Liberatory Practice'. In *Teaching to Transgress: Education as the Practice of Freedom*. New York: Routledge, 1994.
hooks, bell. *All About Love: New Visions*. New York: Routledge, 2000.
hooks, bell. *Salvation*. London: Women's Press, 2001.
Moraga, Cherríe. *Loving in the War Years: lo que nunca paso por sus labios*, expanded 2nd edn. Boston, MA: South End Press, [1983] 2000.
Morrison, Toni. *Beloved*. New York: Knopf, 1987.
Morrison, Toni. 'Home'. In *The House That Race Built*, ed. Wahneema Lubiano. New York: Vintage, 1998, 3–12.
Negrón-Muntaner, Frances. 'Jennifer's Butt'. In *Aztlán: A Journal of Chicano Studies*, 22, Fall 1997.
Pryse, Marjorie and Hortense Spillers (eds). *Conjuring: Black Women, Fiction, and Literary Tradition*. Bloomington, IN: Indiana University Press, 1985.
Rich, Adrienne. 'Compulsory Heterosexuality and Lesbian Experience', *Signs: Journal of Women in Culture and Society*, 4, Summer 1980, 631–60.
Schmuddle, Carol. 'Knowing When to Stop: A Reading of Toni Morrison's Beloved', *CLA Journal*, 37, 2, 1993, 121–35.
Seymour, Craig. 'Revolutions: Foxy Brown, *Broken Silence*', *Vibe*, July 2001, 129–30.
Smith, Barbara. 'Toward a Black Feminist Criticism'. In *All the Women Are White, All*

the Blacks Are Men, But Some of Us Are Brave, eds Gloria T. Hull and Barbara Smith. New York: Feminist Press, 1982, 157–75.

Spelman, Elizabeth V. *Inessential Woman: Problems of Exclusion in Feminist Thought.* Boston, MA: Beacon Press, 1988.

Tate, Claudia. *Psychoanalysis and Black Novels: Desire and the Protocols of Race.* New York: Oxford University Press, 1998.

The Psychedelic '60s: Literary Tradition and Social Change, ed. Josie Pipkin, Web Manager, University of Virginia Library. 17 August 1999. University of Virginia Library, Special Collections Dept., Charlottesville. http://www.lib.virginia.edu/exhibits/sixties/index.html.

Walker, Alice. *The Color Purple.* New York: Washington Square Press, 1982.

Walker, Alice. *In Search of Our Mother's Gardens.* New York: Harcourt Brace Jovanovich, 1983.

Walker, Alice. *Anything We Love Can Be Saved: A Writer's Activism.* New York: Random House, 1997.

Wall, Cheryl A. *Changing Our Own Words.* New Brunswick, NJ: Rutgers University Press, 1989.

NOTES

1. 'Nuyorican' (or 'Neorican' as some prefer it) refers to persons of Puerto Rican heritage born in New York city.
2. Feminists generally assert that gender – that is, the ways in which biological sex are interpreted and played out in society – is socially constructed rather than something which is *essentially* part of a man or a woman (see Sarah Gamble's chapter in this volume on gender and transgender studies). Thus, for example, most feminists would reject the notion that women 'naturally' know more than men when it comes to fashion, or cleaning the house, or making food (and reject, of course the corollary – that women then 'should' be doing these things); this would be conceived of as *essentialist* thinking. However, feminists of color, while acknowledging that 'race', too, is a social construct, also insist on the fact that 'race' has both a social reality and material consequences for women of color. Hence the insistence that there are in fact differences among women that can be attributable to their experiences of what is a socially constructed, yet seemingly 'natural' thing, such as the colour of their skin.
3. Here, we use the phrase 'women's ways of knowing' to indicate what is sometimes generally known as 'feminist epistemology', or more specifically, 'feminist standpoint epistemology'. If 'epistemology' means the study of knowledge, feminist standpoint epistemology maintains that 'knowledge' is not only produced in academies or by empirical means. For a theorist like Sandra Harding, professor of philosophy at the University of Delaware, standpoint epistemology refers to 'socially situated knowledge', that is the knowledge that people have of their own social positions. As Harding puts it: 'In conventional accounts, socially situated beliefs only get to count as opinions. In order to achieve the status of knowledge, beliefs are supposed to break free of – to transcend – their original ties to local, historical interests, values, and agendas' (1998, 50). Feminists, and particularly feminists of color such as Patricia Hill Collins, believe that women of color in particular have developed ways of thinking about, and knowing, their own 'standpoint' – their own social situation – in raced, classed and gendered terms, and that this knowledge which has been barred from academic thought for so long must now be brought into academic Black feminism.
4. *Intersectionality* is a term used by feminist and race theorists to describe the ways race, class and gender converge in women's lives and restructure them in complex and, often, diminishing ways. Intersectionality insists that oppression is not singular in its cause or impact but multiple, with intersecting catalysts and support systems.

5. Further discussion of Anzaldúa is to be found in Kate Rigby's chapter, below, on 'ecocriticism'.

6. Armed with a desire for intense political, cultural, spiritual and introspective awareness, contemporary Black women greet the twenty-first century already engaged in dialogues about bodily recuperation and redefinition (*Recovering the Black Female Body: Self Representations by African American Women*, 2000, edited by Michael Bennett and Vanessa D. Dickerson, for instance), defining and loving self in light of current body politics and pseudo-claims of diversity (Debra King's edited edition of multicultural (multi-racial) essays *Body Politics and the Fictional Double*, 2000), the meaning of liberty and procreative freedom (Dorothy Roberts' *Killing the Black Body: Race, Reproduction and the Meaning of Liberty*, 1997) and the hope of sexual and spiritual awakening (Alice Walker's *By the Light of My Father's Smile*, 1998).

7. 'Anglo' is a term used by Chicanas/os and Latinos/as to describe the white United States' majority population, one which is primarily of European heritage.

8. No group of people has been more successful in marketing this decade's 'Latin explosion' than those in the music industry. As the *All Music Guide*'s on-line notes on Latin Pop explain, 'Latin Pop became the most popular form of Latin music in the United States during the '80s and '90s, even achieving massive crossover success among non-Latino listeners during the late '90s . . . Latin pop's first major crossover star was [Cuban-born singer] Gloria Estefan . . .'. But, as the *Guide* puts it, 'that was nothing compared to Latin Pop's commercial explosion in 1999, thanks to . . . crossover albums by ex-Menudo member Ricky Martin (already a star among Spanish-speaking audiences) and actress Jennifer Lopez'. It is important to note that 'crossover' here is a music industry term, applied only to artists who manage to attract a white majority audience.

9. In fact, these two women's images have been managed by their most important producer to date, Sean 'Puffy' Combs (aka Puff Daddy). Although Puffy has courted a reputation as the producer of what the United States has come to think of as 'real blackness' – tough, inner-city gangsta rap stars – he has in fact spent much of his career producing the likes of Whitney Houston, Lopez, Destiny's Child, Mariah Carey, Apollonia, Taylor Dayne and Lil' Kim.

10. Although the use of the term 'patriarchy' is under debate in feminist thought, we use it here as a shorthand way of indicating a social, political and economic system – or pattern – of 'masculine privilege' wherein more men than women are more often in positions of leadership and authority, and more men than women are afforded correspondingly more resources, both tangible (wages, job positions, entrance into institutions) and intangible (social respect, deference, 'old boy' networks).

DIALOGUES

CHAOS THEORY, COMPLEXITY THEORY AND CRITICISM

Stuart Sim

INTRODUCTION

Chaos theory and complexity theory challenge some of our most deeply held beliefs about the nature of reality. The former claims that natural systems (for example, the weather) are controlled by mysterious forces, called 'strange attractors', such that they are simultaneously random and determined – a conclusion which undermines the laws of logic on which so much of our discourse depends. If chaos theorists are correct, then identity is an even more complex phenomenon than we have supposed it. Given that identity is one of the most pressing concerns of recent criticism and cultural theory (see feminism, deconstruction and postmodernism as cases in point), there are important implications here for literary critical practice which deserve to be explored. This is particularly the case in narratives where the nature of identity is foregrounded – Laurence Sterne's *Tristram Shandy* and Jeanette Winterson's *Gut Symmetries* constituting outstanding examples which will be examined later in the essay. Jean-François Lyotard's observation that 'All that exist are "islands of determinism". Catastrophic antagonism is literally the rule', indicates just how fundamental an adjustment to our world-view is being asked for by the new physics (1984, 59). A key question that arises at such junctures is how much control over our destiny, or environment, we can be said to have as individuals: neither islands of determinism nor catastrophic antagonism constitute particularly congenial locations for the exercise of free will. Another interesting line of inquiry in this context is to consider what the implications of chaos and complexity are for Marxist criticism, given that chaos and complexity problematize classical Marxist conceptions of the nature of the dialectic and materialism.[1]

Complexity takes chaos further, to argue that systems feature a high degree of self-organization: indeed, to claim that at a certain point in the development of a system self-organization spontaneously occurs, projecting the system in question to a more advanced level. When systems – including civilizations and species – are located at the 'edge of chaos' such leaps are more likely to happen. It has even been theorized that the universe itself is such a system, continually in the process of self-organization (the 'strong anthropic principle'). As a component part of the universe, human consciousness, too, is subject to the same laws – although that raises the vexed question, yet again, of control, or lack of it, at the level of the individual. At issue is whether we are independent agents or mere channels. Do we control our consciousness? Or is it simply obeying the dictates of a much larger force, the objectives of which are hidden from us?

When we turn to a text like *Tristram Shandy*, dealing as it does with an earlier version of such problems (also found in the work of the empiricist philosophers David Hume and John Locke), then we find an individual caught up in a world where chance and determinism seem locked in perpetual conflict with each other. Walter Shandy's complaint about the negative impact of 'some retrograde planet' on the Shandy household captures this situation particularly neatly (Sterne, 1983, 164). At any one point in his career Tristram seems to be subject to the operations of both chance and determinism. What is abundantly clear is that he is not in control of his own destiny, or, come to that, the operations of his own consciousness either, which obeys the law of association of ideas instead. In *Gut Symmetries*, on the other hand, we find a character who takes advantage of this state of affairs – as in the operation of the 'wave function' – to overcome human limitations as regards time and space in order to save her lover from death. Whereas Tristram feels severely disadvantaged by the impossibility of a fixed personal identity or self that endures over time, Winterson's female characters are liberated. A complex metaphysical argument about free will is being presented in each case, and any narrative in which free will is a central concern would be a candidate for analysis through the concepts of chaos and complexity.

This chapter will outline the major features of chaos and complexity (strange attractors, the butterfly effect, self-organization, the wave function, the anthropic principle, the edge of chaos, etc.), and tease out the philosophical and cultural implications of theories which problematize our standard world-view – a world-view which is still largely based on notions of continuity and stability. When commentators claim that the realm of matter is structured on the principle of 'deterministic chaos', we are made aware just how much that standard world-view, with its assumption of the uniformity of nature, is now under threat (Coveney and Highfield, 1996, 174). We might reasonably expect to have to deal with one or the other of these phenomena at various points in our lives, but not both simultaneously. There is no very logical response to such a paradox, which leaves us feeling very vulnerable as individuals. *Tristram Shandy* and *Gut Symmetries*, both narratives which self-consciously engage with the problem of identity in terms of the scientific theories of their time, will then be analysed. Chaos and complexity will be seen, therefore, to inform both narrative and critical practice.

CHAOS THEORY

Chaos theory was devised to deal with the dynamics of non-linear systems. Systems such as these are found to be highly sensitive to even very small fluctuations in their initial conditions: the famous 'butterfly effect', whereby the beating of a butterfly's wings in one part of the world could, theoretically, be responsible for the formation of a hurricane thousands of miles away. The weather is an excellent example of just such a critically sensitive system where prediction is notoriously difficult, and can often be spectacularly wrong. It has been noted that:

> Only if an observer knew with infinite accuracy what the starting conditions were in an experimental study of such a chaotic system would he or she be able to make a cast-iron prediction. But the slightest uncertainty – always the case in the real world – denies this, since no matter how small the imprecision, it will be amplified exponentially as time passes. (Coveney and Highfield, 1996, 174)

In chaotic systems randomness and determinism are simultaneously present, which leads to the counter-intuitive conclusion that they are simultaneously predictable and unpredictable in their operation. The same kind of troubling paradox arises in thought experiments in quantum mechanics (the background to chaos and complexity) such as 'Schrödinger's cat', which has been described as follows:

> Schrödinger envisaged a cat incarcerated in a box with a flask of cyanide gas. The box also contains a radioactive source and a geiger counter that can trigger a hammer to smash the flask if a nucleus decays. It is then possible to imagine the quantum state of a nucleus to be such that after, say, one minute, it is in a superposition corresponding to a probability of one-half that decay has occurred and one-half that it has not. If the entire box contents, including the cat, are treated as a single quantum system, we are forced to conclude that the cat is also in a superposition of two states: dead and alive. In other words, the cat is apparently hung up in a hybrid state of unreality in which it is somehow both dead and alive! (Davies, 1995, 169)

Prediction falls apart in such cases, which confound not just our experience of reality but also all our systems of logic (and most particularly the law of identity on which the entire edifice of logic rests). Alive *and* dead is a condition we just cannot comprehend.

Lyotard made a similar point about systems (drawing in this instance on the forerunner to chaos theory, catastrophe theory) when he commented that, 'it is not true that uncertainty (lack of control) decreases as accuracy goes up; it goes up as well' (Lyotard, 1984, 59). In other words, more control equals less control – another conspicuously counter-intuitive conclusion to reach.[2] At every turn our preconceptions about the way systems work in the everyday world are subverted by the new physics. What is also called into question is our ability to know our world in any depth. The mathematician Benoit Mandelbrot has informed us that we cannot even measure a section of the coastline accurately, the reason being that as we go down to greater and greater levels of magnification we find self-similar patterns being repeated endlessly in fractal form:

> Mandelbrot found that as the scale of measurement becomes smaller, the measured length of a coastline rises without limit, bays and peninsulas revealing ever-smaller subbays and subpeninsulas – at least down to atomic scales, where the process does finally come to an end. Perhaps. (Gleick, 1988, 96)

Yet again a total understanding of the system eludes us: at best all we can ever have is a rough approximation of natural systems.

We gain this rough approximation by the unreliable art of measuring, but a further problem arises than the one identified by Mandelbrot – that the very act of measurement alters the system we are dealing with, leading to what has been called the 'collapse' of the wave function:

> Although the microworld is inherently nebulous, and only probabilities rather than certainties can be predicted from the wave function, nevertheless when an actual measurement of some dynamical variable is made a concrete result is obtained. The act of measurement thus transforms probability into certainty by *projecting out* or *selecting* a specific result from among a range of possibilities. Now this projection brings about an abrupt alteration in the form of the wave function, often referred to as its 'collapse', which drastically affects its subsequent evolution . . . The system is therefore capable of changing with time in two completely different ways; one when nobody is looking and one when it is being observed. (Davies, 1995, 168)[3]

Once again we face the paradox of systems having an indeterminable, or multiple, identity that runs counter to our normal understanding of the concept. Collapsing the wave function on Schrödinger's cat does resolve its 'unreal' state of being, but at the considerable risk of killing it.

Behind systems lie mysterious entities known as strange attractors, which dictate what happens within each system. Strange attractors are 'the trajectory toward which all other trajectories converge', and they are inexorable in their operation (Gleick, 1988, 150). We experience their effect in such ordinary natural phenomena as the weather, which is assumed to have its own strange attractor shaping its behaviour – much to the dismay of weather forecasters worldwide, with no access to the underlying programme. An extreme example of a strange attractor would be a black hole, which sucks in all matter that crosses its event horizon. Nothing can escape from a black hole, not even light, and in theory whole galaxies could disappear within such phenomena. Black holes are described as 'singularities', meaning that the laws of physics are suspended inside them. And if, unlike the weather, this all seems very far removed from our everyday experience, we might reflect on the, somewhat alarming, speculation that the universe we live in itself could be a black hole:

> our universe is almost certainly closed . . . The notion that the entire Universe *is* a black hole may seem bizarre at first sight, especially if you are still thinking of black holes only as superdense, compact objects. But remember that the kind of *supermassive* black hole that is thought to lurk at the heart of a quasar can be made out of material scarcely more dense than ordinary water. The bigger the black hole, the lower the density you need to close off spacetime around a collection of matter. (Gribbin, 1995, 238)

It is a moot point whether this should make us feel more or less insecure as regards our sense of identity.

COMPLEXITY THEORY

Complexity carries chaos theory to a new pitch of sophistication, and emphasizes the process of self-organization within systems. Systems are seen to have the ability, at critical points in their development (the edge of chaos), quite spontaneously to self-organize themselves to a higher level of operational complexity. There is 'order for free', as one enthusiast has described the process (Stuart Kauffman, cit. Lewin, 1993, 25). At the extreme end of this theory we find the strong anthropic principle, which treats the universe – including all the life within it – as a system in a constant process of evolution. Forget the forecast heat-death of the universe in around four billion years, argues physicist Paul Davies, 'the universe is as yet "unfinished"' . . . From what can be deduced about astronomical processes, the universe could remain fit for habitation for trillions of years, possibly for ever' (Davies, 1995, 196). Crucially for Davies, human consciousness is part of that universal process: 'there is still a sense in which human mind and society may represent only an intermediate stage on the ladder of organizational progress in the cosmos' (Davies, 1995, 196). Whether being a mere intermediate stage in an amorphous larger process squares with our self-image of ourselves as free-willed independent beings is another question, and at the very least complexity asks for a reassessment of our concept of personal identity – a topic to which we shall return in due course.

The edge of chaos is where systems are at their most creative as well as most unpredictable. It has been described as the state where information gets its foot in the door in the physical world, where it gets the upper hand over energy. Being at the transition point between order and chaos not only buys you exquisite control – small input/big change – but it also buys you the possibility that information processing can become an important part of the dynamics of the system (Chris Langton, quoted in Lewin, 1993, 51).

Systems which allow themselves to become stuck at one stage of development simply ossify, therefore the edge of chaos is the recommended place to be in evolutionary terms. It is certainly the most exciting place to be, although it is also a highly insecure state since it involves a delicate balancing act. Sometimes the balancing act between order and chaos fails, precipitating systems into chaos: 'some perturbations provoke small cascades of change, others trigger complete avalanches, equivalent to mass extinctions' (Lewin, 1993, 62). Critically, we can never know ahead of time whether a small perturbation or a complete avalanche is to be our fate: sometimes, as complexity theorists have noted, civilizations, empires, and species die out quite suddenly, as if overwhelmed by an unexpected turn of events.[4] The edge of chaos can be exciting, but it can also be quite pitiless.

THE PROBLEM OF PERSONAL IDENTITY

The area where chaos and complexity pose most interesting questions for cultural theorists is undoubtedly that of personal identity and its attendant problem of free will. On the one hand, given the coexistence of opposed states (random plus determined) within systems, it suggests that this is even less of a unity than we might have thought, while on the other it raises the spectre of spontaneous self-organization cutting across human endeavour, rendering free will more than somewhat notional. Given the prominent place that free will has in western culture this is a matter of some importance, and certainly one that is of interest to theorists.

Personal identity has become something of a battleground in recent theoretical debate, particularly in continental philosophy circles. From structuralism onwards there has been a tendency in that tradition to view the self as a fragmented entity lacking the unity that western thought generally ascribes to it. Personal identity is a much more fluid concept to structuralists, poststructuralists and postmodernists – and to many feminists, too. What the recent continental tradition seems to be celebrating is the death of man, or as it is sometimes put, the death of the subject: that is, the demise of the particular conception of the individual that has been fostered by the Enlightenment project. The Enlightenment individual is an entity with a unique essence to express and realize in his or her activities, and, at least in theory, western culture is set up to facilitate that self-expression and self-realization. The reality is far more complicated than that (there is not equal access to resources, for a start), but it remains the ideal nonetheless, with totalitarian societies being frowned upon because officially they inhibit the quest for self-realization.

As far as structuralists are concerned, however, individuals are little more than channels through which systems, such as language, operate: 'it is language which speaks, not the author', as Roland Barthes puts it (1977, 143). For poststructuralists, individuals are sites where various drives come into conflict with social norms, and where desire seeks to find means of expression. In Gilles Deleuze and Félix Guattari, for example, we are pictured as 'desiring-machines' confronted by an array of social pressures ('Oedipus' as they collectively refer to these in their book *Anti-Oedipus* (1984)) dedicated to our repression. Schizophrenia becomes for Deleuze and Guattari a way of confounding this repressive regime, since the move into multiple identities renders us more difficult to control (hence their championship of 'schizoanalysis'). One repressed personality is far easier for the authorities to deal with than an unpredictable desiring-machine refusing to conform to social conventions. Postmodernists, too, celebrate our plurality; our ability, as Lyotard perceives it, to make our politics up as we go along, rather than be dictated to by the 'grand narratives' (that is, ideologies) of our time, with their generally reactionary agendas. Politics is for Lyotard a matter of 'little narratives' with delimited objectives rather than authoritarian pretensions. Lyotard's goal is 'svelteness', a condition of being where we can shift from role to role as circumstances demand, instead of having a fixed personality or social role that constrains us to act in a predictable, and thus institutionally controllable, way.[5] Svelte individuals, by implication, cultivate plural identities.

Feminist theorists have also recognized the political advantages of plural identity. Luce Irigaray, for example, uses this model of the individual in *This Sex Which Is Not One* to claim that women can escape from a history of male domination:

> So woman does not have a sex organ? She has at least two of them, but they are not identifiable as ones. Indeed, she has many more. Her sexuality, always at least double, goes even further: it is *plural* . . . the geography of her pleasure is far more diversified, more multiple in its differences, more complex, more subtle, than is commonly imagined – in an imaginary rather too narrowly focused on sameness. (1985, 29)

What Irigaray emphasizes is difference, in this case the difference between male and female sexual identity (just as we shall observe Winterson doing to similar effect in *Gut Symmetries*). Difference becomes a means of evading the designs of patriarchy, which traditionally has constrained women into narrowly defined social roles that make them easier to monitor and control.[6]

Irigaray is deploying deconstructive theory in her concept of female identity. Deconstruction sees difference everywhere, a pervasive aspect of all systems and all discourse (Jacques Derrida's concept of *différance*, where difference combines with deferment, signalling this ubiquity). Its claim to political radicalism is founded on this commitment to difference/*différance*, which works to subvert all attempts to exert authoritarian control over us. According to Derrida, by continually drawing attention to difference/*différance* we take a stance against the incipient totalitarianism of systems, which always seek to eliminate difference from their sphere of operation. Michel Foucault is another thinker to argue that the most characteristic act of authoritarian systems is to set about effacing difference, since this represents a threat to their desire for social conformity as a mechanism of ideological subjection. His various 'archaeologies' are designed to show where and when such effacement has been practised, to the detriment of vulnerable minority groups in Western society (the mentally ill and homosexuals being outstanding examples).

Chaos and complexity provide a scientific background to such theorization, and have infiltrated the discourse of continental philosophers eager to press the cause of difference. Not all commentators agree with this appropriation of recent science, however, as Alan Sokal and Jean Bricmont's celebrated attack on the continental school in *Intellectual Impostures* proves. For the latter, the analogies made between recent science – particularly chaos theory – and cultural politics are highly questionable, and all too often based on a misunderstanding of the scientific concepts involved. Chaos, as Sokal and Bricmont point out, does not have the emotive overtones to a scientist that it does to either a philosopher or political theorist, and they are extremely critical of practically the entire recent continental philosophical tradition for what they regard as a systematic abuse of scientific theory on its part. Nevertheless, the philosophical implications of chaos and complexity are so dramatic that they continue to appeal to cultural theorists concerned to undermine the totalizing imperative of the dominant ideology. The problem remains determining the extent to which events in the micro-world of subatomic particle physics correspond to events in the macro-world in which we conduct our daily lives, but at the very least the analogies being drawn by poststructuralist and postmodernist theorists are thought-provoking and deserve some consideration.

MARXISM AND THE NEW PHYSICS

Marxism has collapsed as a political force of any significant note in the West, but as a generalized cultural theory it continues to have its adherents – enough to have prompted the development of post-Marxism, which attempts to combine the best features of Marxism and postmodernism. The new physics of chaos and complexity poses some particular problems for Marxism, and it is worth examining what these are given that Marxism has been so influential in the area of critical theory. Marxism depends on a conception of the dialectic as something whose trajectory can be manipulated by those who understand its underlying pattern. Thus the communist party can assume that, at some historically determinable point, capitalism will collapse under the weight of its own ideological contradictions (as other social formations, such as feudalism, have been deemed to do in the past), and then plan towards the revolutionary situation that will inevitably occur in the aftermath. The dialectic is held to be a process operating within the material world we inhabit, rather than in the ideal world where Marx's predecessor Hegel had located it (in the guise of the 'World Spirit'). Later Marxists have been critical of this view of the dialectic as a positive phenomenon, with Theodor W. Adorno putting forward his theory of 'negative dialectics' to counter the official Marxist interpretation. Negative dialectics regards difference as a constant element of the dialectical process, such that it can never really be relied on by the Marxist theorist, for whom it is assumed to have a predictable trajectory. The continual creation of contradictions undermines the concept of identity in Adorno's view. Contradiction reveals 'the untruth of identity', the fact that we can never grasp any process in its entirety, encouraging us to develop 'nonidentity thinking' instead (Adorno [1966], 1973, 5). At such points, with identity instantly generating nonidentity, Adorno comes very close to the theory of deterministic chaos, where randomness and determinism are simultaneously present.

The nature of matter is, if the pun will be allowed, a matter of some considerable importance to the classical Marxist theorist, who wants the dialectic to be the critical component of all natural processes, rather than the more abstract phenomenon envisaged by Hegel. Engels identified the development of a grain of barley into a plant as a classic case of the dialectic in action in nature, and this particular example of the 'negation of the negation' (with each stage of the development held to be negating the former) has been much debated in Marxist circles since (Engels [1878], 1976, 172–3). Many have questioned it, dismissing it as 'vulgar materialism', but the desire to locate the dialectic right at the heart of the workings of matter is well engrained in the Marxist outlook all the same.[7] Classical Marxism is, in fact, tied to a particular conception of matter as predictable in its operation, and it has to be considered at risk if that conception of matter is seriously challenged – as it certainly has been by scientific inquiry from the later twentieth century onwards. Some commentators have even spoken of the 'death of materialism' as we move away from our mechanistic models of the universe to a new paradigm based on quantum considerations (Davies and Gribbin, 1991, 2). The death of materialism is not good news for Marxism, which still essentially adheres to a mechanistic world-view, with broadly determinable patterns of cause and effect, and whatever undermines Marxist philosophy also undermines Marxist critical theory, the authority of which derives from the philosophy in the first instance.

The notion of the edge of chaos has interesting implications for Marxist theory. At the point when a system is on the verge of collapsing under the weight of its own contradictions it would seem to be poised at the edge of chaos. For Marxists this would be the point at which capitalism, having created its antithesis in a revolutionary-minded proletariat which has grasped the fact of its exploitation by the system, is at its most vulnerable. Equally, one could say that it is when capitalism is potentially at its most creative, and that it may well find ways to resolve the situation to its own benefit such that it evolves to a new level of sophistication and thus extends its life-span. It could be argued that something like this has indeed happened on several occasions since Marx put forward the theory of dialectical materialism, providing some explanation as to why the final 'crisis of capitalism' that Marxism has so often confidently forecast has never quite occurred (adherents are still claiming we are on the verge of it in the early twenty-first century despite Marxism's many recent setbacks[8]). Later capitalism (or 'late', as some Marxists optimistically refer to it) is not the same beast with which Marx was grappling.

From this perspective the outcome of the dialectical process is not specifiable in advance: the system may collapse, or alternatively the system may regenerate itself, self-organizing to a higher level of operational complexity in the process. Socialism may or may not prove to be the next level of complexity to capitalism. If outcomes to conflicts at the edge of chaos are indeed this open, then Marxism loses its predictive power, and with that, much of its prestige as a cultural theory. We could still identify something like a dialectical process being worked out, between order and chaos in this instance, but not one whose outcome could be predicted with any certainty by the participants. Marxism has always prided itself on being a 'science' of history, but it ceases to be a science if its projections are surrounded by so much doubt and confusion. The 'edge of chaos' test reveals significant gaps in Marxism's pretensions to theoretical supremacy.

CONCLUSION

Looking at fictional texts from the past through the prism of current scientific theories might seem like an anachronistic exercise, but in the case of chaos and complexity there is a ready defence to hand. Chaos and complexity are simply more scientific ways of describing unresolved problems in human affairs that other ages experienced in a more empirical fashion. Where now we wrestle with the paradox of randomness and determinism coexisting within systems, earlier times mused over the conflict between chance and fate, and fortune or fate, and saw individuals as being just as vulnerable to the vagaries of these entities as we do to strange attractors and black holes. A recurrent theme throughout the history of the novel in western literature has been the conflict between individual and system, with the issue of free will looming large in consequence. Chaos and complexity, appropriately enough, add extra layers of complexity to this debate, and enable us to see the debates over free will and personal identity in the novel in a more scientific light than hitherto. These theories generate essentially the same dilemmas that faced an author like Sterne, who is similarly bemused by the individual's problematical relationship to natural systems – as well as exercised by whether our consciousness is part of those natural systems or not.[9] How chaos and complexity help us to go deeper into a text such as *Tristram Shandy* we shall now consider.

NOTES TOWARDS READINGS OF
TRISTRAM SHANDY AND *GUT SYMMETRIES*

Tristram Shandy pictures a world in which chance and fate conspire to prevent the formation of a fixed personal identity, and in both its themes and structure it looks forward to the discourse of chaos and complexity.[10] Here is a world where systems take no account of individual desires, and where disaster is seemingly always waiting just around the corner to entrap one. Tristram's concern is to establish a pattern to his life such that he can come to understand his place in the universal scheme of things, but all he can find looking back on his career, stretching from the moment of conception onwards, is disorder and digression. Linear coherence consistently eludes Tristram, try as he might to make his life add up to a unity.

The narrative takes its lead from the concept of association of ideas outlined in John Locke's *An Essay Concerning Human Understanding*, where it is postulated that ideas can bond together in an arbitrary manner:

> Some of our ideas have a *natural* correspondence and connexion one with another; it is the office and excellency of our reason to trace these, and hold them together in that union and correspondence which is founded in their peculiar beings. Besides this, there is another connexion of ideas wholly owing to *chance* or *custom*. Ideas that in themselves are not at all of kin come to be so united in some men's minds that it is very hard to separate them; they always keep in company, and the one no sooner at any time comes into the understanding but its associate appears with it; and if they are more than two which are thus united, the whole gang, always inseparable, show themselves together . . . This strong combination of ideas, not allied by nature, the mind makes in itself either voluntarily or by chance; and hence it comes in different men to be very different, according to their different inclinations, educations, interests, &c. (1964, 250–1)

Such conjunctions are unique to the individual (all of us could provide our own examples if required), and they defy any laws of logic in their sheer contingency. David Hume's inquiries into the nature of personal identity draw heavily on the principle of association of ideas, to reach conclusions very similar to that of Sterne. For Hume, personal identity is a state of flux where we are bombarded by sense perceptions:

> when I enter most intimately into what I call myself, I always stumble on some particular perception or other, of heat or cold, light or shade, love or hatred, pain or pleasure. I never can catch myself at any time without a perception, and never can observe anything but the perception . . . I may venture to affirm of the rest of mankind, that they are nothing but a bundle or collection of different perceptions, which succeed each other with an inconceivable rapidity, and are in a perpetual flux and movement. (1962, 301–2)

Given this state of affairs a unified self is all but impossible: there is no magic moment when we can have a consciousness of such unity, simply the unending flow of sense perceptions. Hume's rather despairing conclusion is 'that all the nice and subtle questions concerning personal identity can never possibly be decided' (1962, 311).

Tristram is no more successful in solving 'all the nice and subtle questions concerning personal identity', and thus finding some meaning for his life. All he can identify in retrospect is a series of 'pitiful misadventures and cross accidents'

(Sterne, 1983, 10) that prevent his life from conforming to any kind of recognizable pattern. The narrative of *Tristram Shandy* resolves itself into a stream of digressions with only the most tenuous of linking threads. At any one point Tristram is subject to the operation of association of ideas, which deflect all his attempts to construct a linear path through life. That path will be decided by a combination of chance and determinism, forces outside Tristram's control, rather than by any effort of Tristram himself.

Newtonian physics emphasized the order of the natural world, but Sterne implicitly calls this paradigm into question through the misadventures of his hero.[11] Disorder is a more pervasive feature of Tristram's life, and it often seems to stem from the operation of the butterfly effect. In the case of Tristram's naming, for example, the transformation of Trismegistus, his intended name, into Tristram as it passes along a chain of individuals to the curate baptizing him, is subsequently amplified into a melancholy disposition that will haunt Tristram for the rest of his days. Equally, his mother's question at the moment of Tristram's conception, '*Pray my dear . . . have you not forgot to wind up the clock?*', disperses the 'animal spirits' leading to a disordered, chaotic life (Sterne, 1983, 5). Apparently small inputs into Tristram's life can have catastrophic effects on his development at later stages, and his description of himself as 'the continual sport of what the world calls Fortune' seems entirely justified (Sterne, 1983, 10).

Being at the edge of chaos proves to be a nightmare for the entire Shandy family, who seem fated to be tipped over into chaos itself with monotonous regularity; Uncle Toby's war injury, Bobby Shandy's unexpected early death, Tristram's series of unfortunate personal mishaps (instances of physical maiming not least among them), and Walter Shandy's many failed schemes all providing hard evidence of just how dangerous deterministic chaos can be. Catastrophic antagonism certainly gives the impression of being the rule in Shandy family affairs, as if some strange attractor were directing them:

> Confusion! cried my father (getting up upon his legs a second time) – not one single thing has gone right this day! had I faith in astrology, brother (which by the bye, my father had), I would have sworn some retrograde planet was hanging over this unfortunate house of mine, and turning every individual thing in it out of its place. (1983, 163–4)

When it comes to such confusion, reason is no help. The Shandy family is instead thrown back on sentiment as a method of coping with its vulnerability to the operations of fate and chance. Sentiment represents an emotional response to a world beyond our control: a recognition that 'the nice and subtle questions concerning personal identity' defeat all of us in the end. In the absence of any practical solutions, sympathy with each other's plight is all that can be put forward by the author.

Gut Symmetries very self-consciously structures itself on recent physics, using the wave function and superstring theory as integral elements of the narrative.

The story itself is a postmodern version of 'the eternal triangle', where two of the characters, one male, one female, are physicists searching for a Grand Unified Theory to explain the workings of the universe (superstrings being one such highly regarded candidate). They start an affair, which is later complicated by the female physicist entering into another affair with the male physicist's wife. The novel is also an exploration of the differences between male and female nature, where the latter is held to be much the more flexible and adaptable, and, because of that, able to take advantage of the wave function and breach the laws of space and time. Male characters, on the other hand, are found to be earth-bound and lacking in the imaginative skills needed to access the wave function (Winterson is something of an essentialist thinker in this regard). As Jove, the male partner in the triangle, puts it:

> Matter is energy. Of course. But for all practical purposes matter is matter. Don't take my word for it. Bang your head against a brick wall. The shifting multiple realities of quantum physics are real enough but not at a level where they affect our lives. I deal in them every day and I, like you, still have to wash my underpants. In a parallel universe somewhere near here I may never have to wash my underpants, but until then, no mystical union with the One will muffle the stink. (Winterson, 1997, 191–2)

Jove reveals his limitations at such points, whereas the female characters find something like that mystical union in their love for each other. The latter are dismissive of Jove's masculine 'realism'. 'Why not join the Flat Earth Club?' he is asked, while being reminded that 'quantum mechanics is not interested in our logic' (Winterson, 1997, 192, 160). The female self is more attuned to shifting multiple realities than the male is, and evinces a nostalgia for the unity that preceded our current form of the universe:

> In the beginning was a perfect ten-dimensional universe that cleaved into two. While ours, of three spatial dimensions and the oddity of time, expanded to fit our grossness, hers, of six dimensions wrapped itself away in tiny solitude. This sister universe, contemplative, concealed, waits in our future as it has refused our past. (Winterson, 1997, 4)

Gut Symmetries probes into the connection between the subatomic world and the everyday world we inhabit, with Winterson drawing freely on superstring theory to suggest that all matter is linked in such a way that we can actually experience the connection if we have the right temperament (matter being, as she tells us, simply 'that which has a tendency to exist' (Winterson, 1997, 7)). Superstrings mean that actions at one point in the space-time continuum vibrate at others far distant, enabling Alice, in somewhat science-fictional fashion, to reach Stella, lost at sea with Jove, and to save her from imminent death at Jove's hands. The female characters, we are to assume, have tuned into that sister universe (the gendering is highly significant), and turned its shifting multiple realities to their own advantage against the malign forces of patriarchy.

In general, the female self pictured in *Gut Symmetries* has a fluidity characteristic of postmodern science, that the masculine self signally lacks – hence the appeal of lesbian love to the female characters. Love is hardly possible between the male and female characters of Winterson's world, since the masculine consciousness cannot really countenance the loss of ego, and surrender to the workings of the superstring network, that love demands and that the female consciousness is so willing to embrace. Men are simply too self-absorbed to respond to the patterns of what for Winterson is a 'symphonic' universe (Winterson, 1997, 98).[12] The female consciousness, especially as expressed in lesbianism, represents a serious threat to the masculinist world-view, and in a rather neat trick, scientific theory, traditionally a male preserve, is turned into a method of furthering the female cause. Female consciousness seems to be an expression of the strong anthropic principle, and for Winterson and her characters this marks an advance for humanity.

QUESTIONS FOR FURTHER CONSIDERATION

1. We do not experience the subatomic level of matter: how valid is it to make analogies between this micro-world and the macro-world of which we do have direct experience?
2. Is there any justification for Winterson's belief that women are more in tune with the natural world (including its physics) than men are?
3. What scope can there be for free will in a world governed by 'deterministic chaos'?
4. Might we see association of ideas in *Tristram Shandy* as an example of deterministic chaos in action?
5. Should we embrace the edge of chaos in our own lives? Or does it make more sense to protect ourselves against such a state of insecurity?
6. Tristram seems to use sentiment as a method for reconciling himself to his lack of control over his environment or personal destiny: how effective do you find this response?

ANNOTATED BIBLIOGRAPHY

Coveney, Peter, and Roger Highfield. *Frontiers of Complexity: The Search for Order in a Chaotic World*. London: Faber & Faber, 1996. Comprehensive study of the physics of chaos and complexity, ranging through such diverse phenomena as artificial life, neural networks, robotics, game theory, evolution and genetics. A more technical study than either Gleick (1988), or Lewin (1993), but worth persevering with for its mine of information.

Davies, Paul. *The Cosmic Blueprint: Order and Complexity at the Edge of Chaos*. Harmondsworth: Penguin, 1995. Examines the creative aspect of complex systems, particularly their ability spontaneously to self-organize to higher levels of operational complexity. Argues that our universe has this capacity, which may enable it to overcome its current apparent physical limitations and escape its forecast 'death'.

Gleick, James. *Chaos: Making a New Science*. London: Cardinal, 1988. General introduction to the science of chaos aimed at a popular market. Emphasizes that chaos is a part of our everyday world, with chaotic behaviour being a standard component of natural systems such as the weather. Provides detailed analyses of such key phenomena as the butterfly effect and fractals.

Gribbin, John. *In Search of the Edge of Time: Black Holes, White Holes, Wormholes*. Harmondsworth: Penguin, 1995. Fascinating study of the physics of black holes, and the possibilities they raise for time travel (such as 'wormholes' between universes). Expertly takes the reader through such complex topics as the warping of space and time, and provides detailed exposition of the various kinds of 'dense' stars.

Hayles, N. Katherine. *Chaos and Order: Complex Dynamics in Literature and Science*. Chicago, IL: University of Chicago Press, 1991. Collection of essays by various writers, investigating the connections between science and literature from the eighteenth century to the present. An overall concern is the dialectic between order and disorder in both literary and scientific inquiry, and topics covered include the impact of Newtonian physics on literary practice.

Lewin, Roger. *Complexity: Life on the Edge of Chaos*. London: Phoenix, 1993. Accessible introduction to the basic concepts of complexity, which concentrates on explaining the theory through the work and ideas of the major figures in the field. Argues that complexity is a unifying theory that shows how all complex systems can be reduced to the operation of a few simple rules.

Sim, Stuart. ' "All that exist are 'islands of determinism' " ': Shandean sentiment and the dilemma of postmodern physics'. In *Laurence Sterne in Modernism and Postmodernism*, eds David Pierce and Peter de Voogd. Amsterdam, and Atlanta, GA: Editions Rodopi, 1996: 109–21. Explores the correspondences between Sterne's fiction and chaos theory, the premise being that the metaphysical problems encountered in *Tristram Shandy* (lack of control over one's destiny, the contingent nature of self and personal identity) are strikingly similar to those posed by the physics of chaos, with the latter's paradoxical mixture of randomness and determinism.

Sim, Stuart. *Post-Marxism: An Intellectual History*. London and New York: Routledge, 2000. Wide-ranging survey of the growth of post-Marxism as a cultural movement, which traces the debate over the nature of the dialectic within Marxism over the course of the twentieth century. Chapter 9 questions whether dialectical materialism can survive exposure to the less mechanistic conceptions of matter to be found in chaos and complexity theory.

Sim, Stuart. 'Sterne●Chaos●Complexity'. In *The Eighteenth-Century Novel 1*, ed. Susan Spencer. New York: AMS Press, 2001. Develops the arguments in Sim (1996) (above) to take account of complexity theory. Links are established between Laurence Sterne's world-view, David Hume's philosophical inquiries, and such aspects of complexity theory as spontaneous self-organization and the 'edge of chaos'.

SUPPLEMENTARY BIBLIOGRAPHY

Adorno, Theodor W. *Negative Dialectics*, trans. E. B. Ashton. London: Routledge & Kegan Paul, 1973.

Barthes, Roland. *Image-Music-Text*, ed. and trans. Stephen Heath. Glasgow: Fontana/ Collins, 1977.

Davies, Paul and John Gribbin. *The Matter Myth: Towards 21st-Century Science*. Harmondsworth: Penguin, 1991.

Deleuze, Gilles and Félix Guattari. *Anti-Oedipus: Capitalism and Schizophrenia*, trans. Robert Hurley, Mark Seem and Helen R. Lane. London: Athlone Press, 1984.

Engels, Friedrich. *Anti-Dühring: Herr Eugen Dühring's Revolution in Science*. Peking: Foreign Languages Press, 1976.

Hume, David. *A Treatise of Human Nature*, ed. D. G. C. Macnabb. Glasgow: William Collins, 1962.

Irigaray, Luce. *The Irigaray Reader*, ed. Margaret Whitford. Oxford: Blackwell, 1991.

Irigaray, Luce. *This Sex Which Is Not One*, trans. Catherine Porter, with Carolyn Burke. Ithaca, NY: Cornell University Press, 1985.

Locke, John. *An Essay Concerning Human Understanding*, ed. A. D. Woozley. Glasgow: William Collins, 1964.

Lyotard, Jean-François. *Political Writings*. Trans. Bill Readings, with Kevin Paul Geiman. London: UCL Press, 1993.

Lyotard, Jean-François. *The Postmodern Condition: A Report on Knowledge*, trans. Geoff Bennington and Brian Massumi. Manchester: Manchester, University Press, 1984.

Penrose, Roger. *Shadows of the Mind: A Search for the Missing Science of Consciousness*. Oxford: Oxford University Press, 1994.

Pierce, David and Peter de Voogd (eds). *Laurence Sterne in Modernism and Postmodernism*. Amsterdam and Atlanta, GA: Editions Rodopi, 1996.

Smethurst, D. P. and H. C. Williams. 'Power Laws: Are Hospital Waiting Lists Self Regulating?' *Nature*, 410, 5 April 5 2001, 652–3.

Sokal, Alan, and Jean Bricmont. *Intellectual Impostures: Postmodern Philosophers' Abuse of Science*. London: Profile Books, 1998.

Sterne, Laurence. *The Life and Opinions of Tristram Shandy, Gentleman*, ed. Ian Campbell Ross. Oxford: Oxford University Press, 1983.

Timpanaro, Sebastian. *On Materialism*, trans. Lawrence Garner. London: NLB, 1975.

Winterson, Jeanette. *Gut Symmetries*. London: Granta, 1997.

Woodcock, Alexander and Monte Davis. *Catastrophe Theory*. Penguin: Harmondsworth, 1980.

NOTES

1. I deal with this issue in some detail in Sim (2000), Chapter 9.
2. A recent study conducted at the Queen's Medical Centre, Nottingham, has claimed that government intervention in the National Health Service, to cut down patient waiting lists, falls victim to the same principle (see Smethurst and Williams, 2001). For an exposition of catastrophe theory, see Woodcock and Davis (1980).
3. The problem with measurement was first identified in Heisenberg's uncertainty principle.
4. See Lewin (1993) for a discussion of this in relation to the Anasazi civilization of the American south-west, a favourite study of theorists in this area of inquiry.
5. See Jean-François Lyotard, 'A Svelte Appendix to the Postmodern Question' (Lyotard, 1993, 25–9).
6. It should be noted that Irigaray's conception of difference has altered over the course of her career, and, as Margaret Whitford has remarked of works like *This Sex Which Is Not One*, 'her early statements about *parler femme* (speaking (as) woman) may seem rather optimistic, corresponding perhaps to the political climate of the early 1970s and the initial euphoria of the women's movement. She now makes it clear that big shifts in society and culture will be necessary if transformations in language are to come about' (1991, 4).
7. Some recent theorists have also defended it; see particularly Timpanaro (1975).
8. The anti-globalization movement, with its protests at recent World Trade Organization meetings, is taken to be evidence of yet another 'final crisis', although it hardly conforms to Marxist notions of the development of class consciousness.
9. Debate still rages as to the anti-mechanistic or otherwise nature of consciousness. See, for example, the anti-mechanistic arguments put forward in Penrose (1994).
10. See Sim (1996 and 2001) for more detailed studies of the correspondences between Sterne's text and the two theories in question.
11. For an analysis of the dialectic between order and chaos in eighteenth-century culture, see Robert Markley, 'Representing Order: Natural Philosophy, Mathematics, and Theology in the Newtonian Revolution', in Hayles (1991, 125–48).

12. This symphonic nature comes out in Paul Davies's observation that, 'In principle, all particles that have ever interacted belong to a single wave function – a global wave function . . . One could even consider (and some physicists do) a wave function for the entire universe. In such a scheme the fate of any given particle is inseparably linked to the fate of the cosmos as a whole' (Davies, 1995, 177).

CHAPTER 5

ETHICAL CRITICISM

Kenneth Womack

INTRODUCTION

Questions about ethics continue to exert a profound influence upon the direction of contemporary literary criticism. Yet, as Geoffrey Galt Harpham observes in *Shadows of Ethics: Criticism and the Just Society*, ethical criticism functions in the eyes of many literary scholars as an 'alien discourse' that challenges or undermines the theoretical project's capacity for promoting 'literature's immediacy, concreteness, vitality, and affective richness' (Harpham, 1999, ix). During the last two decades, ethical criticism's fusion with continental philosophy has produced a more theoretically rigorous form of literary critique that continues to elevate its status as a viable interpretive mechanism. In contrast with North American variations of the paradigm that find their origins in Kantian moral philosophy and troll dangerously close to the shoals of moral relativism, ethical criticism's European manifestations offer a more forceful analysis by emphasizing continental philosophy's various and ongoing accounts of alterity, otherness and phenomenology. While both schools of thought may hale from decidedly different venues of intellectual thought, ethical criticism's various manifestations demonstrate the theoretical project's larger interest in assessing the value systems that inform our textual interpretations.

In North America, ethical criticism finds its contemporary origins in the works of such scholars as Wayne C. Booth, Martha C. Nussbaum and J. Hillis Miller. Volumes such as Booth's *The Company We Keep: An Ethics of Fiction* and Nussbaum's *Love's Knowledge: Essays on Philosophy and Literature* demonstrate the interpretive power of ethical criticism, as well as the value of its critical machinery to scholarly investigations regarding the nature of literary character, the cultural landscapes of fiction and the ethical motivations of satire – the narrative manoeuvre that Booth ascribes to our desire to 'make and remake ourselves' (Booth, 1988, 14). Critics such as Booth and Nussbaum avoid the textual violence of censorship to advocate instead a form of criticism that explores the moral sensibilities that inform works of art. In *Love's Knowledge*, Nussbaum illustrates the nature of ethical criticism's recent emergence as a viable interpretive paradigm: 'Questions about justice, about well-being and social distribution, about moral realism and relativism, about the nature of rationality, about the concept of the person, about the emotions and desires, about the role of luck in human life – all these and others are debated from many sides with considerable excitement and even urgency', she writes (Nussbaum, 1990, 169–70). In its desire to examine the ethical nature of these artistic works, ethical criticism seeks to create a meaningful bond between the life of the narrative and the life of the reader. Although ethical criticism hardly functions as a conventional interpretive paradigm in the tradition of Marxist, Lacanian or gender textual readings, it serves effectively nevertheless as a self-reflexive means for critics to explain the contradictory emotions and problematic moral stances that often mask complex and fully realized literary characters. Ethical criticism provides its practitioners, moreover, with the capacity to posit socially relevant interpretations by celebrating the Aristotelian qualities of living well and flourishing. In this way, ethical criticism evokes the particularly 'human character' of literature that Tobin Siebers extols the merits of in *The Ethics of Criticism*.

Principal among continental philosophy's turn towards ethics are such thinkers as Emmanuel Levinas[1] and Jacques Derrida. Levinas's moral philosophy highlights notions of responsibility, the concept of the gift and a more universalized cognizance of otherness in the western philosophical tradition. In addition to analysing the nature of our relationships with others as well as ourselves, Levinas's ethical theories intersect a wide array of contemporary theoretical debates regarding feminist studies, pluralistic models of reading and cultural criticism. As Jill Robbins observes in *Altered Reading: Levinas and Literature*, Levinasian ethics 'denotes the putting into question of the self by the infinitizing mode of the face of the other' (Robbins, 1999, xiii). In addition to demonstrating the notion of an 'unconditional ethical imperative', in the words of Simon Critchley, Derrida's conceptions of deconstructive reading provide us with a powerful mechanism for comprehending the ethical implications of philosophy, politics and democracy. In *The Ethics of Deconstruction: Derrida and Levinas*, Critchley contends that Derrida's ethical problematics can be valuably understood in terms of the philosopher's ongoing textual dialogue with Levinas. 'An ethical moment is essential to deconstructive reading', Critchley writes, and 'ethics is the goal, or horizon, towards which Derrida's work tends' (Critchley, 1992, 2).

In addition to examining the most significant strands of North American postulations of ethical criticism and continental philosophy's various forms of ethical critique, this chapter will offer an exemplary reading of the intersections between ethics and literature via interpretive sketches of George Eliot's *Silas*

Marner and Spike Jonze's *Being John Malkovich*. Eliot's novel, for example, provides readers with a narrative that illustrates Levinasian notions of responsibility and the gift as Silas Marner, a friendless weaver, finds redemption through his love for the orphan Eppie rather than a treasured cache of gold. Jonze's *Being John Malkovich* examines a variety of metaphysical and existential questions, while also offering a useful forum for addressing Critchley's concept of an 'unconditional ethical imperative'. Jonze's film, with its powerful depiction of moral philosophy's phenomenological concept of a cataleptic impression, functions as a revelatory means for discussing the dimensions of ethics that mark its narrative, as well as our understanding of various aspects of *Being John Malkovich*'s larger ethical spaces.

ETHICAL CRITICISM IN NORTH AMERICA

In many ways, the recent revival of ethical criticism in North American intellectual circles finds its roots in the desire by literary theorists to re-examine our complicated relationships with literary texts. In one of the more forceful ethical critiques of literary theory, *The Ethics of Criticism*, Siebers identifies the crisis that confronts modern criticism – an interpretive dilemma that 'derives in part from an ethical reaction to the perceived violence of the critical act' (Siebers, 1988, 15). He further argues that an ethical approach to literary study requires critics to engage their subjects self-consciously with sustained attention to the potential consequences of their interpretive choices: 'The ethics of criticism involves critics in the process of making decisions and of studying how these choices affect the lives of fellow critics, writers, students, and readers as well as our ways of defining literature and human nature.' Siebers ascribes the aforementioned crisis in criticism to a linguistic paradox that inevitably problematizes critical practice. 'Modern literature has its own cast of characters,' he writes. 'It speaks in a discourse largely concerned with issues of language, but behind its definitions of language lie ideals of human character' (Siebers, 1988, 10). Siebers argues that acknowledging the place of ethics in critical theory affords practitioners of the discipline with the autonomy to offer relevant conclusions about literary texts and their considerable social and ideological import. 'Literary criticism cannot endure without the freedom to make judgments', Siebers notes, 'and modern theory urgently needs to regain the capacity to decide' (Siebers, 1988, 41). The ability to render sound, moral interpretations, then, provides the foundation for an ethical criticism that fully engages the remarkably human nature of literary study. Such a reading methodology allows for the self-conscious reassessment of our evaluative procedures and their potential for the production of meaningful critiques. As Siebers concludes: 'To criticize ethically brings the critic into a special field of action: the field of human conduct and belief concerning the human' (Siebers, 1988, 1).

For many practitioners of ethical criticism, Louise M. Rosenblatt's *The Reader, the Text, the Poem: The Transactional Theory of the Literary Work* supplies ethical critics with an interpretational matrix for explaining the motives of readers and their 'transactions' with literary texts. Rosenblatt identifies two different types of reading strategies – aesthetic reading, in which the reader devotes particular attention to what occurs *during* the actual reading event, and non-aesthetic reading, a reading strategy in which the reader focuses attention upon the traces of knowledge and data that will remain *after* the event. Rosenblatt designates the latter strategy as a kind of 'efferent' reading in which readers primarily interest themselves in what will be derived materially from the experience (Rosenblatt, 1978, 23–5). Efferent readers reflect upon the verbal symbols in literature, 'what the symbols designate, what they may be contributing to the end result that [the reader] seeks – the information, the concepts, the guides to action, that will be left with [the reader] when the reading is over' (Rosenblatt, 1978, 27). Booth argues that ethical criticism functions as a methodology for distinguishing the 'efferent freight' that results from this reading strategy (Booth, 1988, 14). Rosenblatt describes the act of reading itself – whether aesthetic or non-aesthetic – as a transaction that derives from the peculiar array of experiences that define the reader's persona: 'Each reader brings to the transaction not only a specific past life and literary history, not only a repertory of internalized "codes", but also a very active present, with all its preoccupations, anxieties, questions, and aspirations,' she writes (Rosenblatt, 1978, 144). This recognition of the complexity of the reading transaction underscores the deep interconnections between readers and the human communities in which they live and seek personal fulfilment.

Rosenblatt argues that the transaction of reading involves 'laying bare the assumptions about human beings and society and the hierarchy of values that govern the world derived from the text' (Rosenblatt, 1978, 149–50), a conclusion regarding the ethical value of art in the human community that John Gardner illuminates in his influential volume, *On Moral Fiction*. He argues that literary works should offer readers the opportunity for receiving knowledge from its pages, the possibility – rather than the didactic requirement – of emerging from a reading experience with a heightened sense of communal awareness. Gardner writes:

> We recognize art by its careful, thoroughly honest search for and analysis of values. It is not didactic because, instead of teaching by authority and force, it explores, open-mindedly, to learn what it should teach. It clarifies, like an experiment in a chemistry lab, and confirms. As a chemist's experiment tests the laws of nature and dramatically reveals the truth or falsity of scientific hypotheses, moral art tests values and rouses trustworthy feelings about the better and the worse in human action. (Gardner, 1978, 19)

The role of the ethical critic, then, involves the articulation of a given text's ability to convey notions of knowledge and universal good to its readers, whether through the auspices of allegory, satire, morality plays, haiku or any other fictive means of representation. In Gardner's estimation, ethical critics can only accomplish this end through the fomentation of understanding in their readership. 'Knowledge may or may not lead to belief,' he writes. But 'understanding always does, since to believe one understands a complex situation is to form at least a tentative theory of how one ought to behave in it' (Gardner, 1978, 139). Thus, ethical criticism examines the ways in which literary characters respond to the divergent forces they encounter in the fictional landscapes that they occupy. Their human behaviours and actions provide the interpretive basis for moral reflection and conclusion.

As Gardner notes in *On Moral Fiction*, however, practitioners of ethical criticism must invariably confront the spectre of censorship, a dangerous commodity rooted in the human tendency to instruct without regard for the plurality of competing value systems at work in both the theoretical realm of literary criticism and the larger world of humankind. 'Didacticism', he cautions, 'inevitably simplifies morality and thus misses it' (Gardner, 1978, 137). Similarly, critics must avoid the perils of attempting to establish models of behaviour and codified moral standards of acceptability, for such practices inevitably lead to the textual injustice of censorship. Gardner writes: 'I would not claim that even the worst bad art should be outlawed, since morality by compulsion is a fool's morality' (Gardner, 1978, 106). Despite his own admonitions to the contrary in *On Moral Fiction* – and because of the dearth of genuine scholarly wisdom inherent in his study of moral criticism – Gardner himself nevertheless trolls dangerously close to the shores of censorship when he speaks of carrying out 'art's proper work': art 'destroys only evil', he argues. 'If art destroys good, mistaking it for evil, then that art is false, an error; it requires denunciation' (Gardner, 1978, 15). Such a proposition inevitably leads to the establishment of singular standards of good and evil in the heterogeneous, pluralistic spheres of criticism and human reality. Can *ethical* critics, in good conscience, operate from superior positions of moral privilege and arrogant didacticism?

Understanding the place of moral philosophy in the latest incarnation of ethical criticism offers a means for exploring this dilemma. Bernard Williams's *Ethics and the Limits of Philosophy*, for instance, discusses the ways in which the tenets of moral philosophy provide a context for us 'to recreate ethical life' in the sceptical world of contemporary western culture (Williams, 1985, vii). In addition to examining the Johnsonian question of how to live, Williams devotes particular attention to assessing the role of the ethical critic. 'Given people who are in some general sense committed to thinking in ethical terms, how should they think?' he asks. 'Are their ethical thoughts sound?' (Williams, 1985, 71). The issue of a valid ethical criticism itself poses a spurious philosophical quandary, for it requires the critic to define standards of moral correctness, or, as Williams concludes, to dispense with establishing them altogether. 'An ethical theory is a theoretical account of what ethical thought and practice are,' he writes, which 'either implies a general test for the correctness of basic ethical beliefs and principles or else implies that there cannot be such a test' (Williams, 1985, 72). Williams suggests that critics can only surmount this dilemma by interpreting a given set of events from an empathetic position, and, moreover, through their 'ability to arrive at shared ethical judgments' (Williams, 1985, 97). In this way, ethical critics and moral philosophers alike engage in a form of ethical practice that allows for the reflexive process of critical contemplation, a self-conscious methodology for critically articulating the pluralistic nuances of that which constitutes a shared sense of moral correctness.

In addition to questioning the nature of our communal sense of ethical propriety, moral philosophers such as Williams attempt to account for the motives of those critics who dare to engage in the interpretation of human values. Such critics must assume the risks – whether or not they employ an equitable and pluralistic system of evaluation – of impinging upon the current direction of the philosophical conversation regarding human ethics. 'Critical reflection should seek for as much shared understanding as it can find on any issue, and use any ethical material that, in the context of the reflective discussion, makes some sense and commands some loyalty,' Williams notes, although 'the only serious enterprise is living, and we have to live after the reflection' (Williams, 1985, 117). For this reason, the principles of moral philosophy charge ethical critics with the maintenance of a sense of free intellectual discourse, in addition to obliging them to render sound moral conclusions. 'We should not try to seal determinate values into future society,' he warns, for 'to try to transmit free inquiry and the reflective consciousness is to transmit something more than nothing, and something that demands some forms of life more rather than others' (Williams, 1985, 173).

Ethical criticism endeavours, as a matter of course, to communicate the meaning of this 'something' and its greater social relevance through the interpretation of literary works. In *The Company We Keep*, Booth offers an expansive account of ethical criticism and its potential for literary study, while also attempting to allay any fears that his heuristic rests upon dogmatic foundations. Booth affords particular attention to the range of hermeneutic functions that ethical criticism performs, as well as to its unfortunate lack of clarity as an interpretive paradigm:

> We can no longer pretend that ethical criticism is passé. It is practiced everywhere, often surreptitiously, often guiltily, and often badly, partly because it is the most difficult of all critical modes, but partly because we have so little serious talk about why it is important, what purposes it serves, and how it might be done well. (Booth, 1988, 19)

Booth notes that ethical criticism's opponents often misread the paradigm's intent as didactic in nature. Instead, Booth argues, 'ethical criticism attempts to describe the encounters of a story-teller's ethos with that of the reader or listener. Ethical critics need not begin with the intent to evaluate, but their descriptions will always entail appraisals of the value of what is being described.' In this way, Booth supports a reflexive interpretational methodology, an ethical criticism that allows for the recognition of the interconnections between the reading experience and the life of the reader. Ethical criticism acknowledges, moreover, the powerful factors of language and ideology in its textual assessments. 'There are no neutral ethical terms', Booth writes, 'and a fully responsible ethical criticism will make explicit those appraisals that are implicit whenever a reader or listener reports on stories about human beings in action' (Booth, 1988, 8–9).

Booth defines these instances of appraisal – these practical applications of ethical criticism – as acts of 'coduction', referential moments in which critics compare their reading experiences with the conclusions of others. Like Siebers, who argues that 'the heart of ethics is the desire for community' (Siebers, 1988, 202), Booth notes that the act of 'judgment requires a community' of trustworthy friends and colleagues (Booth, 1988, 72). Coduction, in Booth's schema, valorizes the reflexive relationship that develops between texts and their readers, as well as the equally reflexive manner in which texts postulate meaning. 'The question of whether value is in the poem or in the reader is radically and permanently ambiguous, requiring two answers,' Booth writes. 'Of course the value is not in there, *actually*, until it is actualized, by the reader. But of course it could not be actualized if it were not there, *in potential*, in the poem' (Booth, 1988, 89). Booth also notes ethical criticism's pluralistic imperatives and their value to the understanding and operation of ideological paradigms. In his analysis of feminist criticism, for example, Booth discusses the ways in which 'the feminist challenge' derives from fundamental ethical dilemmas inherent in the construction of literary texts: 'Every literary work implies either that women can enter its imaginative world as equals or that they cannot – that instead they must, in reading, decide whether or not to enter a world in which men are a privileged center' (Booth, 1988, 387). As Booth reveals, feminist criticism itself functions as a type of ethical criticism, a means of literary interpretation that seeks to repair an abiding social injustice that, through its misogyny, problematizes the lives of the larger community of readers.

In *The Ethics of Reading: Kant, de Man, Eliot, Trollope, James, and Benjamin*, Miller posits an 'ethics of reading' that seeks to explain the reflexive process that occurs between the text and the reader, in addition to offering testimony to the ethical possibilities of poststructuralism, particularly deconstruction. Miller argues that the act of reading ethically transpires when 'an author turns back on himself, so to speak, turns back on a text he or she has written, re-reads it' (Miller, 1987, 15). For Miller, such a process allows readers – the *de facto* authors of the texts that they appraise – to offer relevant conclusions about the moral properties of literary works and the ethical sensibilities of the readers' theoretical premises, whether they be deconstructive or otherwise. In *Versions of Pygmalion*, Miller proffers a similar argument regarding the 'ethics of narration' and the shifting, performative aspects of reading experiences. Miller derives the title of his volume from the story of Pygmalion in Book 10 of the *Metamorphoses* – a narrative in which something inanimate comes alive, just as reading ethically creates a vital, living relationship between the text and the reader. Miller devotes special attention to the ways in which reading defies stasis, as well as to the manner in which reading ethically, moreover, evolves during successive readings of a given text: 'Reading occurs in a certain spot to a certain person in a certain historical, personal, institutional, and political situation, but it always exceeds what was predictable from those circumstances,' he observes. 'It makes something happen that is a deviation from its context, and what happens demands a new definition each time' (Miller, 1990, 22). In his paradigm for the ethics of reading, Miller allows for the negative possibilities of reading, aspects that Booth, in his effort to celebrate ethical criticism and its myriad of affirmative outcomes, prefers to ignore: 'A theory of the ethics of reading that takes seriously the possibility that reading might lead to other morally good or valuable actions would also have to allow for the possibility that the reading even of a morally exemplary book might cause something morally deplorable to occur,' Miller writes (Miller, 1990, 21). In this manner, Miller postulates a valuable corollary to the reflexive properties of ethical criticism and the ways in which context and temporality possess the propensity to alter the quality of reading experiences.

Like Williams, Nussbaum advocates an ethical criticism with tenable foundations in moral philosophy, as well as an interpretive mechanism that functions as an impetus for sustaining moral discourse and social interconnection. In addition to her enthusiastic subscription to many of the arguments inherent in Booth's ontology for an ethical criticism, Nussbaum proffers a series of essays in *Love's Knowledge* that sharpen the ethical paradigm's focus through her discussion about the interrelations between philosophy and literature, as well as through her close, ethical readings of a diversity of writers, including Henry James, Proust, Ann Beattie and Samuel Beckett, among others. Drawing upon selected works by these figures, Nussbaum examines the ways in which style and content impinge upon ethical issues, while also deliberating about the manner in which the ethical interpretation of literary works offers readers a means for exploring the moral import of emotions and locating paths to self-knowledge. Nussbaum affords particular attention to the roles that stylistics, linguistics and structure play in articulating the moral essence of a given narrative. In Nussbaum's schema, the literary artist bears the responsibility for honourably positing narratives that allow readers the opportunity to discover their own paths to self-understanding and meaning, to formulate their own strategies for living well. Like Booth, Nussbaum equates the quality of life with the ethical dimensions of literature. 'The novel is itself a moral achievement', she writes, 'and the well-lived life is a work of literary art' (Nussbaum, 1990, 148).

In addition to advancing the ethical notion of community in her work, Nussbaum argues for the place of love as a subject in the evolving discourse of ethical criticism. 'The subject of romantic and erotic love is not often treated in works on moral philosophy,' she admits (Nussbaum, 1990, 336). For this reason, Nussbaum differentiates between the Kantian notions of 'pathological' and 'practical' love in her analysis. Pathological love, she notes, signifies the often irrational emotions of romantic love in sharp contrast to the more enduring qualities of practical love, an emotion that Nussbaum defines as 'an attitude of concern that one can will oneself to have toward another human being, and which is, for that reason, a part of morality'. The moral dimensions of practical love, therefore, merit considerable attention as a methodology for understanding the many ways in which readers respond ethically to literary texts. Moreover, 'if one believes, in addition, that the realm of morality is of special and perhaps of supreme importance in human life . . . one will be likely, having once made that distinction, to ascribe high *human* worth to practical love' (Nussbaum, 1990, 336–7). In this way, the acknowledgement of practical love provides additional insight into human conceptions of living well and the manner in which literary texts depict love's capacity to produce personal fulfilment. Nussbaum also refines the communal aspects that mark the ethical paradigm. She extends the metaphor that ethical criticism forges a type of community between text and reader to allow for not only the possibility of living well as an individual, but living together well in a much larger sense of the word. 'A community is formed by author and readers,' she writes. 'In this community separateness and qualitative difference are not neglected; the privacy and the imagining of each is nourished and encouraged. But at the same time it is stressed that living together is the object of our ethical interest' (Nussbaum, 1990, 48). In *Poetic Justice: The Literary Imagination and Public Life* (1995), Nussbaum advances this concept through her exploration of the value of ethical reading as a means for influencing political theory and public discourse: 'If we think of reading in this way, as combining one's own absorbed imagining with periods of more detached (and interactive) critical scrutiny, we can already begin to see why we might find in it an activity well suited to public reasoning in a democratic society' (Nussbaum, 1990, 9). By widening the scope of the ethical paradigm to account for a range of emotional states, as well as a variety of public and private modes of discourse, Nussbaum shares in the creation of an ethical criticism that provides for the relevant interpretation of the social, political and cultural nuances of the human community.

Despite the publication in recent years of a number of volumes devoted to the humanistic study of literary works – a roster of monographs that includes Cora Diamond's *The Realistic Spirit: Wittgenstein, Philosophy, and the Mind*, Adam Zachary Newton's *Narrative Ethics*, and Kim L. Worthington's *Self as Narrative: Subjectivity and Community in Contemporary Fiction* – ethical criticism, particularly in its North American manifestations, must still successfully contend with several issues of historical and contemporary import in order to authenticate itself as a viable interpretive paradigm. Apart from continuing to underscore its usefulness to literary study, ethical criticism must effectively differentiate itself from the contemporary critical prejudice associated with the 'traditional humanism' previously associated with such figures as F. R. Leavis and Northrop Frye. Practitioners of ethical criticism are succeeding in this regard in a variety of ways, including their critical alliance with the ethical philosophies of Emmanuel Levinas and via the recent emergence of the law and literature movement. By also demonstrating its significant pedagogical value, as well as establishing itself as a meaningful component in the future of the theoretical project, the ethical paradigm may yet realize Booth's vision in *The Company We Keep* of a reading methodology that shuns theoretical dogma in favour of 'critical pluralism' and highlights the ethical interconnections between the lives of readers and their textual experiences (Booth, 1988, 489).

ETHICAL CRITICISM AND CONTINENTAL PHILOSOPHY

In European critical circles, Levinas's fundamental ethical concepts function at the core of their advancement of an ethical criticism. Such philosophically vexed issues as obligation and responsibility, for instance, are perhaps most usefully considered via Levinas's conceptions of alterity, contemporary moral philosophy's *sine qua non* for understanding the nature of our innate responsibilities to our human others. In 'Is Ontology Fundamental?' Levinas discusses the ethical significance of other beings in relation to the needs and desires of ourselves. Our ethical obligations to others, Levinas reasons, find their origins in our inability to erase them via negation. Simply put, unless we succeed in negating others through violence, domination or slavery, we must comprehend others as beings *par excellence* who become signified as 'faces', the Levinasian term that refers to the moral consciousness and particularity inherent in others. This 'primacy of ontology', in Levinas's words, demonstrates the nature of the collective inter-relationships that human beings share with one another (Levinas, 1996, 10). In 'The Trace of the Other', Levinas argues that 'the relationship with the other puts me into question, empties me of myself' (Levinas, 1986, 350). More importantly for our purposes here, Levinas describes the concept of the face as 'the concrete figure for alterity' (Levinas, cit. Robbins, 1999, 23). The notion of alterity itself – which Paul-Laurent Assoun characterizes as 'the primal scene of ethics' (Assoun, 1998, 96) – refers to our inherent responsibilities and obligations to the irreducible face of the other. These aspects of our human condition find their origins in the recognition of sameness that we find in others. This similarity of identity and human empathy establishes the foundation for our alterity – in short, the possibility of being 'altered' – and for the responsibilities and obligations that we afford to other beings.

In *Time and the Other*, Levinas identifies the absolute exteriority of alterity, as opposed to the binary, dialectic or reciprocal structure implied in the idea of the other. Hence, alterity implies a state of being apprehended, a state of infinite and absolute otherness. In 'Philosophy and the Idea of Infinity', Levinas writes that 'we can say that the alterity of the infinite is not cancelled, is not extinguished in the thought that thinks it. In thinking infinity the I from the first *thinks more than it thinks*. Infinity does not enter into the *idea* of infinity, is not grasped; this idea is not a concept,' he continues. 'The infinite is radically, absolutely, other' (Levinas, 1987, 54). Alterity's boundless possibilities for registering otherness, for allowing us to comprehend the experiences of other beings, demonstrates its ethical imperatives. Its exteriority forces us to recognize an ethics of difference and of otherness. Such encounters with other beings oblige us, then, to incur the spheres of responsibility inherent in our alterity. When we perceive the face of the other, we can no longer, at least ethically, suspend responsibility for other beings. In such instances, Levinas writes in 'Meaning and Sense', 'the I loses its sovereign self-confidence, its identification, in which consciousness returns triumphantly to itself to rest on itself. Before the exigency of the Other (*Autrui*), the I is expelled from this rest and is not the already glorious consciousness of this exile. Any complacency', he adds, 'would destroy the straightforwardness of the ethical movement' (Levinas, 1996, 54).

Levinas's ethical thought – with its accent upon the moral necessity for establishing altered relationships among the human community – exerts a considerable influence upon the direction of European moral philosophy, as evidenced by Derrida's various forays into ethical theory. In his important essay, 'Donner la mort' – published as *The Gift of Death* in 1995 – Derrida examines the concepts of giving, faith, and responsibility. As central components at the foundation of any genuinely altered relationship, these issues demonstrate what Derrida refers to as the 'very ordeal of the undecidable', which denotes the risk inherent in venturing into such relationships in the first place (Derrida, 1995, 5). The act of giving, for example, demands that the giver engage in altruistic behavior that may not be appreciated or accepted by the recipient of his or her generosity; similarly, an act of faith obliges its participants to behold themselves to powers and belief systems beyond the boundaries of their selves. Perhaps even more interestingly, the concept of responsibility requires that the ethical agent assume responsibility for others who may or may not accept, respect or understand the agent's munificent behaviour. As Derrida posits in his essay, even the gift of death itself is problematized by divergent arenas of meaning. Sacrificing one's own life in the service of one's country depends upon the length and degree of human memory regarding the sacrificer's selfless act, an act that, intriguingly enough, may result in the 'gift' of death for one's enemy. Ironically, then, the sacrificial agent nobly exchanges his or her own life without recognizing the alterity – in a Levinasian sense – of a faceless enemy.

Ethical critics confront similarly problematic moral conundrums regarding our motivations for engaging in ethical behaviour. 'What is given – and this would also represent a kind of death', Derrida observes, 'is not some thing, but goodness itself, a giving goodness, the act of giving or the donation of the gift'. For Derrida, this is a 'goodness that must not only forget itself but whose source remains inaccessible to the donee' (Derrida, 1995, 41). In short, the giver must be able to engage in the act of giving for motives that spring from pure goodness. Any residual expectations would serve to undermine the original act of altruism on behalf of the giver. The gift of death presents even more vexing dilemmas for the giver bent on delivering an act of goodness. 'Death is very much that which nobody can undergo or confront in my place. My irreplaceability is there conferred, delivered, "given", one can say, by death' (Derrida, 1995, 41). The gift of death, then, necessarily encounters the discrepancy between individual and collective acts of goodness. Giving one's life ensures a personal level of responsibility for an act that might result in collective degrees of goodness. Hence, the giver may enjoy the effects of an altered relationship that the recipients of his or her gift may never fully comprehend, recognize or even accept. Yet, as Derrida notes, it is only through these acts of giving – risky and potentially unknowable as they may be – that we create opportunities for glimpsing the face of our human others.

Luce Irigaray grapples with ethical issues of another sort in her classic work of literary criticism, *An Ethics of Sexual Difference*, a volume in which she maintains that genuine notions of sexual difference between the masculine and the feminine – as well as between their highly contingent outlooks and perspectives – will only occur after the advent of an ethical revolution in which men no longer control the nature of discourse and speech-acts. Only then, Irigaray writes, will everyone, male as well as female, have equal 'access to transcendence' (Irigaray, 1993, 217). Irigaray's ethical theories of sexual difference find their origins in her postulation of intersubjective relations in which males and females weigh their senses of self-love in relation to their capacities for registering the otherness of their gendered counterparts. Irigaray argues that masculine versions of love of the self concern how men relate to themselves. According to Irigaray, males reveal their love of self in terms of their nostalgia for maternal love, a quest for finding God through their fathers and sexual love. Conversely, Irigaray's feminized model of self-love involves a complex interrelationship between maternity, the socialized gratification of her male counterparts' love of self and an inherent senses of altruism. Hence, Irigaray's sexual ethics of difference concerns the manner in which males and females see themselves in relation to the larger worlds in which they live. 'Whatever identifications are possible', Irigaray remarks, 'one will never exactly occupy the place of the other – they are irreducible one to the other' (Irigaray, 1993, 13). Irigaray asserts that a recognition of these fundamental distinctions points to signal ways in which males and females might form more fulfilling and evenly balanced relationships.

In *Ethics of Eros: Irigaray's Rewriting of the Philosophers*, Tina Chanter ascribes this most ethical of Irigaray's philosophical conclusions to the thinker's Hegelian observations about woman's place in the dialectic of nature and history. Ultimately, Irigaray's theories of sexual difference elevate the needs of the community over the individual. In Irigaray's schema, masculinized controls over speech-acts and language must be unloosed in order to enrich the entire human community of males and females alike. Yet the rights of the individual remain sacrosanct in Irigaray's philosophy as well. 'The possibility of articulating an ethic of sexual difference is bound up with the need to insist on recognizing the validity of the specific rights and duties of specific groups distinct from their identity as defined by the social whole,' Chanter writes. 'Insofar as this project appeals to the importance of specifying multiple ways of existing in a society', she adds, 'it opens the way for an ethics that extends beyond sexual difference' (Chanter, 1995, 126). In *Beyond Accommodation: Ethical Feminism, Deconstruction, and the Law*, Drucilla Cornell explains Irigaray's philosophy in terms of its attention to the nature of females' various means of identifying themselves with the world. Cornell argues that women often live in states of 'dereliction' that force them to live as outcasts of sorts in their own social and familial environments. 'The politics of identification signify Woman and let her "speak",' Cornell asserts. 'But this battle takes place only within the shared framework based on a rejection of ego psychology' (Cornell, 1999, 75). Because masculine desires frequently mitigate female relations with themselves and others via language, Cornell argues, we are left with an 'uncapturable' feminine *jouissance*. This aporia exists at the core of Irigaray's ethics of sexual difference, an ethical system that seeks to explain the socialized interpersonal discrepancies that continue to problematize male–female relationships, as well as the ways in which women see themselves in relation to the world.

In recent years, Alain Badiou has emerged as one of France's most influential moral philosophers. Badiou's philosophical project can be usefully understood in terms of the two principal thrusts of his ethical theory regarding the nature of human interaction: (1) that the creation and approval of knowledge establishes, names and recognizes various forms of consolidated identity in the human community; (2) that some singular truths do persist within human discourse, despite contemporary philosophy's various challenges against the notion of universal truth. Perhaps even more significantly, Badiou argues for the abandonment of the ethics of otherness that has pervaded continental philosophy – and especially the work of such eminent thinkers as Levinas, Derrida and Irigaray, among others. In Badiou's ethical schema, genuine ethical issues emerge in specific situations and under sets of circumstances that exist without regard for the nature of a person's differentiation or otherness. For this reason, Badiou posits a theory of ethical deliberation in which a plurality of human beings considers the particularized events and situations that produce a given ethical dilemma. Through their act of deliberation, the participants would concoct a series of procedures germane to the circumstances of the issue at hand. In this manner, the deliberators would subsequently produce their own ethical norms and truths in order to respond to the contingencies inherent in the ethical dilemma of the moment. By relying upon a sustainable theory of ethical evaluation, Badiou's ethical philosophy elevates human interaction over otherness. In short, the needs of the community trump the desires of the individual.

Badiou devotes considerable attention to the identification of evil as a state of being that evidences itself in particular events and circumstances. In addition to differentiating evil from violence – which he defines as the means via which human beings persevere beyond (or beneath) good and evil – Badiou contends that evil is a subjective category of the self. 'Evil is the process of a simulacrum of truth,' Badiou writes. 'And in its essence, under a name of its invention, it is terror directed at everyone' (Badiou, 2001, 77). According to Badiou, our recognition of evil is only made possible by the contrastive existence of goodness, which allows us, then, to perceive evil as a condition of human experience that evolves under a given set of circumstances. Hence, evil emerges through our encounters with goodness, a concept that, in itself, assists us in our communal goal of warding off evil. Because evil necessarily exists at the margins of goodness Badiou suggests that philosophers abandon any interest in elevating certain manifestations of evil – what contemporary moral philosophers refer to as 'radical evil', for example – over others. Evil assumes different types and various levels of scale in direct relationship to the nature of the circumstances under which it develops. Badiou argues that the horrors of Nazism and ethnic extermination, for instance, underscore 'both that which measures all the Evil our time is capable of, being itself beyond measure, and that to which we must compare everything (thus measuring it unceasingly) that we say is to be judged in terms of the manifest certainty of Evil. As the supreme negative example', Badiou adds, 'this crime is inimitable, but every crime is an imitation of it' (Badiou, 2001, 63). Simply put, evil exists, as with goodness, as one of the inalienable (albeit enduring and unfortunate) truths of human interaction.

In *Getting It Right: Language, Literature, and Ethics*, Geoffrey Galt Harpham examines ethical criticism's potential as an interdisciplinary means of interpretation. Perhaps more significantly, though, he usefully (and indeed, uniquely) merges the scholarship of continental philosophy – especially Levinasian philosophy – with North American conceptions of moral philosophy's role in the creation of an evaluative criticism. Ethical criticism should be 'considered a matrix, a hub from which the various discourses and disciplines fan out and at which they meet, crossing out of themselves to encounter each other', he writes. 'Ethics is perhaps best conceived as a "conceptual base" – neither as organic drive nor as properly conceptual superstructure, but rather as a necessary, and necessarily impure and unsystematic, mediation between unconscious and instinctual life and its cognitive and cultural transformation' (Harpham, 1992, 17–18). Harpham supports this endeavour through his examinations of such 'ethical terms' as 'obligation', '*ought*', 'ethical duty' and 'ethicity'. Through their delineation, he seeks to establish meaningful interconnections between ethical criticism and other means of textual inquiry. Harpham argues that the issue of choice lies at the heart of obligation. 'One can – one must – choose which principle to be governed by,' he observes. 'Ethics in general is a species of risk that affords no rigorous way to tell ethical reasons from other reasons, choices from obligations' (Harpham, 1992, 37). Harpham further asserts that 'at the dead center of ethics lies the *ought*', or the ethical obligation. This notion of an *ought* – the moral obligations of an ethical person – reveals that person's 'commitments, values, character. To be ethical, an *ought* must not refer itself to threats or desires, coercion or self-ends' (Harpham, 1992,

18). Harpham defines 'ethical duty' as a form of critical reflection: 'One must always reflect,' Harpham writes. 'This is the law that ethical discourse virtually presumes as well as teaches' (Harpham, 1992, 42).

In Harpham's conception of an ethical terminology, 'ethicity' refers to the interpretive moment in ethical criticism: 'the most dramatic of narrative turnings, the climactic point just between the knitting and unravelling of the action, the fort and the da, the moment when the rising line of complication peaks, pauses, and begins its descent into the dénouement'. Addressing the narratological and characterological essences of this evaluative instance – what Harpham calls the 'macro-turn' – enables ethical critics, through their obligations to their own sets of values and commitments, to reflect upon and interpret the moral choices depicted in narratives (Harpham, 1992, 171). In many ways, this notion highlights the central attributes that undergird both European and North American manifestations of ethical criticism. Drawing upon Levinasian notions of alterity, scholars such as Harpham clearly represent the best of both philosophical worlds in which continental philosophy's interest in otherness tempers the North American academy's risky forays into moral relativism. Both scholarly worlds – different and confrontational as they may seem at times – ultimately recognize that it is our perceptions of the ethics of the texts themselves, and our experiences with them, that truly matter.

NOTES TOWARDS READINGS OF GEORGE ELIOT'S *SILAS MARNER* AND SPIKE JONZE'S *BEING JOHN MALKOVICH*

As a reading paradigm, ethical criticism offers a valuable lens for examining the manner in which literary characters experience moments of moral clarity and interpersonal change. Originally published in 1861, Eliot's *Silas Marner* illustrates a variety of ethical principles inherent in the evolving critical vocabulary of continental philosophy's postwar ethical turn. In many ways, the novel's protagonist enjoys an altered relationship not only with Eppie, the little orphan girl who punctures the self-imposed asceticism of his insular world, but with himself. Eliot's novel also affords us with a useful exemplar of the gift in a Derridean sense, particularly in terms of the aspects of responsibility and self-sacrifice that giving necessarily entails. Readers often celebrate *Silas Marner* because of its intriguing psychological interplay, as well as for its heart-warming conclusion. An ethical reading of the novel, though, allows us to consider the intra- and interpersonal predicaments that act as important precursors to *Silas Marner*'s moving denouement.

For Silas, enjoying a genuinely altered relationship with anyone – much less himself – would seem to test the bounds of probability. Afflicted by periodic, trance-like bouts of protracted catalepsis, Silas endures a lonely existence in which only the mounting guineas in his treasured iron pot inspire any real passion in him for living. Thunderstruck after experiencing the theft of his gold, Silas's psyche slowly erodes as he realizes the extent of his loss, artificial as it may be: 'He put his trembling hands to his head, and gave a wild ringing scream, the cry of desolation,' Eliot writes (Eliot, 1996, 34). The shock of his new reality, with its contingent uncertainty and personal malaise, prepares Silas for the gift that he enjoys literally in the company of Eppie, the orphan who changes his life when she happens upon his cottage. Believing that 'the gold had turned into the child' (Eliot, 1996, 103), Silas accepts the burden of the gift when he recognizes the responsibility involved in his act of altruism: 'Unlike the gold, which needed nothing, and must be worshipped in close-locked solitude', Eliot writes, 'Eppie was a creature of endless claims and ever-growing desires, seeking and loving sunshine, and living sounds, and living movements; making trial of everything, with trust in new joy, and stirring the human kindness in all eyes that looked on her' (Eliot, 1996, 105–6). Later, when her birth-father arrives on the scene and threatens to come between the girl and Silas, her loving surrogate, Eppie validates the power of the weaver's gift and the genuine extent of Silas's altered outlook upon the increasingly wide world that exists beyond his lonely cottage walls: 'We've been used to be happy together every day, and I can't think o' no happiness without him. And he says he'd nobody i' the world till I was sent to him, and he'd have nothing when I was gone. And he's took care of me and loved me from the first, and I'll cleave to him as long as he lives, and nobody shall ever come between him and me' (Eliot, 1996, 143).

In this manner, Eliot illustrates love's remarkable capacity for altering our perspectives and establishing genuine interpersonal transcendence. In his highly original film, *Being John Malkovich*, director Spike Jonze and screenwriter Charlie Kaufman examine another gift of sorts that affords them with a mechanism for investigating the manner in which literary and filmic stylistics contribute to the ethical impressions that often exist within a given narrative's textual recesses. As Nussbaum notes, an artist's sense of style – whether visual, literary or otherwise – often functions as a means for rendering ethical judgements. In *Love's Knowledge*, Nussbaum argues that 'form and style are not incidental features. A view of life is *told*. The telling itself – the selection of genre, formal structures, sentences, vocabulary, of the whole manner of addressing the reader's sense of life – all of this expresses a sense of life and of value, a sense of what matters and what does not, of what learning and communicating are, of life's relations and connections,' she writes; 'life is never simply *presented* by a text; it is always *represented as* something' (Nussbaum, 1990, 5). Jonze's ethics of style finds its origins in the film's clever plot device involving a mysterious portal that allows curiosity seekers the opportunity to venture into the mind of actor John Malkovich. For much of the film, a kind of absurdist comedy functions as Jonze's stylistic *métier* and as the prelude to the larger ethical implications that he will explore in the film's final, stunning reel.

The film itself devotes much of its initial energy to contending with what appears to be its singular narrative thrust, a gimmick of sorts in which people pay $200 for the opportunity to spend 15 minutes inside Malkovich's brain before being expelled, rather amazingly, on a grassy median near the New Jersey Turnpike. Orchestrated by dejected puppeteer Craig (John Cusack) in cahoots with his dowdy wife Lotte (Cameron Diaz) and his devious co-worker Maxine (Catherine Keener), the trio's scheme for exploiting the portal begins to unravel when their relationship devolves into a love triangle and they start asking questions about the origins of this freak of time and space that has altered their lives. At times, *Being John Malkovich* seems to be grappling with issues of celebrity, addiction and identity politics, yet the film's simultaneously evocative and disturbing final scene utterly changes everything that comes before it in the screenplay. In this way, *Being John Malkovich* both aspires to more substantial literary pretensions *and* takes on greater significance. Jonze and Kaufman accomplish this end by self-consciously staging a scene that allows their audience to experience a 'cataleptic impression' – a cognitive, philosophical phenomenon that, according to Nussbaum, 'has the power, just through its own felt quality, to drag us to assent, to convince us that things could not be otherwise. It is defined as a mark or impress upon the soul' (Nussbaum, 1990, 265). In the scene – a surreal, simplistic image of a young girl tranquilly swimming in a suburban pool that could be located, rather pointedly, anywhere – Jonze and Kaufman ask questions about the ethics of our desires and the often perplexing interrelationship between the desires of the self and the needs of the community. We become transfigured by the experience of viewing the scene, alarmed by the sinister possibilities that it entails, and cognizant, for the first time in the film's duration, that *Being John Malkovich* seeks to interrogate ethical issues that exist at the core of our very being.

QUESTIONS FOR FURTHER CONSIDERATION

1. What are the principal differences between ethical criticism's incarnations in North America and Europe, respectively? What are each movement's fundamental similarities?
2. What historical issues might have led to the academy's general interest in ethical issues in the latter half of the twentieth century?
3. How has the ethical turn impacted the direction of literary criticism since the 1980s? Is there any evidence of an ethical renewal of sorts in the academy?
4. What are the principal strengths of ethical criticism as an interpretive paradigm? What seem to be its overall weaknesses as a form of literary critique?
5. Compare the ethical premises exhibited by such thinkers as Wayne C. Booth, Martha C. Nussbaum, Jacques Derrida and Luce Irigaray. How are they similar? How do they diverge from each other's views about ethics?
6. Drawing upon other novels and films in addition to the aforementioned works by George Eliot and Spike Jonze, how does a consideration for ethical issues alter your understanding of the ideological imperatives inherent in various literary and filmic texts?

ANNOTATED BIBLIOGRAPHY

Badiou, Alain. *Ethics: An Essay on the Understanding of Evil*, trans. Peter Hallward. London: Verso, 2001. Badiou addresses the various assumptions behind the contemporary ethical turn that continue to impact a wide range of thinkers across the disciplines. In addition to arguing that our ethical principles often reinforce an ideology of the status quo, Badiou suggests that prevailing ethical norms find their origins in unsubstantiated opinion, legalistic formalism and theological mystification. Badiou identifies an 'ethic of truths' in an effort to outline a functional concept of evil.

Booth, Wayne C. *The Company We Keep: An Ethics of Fiction*. Berkeley, CA: University of California Press, 1988. Booth's volume defines the shape and nature of ethical criticism as a reading paradigm. Booth argues that ethical critics must devote particular attention to the notion of an *ethos*, or the total character or quality of storytellers and listeners. In addition to exploring the ethics of reading, Booth addresses the ethical imperatives inherent in texts by such figures as Jane Austen, D. H. Lawrence and Mark Twain, among others.

Davis, Todd F. and Kenneth Womack (eds). *Mapping the Ethical Turn: A Reader in Ethics, Culture, and Literary Theory*. Charlottesville, VA: University Press of Virginia, 2001. Davis and Womack's anthology assembles many of ethical criticism's most significant voices, including Wayne C. Booth, Martha C. Nussbaum, Charles Altieri, J. Hillis Miller, Susan Gubar, Adam Zachary Newton, Cora Diamond and Margaret Urban Walker, among others. In addition to providing a range of different kinds of readers with an introduction to the paradigm, this volume affords readers with a comprehensive study of ethical criticism, its terminology and its application to a variety of genres and disciplines.

Derrida, Jacques. *The Gift of Death*, trans. David Wills. Chicago, IL: University of Chicago Press, 1995. Derrida's classic volume examines the issues of giving or granting in relation to the notion of death. In addition to devoting particular attention to human rights and its various ethical and legalistic aspects, Derrida discusses such concepts as taking, teaching and learning. Derrida also reflects upon the notion of otherness in terms of Europe's ethical responsibilities on the international stage.

Eaglestone, Robert. *Ethical Criticism: Reading after Levinas*. Edinburgh: Edinburgh University Press, 1997. Eaglestone explores the relationship between literature and ethics. In addition to discussing the ethical nature of literary study in what he defines as the post-theory era, Eaglestone traces the historical emergence of ethical criticism. Eaglestone provides readings of the critical positions of such figures as Martha C. Nussbaum, J. Hillis Miller and Paul de Man, among others.

Irigaray, Luce. *An Ethics of Sexual Difference*, trans. Carolyn Burke and Gillian C. Gill. Ithaca, NY: Cornell University Press, 1993. Irigaray discusses the manner in which thought and language impact the ethical question of sexual difference. Drawing upon recent insights in philosophy, science and psychoanalysis, Irigaray offers various meditations on love in relation to classic philosophical texts by Plato, Aristotle and Emmanuel Levinas, among others. Irigaray devotes particular attention to a range of dualities that impact ethical questions regarding sexual difference, including inside/outside, form/content, subject/other and self/other.

Newton, Adam Zachary. *Narrative Ethics*. Cambridge, MA: Harvard University Press, 1995. Newton examines the interrelationships that exist between narrative and ethics. Drawing upon the philosophical insights of Emmanuel Levinas, Newton discusses the role of ethics in works by Joseph Conrad, Henry James, Herman Melville and Sherwood Anderson, among others.

Nussbaum, Martha C. *Love's Knowledge: Essays on Philosophy and Literature*. New York: Oxford University Press, 1990. Drawing upon the ethical philosophies of such figures as Plato and Wayne C. Booth, Nussbaum addresses the moral properties inherent in the works of a variety of authors, including Proust, Henry James and Ann

Beattie, among others. Nussbaum devotes special attention to the manner in which these works possess the ability to impinge upon the inner moral lives of their readers.

Robbins, Jill. *Altered Reading: Levinas and Literature*. Chicago, IL: University of Chicago Press, 1999. Robbins provides readers with a wide-ranging analysis of Emmanuel Levinas's ethical philosophy. In addition to offering chapters regarding all of the philosopher's major works, Robbins addresses Levinas's principal terminology, including the concept of the gift, alterity, the face of the other and the claims of figural interpretation. Robbins also considers Levinasian philosophy's interrelationship with aesthetics and literary criticism.

SUPPLEMENTARY BIBLIOGRAPHY

Assoun, Paul-Laurent. 'The Subject and the Other in Levinas and Lacan', trans. Dianah Jackson and Denise Merkle. In *Levinas and Lacan: The Missed Encounter*, ed. Sarah Harasym. Albany, NY: State University of New York Press, 1998, 79–101.

Bernasconi, Robert and Simon Critchley (eds). *Re-Reading Levinas*. Bloomington, IN: Indiana University Press, 1991.

Burke, Seán. 'The Aesthetic, the Cognitive, and the Ethical: Criticism and Discursive Responsibility'. In *The Arts and Sciences of Criticism*, eds David Fuller and Patricia Waugh. Oxford: Oxford University Press, 1999, 199–216.

Champagne, Roland. *The Ethics of Reading According to Emmanuel Levinas*. Amsterdam: Rodopi, 1998.

Chanter, Tina. *Ethics of Eros: Irigaray's Rewriting of the Philosophers*. London: Routledge, 1995.

Chow, Rey. *Ethics after Idealism: Theory, Culture, Ethnicity, Reading*. Bloomington, IN: Indiana University Press, 1998.

Cohen, Tom. *Ideology and Inscription: 'Cultural Studies' after Benjamin, de Man, and Bakhtin*. Cambridge: Cambridge University Press, 1998.

Cornell, Drucilla. *Beyond Accommodation: Ethical Feminism, Deconstruction, and the Law*. Lanham, MD: Rowman & Littlefield, 1999.

Critchley, Simon. *Very Little . . . Almost Nothing: Death, Philosophy, Literature*. London: Routledge, 1997.

Critchley, Simon. *The Ethics of Deconstruction: Derrida and Levinas*, [1992]. West Lafayette, IN: Purdue University Press, 1999.

Derrida, Jacques. '. . . and Pomegranates', trans. Samuel Weber. In *Violence, Identity, and Self-Determination*, eds Hent de Vries and Samuel Weber. Stanford, CA: Stanford University Press, 1997, 326–44.

Eliot, George. *Silas Marner*, [1861]. New York: Dover, 1996.

Gardner, John. *On Moral Fiction*. New York: Basic, 1978.

Gibson, Andrew. *Postmodernity, Ethics, and the Novel: From Leavis to Levinas*. London: Routledge, 1999.

Harpham, Geoffrey Galt. *Getting It Right: Language, Literature, and Ethics*. Chicago, CA: University of Chicago Press, 1992.

Harpham, Geoffrey Galt. *Shadows of Ethics: Criticism and the Just Society*. Durham, NC: Duke University Press, 1999.

Jonze, Spike (dir.). *Being John Malkovich*. Gramercy Pictures, 2000.

Levinas, Emmanuel. *Time and the Other*, trans. Richard Cohen. Pittsburgh, PA: Duquesne University Press, 1985.

Levinas, Emmanuel. 'The Trace of the Other', trans. Alphonso Lingis. In *Deconstruction in Context: Literature and Philosophy*, ed. Mark C. Taylor. Chicago, IL: University of Chicago Press, 1986, 345–59.

Levinas, Emmanuel. 'Philosophy and the Idea of Infinity'. In *Collected Philosophical Papers*, trans. Alphonso Lingis. Dordrecht: Martinus Nijhoff, 1987, 47–59.

Levinas, Emmanuel. *Basic Philosophical Writings*, eds Adriaan T. Peperzak, Simon Critchley and Robert Bernasconi. Bloomington, IN: Indiana University Press, 1996.

Levinas, Emmanuel. 'Is Ontology Fundamental?', trans. Simon Critchley, Peter Atterton and Graham Noctor. In Levinas, *Basic Philosophical Writings* (1996, 2–10).

Levinas, Emmanuel. 'Meaning and Sense' (trans. Alphonso Lingis. In Levinas, *Basic Philosophical Writings* (1996, 33–64).

Lyotard, Jean-François. *The Postmodern Condition: A Report on Knowledge*, trans. Geoffrey Bennington and Brian Massumi. Minneapolis, MN: University of Minnesota Press, 1984.

McGinn, Colin. *Ethics, Evil, and Fiction*. Oxford: Clarendon, 1997.

Miller, J. Hillis. *The Ethics of Reading: Kant, de Man, Eliot, Trollope, James, and Benjamin*. New York: Columbia University Press, 1987.

Miller, J. Hillis. *Versions of Pygmalion*. Cambridge, MA: Harvard University Press, 1990.

Norris, Christopher. *Truth and the Ethics of Criticism*. New York: St Martin's, Press, 1994.

Nussbaum, Martha C. *Poetic Justice: The Literary Imagination and Public Life*. Boston, MA: Beacon, 1995.

Parker, David. *Ethics, Theory, and the Novel*. Cambridge: Cambridge University Press, 1994.

Rosenblatt, Louise M. *The Reader, the Text, the Poem: The Transactional Theory of the Literary Work*. Carbondale, IL: Southern Illinois University Press, 1978.

Siebers, Tobin. *The Ethics of Criticism*. Ithaca, NY: Cornell University Press, 1988.

Walker, Margaret Urban. *Moral Understandings: A Feminist Study in Ethics*. New York: Routledge, 1998.

Williams, Bernard. *Ethics and the Limits of Philosophy*. Cambridge, MA: Harvard University Press, 1985.

Worthington, Kim L. *Self as Narrative: Subjectivity and Community in Contemporary Fiction*. Oxford: Clarendon, 1996.

NOTE

1. For further discussion of Levinas, particularly in relation to the question of the practice and theory of literary and cultural criticism, see Frederick Young's chapter in this volume, below.

CHAPTER 6

TRAUMA, TESTIMONY, CRITICISM: WITNESSING, MEMORY AND RESPONSIBILITY

Julian Wolfreys

> For history to be a history of trauma means that it is referential precisely to the extent that it is not fully perceived as it occurs; or to put it somewhat differently, that a history can be grasped only in the very inaccessibility of its occurrence.
>
> Cathy Caruth

> In order to cope with a trauma, we symbolize.
>
> Slavoj Žižek

Although there is a significant number of critical works addressing the figure and effects of trauma, or what Ulrich Baer calls 'unresolved experience' (2000, 1) and the related role of testimony in literature, there is no single school of criticism, no one methodology as such, dealing with these issues. It is not the purpose of this chapter to read this apparent absence as a deficiency. Nor is it my intention to supply an 'introductory' discussion or objective summary of the work so far done in order to supplement that work and thereby make up for any supposed lack. On the contrary, it must be admitted from the outset that any gesture in the direction of regulating a response to trauma or establishing a methodology or mode of analysis should be resisted, if one is to do justice to trauma and the work of testimony. As Dominick LaCapra has suggested, 'a post-traumatic response . . . becomes questionable when it is routinized in a methodology or style that enacts compulsive repetition' (2001, 47). Equally, it has to be acknowledged that what is being named as an interest in critical studies and what I wish to explore in this chapter as the possibility of a critical modality could come under the headings of 'mourning', 'memory work', 'acts of bearing witness' (another possible description of testimony) or, more obliquely and generally, 'responsibility' in the acts of reading we call criticism. Perhaps that in reading which we will approach here might most appropriately be understood as 'a grammar of shock, absorption and loss', to cite Avital Ronell (1989, 89). Therefore, however one orientates oneself, the emphasis must be placed on a careful reading in response to that which marks the text, hence Ronell's apposite use of the term 'grammar', rather than any application of paradigmatic procedures or protocols.

To speak of a 'grammar' is not to deny the material horror and after-effects of a historical event such as the Holocaust; nor is such a remark the sign of some formalist retreat into language games and trivializing quibbles over truth claims, into 'hyperbolic or speculative acts' as Dominick LaCapra argues in *Writing History, Writing Trauma* (2001, 185, 195), against what he perceives to be the occasional linguistic 'excesses' of so-called poststructuralist discourse. It is, instead, to acknowledge and observe how 'absence is a structural part of witness', as Michael Bernard-Donals and Richard Glejzer put it (2001, 56). As they continue: 'the act of witness is only ever available in another place and in another time [than that of the experience of the traumatic event] . . . Witness can only be accessible to the extent that it is not fully perceived or experienced as it occurs, and it can only be grasped in the very inaccessibility of its occurrence' (2001, 58). It is this 'grammatical' register that Cathy Caruth also addresses, and to which we will return, below. However, it has to be said, concerning the figures of 'loss' and 'absence', that these are not simply figures which speak 'transhistorically to absolute foundations . . . induc[ing] either a metaphysical etherealization, even obfuscation, of historical problems or a historicist, reductive localization of transhistorical, recurrently displaced problems – or perhaps a confusingly hybridised, extremely labile discourse . . . that seems to derive from the deconstruction of metaphysics', in the words of LaCapra (2001, 195). What is 'transhistorical' is, in fact, LaCapra's own analysis here. For he reduces and generalizes, in what seems a fairly metaphysical way, the reading of loss and absence, precisely to the extent that he assumes that each figure is conceptualized in an undifferentiated manner, in the theoretical analyses he addresses. What it is important to realize, in any reading of absence or loss as that which necessitates structurally any response to trauma, is that what is absent or lost is singular, particular to the historial instant of the traumatic event and its subsequent reading or writing. As Ulrich Baer suggests, there is an 'obligation to recognize another's experience of trauma as irreducibly *other* and irreducible to generalizations' (2000, 11); moreover, to cite Baer again, every text, every other, attesting to the traumatic makes 'an uncompromising claim . . . to be read in its own terms. Yet at the same time . . . each . . . opens itself to iteration, under-standing, and address' (2000, 11). There is thus the 'necessity of considering the poetic representation of unresolved experience [that is to say, trauma] . . . as absolutely singular' (2000, 9).

This is of course to point to the very difficult ground on which we find ourselves, hence my own caution concerning the questions of terminology and of methodological regulation. It is doubtless the case that such terms and phrases as those towards which I express an initial wariness, if not suspicion, might resonate in various ways in relation to particular protocols or programmes, certain manifestations of institutionalized analysis more or less obviously. You might believe on the evidence of words such as 'trauma' or phrases such as 'memory work', for example, that there is a certain 'psychoanalytic' register at work in my discourse. This is so of course, undeniably, as the discussions of Freud below indicate. It has to be said, however, that, while the question of 'reading and writing trauma' is indebted in particular ways to psychoanalysis and psychoanalytic literary criticism – or, to be more precise, certain strands within these nominations – there will also be other aspects to the critique in the present chapter that are not directly accounted for in psychoanalysis, and which therefore exceed the institutional, discursive parameters of such work, while also acknowledging other epistemological models and critical discourses.

There is observable, for example, the matter of a reorientation towards reading history, of reading 'history' and its representations differently in relation to trauma, as Caruth makes plain in my first epigraph. Whether or not history can be thought as *always* or *only* a history of trauma, it is important to note two aspects of Caruth's complication of the notion of history: first, that there is the matter of referentiality, of the signs, traces or marks by which we attempt to recover or reconstruct history. History, in this account, is comprehended as textual. This is not, to stress the point once more, to suggest that historical events do not happen. Instead, as Caruth informs us, the materiality of the historical event is *only ever available* through the relay and concomitant deferral that is the condition of the materiality of signifiers. Therefore, what we call history always comes down to a matter of reading and, equally, rereading and rewriting in as responsible a manner as possible, however neutral we seek to be, or (mis)believe we can be. Second, and at the same time, the work of reading history must necessarily take place precisely because the historical occurrence is neither fully perceivable in the event nor subsequently accessible after the fact of its occurrence.

As another particular dimension to the problem of reading, there can be discerned also, and especially in the use of the word *responsibility*, an indebtedness to ethical demands and requirements and the question of ethics in general.[1] This is also true.[2] If, as Shoshana Felman has remarked apropos of trauma and testimony, that there is 'a parallel between [a] kind of teaching [and, we would add, reading] (in its reliance on the testimonial process) and psychoanalysis', the former is not reducible to the latter. Despite this, both 'are called upon to be *performative* . . . both strive to produce, and to enable, *change.*

Both . . . are interested not merely in new information, but, primarily, in the capacity . . . to *transform*' (Felman and Lamb, 1992, 52). It is precisely in this demand for the performative dimension[3] and the transformation it entails that responsibility is heard. What amounts to an ethical call announces itself as the possibility of exceeding analysis and, indeed, representation. So, to recap: while there are, or may be, parallels between discourses, there is neither a method nor a school. There is only the necessity, and the risk, of enabling reading as transformative critique. This being the case, it is perhaps best to begin approaching the subject in hand by offering the following provisional statement as a means of initial orientation, or, indeed, an affirmation of responsibility: all critical acts should manifest responsibility to texts being read beyond, and in excess of, the calculation of any programme of reading (within limits), methodology or school of thought, but what that responsibility might be cannot be decided ahead of the encounter.

Paradoxically, though, no reading can ever account for everything in a text. Reading, therefore, can never be completed. There will always be (and have been, always already) some trace, some haunting remainder, with which we have to live, which we must admit, and yet for which we cannot account, finally. As Gayatri Spivak has remarked, 'One cannot be mindful of a haunting, even if it fills the mind' (Spivak, 2001, 221), and this is chiefly because, with regard to trauma, there is what Baer calls a 'twofold *structural* disjunction between an experience and its integration into narrative memory, understanding, and communicability . . . All such experiences . . . [are] located somewhere outside memory yet within the psyche' (Baer, 2000, 10). That this paradox or impasse exists in no way lets the reader off the hook from assuming responsibility. Rather, reading, considered as precisely the response which recognizes its responsibility in the face of the impossibility that reading also entails, must continue, must respond to the other, all the while accepting and acknowledging that, in bearing witness to the other, one cannot master, control, determine or domesticate the other through some normative ontological or epistemological process. This is all the more so when it is a question of seeking to represent traumatic events, of seeking the adequate or appropriate mode of representation. As Bernard-Donals and Glejzer make clear throughout *Between Witness and Testimony: The Holocaust and the Limits of Representation*, there is that about the trauma of an event such as the Holocaust beyond representation or narrative adequation, so excessive is its horror. All responsible criticism engages in both a recognition of its own responsibility and the impossibility of such an endless demand, a call to conscience if you will. Reading trauma as a material manifestation of the other in a given text may well be asked to call on the discourses or disciplines of psychoanalysis, history and ethics (considered narrowly as one 'strand' in the discipline of philosophy), but it is irreducible to any disciplinary economy, or the calculation implied by accommodation between programmatic discourses. Reading and writing trauma, always as the response to singularity, effect its transformation, if this happens at all, not in any calculable control of critical position or the representation which any critical or historical modality may believe it can make possible, but in the production of a reiteration of the traumatic excess 'which troubles testimony and narrative and forces the reader to confront the horror of the limit' (Bernard-Donals and Glejzer, 2001, 5).

At the risk of repeating myself, let me re-emphasize these issues in other words: the act of criticism as the manifestation of nothing more nor less than good reading in these terms becomes, therefore, a form of testimony, a bearing witness or being called to witness. This is good reading as such. But the radical otherness, the alterity of that to which we must respond, is understood when it comes to be recognized that testimony, as with responsibility and in order to be responsible, *in order to be testimony and not merely an account generated according to some protocol,* has to be transformative or inventive. It must take that risk. It cannot be dictated according to the prescription of certain rules operative in the same fashion every time reading takes place. On the subject of a responsibility exceeding any programme or protocol, Jacques Derrida remarks:

> I will even venture to say that ethics, politics, and responsibility, *if there are any*, will only ever have begun with the experience and experiment of the aporia. When the path is clear and given, when a certain knowledge opens up the way in advance, the decision is already made, it might as well be said that there is none to make: irresponsibly, and in good conscience, one simply applies or implements a program. Perhaps, and this would be the objection, one never escapes the program. In that case, one must acknowledge this and stop talking with authority about moral or political responsibility. The condition of possibility of this thing called responsibility is a certain *experience and experiment of the possibility of the impossible: the testing of the aporia* from which one may invent the only *possible invention, the impossible invention.* (Derrida, 1992, 41)

Testimony, therefore, and 'testimonial criticism', if such a thing takes place, cannot be prepared or prepared for ahead of the event, the arrival of the other. Testimony, in order to be such, cannot be calculated, for every testimony must respond to the singular specificity of the traumatic experience. If responsibility is understood, then both the alterity and the singularity of the other have to be admitted. If, as Shoshana Felman suggests, we live 'in the age of testimony' (1992, 53), by which name she indicates 'the era of the Holocaust, of Hiroshima, of Vietnam' (53), and to which it would be necessary to add '11 September 2001', then it has to be recognized at the same time that what is called an era or an age is marked by the registration of historical events incommensurate either with one another or with that very epochal similitude that the notion of the era or age, in the naming of an identity based on sufficient, that is to say calculable, resemblance suggests. Testimony is irreducible to some concept or figure, some genre or species of narrative within historical narrative or literature.

The aporia of responsibility that I have sketched above demonstrates this in showing how conceptual thinking operates within limits and with the imagined horizon of some limit, as does Felman's invocation of 'age' or 'era'.[4] To speak of either 'trauma' or 'testimonial criticism' is both to assume that one knows what both trauma and testimony are, i.e. that there are stable concepts appearing in the same form, time after time, and to believe also that such a criticism is, in fact, a delineable or delimitable conceptual form. Yet, as Ulrich Baer cautions, 'in addition to historical differences [the very differences that the thinking of an 'era' occludes], "trauma" is not a stable term. An experience registers as . . . traumatic. And this remains fundamentally unresolved, not because of the event's *inherent content*, but because recourse to an external frame of reference is unavailable' (2000, 9). To risk a somewhat counterintuitive formula at this juncture therefore, which doubtless says too little and tries to say too much, literature *just is* testimony and it is this which imposes upon the reader and the act of criticism the burden of an incalculable responsibility. (Another way to think this would be to recall Walter Benjamin's well-known comment that all documents of civilization are also documents of barbarity.) Reading is the act of bearing witness to literature's memory work, where the reader must respond, must make impossible decisions, in response to the attestation of impersonal memory. And the responsibility entailed herein truly *is* incalculable, for, in every act of witnessing, every response to the other in its singularity, I sacrifice countless others (Kronick, 1999, 15).[5] Yet, it is for this reason that we cannot reductively assume similarity through the act of reading by a gesture of generalization. In a very risky gesture, Jacques Derrida identifies the dangers of such thought, precisely around what is taken by many as the name of trauma par excellence, Auschwitz. While, to quote Alexander García Düttman, it is undeniable that the singularity of Auschwitz 'is incommensurable: not only because *nothing similar* can be thought or imagined but above all because something unlike anything else compels us to think and act in such a way that *nothing similar* ever happens' (2000, 97), Derrida – as Düttman points out – 'warns us against discourses, which, taking Auschwitz as the model'

> are in danger of reconstituting a sort of centrality, a 'we' which is certainly not that of speculative dialectics but which is related to the unanimous privilege which we occidental Europeans accord to Auschwitz in the fight or the question which we oppose to speculative dialectics, to a certain type of occidental reason. The danger is that this 'we' would take from memory or sideline proper names other than Auschwitz, ones which are just as abominable, names which have names and names which have no name. (Derrida, 1981, 311, cit. Düttman, 2000, 99)

It would be a gross misreading to see in this statement some kind of denial of either the historical event or the traumatic significance of Auschwitz. It is, though, crucially, urgently important that we comprehend how Derrida is illustrating the dangers in a certain limit-thinking with regard to certain aspects of normative historical representation and, equally, the dangers of letting the proper name do your thinking for you. In fact, the danger of the proper name is that, in letting it come to assume some privileged position in one's discourse, thinking – and, therefore, responsibility – stops. There is, then, the difficult business of thinking Auschwitz, and, indeed, any traumatic event, in all its inexpressible, irreducible singularity, a difficulty which remains with regard to any narrative of trauma. For what remains, as the trace of the traumatic figuring, the articulation of a name such as Auschwitz or the name which has no name, such as 11 September 2001, is what Alexander García Düttman calls 'the possibility of survival, of another memory and another promise, [which] depends on a certain unreadability' (2000, 74).

The work of criticism that addresses trauma, testimony and memory must then necessarily explore what Cathy Caruth has described as the 'enigma of the otherness' in the revenance and articulation of trauma, which the human agent 'cannot fully know' (1996, 3). Caruth demonstrates a two-part disruptive or disjunctive structure in the nature of narrative form, of which more, in relation to trauma, below in the second section of this chapter. This structure allows for the articulation of the subject's act of witnessing and responsibility involved in acts of memory and witnessing through the other's arrival which forces on the subject a knowledge which had previously been withheld. The return of the other opens the subject's complicity to him- or herself, not necessarily as a specific guilt for a specific act, but as the culpability, and the responsibility which *that* entails, as a condition of Being, in which, as beings, we all share, and which has itself to be acknowledged (as Martin Heidegger makes plain in his analysis of *Dasein*, in *Being and Time*).

In exploring this mode of narrative, then, I am seeking to show how criticism's function is to reiterate, and thereby bear witness itself, to the disarticulating modality already installed in various forms of fiction or 'the literary' as so many acts of witnessing and memory. The question of trauma and testimonial criticism becomes one, I will argue, of a patient tracing of that which constitutes the literary text as both a function of memory and responsibility and as a mode of technicity, a making appear, to which, in every act of reading, all readers must bear witness and for which they must take responsibility as a definition of the act of reading itself. There is implied an open series of responses, each opening itself to, and in, a potentially infinite disjunctive chain.

Such a model of reading and the understanding of the literary which it invokes has at least two effects, which it will be the function of this chapter to examine and explain: (1) The motion of the return or supplement, the revenance of testimony, implies the call of the other as intrinsic to the act of narration; as such, it inscribes an iterable circulation. In this, we may read a narrative modality which functions against the facts of history and which is suggestive of a poetics of witnessing and of the work of trauma as the work of memory irreducible to any historical model. (2) At the same time, such return, and the persistence of witnessing which it implies, is suggestive of the fact, once again, that we can never be let off the hook as regards our acts of responsible reading. In short, the function in part of testimonial criticism is to open to the reader through a recognition of the other's articulation a recognition that what Heidegger calls the 'call of conscience' is not simply always already in effect but always remains to come. Thus we will never have done with reading, and reading remains also that which is to come. The folding and unfolding of structure traced by Caruth thereby is read as the necessary ethical figure of a reading resistant on the one hand to closure and on the other hand to any simple sense of continuity or linearity in narrative motion. As Ulrich Baer puts it, trauma remains open and undecidable because there is no possible immediate recourse to 'an external frame of reference' (2000, 9). The very idea of narrative itself, or, more generally, textuality, involves the 'epistemological possibility and the moral necessity of considering the poetic representation of unresolved experience . . . as absolutely *singular*' (Baer, 2000, 9), and knowable only, paradoxically, in its singularity through the open seriality which narrative makes possible.

In exploring the work of critics such as Baer and Caruth, Derrida and Felman, among others, I am therefore attempting to engage with these particular exemplary interventions by tracing, albeit briefly, the fractured intercessions between and exceeding various discourses, as these concern themselves with matters of memory and subjectivity, guilt and being. The impossibility of a representation in relation to the singularity *and* iteration of trauma ties the question of testimony both to the idea of the secret and the question of the unrepresentability of the instant of the traumatic event, as Derrida has made clear in *Demeure*. However, as I wish to argue, our inability to represent the traumatic instant is neither simply a moment of replaying the silencing of articulation by which the traumatized subject is produced, nor is it, equally simply, an acknowledgement of empathy and, therefore, an undifferentiated identification with the victim of trauma;[6] instead, the work of criticism becomes a matter of addressing the 'impossibility and necessity' of bearing witness to the 'unexperienced experience' (Derrida, 2000, 47), and it is through the structural gap, in that grammar of absence and loss, that the other comes to be heard.

Trauma, then, might be said to be a ghost. Given that 'the essential character of traumatism' is best described as a 'nonsymbolizable wound' (Ronell, 1994, 327), to read trauma is to register the sign of a secondary experience and recognition of the return of something spectral in the form of a trace or sign signifying, but not representing directly, that something, having occurred, has left its mark, an inscription of sorts on the subject's unconscious, and one which, moreover, can and does return repeatedly, though never as the experience as such. This is not to say that the traumatic event, that factual or historical event which one day took place, never happened or was not real. It is to register, however, that for trauma to be comprehended as trauma, as that which, in appearing, inflicts itself on the subject and thereby causes suffering, is never experienced for the first time *as trauma*. As Dominick LaCapra rightly remarks, '[s]omething of the past always remains, if only as a haunting presence or symptomatic revenant' (2001, 49). The traumatic is that, therefore, which is phantomatic or phantasmatic. Structural through and through, the traumatic phantasm – and, indeed, all phantasms in general – are contradictory, as Louis Althusser suggests. As he puts it, 'something occurs . . . but nothing happens . . . everything is immobile' (1996, 103). The subject of trauma is rendered immobile, unable to move beyond the haunting effects left by trauma, and can only experience in a damaging, repetitive fashion, the disjunctive spectres, remains of what is 'nonsymbolizable'. And yet, paradoxically, the phantasm is a symbol; what has to be understood, however, is that the symbol is not a mimetic representation, it is not an image of the experience itself. It belongs to the order of apperception rather than perception. As Althusser argues, Freud's notion of the phantasm is analogous with the workings of figural language:

> [w]e are obliged to observe that in the phantasm Freud designates something extremely precise, an existent – though nonmaterial – reality, concerning which no misunderstanding is possible, and a material reality that is the very existence of its object: the unconscious. But we are also obliged to observe that the name Freud gives to that reality . . . is the name of a *metaphor*: phantasm . . . the concept of the phantasm in Freud . . . can . . . be, *for us*, the concept *of the limit* . . . (Althusser, 1996, 104)

While I would revise Althusser's understanding by suggesting that, at least as far as the phantasm of trauma is more of the order of catachresis than metaphor, it is clearly incontestable that the phantasm thus remarks both the otherwise unsymbolizable, and also the grammatical or structural displacement, as the necessary movement in the production of meaning; in doing so, it becomes available – it is only ever available – as the inscription of (and, indeed, *at*) the very limit of representation, rather than being or belonging to representation. The haunting trace not only attests to that which is 'outside memory yet within the psyche', to recall Ulrich Baer's words, it also reveals an irreversible and therefore structural passage between, in Dianne Sadoff's words, 'the material, physiological realm and the correlate mental realm' (1998, 45). In coming to terms with this disjunctive passage as intrinsic to the psychic incorporation of trauma, and the subsequent ghostly reiteration by which trauma came to be comprehended, Freud 'stumbled', as Sadoff continues, 'on the concept of representability . . . Mnemic symbols, reproduced scenes, and dreams . . . situated images . . . in a pictorial and verbalized spaced, traversed by memories, fears and desires' (1998, 50).

Interested by what Cathy Caruth describes as the 'peculiar and *uncanny* way in which catastrophic events seem to repeat themselves for those who have passed through them' (1996, 1; emphasis added), Freud sought to explain the experience of trauma through Tasso's story of Tancred and Clorinda. Tancred:

> unwittingly kills . . . Clorinda . . . when she is disguised in the armour of an enemy knight. After her burial he makes his way into a strange magic

forest which strikes the Crusaders' army with terror. He slashes with his sword at a tall tree; but blood streams from the cut and the voice of Clorinda . . . is heard complaining that he has wounded his beloved again. (Freud, 1989, 24)

As Tasso's narrative, recounted by Freud, illustrates, the protagonist is lead inadvertently to repeat his initial act, and it is only through the structural repetition, that unconscious re-enactment and the resulting haunting traces of Clorinda's fate – the blood, the voice – whereby she 'returns', not as herself but as a phantasm of herself, that Tancred receives the forceful shock of under-standing the significance of his earlier action. Structurally, the event becomes dislocated, doubled *and* displaced in reiterative fashion in both Tasso's and Freud's accounts, its meaning *for its subject* produced through the spatio-temporal disjunctive inscription that Derrida names différance between the 'first' recounting of act, the historical fact, and the subsequent, supplementary textual remarking in the revenant signs. As Cathy Caruth says, 'this under-standing of trauma in terms of its indirect relation to reference does not deny or eliminate the possibility of reference but insists, precisely, on the inescapability of its belated impact' (1996, 7). And it is for this reason that, in Freud's account, trauma is 'understood as a wound inflicted not upon the body but upon the mind' (1), whereby 'knowing and not knowing are entangled in the language of trauma' (4).

Cathy Caruth elucidates further the structural significance of trauma, ex-panding Freud's insights beyond the already undeniably significant recognition of that which haunts through the traces of its reiteration. What the critic finds powerfully moving in this scene is not only Tancred's illumination. It is also Clorinda's voice: 'a voice that is paradoxically released *through the wound*' (1996, 2). Caruth explains: '[t]he voice of his beloved addresses him and, in this address, bears witness to the past he has unwittingly repeated. Tancred's story thus represents traumatic experience' (3) as double. On the one hand, there is that dimension already acknowledged by Freud, where trauma is figured and read as 'the enigma of the human agent's repeated and unknowing acts' (3). On the other hand, the story admits for Cathy Caruth the 'enigma of the otherness of a human voice . . . that witnesses a truth' (3) not completely comprehended by the subject. It is thus a matter of giving acknowledgement to the other, of bearing witness to that alterity. In learning how to read and write in response to trauma one must therefore acknowledge the crucial problem 'of listening, of knowing, and of representing' (Caruth, 1996, 5). Critical readings and literary or filmic texts concerned with such issues are obligated to bear witness by asking 'what it means to transmit and to theorize around a crisis that is marked, not by a simple knowledge [by which one might suggest a knowledge available to adequate representation, if such exists], but by the ways it simultaneously defies and demands our witness' (Caruth, 1996, 5).

Such is the '"technical" difficulty', to use a phrase of Avital Ronell's, regarding any critical or literary act concerning trauma and testimony (1994, 313). I believe that Ronell employs the word 'technical', simultaneously marking it off through the cautionary use of quotation marks, in order to emphasize the fundamental condition of technicity, that is, as remarked above, an act of making something appear. How does one verbalize or visualize where there is nothing present as such, and yet where there is a non-material reality and its material effects? The difficulty, Ronell suggests, 'consists in the fact that trauma can be experienced in at least two ways . . . as a memory that one cannot integrate into one's own experience, and as a catastrophic knowledge that one cannot communicate to others' (1994, 313–14). Slavoj Žižek puts the problem another way:

> There is an inherent link between the notions of trauma and repetition, signalled in Freud's well-known motto that what one is not able to remember, one is condemned to repeat: a trauma is by definition something one is not able to remember, i.e. to recollect by way of making it part of one's symbolic narrative; as such, it repeats itself indefinitely, returning to haunt the subject – more precisely, what repeats itself is the very failure, impossibility even to repeat/recollect the trauma properly. (Žižek, 2001, 36–7)

The difficulty explained by Žižek and Ronell is that of some impassable point in thinking, where what comes to be revealed, even though we cannot say what it is, is the acknowledgement of a radically discontinuous structure between self and other. As Derrida remarks 'one needs the other to be determined, in order to relate to history, to memory, to what is kept as a nameable or nameless secret. There is some sealed memory, kept as a crypt or as an unconscious, which is encrypted here' (1997, 115).

Acknowledging that the aporia of trauma is impassable, to the extent that the experience cannot either be integrated into memory or remembered in such a fashion that one can 'overcome' trauma through a kind of mimetic reassembly of the absent experience, perhaps it remains the case that one's response and responsibility has to assume different forms, different modalities, different readings. Such possibilities, in acknowledging the limit of representation, open themselves to other articulations, might make it possible to 'begin again' in such a way that the traces of the traumatic are comprehended in their irrecoverable condition so as to allow for what architect Daniel Libeskind describes as a 'hopeful future' (1997b, 102). Clearly, it would seem that the question of how one responds is not so much a matter of *mimesis* as it is of *poiêsis*.

Libeskind has, himself, confronted just such a problem as an architect asked to respond in the appropriate manner to the Holocaust, and to the relation between the violence of forgetting imposed by trauma and what he describes as the 'invisible matrix or anamnesis of connections in relationship . . . between figures of Germans and Jews' (1997a, 34) on several projects. One such project is the Jewish Museum, Berlin, in which the architect has sought to address the memory of the relation between Jewish culture and tradition and German culture, not simply in dialectical terms but, instead, through the material reality offered by the memory and history of the city of Berlin, as one space wherein traumatic erasure and silencing took place. Libeskind's project was thus to be able to speak of the invisible within the visible, the unspeakable within the articulated, thereby symbolizing indirectly the unsymbolizable of the traumatic event. To this end, the museum could not be merely a memorial, imposing itself as another form of silencing by gathering so many 'representations' of absence as though these were somehow representative of all the facts that were the case of the Holocaust, and thereby allowing for the possibility of the necessary act of witnessing to slide into some form of empathic voyeurism. Instead, Libeskind chose to rethink the very space of the museum, and passage through it, in order that every 'participant', as he puts it, 'will experience [the museum] as his or her own absent present' (1997a, 34); in order that every visitor's 'role', as it were, is not defined solely as objective or constative – as a visitor, I do not simply observe and reflect on represented events to which I believe I have little or no relationship, as is the case in conventional museums – but is, also, inescapably, participatory and performative (and therefore transformative, auto-transformative) – in the act of passage I experience and thus am asked to remember, to symbolize, the invisible, the silenced, the erased, of Berlin *within* the visible, present, articulated structure of the museum, which both belongs to Berlin and yet which also traces Berlin's alterity. This is achieved by Libeskind through the very nature of the spatial and architectural experience rather than because of any single item in the museum's collection, each of which is always in danger of functioning as synecdoche for the trauma of the *Shoah* as a whole, and thereby falling into mimetic representation inappropriate to the 'anamnesis of connections in relationship'. Specifically, Libeskind has sought to rethink the museum in performative terms through the incorporation of 'roads' and 'voids' between the galleries, and between the previously existing Berlin Museum and the Jewish Museum designed by Libeskind. Libeskind's comments from his website are worth quoting at length:

> In specific terms the building measures more than 15,000 square meters. The entrance is through the Baroque Kollegienhaus and then into a dramatic entry Void by a stair which descends under the existing building foundations, crisscrosses underground and materializes itself as an in-dependent building on the outside. The existing building is tied to the extension underground, preserving the contradictory autonomy of both the old building and the new building on the surface, while binding the two together in the depth of time and space.
>
> There are three underground 'roads' which programmatically have three separate stories. The first and longest 'road', leads to the main stair, to the continuation of Berlin's history, to the exhibition spaces in the Jewish Museum. The second road leads outdoors to the E.T.A. Hoffmann

Garden and represents the exile and emigration of Jews from Germany. The third axis leads to the dead end – the Holocaust Void.

Cutting through the form of the Jewish Museum is a Void, a straight line whose impenetrability forms the central focus around which the exhibitions are organized. In order to cross from one space of the Museum to the other, the visitors traverse sixty bridges which open into the Void space; the embodiment of absence.

The work is conceived as a museum for all Berliners, for all citizens. Not only those of the present, but those of the future who might find their heritage and hope in this particular place. With its special emphasis on the Jewish dimension of Berlin's history, this building gives voice to a common fate – to the contradictions of the ordered and disordered, the chosen and not chosen, the vocal and silent.

I believe that this project joins Architecture to questions that are now relevant to all humanity. To this end, I have sought to create a new Architecture for a time which would reflect an understanding of history, a new understanding of Museums and a new realization of the relationship between program and architectural space. Therefore this Museum is not only a response to a particular program, but an emblem of Hope. (Daniel Libeskind, www.daniel-libeskind.com/projects)

Libeskind's architecture responds to the singularity of historic catastrophe and its material effects. His work does this moreover in taking into account the urgent need, the responsibility once again, to make possible an event that can exceed the programming of institutional representation, and the calculability, the economy, of witnessing and memory within any mimetic paradigm. As his commentary makes clear, we can only attest to what is absent, not bring that which cannot be symbolized back. In bearing witness, however, there is always a question of a poetics of witnessing which is affirmative in that it is open, and opens itself, in radical ways in relation to an understanding to come, incommensurable with any knowledge.

On another occasion, Libeskind was asked to design an urban project for the site belonging to the SS surrounding Sachsenhausen concentration camp. The initial suggestion that the site could be used for housing, thereby effectively 'domesticating' and forgetting the experience which haunted the location, was rejected by the architect as being inadequate to, and incommensurate with, any project of 'mental rehabilitation' (Libeskind, 1997b, 102), necessary in Germany. As Libeskind describes it, 'the paradoxical challenge of the work is to retain a strong memory for generations to come and at the same time to formulate a response which provides new possibilities, new activities' (102). One of the ways in which this was achieved was through decentralizing the site of the concentration camp, originally to have been the 'monumental central' location of the proposed housing development; deregulating the order of the site provided for Libeskind a way of displacing the camp from its axial prominence, which would simply have repeated without transforming what was represented. Another transformation proposed was to use the land in such a way as to effect 'ecological intervention and invention' (102), allied to the economic needs of the city of Oranienberg. Libeskind saw the necessity of providing training facilities for the unemployed, as well as other public services such as 'physical and mental health clinics', 'a library, archive, museum', and the accommodation of small companies, specifically those 'connected to cultural production, such as instrument makers, furniture restorers or ceramicists' (102). Libeskind's responses to the Sachsenhausen location suggests an affirmation of responsibility in the face of one singular instance of trauma, a responsibility which manifests itself in the resistance to a predictable programming of redevelopment and which therefore situates its own affirmative singularity. Yet, while retaining the singularity of both trauma and response as the work of an act of 'reading' (in the broad sense) as discussed above, Libeskind also acknowledges a more theoretically broad comprehension of the task engendered after trauma, without reducing that to a method in itself. He writes: 'The task of urbanizing the territories formerly connected with the Sachsenhausen concentration camp raises the most fundamental political, cultural and spiritual issues of the 20th century.'

> What must be faced in any endeavour to recreate and redevelop such an area is the need to mourn an *irretrievable* destiny, in the hope that this mourning will *affect* the connection between the political program, the area's topography and its social use. (102; emphases added)

Libeskind's language gives full recognition to the condition of trauma, but also demonstrates how the possibility of thinking transformatively according to a poetics of mourning and memory irreducible to any simple act of representation can bring about the translation from 'mourning' to 'morning'. A new start which does not forget and yet which moves forward is signified precisely in Libeskind's erasure of the 'u', yet leaving both the letter and the erasure to remain, in order that the necessity for mourning is not abandoned, while, also indicating that it not become a form of passive identification with the victims of the camp, thereby forestalling any hope of political or spiritual change.

NOTES TOWARDS READINGS OF
FRANKENSTEIN AND *HEART OF DARKNESS*

Trauma effects an incision in the self, so that one effectively becomes two (Felman and Laub, 1992, 178), by a process of what Nicolas Abraham and Maria Torok have called an 'internal psychic splitting' (1994, 100). These two selves are the one who experiences and the one who survives (King, 2000 17–19). This is the case, whether by 'self' one indicates a single subject, an individual subjected to a catastrophic experience, or a national, communal or cultural subject, such as a nation or race.

Yet this splitting, this division and doubling that produces the discontinuous subject, doomed to be haunted by the repetitive return of the spectres of trauma, is not only a form of forgetting brought on by the extremity of some original experience; it is also, as Freud's narrative example makes clear, a manifestation of incorporation. The subject incorporates into him- or herself the signs of the traumatic, thereafter being unable to comprehend them. What distinguishes such incorporation as traumatic, however, is that the signs do not become assimilated in that psychic process termed 'introjection', whereby the subject grows in 'continual process of self-fashioning . . . introjection represents our ability to survive shock, trauma, or loss' (Rand, in Abraham and Torok, 1994, 14). As Abraham and Torok put it, '*incorporation results from those losses that for some reason cannot be acknowledged as such . . .*'

> There can be no thought of speaking to someone else about our grief under these circumstances. The words that cannot be uttered, the scenes that cannot be recalled, the tears that cannot be shed – everything will be swallowed along with the trauma that led to the loss. Swallowed and preserved. Inexpressible mourning erects a secret tomb inside the subject . . . Sometimes . . . the ghost of the crypt comes back to haunt the cemetery guard, giving him strange and incomprehensible signals, making him perform bizarre acts, or subjecting him to unexpected sensations. (1994, 130)[7]

Where the phantasm had been for Althusser a metaphor, for Abraham and Torok, the spectre of trauma, in its incorporation, is *antimetaphor*, as they term it, because it effectively blocks all access to figurative contiguity or correlation, and therefore to any proper or appropriate narrative or symbolic reassembly. Hence, my suggestion that we would do well to understand the trace of trauma, in its resistance to any naturalization or domestication, as a figure of catachresis, the absolutely monstrous trope without discernible or otherwise accessible relation to its source or origin.

The figural paradox of incorporation and that amnesiac mechanism belonging to trauma may be comprehended if, in following Slavoj Žižek's reading of Primo Levi on the Holocaust (2001, 37–8), we make the distinction between understanding and knowledge, which, in other terms, is also the distinction already alluded to between representation as *poiêsis* and as *mimesis*. While, rationally, we may know or be able to have access to all the historical facts (or as many of the facts as can be discovered) concerning a particular traumatic historical event, neither historical facts nor statistics, nor any historical account aiming to represent faithfully the past solely through the narrative ordering of such factual details, will ever wholly help either those witnesses who survive or those who after the event bear witness to what took place *understand*. There is always already opening, once again, that incommensurable gap, and with it, the fateful repetition. Understanding does not belong to the rational, the logical, the mimetic; it arrives, if it arrives at all, through articulating a certain relationship to that of which the facts cannot speak, and whereof they must, therefore, keep silent. Understanding is only possible – and this is not some guarantee or promise – if one begins by comprehending the process of a certain 'translation' already discussed – where the corporeal registration of shock and horror is effectively *decorporealized* and simultaneously *incorporated*.

Thus, if, as I have already claimed, literature just names, or is understood as the name of, *for*, the work of witnessing and memory, and if it does bear witness and remember, moreover, through the symbolization of what remains unsymbolizable and unrepresentable, it has to be appreciated and grasped that reading literature, in order to be responsible, cannot merely content itself with a reading of character motivation, of plot summary, or, indeed, with an analysis the epistemological grounding for which is to be located in an assumption of literature as conforming to realist criteria of representation. Rather, as one possible hypothesis, narrative takes place through the assembly of signifying fragments moving through various flows, the intersections of which gather in moments of intensity so as to project phantasmatic symbolizations of that which otherwise cannot be articulated. In such terms, narrative or, perhaps, even literature itself is the indirect articulation of what Maurice Blanchot has described as 'a speech unheard, inexpressible, nevertheless unceasing, silently affirming that where all relation is lacking there yet subsists, there already begins, the human relation in its primacy' (1993, 135).

Take, for example, the narrative of Mary Shelley's *Frankenstein, or the Modern Prometheus* (1818). The story of a man, Victor Frankenstein, who assembles something almost human but not quite – something other than human which, in its uncanny resemblance to the human animal, constantly reminds its maker of a disturbing otherness within any notion of self or being – is, in one sense, clearly fantastic, impossible. The narrative thus represents what is, strictly speaking, unrepresentable, even though Mary Shelley is at pains to point out that there are those in the scientific community who have suggested that her narrative represents a not 'impossible occurrence' (1994, 3). The author goes on to remark, in a form of qualification, that 'however impossible as a physical fact, [the narrative event of the construction of a human being] affords a point of view to the imagination for the delineating of human passions more comprehensive and commanding than any which the ordinary relations of existing events can yield' (1994, 3). At pains to point out that *Frankenstein* is not merely some supernatural tale of spectres, Shelley clearly wishes it to be understood that the story concerns the articulation of a certain imaginative, psychological understanding – a poetics, in short – incommensurable with any strictly realistic representation or adequate knowledge.

Thus we find ourselves witness to a particular, singular narrative responding to that process of transition between physical and mental realms and, at the same time, that narrative's inability to verbalize or bear witness to epistemological crisis. Historically, *Frankenstein* is available to us as being both caught in and traversing the space between the external and internal, symbolizing, we might say, the registration of a cultural experience of trauma in the face of the epistemological shock to the self of then 'new' sciences. It moves between differing modalities of comprehension concerning self and other, or the two halves of the split self, which it remarks materially through the characters of Victor Frankenstein and his creature. The novel is suspended in its traversal between external physical world and internal psychic states, however, in that – and this is a sign of the materiality, the historiality of the narrative's attempt to respond to the traumatic reception of new knowledge, and out of which comes the narrative's imaginative understanding – it still finds it necessary to apprehend its concerns through the ostensible depiction of creator and creature as essentially separate, and yet inseparable, characters.

Yet, what is really fascinating in Shelley's narrative, despite the corporeal externalization – and thus as a manifestation of anthropomorphic representation signalling the inability to move beyond the otherwise inaccessible, inexpressible experience of trauma – is the movement of structural repetition. Victor Frankenstein's creation pursues his creator relentlessly, returning and haunting both Victor and the narrative itself. Significantly, apropos of the question of traumatic revenance, we should read such returns and reiterations not as the arrival of a significant character so much as we should comprehend how the narrative is itself marked and interrupted, traumatized, by this iterable interruption. And while Victor Frankenstein may have scientific knowledge, he has no understanding of what he has done; its meaning is inaccessible to him, and so he is pursued by this monstrous phantasm of his own making. Similarly, the narrative can only function through its various doublings and repetitions, and its material, uncloseable fissure between externality and internality, its constant reminders of the divisions of the subject announcing, in a quite singular manner, the trauma of modernity. The reciprocal shuttling of its various 'voices' render the text as a weaving machine, the sovereign narrator dismembered through a technology of witnessing. And the reader is confronted, perhaps traumatized, by an image of a possibly traumatized creator unable to take responsibility for the other, a figure of abjection, trauma and alterity, not-quite-human enough and yet all-too-human in a particularly modern sense: technologically reproduced, grafted, re-marked, commodified and made monstrous. And yet, to conclude this brief sketch by reiterating what is, for me, the key issue here, this is not only to describe Frankenstein's creature, or even Victor Frankenstein's non-recognition; it is also to say something, albeit indirectly, about *Frankenstein*, the text:[8] for, arguably, it bears all the hallmarks of traumatic narrative unable to escape its own condition, doomed to fold onto itself that otherness which haunts it throughout.

It might be said that it took less than a hundred years for literature to respond to the processes of internalization which trauma simultaneously names and encrypts.[9] That wholesale internalization finds itself remarked in Joseph Conrad's *Heart of Darkness* (1902). While *Frankenstein*'s registration of the traumatic is fundamentally epistemological in nature, Conrad's narrative strives to address the trauma of the colonial enterprise, and to bear witness to that. Were we simply interested in reading characters as traumatized, we could, doubtless, focus on Kurtz. (And, indeed, I do wish to turn, if not to Kurtz entirely, then, at least, to his final words.) However, I want to stress that *Heart of Darkness* records trauma at its most basic lexical levels, through the very choice of words by which the attempt at representation takes place. (Again, given that Conrad's novel offers its readers a first-person narrative, it would be easy enough to domesticate the reading of trauma by seeing its articulation as, simply, only, the articulation of the narrator, Marlowe's, psychological condition.) The narratorial voice (which, it has to be stressed, cannot be equated simply with Marlowe's, if only because Marlowe's account is both marked by the voices of others, as well as being a response to, and therefore framed by, an anonymous, invisible narrator who begins *Heart of Darkness*) is traced by a poetics of the limit, a materiality of the letter attesting to both the limit and inadequacy of representation in the face of catastrophe and horror, and the importance of bearing witness to the fact, and in the face, of the inexpressible.

This 'limit-language' occurs throughout the novel through the use of several hundred words, all sharing prefixes the work of which is either to say that determinate knowledge or representation cannot take place or that knowledge and representation are only this admission that one cannot know, one cannot represent trauma. These are words such as *interminable, immensity, imperceptible, untitled, inscrutable, incomprehensible, inconclusive, uncanny, unknown, insoluble, impossible, unfamiliar, incredible, impenetrable, unspeakable, inconceivable, inexorable, unforeseen, invisible, indistinct*. Their frequency both maintains the narrative and yet interrupts, disables the narrative at every point. Such words speak to the obligation to read and to the impossibility of a reading.

Thus, one aspect of Conrad's writing situates the responsible act *in* the materiality of the letter in order to respond *to* the materiality of history, and in order to acknowledge how, on the one hand, it is impossible to record historical events in any direct representation, while, on the other, to show indirectly, how any such mimetic act is inadequate to the intensity, the immensity, of traumatism. Rather, Conrad's poetics of indirection attest to history as a history of trauma, to recall Cathy Caruth's words. In its deployment of a limit-language, Conrad's novel attests to the technical difficulty concerning trauma spoken of by Avital Ronell, for it undeniably inscribes the trauma of colonialism as (in Ronell's words) 'a memory that one cannot integrate into one's own experience, and as a catastrophic knowledge that one cannot communicate to others'. What such language also gives us to understand is how 'repetition [is] at the heart of catastrophe' (Caruth, 1996, 2). Nowhere is this, along with Ronell's traumatic double bind, articulated more clearly, than in Kurtz's final moments:

> Did he live his life again in every detail of desire, temptation, and surrender during that supreme moment of complete knowledge? He cried in a whisper at some image, some vision, – he cried out twice, a cry that was no more than a breath –
>
> "'the horror, the horror!'" (Conrad, 1995, 112)

If repetition is at the heart of catastrophe, it is also at the heart of darkness, a darkness naming the absolute inaccessibility of the traumatic event. Kurtz's words clearly repeat themselves in the rhythm of trauma's return and which iteration 'splits the mark [in this example, Kurtz's doubling, dividing articulation] into a past that can never be fully rendered present and a future which is always about to arrive' (Weber, 1996, 149). Structurally, what has to be acknowledged here is that not only is Kurtz not experiencing the traumatic as such, but is only responding to its inaccessibility, while expressing the mark it has indelibly inscribed upon him; also, his articulation – one which, in its reiteration, has the possibility of echoing and remarking itself endlessly – is itself doubled by Marlowe's memory of it (a memory which haunts Marlowe, and which returns on Marlowe's visit to Kurtz's fiancée (118)). It is to be noticed that Marlowe cannot say for certain what Kurtz is witness to, he can only pose an unanswerable question. Furthermore, that repetition is worked out in Marlowe's own words. He says twice of Kurtz that 'he cried', 'he cried out twice', and that, whatever Kurtz bears witness to, it is both an image and a vision. There is a splitting and duplication at work here, once again, both of which are the signs of traumatic incorporation; these effects do not merely 'belong' to a particular character's psyche, but are inscribed at the heart of the language. Moreover, the extent to which trauma is both witnessed and replayed is to be comprehended in the way in which, in the iterable movement of Marlowe's response, constative description appears to fall into performative speech act. What this suggests, *what it imposes*, is an open structure of witnessing. Marlowe does not know how to assimilate Kurtz's words, but bears witness to them and to the trauma they appear to signal, thereby enacting otherwise, transformatively, the act of attestation, and, in the process, opening an ethical relay. The structure of *Heart of Darkness* is thus mobilized by what J. Hillis Miller has called a 'proliferating relay of witnesses . . . The relay of witness behind witness behind witness, voice behind voice behind voice . . .' (1990, 188). That we as readers comprehend this means that we are only the latest, not the last, in the relay of witnesses to the unspeakable in every singular traumatic event. This is the impossible responsibility we bear. For, to recall the words of Maurice Blanchot, what is encrypted in those words, 'the horror, the horror', and in the relay they interrupt and maintain, is 'a speech unheard, inexpressible, nevertheless unceasing, silently affirming that where all relation is lacking there yet subsists, there already begins, the human relation in its primacy'. And what is important, as Blanchot reminds us, and as we come to understand from *Heart of Darkness*, 'is not to tell, but to tell once again, and, in the retelling, to tell again each time a first time' (1993, 314).

QUESTIONS FOR FURTHER CONSIDERATION

1. Consider how trauma is structured like a language.
2. If trauma is unsymbolizable as such, what in narratives such as *Frankenstein* and *Heart of Darkness* make the effects of trauma readable (if they are)?

3. In what ways might *Heart of Darkness* be said to 'tell again each time for the first time'?

4. In what ways does the psychological concept of trauma challenge conventional understandings of historical event and representation?

5. If conventional, particularly mimetic, acts of representation are inadequate in their response to catastrophic historical events, what other modalities of representation do literature and film make available to us?

6. To what extent does the narrative inability to articulate an adequate or final response to 'the horror, the horror' in *Heart of Darkness*, while showing how it can only say that it cannot say, address the condition of trauma while making the reader aware of her/his own responsibility?

ANNOTATED BIBLIOGRAPHY

Baer, Ulrich. *Remnants of Song: Trauma and the Experience of Modernity in Charles Baudelaire and Paul Celan*. Stanford, CA: Stanford University Press, 2000. Developing his analysis of modernity and modern poetics from studies of trauma and testimony, and research on the Holocaust, Baer's study explores how the act of critical engagement with poetic utterance offers one possible ethical intervention and response to the haunting effects of traumatic experience. Baer provides an indispensable reading of psychological and historical catastrophe through close reading of the 'modern' experience of the aporetic, and its equally 'modern' traumatic condition, as articulated in the poetry of Charles Baudelaire and Paul Celan.

Bernard-Donals, Michael and Richard Glejzer. *Between Witness and Testimony: The Holocaust and the Limits of Representation*. Albany, NY: State University of New York Press, 2001. Addressing the problems of bearing witness to the unspeakable, Bernard-Donals and Glejzer provide an indispensible interdisciplinary study of the challenges to acts of testimony and representation in any consideration of the Holocaust. Making careful distinctions between the concepts of 'witnessing' and 'testimony', the authors stress that we are obligated to testify despite the ineffable extremity of the *Shoah*, and to find means of articulation in the face of the limits and inadequacy of conventional historical representation.

Blanchot, Maurice/Jacques Derrida. *The Instant of My Death/Demeure: Fiction and Testimony*. Stanford, CA: Stanford University Press, 2000. Comprising a bilingual edition of Blanchot's short narrative, *L'instant de ma mort/The Instant of My Death*, in which a young man finds himself before a firing squad during the Second World War, and Derrida's careful reading of this story. Derrida's essay explores the fraught relation between writing and history, and the problematic of writing about an experience that is not available to one, thereby addressing the limits and (im)possibilities of any act of witnessing or testimony.

Caruth, Cathy. *Unclaimed Experience: Trauma, Narrative and History*. Baltimore, MD: The Johns Hopkins University Press, 1996. Caruth's volume challenges the efficacy of any understanding of history based on models of experience and reference through a recognition of the significance of the impact of trauma on historical comprehension in the twentieth century. Given that trauma prohibits any immediate understanding of historical catastrophe, *Unclaimed Experience* seeks to consider, through readings of Freud, Kleist, Kant, de Man and Alain Resnais' film *Hiroshima mon amour*, what other means for coming to terms with trauma might be available.

Felman, Shoshana and Dori Laub. *Testimony: Crises of Witnessing in Literature, Psychoanalysis, and History*. London: Routledge, 1992. Literary critic Shoshana Felman and psychoanalyst Dori Laub explore the nature of testimony, witnessing and memory, in particular relation to the Holocaust, in an interdisciplinary study which encompasses readings of poetic, critical and autobiographical texts, as well as examining film and videotaped testimony of Holocaust survivors. In doing so, they offer a reconceptualization of the relationship between art and culture and the witnessing of traumatic historical events.

Freud, Sigmund. *Beyond the Pleasure Principle*. In *The Standard Edition of the Complete Psychological Works of Sigmund Freud*, trans. and gen. ed. James Strachey. London: Hogarth, 1953–74, Vol. 18. Rpt. as *Beyond the Pleasure Principle*, trans. and ed. James Strachey, intro. Gregory Zilboorg, biographical intro. Peter Gay. New York: Norton, 1989. Originally published in 1920, Freud's significant statement on the nature of 'drives' as the motivating forces of the human psyche contains his articulation on the fundamentally structural condition of traumatic repetition and its relationship to forms of communication and narrative.

LaCapra, Dominick. *Writing History, Writing Trauma*. Baltimore, MD: Johns Hopkins University Press, 2001. A crucial intervention in its questioning of the efficacy of any normative historicizing of traumatic events. LaCapra's volume extends both the modalities of historical representation and critical language in relation to literary testimony through both a critique of the limits of various aspects of literary criticism and history as a discipline and also in sustained consideration of what it means to write the event.

SUPPLEMENTARY BIBLIOGRAPHY

Abraham, Nicolas and Maria Torok. *The Shell and the Kernel. I.* (1987), ed., trans. and intro. Nicholas Rand. Chicago: University of Chicago Press, 1994.

Althusser, Louis. *Writing on Psychoanalysis: Freud and Lacan* [1993], trans Jeffrey Mehlman. New York: Columbia University Press, 1996.

Blanchot, Maurice. *The Infinite Conversation* (1969), trans. and Foreword Susan Hanson. Minneapolis: University of Minnesota Press, 1993.

Castle, Terry. *The Female Thermometer: Eighteenth-Century Culture and the Invention of the Uncanny*. Oxford: Oxford University Press, 1995.

Conrad, Joseph. *Heart of Darkness* (1902). In *Heart of Darkness with The Congo Diary*, ed. and intro. Robert Hampson. London: Penguin, 1995, 1–140.

Derrida, Jacques. *The Other Heading: Reflections on Today's Europe* (1991), trans. Pascale-Anne Brault and Michael Naas. Chicago: University of Chicago Press, 1992.

Derrida, Jacques. *The Gift of Death* (1992), trans. David Wills. Chicago: University of Chicago Press, 1995.

Derrida, Jacques. 'Response to Daniel Libeskind'. In Daniel Libeskind, *Radix-Matrix: Architecture and Writings*. Munich: Prestel, 1997, 110–15.

Düttman, Alexander García. *The Gift of Language: Memory and Promise in Adorno, Benjamin, Heidegger, and Rosenzweig*. London: Athlone Press, 2000.

Germain, Sylvie. *The Weeping Woman on the Streets of Prague* (1992), trans. Judith Landry, intro. Emma Wilson. London: Dedalus, 1993.

Keenan, Thomas. *Fables of Responsibility: Aberrations and Predicaments in Ethics and Politics*. Stanford, CA: Stanford University Press, 1997.

King, Nicola. *Memory, Narrative, Identity*. Edinburgh: Edinburgh University Press, 2000.

Kronick, Joseph G. *Derrida and the Future of Literature*. Albany, NY: State University of New York Press, 1999.

Libeskind, Daniel. 'Between the Lines'. In *Radix-Matrix: Architecture and Writings*. Munich: Prestel, 1997, 34–56.

Libeskind, Daniel. 'Mourning: Sachsenhausen, Oranienberg'. In *Radix-Matrix: Architecture and Writings*. Munich: Prestel, 1997, 102–9.

Libeskind, Daniel. www.daniel-libeskind.com/projects.

Miller, J. Hillis. 'Heart of Darkness Revisited'. In Tropes, Parables, Performatives: Essays on Twentieth-Century Literature. Hemel Hempstead: Harvester Wheatsheaf, 1990, 181–94.

Ronell, Avital. The Telephone Book: Technology-Schizophrenia-Electric Speech. Lincoln, NE: University of Nebraska Press, 1989.

Ronell, Avital. Finitude's Score: Essays for the End of the Millennium. Lincoln, NE: University of Nebraska Press, 1994.

Sadoff, Dianne. Sciences of the Flesh: Representing Body and Subject in Psychoanalysis. Stanford, CA: Stanford University Press, 1998.

Shelley, Mary. Frankenstein, or the Modern Prometheus (1818), ed. and intro. Marilyn Butler. Oxford: Oxford University Press, 1994.

Spivak, Gayatri Chakravorty. 'A Moral Dilemma'. In Howard Marchitello (ed.), What Happens to History: The Renewal of Ethics in Contemporary Thought. New York: Routledge, 2001, 215–36.

Weber, Samuel. Mass Mediauras: Form Technics Media. Stanford, CA: Stanford University Press, 1996.

Žižek, Slavoj. On Belief. London: Routledge, 2001.

NOTES

1. See, for example, the conclusion to Sudesh Mishra's chapter in this volume (Chapter 1, 'Diaspora Criticism'), which urges the recognition of the diasporic experience in terms of trauma, and the subsequent obligation which such recognition places on the act of critical reading.

2. In pointing to a 'psychoanalytic' or an 'ethical' criticism, I am merely alluding to two of the more obvious 'contexts' or frameworks, conceptual languages or institutionally recognized discourses, which someone reading this might highlight in order to 'explain' the origins of the present critical act. Thus there is the possibility for recognizing a degree of overlap or resemblance between this chapter and, say, that on the subject of 'ethical criticism' by Kenneth Womack, or the specific project of the work of Emmanuel Levinas, as explored by Frederick Young, both in the present volume.

   The psychoanalytic and ethical registers are not the only ones at work here, however. Equally, the question of history is announced. One might also suggest that, within the current volume, there are aspects of my chapter touching on those raised by David Punter, in his chapter on 'spectrality', or in Tom Cohen's consideration of materiality. Another way of commandeering the chapter in terms of a master discourse might be to see it as an articulation of particular aspects of Jacques Derrida's recent work, and therefore, by the usual, wholly predictable extension, to apprehend this chapter as an example of so-called deconstruction. Such assumptions or, to be more accurate, calculations, exemplify the ways in which conceptualization proceeds, and which the introduction of this chapter seeks to unpack in relation to the motifs of 'testimony', 'trauma', 'witnessing' and 'responsibility'.

3. On the subject of performativity, see Sarah Gamble, Frederick Young and Tom Cohen's chapters in this collection.

4. I am borrowing the contours of this commentary from the work of Jacques Derrida, who, in The Gift of Death, has commented that '[t]he simple concepts of alterity and singularity constitute the concept of duty as much as that of responsibility. As a result, the concepts of responsibility, of decision, or of duty, are condemned a priori to paradox, scandal, and aporia. Paradox, scandal, and aporia are themselves nothing other than sacrifice, the revelation of conceptual thinking at its limit, its death and finitude' (1995, 68). Elsewhere, in the same work, Derrida remarks: 'I am responsible to any one (that is to say to any other) only by failing in my responsibility to all others, to the ethical or political generality, and I can never justify this sacrifice' (1995, 70).

5. Kronick elaborates this point from a discussion of Derrida's in the third chapter of *The Gift of Death*: 'I can respond only to the one (or to the One), that is, to the other, by sacrificing that one to the other. I am responsible to any one (that is to say to any other) only by failing in my responsibility to all the others, to the ethical or political generality. And I can never justify this sacrifice, I must always hold my peace about it. Whether I want to or not, I can never justify the fact that I prefer or sacrifice any one (any other) to the other . . . What binds me to singularities, to this one or that one . . . remains finally undecidable . . . as unjustifiable as the infinite sacrifice I make at each moment. These singularities represent others, a wholly other form of alterity: one other or some other persons, but also places, animals, languages. How would you ever justify the fact that you sacrifice all the cats in the world to the cat that you feed at home every morning for years, whereas other cats die of hunger at every instant.' Jacques Derrida, *The Gift of Death* (1992), trans. David Wills. Chicago: University of Chicago Press, 1995, 70–1.

6. It has to be acknowledged, of course, that the act of 'secondary witnessing', a kind of working-through the trauma of others, is a problem fraught with the dangers of identification. As LaCapra remarks, 'a difficulty arises when the virtual experience involved in empathy gives way to vicarious victimhood, and empathy with the victim seems to become an identity' (2001, 47).

7. Uncannily enough, this quotation, or a part of it at least, returns below, in David Punter's essay on spectral criticism.

8. In a possible development of this sketch of a reading of Shelley's novel, it can be argued that Shelley's comprehension of the aberrant, the traumatic and the monstrous that inform modernity figures cultural experience in a proleptic, if not prosthetic manner, as that comes to be analysed by Karl Marx at the beginning of *Capital*. As Thomas Keenan's persuasive analysis of Marx's opening rhetorical gestures makes plain, Marx addresses the ways in which the economic 'shows itself by hiding itself, by announcing itself as something else or in another form'; wealth is figured as something monstrous, 'compounded of elements from different forms . . . grown beyond the control of its creators'. This monster cannot be domesticated; neither can it be rendered as an organic unity, being 'nothing but parts, unnatural and uncommon . . . [a]berrant, deviant . . . This figure of monstrosity, living and dead (the *Wahrig* [*Deutsches Wörterbuch*] links *ungeheuer* [*enormous, immense, monstrous*] to *unheimlich*, [*uncanny*, lit. *unhomely*] unhomely monstrosity to ghostly recurrence), haunts the chapter' (Keenan 1997, 104). Marx even quotes himself, thereby engaging in an act of mechanical grafting, according to Keenan, where this monstrous or ghostly act serves only to point further for the critic to the ways in which words themselves are 'nothing but commodities, to be accumulated, moved and removed . . . transferred like (*als*) property or the mechanical limb . . . on a monster' (1997, 105). It is arguable that, while Keenan does not speak directly of trauma in the context of reading the opening passages from Marx, he does mobilize through his analysis of the monstrous and spectral rhetoric that Marx engages around the subject of the commodity, a transformative critique of the essentially traumatic effect on cultural identity (including Marx's own, given his choice of words) of capitalist economics.

9. Terry Castle provides a compelling account of the nineteenth century as a century of incorporation and internalization, through an analysis of the figure of 'phantasmagoria' and its transformation from the literal meaning, pertaining to the technological production and representation of ghosts in exhibitions and other public entertainments to the wholly internal 'successions of . . . phantasms . . . as called up by the imagination, or as created by literary description' (Castle, 1995, 141).

SPACE AND PLACE

ECOCRITICISM

Kate Rigby

REMEMBERING THE EARTH

In 1756, the vicar of Selbourne planted four lime trees between his house and the butcher's yard opposite, '"to hide the sight of blood and filth"' (White, cit. Thomas, 1983, 299). Gilbert White was a great naturalist and went on to write *The Natural History of Selbourne* (1789), a text much prized by ecocritics as environmental literature. White's arboreal screening out of the slaughterhouse is, in a sense, equally significant, for it exemplifies one of the key developments Keith Thomas charts in his history of changing attitudes towards the natural world in England between 1500 and 1800: namely, a growing uneasiness about killing animals for food. Towards the end of the eighteenth century this change in sensibilities led some, including the English poet Shelley, to become vegetarian.[1] The vast majority of people, including the vicar of Selbourne, nonetheless continued to eat animals. What changed was rather that slaughterhouses were banished from the public gaze, while meat increasingly was sold and prepared as faceless flesh – that is, minus the head. What concerns me here for the moment is less the ethics of meat consumption than the concealment of its price. For it is this kind of concealment that would become characteristic of society's relationship to the natural world in the modern era – an era which with the dramatic disclosure of global ecological imperilment has perhaps now begun to come to an end.

Since the eighteenth century, the necessity of recalling the true cost, both to subordinate humans and to the earth, of our production processes and consumption habits has grown in equal measure to its difficulty. For at the same time that the ecosystems sustaining all life on earth have become ever more critically endangered by our growing numbers and levels of consumption, ever more people (above all, those whose ecological debt is the largest) live at an ever greater remove from the natural world, unmindful of their impact upon the earth. In addition, as Slavoj Žižek has observed, to the extent that the ecological crisis pertains to what Lacan terms the 'real', that which precedes, defies and disrupts symbolic representation, it remains strangely elusive to thought, even while pressing in upon us daily, shifting the literal ground of our being (Žižek 1991, 35–9; see also Kerridge 1998a, 1–4 and 1998b). Within the academy especially, the recollection of our embeddedness within an increasingly endangered earth has not come easily to those disciplines devoted to the study of cultural artefacts. Literary critics and cultural theorists in particular have been notoriously slow to register those changes in thinking about the relationship of culture and society to the natural world which began to be articulated in neighbouring disciplines, above all philosophy, but also theology, politics and history, from the early 1970s. 'If your knowledge of the outside world were limited to what you could infer from the major publications of the literary profession', observed Cheryll Glotfelty in 1996 in her introduction to the first ecocriticism reader,

> you would quickly discern that race, class and gender were the hot topics of the late twentieth century, but you would never know that the earth's life support systems were under stress. Indeed, you might never know that there was an earth at all. (Glotfelty, 1996, xvi)

There were in fact some isolated calls for an ecologically oriented criticism during the 1970s.[2] However, it was not until the end of the twentieth century that the study of literature and the environment was finally recognized as 'a subject on the rise'.[3] In some respects it is perhaps not surprising that the study of literary texts should be coupled with such forgetfulness of the earth. Although the practice of criticism has ancient origins in the exegesis of biblical and classical Greek texts, modern literary criticism only began to be institutionalized as an academic discipline in the early nineteenth century. This was precisely the time when a rigid separation began to be drawn between the 'natural' and the 'human' sciences. This is a divide that few literary critics and cultural theorists have dared to cross, until relatively recently. The compartmentalization of knowledge effected by this divide is central to what Bruno Latour (1993) terms the 'Modern Constitution', which sunders the human from the non-human realm, while defining society's relationship to nature predominantly in terms of mastery and possession. It is the Modern Constitution, which facilitates also that characteristically modern (and especially urban) form of self-deception, whereby the consumption of meat can be disconnected from the suffering and death of animals. Thus, to regain a sense of the inextricability of nature and culture, *physis* and *techne*, earth and artefact – consumption and destruction – would be to move beyond both the impasse of modernism and the arrogance of humanism.

What, then, might such a posthumanist, postmodernist remembering of the earth entail for the literary critic or cultural theorist? In her poem 'Parchment', Michelle Boisseau gives us some valuable leads:

I'm holding in my hand the skin of a calf
that lived 600 years ago, translucent
skin that someone stretched on four strong poles,
skin someone scraped with a moon-shaped blade.
Here is the flesh side, it understood true dark.
Here is the hair side that met the day's weather,
the long ago rain. It is all inscribed
with the dark brown ink of prayer,

the acid galls of ancient oaks, though these reds,
deluxe rivulets that brighten the margins,
are cinnabar ground too a paste, another paste
of lapis for these blue medieval skies,
and for flowering meadows or a lady's long braids-
the orpiment – a yellow arsenic –
whose grinding felled the illuminator's
boy assistants like flies, or the insect kermes

whose pregnant bodies gave pigment, and the goose
who supplied quills, the horse its hair, and flax
the fine strong thread that held the folded skins
into a private book stamped with gold for a king.
(Boisseau, 2000, 177)

The parchment that Boisseau describes here is a product of *techne*, an artefact of considerable beauty, embodying something of the religious traditions and aesthetic sensibilities of a rich cultural tradition: it is, we learn, a late medieval illuminated prayerbook. In her poetic presentation of this prayerbook, Boisseau calls attention not to its meaning as a text, nor to its economic or antiquarian value, but to its materiality. Or rather, she asks us to reconsider its potential meaning and value in relation to its materiality, perceived in terms of its cost to the natural world. Thus, she recalls the slaughtered calf, whose skin supplied the parchment, the oak trees, the insect-engendered galls which supplied dark ink for the written text, and all the other animals, vegetables and minerals which made possible the material production of this artefact. Recalling too the illuminator's boy assistants, who died 'like flies' from arsenic poisoning as a result of their labour, Boisseau reminds us that the price of production is borne by subordinate humans, as well as by non-human others. This link between social domination and the exploitation of nature is hinted at again in the close of the poem, where we learn the purpose for which this book had been produced at such cost: namely, for the private use of a king.

In one of his 'Theses on the Philosophy of History' Walter Benjamin observes that, to the historical materialist, there is 'no document of civilization which is not at the same time a document of barbarism' (Benjamin, 1973, 258). Most ecocritics would agree with this, but they would add that there is also no work of culture which is not simultaneously exploitative of nature. This is of course also true of Boisseau's 'Parchment' (and, indeed, this chapter), the writing, publication and distribution of which has taken its own toll on the natural environment. And yet, the relationship between nature and culture is not one way. Of this too we might be reminded by Boisseau's poem. For the written prayers and visual images contained in this prayerbook convey ideas about nature, and about the relationship between nature, humanity and the divine, which crucially conditioned medieval perceptions and practices regarding the natural world, and which continue to resonate in complex and contradictory ways up to the present. Culture constructs the prism through which we know nature. We begin to internalize this prism from the moment we learn to speak; the moment, that is, that we are inducted into the *logos*, the world as shaped by language. 'Nature', which, as Raymond Williams has remarked, is 'perhaps the most complex word in the language' (Williams, 1983, 219), is in this sense a cultural and, above all, a linguistic construct. The physical reality of air, water, fire, rock, plants, animals, soils, ecosystems, solar systems etc., to which I refer when I speak of 'the natural world', nonetheless precedes and exceeds whatever words might say about it. It is this insistence on the ultimate precedence of nature vis-à-vis culture, which signals the ecocritical move beyond the so-called 'linguistic turn' perpetuated within structuralism and poststructuralism.[4] For some ecocritics, this precedence extends to a consideration of the ways in which human languages, cultures and textual constructs are themselves conditioned by the natural environment.

It might be countered that at a time when there is allegedly no place on earth that has not been affected in some way by humanity's alteration of the natural environment, the precedence of nature has now become questionable. It is, however, precisely the imperilment of the biosphere wrought by that alteration which impels the ecocritical reinstatement of the referent as a matter of legitimate concern. For the ecocritic, it is vital to be able to say, with Kate Soper, that 'it is not language that has a hole in its ozone layer; and the "real" thing continues to be polluted and degraded even as we refine our deconstructive insights at the level of the signifier' (Soper, 1995, 151). Moreover, the fact that ever more of the earth's surface is currently being refashioned by *techne* does not mean that *physis* has ceased to exist. All human making, including the largely unintentional remaking (or rather, undoing) of the earth's ecosystems, remains dependent upon physical processes which precede and exceed human knowledge and power. All human being, meanwhile, remains interwoven, albeit often invisibly, with the life of countless non-human beings, who continue as best they can to pursue their own ends in the midst of an increasingly anthropogenic environment.

Ecocriticism, then, remembers the earth by rendering an account of the indebtedness of culture to nature. While acknowledging the role of language in shaping our view of the world, ecocritics seek to restore significance to the world beyond the page. More specifically, they are concerned to revalue the more-than-human natural world, to which some texts and cultural traditions invite us to attend. In this way, ecocriticism has a vital contribution to make to the wider project of Green Studies, which, in Laurence Coupe's words, 'debates "Nature" in order to defend nature' (Coupe, 2000, 5). For many ecocritics, moreover, the defence of nature is vitally interconnected with the pursuit of social justice. As Scott Slovic reminds us (citing Walt Whitman), ecocriticism is 'large and contains multitudes' (Slovic, 1999, 1102). Ecocritics are increasingly many and varied, drawing on a range of analytical strategies and theoretical approaches, and addressing a diversity of cultural phenomena, from Shake-spearean drama to wildlife documentaries, romantic pastoral to sci-fi ecothril-lers, the Bible to Basho.[5] This is a fast growing field which cannot be explored fully within the limits of this chapter. In what follows, I will nonetheless seek to trace some of the primary ways in which ecocriticism is currently transforming the practice of literary studies.

CRITIQUING THE CANON

In 1967, the American historian Lyn White Jr published a slim article entitled 'The Historical Roots of Our Ecologic Crisis' (White, 1996). The fact that this key early work of ecological cultural criticism first appeared in the journal *Science* reflects the extent to which environmental destruction was at that stage still seen as a largely scientific and technical issue. Yet the burden of White's article was precisely that science provided an inadequate basis for understanding, let alone resolving, a problem which was cultural and social in origin. Pre-empting Arne Naess' influential critique of 'shallow ecology' (1972), White argued that, '[w]hat people do about their ecology depends on what they think about themselves in relation to things around them. Human ecology is deeply conditioned by beliefs about our nature and destiny – that is, by religion' (White, 1996, 6). For this reason, White maintained that it was necessary to look to the dominant religious traditions of the West in seeking to identify the primary source of those attitudes towards the natural world, which in his view had led to the current crisis. The main target of White's critique is the Hebrew creation story in Genesis 1, which 'not only established a dualism of man and nature but also insisted that it is God's will that man exploit nature for his proper ends' (White, 1996, 10). As White is well aware, however, the Bible, like all texts, is a complex and multivalent document, conveying highly mixed messages about the relationship between God, humanity and the rest of creation. In his analysis, the problem lay not so much with the biblical text itself, but rather with the way in which it began to be interpreted in western Christianity from about the twelfth century: namely, as legitimating that scientific exploration, technological manipulation and economic exploitation of the natural world which has today reached a level that would have been unimaginable, and quite possibly appalling, to the authors of Genesis.

White's article inaugurated the ecologically oriented critique of the way in which nature is constructed in certain canonical texts of the western tradition. The first extended deployment of an ecocritical hermeneutics of suspicion to literature was Joseph Meeker's *The Comedy of Survival* (1972). Meeker's disapprobation falls in particular upon classical tragedy, which, he contends, reinforces the anthropocentric 'assumption that nature exists for the benefit of mankind, the belief that human morality transcends natural limitations, and humanism's insistence on the supreme importance of the individual' (Meeker, 1972, 42–3). Meeker is also highly critical of the pastoral tradition, which he sees as a form of escapist fantasy, valorizing a tamed and idealized nature over wild no less than urban environments. This kind of critique continues to have an important place in the ecological recasting of the canon. However, the charge that Christianity, or any other key element in western culture (tragedy, pastoral, rationalist metaphysics, phallogocentrism, etc.), 'bears a huge burden of guilt' (White, 1996, 12) for today's ecological crisis needs to be qualified in at least three ways.

Firstly, and most obviously, it is important to note that the West does not have a monopoly on ecological errancy. Many other cultures and societies have also failed to live sustainably in the past. Secondly, western religious and literary traditions are not monolithic ideological constructs, but complex and ambivalent cultural legacies. As we will see, much recent ecocriticism has been directed towards revaluing some of these traditions, including pastoral. As yet, no ecocritics have to my knowledge attempted a sustained defence of tragedy, but it could be argued that in some forms and contexts, its force is precisely to question, rather than endorse, the hubris of human self-assertion. In recent times, the tragic mode has been effectively redeployed in environmental apocalyptic, such as Rachel Carson's 'Fable of Tomorrow' (Carson, 1982, 21–2), in which the prefiguration of the potentially disastrous consequences of society's tragic blindness functions as a call to environmental action in the present. Similarly, it is increasingly clear that Christian arguments can be and have been called upon to justify very different, even contradictory, ways of relating to the natural world. Thus, for example, while Francis Bacon (1561–1626), the so-called 'father' of modern science, could appeal to the Bible in presenting the conquest of nature by man as divinely ordained,[6] many of the opponents of precisely this kind of human chauvinism from the late sixteenth century onwards have also couched their arguments in Christian terms. During the medieval period, too, divergent interpretations of Christian texts and traditions are evident even within the West, as White's own endorsement of St Francis as a 'patron saint for ecologists' (White, 1996, 14) attests. Moreover, the fact that the period of the greatest despoliation of the earth has coincided precisely with the waning of the earlier theocentric view of nature as God's creation suggests, at the very least, that the culpability of Christianity is indirect.

There is finally also the tricky question of causality. While it might be true that 'what people do about their ecology depends upon what they think about things around them', as White puts it, we still have to ask what conditions the discursive practices and cultural traditions within which those thoughts are embedded. To leave the analysis on the level of cultural critique would be to fall prey to the fallacy of idealism, especially if there is any truth in the Marxist view that the material forces and relations of production are the real drivers of cultural and social change. Although we might not want to subscribe to the alternate ('materialist') fallacy of economic determinism either, it is important to acknowledge the influence of social, political and economic structures in the perpetuation, transformation and displacement of those views of nature which are conveyed by the texts of culture. As Carolyn Merchant and others have demonstrated, the Baconian reinterpretation of Providence, in conjunction with the mechanistic and atomistic view of nature that came to prominence in the seventeenth century, proved highly congenial to the laissez-faire mercantile capitalism, and associated colonialist ventures, that took off in northwestern Europe at the time.[7] These socio-economic developments might not have *generated* the new conception of Nature as totally knowable, manipulable, and predestined to be conquered and transformed by man, but they almost certainly *guaranteed the success* of this view as a dominant paradigm in the modern era.

REFRAMING THE TEXT

And yet, a consideration of social context alone cannot produce a fully ecological reading of cultural texts and traditions. Here too, White's brief article is instructive. A critique of capitalism is notably absent from his account. However, White's argument is in another respect profoundly materialist. For the somewhat aggressive interpretation of Genesis that emerges in the West is in his view connected, albeit indirectly, with something no less material than the nature of northern European soils. Unlike the lighter soils of the Mediterranean region, these are typically heavy and sticky, necessitating the use of a correspondingly heavy iron plough in farming the land effectively. Such a plough, 'equipped with a vertical knife to cut the line of the furrow, a horizontal share to slice under the sod, and a moldboard to turn it over' (White, 1996, 8) appeared in northern Europe towards the end of the seventh century. Whereas the older wooden plough merely scratched the surface of the soil, the new plough, which required eight oxen to pull it, 'attacked the land with such violence that cross plowing was not needed, and fields tended to be shaped in long strips' (White, 1996, 8). Intriguingly, within about fifty years of the development of this plough, which, as White stresses, is unique to northern Europe, a change can be noted in the western illustrated calendars. In place of the old passive personifications of the seasons, the 'new Frankish calendars [. . .] show men coercing the world around them – plowing, harvesting, chopping trees, butchering pigs' (White, 1996, 8). The burden of these images, in White's view, is that 'Man and nature are two things, and man is master' (White, 1996, 8).

Whether or not the connections that White makes between soils, ploughs, calendars, biblical interpretation and, ultimately, industrial modernity can be substantiated, his introduction of the earth as a *player* in his historical narrative is methodologically and philosophically significant. For White, as for subsequent ecocritics and environmental historians, the natural world is no longer a passive recipient of human interventions and projections but an active participant in the formation and transformation of human culture and society. As Aldo Leopold observed in 1949, many historical events, 'hitherto explained solely in terms of human enterprise, were actually biotic interactions between people and land', the outcome of which was determined as much by the character of the land as by the culture and character of its human occupants (Leopold, 1998, 89). Transposed to literary studies, it is clear that this principle necessitates a radical shift in the way in which texts are interpreted and contextualized. This is the second way in which ecocriticism recasts the canon, and it demands of the critic an acquaintance with new areas of knowledge and understanding. Whereas, in the past, literary critics might have leant on history, philosophy or the social sciences in framing their readings of particular texts, ecocritics need to draw also on geography, ecology and other natural sciences.

A striking example of this procedure is provided by Jonathan Bate (1996), when he rereads Byron's apocalyptic poem 'Darkness' (1816), together with Keats's idyllic ode 'To Autumn' (1819), against meteorological records for the places and time periods in which these texts were written. Pitting himself against the literary critical convention of reading apocalyptic writing such as Byron's either intertextually, with reference to earlier apocalyptic writing, or as a product of imagination bearing a largely metaphoric relation to the world beyond the page, Bate explores what happens if Byron's image of a darkened earth is taken literally. This leads him to the discovery that the highly inclement weather conditions described by Byron in his letters of the time, and confirmed by the meteorological records, can be traced to the eruption in 1815 of the Tambora volcano in Indonesia. This huge eruption caused an estimated 80,000 deaths locally, and lowered global temperatures for three years, leading to failed harvests, food riots and increased respiratory problems as far away as Europe. Bate's ecocritical strategy of foregrounding the role of the natural environment in the genesis of this text is in fact entirely in keeping with the perspective of the poem itself, which dramatizes the potentially catastrophic consequences of a dramatic change in the natural environment: in this case, the loss of the life-giving rays of the sun. Read in this meteorological context, 'To Autumn' also appears in a different light. Keats's pastoral idyll was written in the autumn following the first good summer since 1815, at a time when clear air and warm weather was especially important to its consumptive author. Far from being an escapist fantasy, this is in Bate's view a valuable 'meditation on how human culture can only function through links and reciprocal relations with nature' (Bate, 1996, 440).

As Karl Kroeber (1994) has observed, the literary critical preoccupations and disputations of the 1960s, 1970s and 1980s, appear in retrospect to owe much to the ideological context of the Cold War. Focusing on questions of human creativity, human agency and human social relations, 'Cold War criticism' can also be seen to perpetuate that binary opposition of the human to the non-human, culture to nature, which has a long history in western rationalism. By contrast, 'Global Warming criticism', as Bate terms his new approach, attends to the inextricability of culture and nature, the primary sign of which he considers to be the weather (Bate, 1996, 439). Informed not only by meteorology and ecology, but also by the new science of non-linear dynamic systems popularized as 'Chaos Theory', Global Warming criticism presupposes a natural world which can no longer be thought of as passive, orderly and compliant, but which is rather volatile, unpredictable and responsive to our interventions in ways that we can neither foresee nor control. Acknowledging the ecologically embedded, embodied and hence vulnerable nature of human existence, Global Warming criticism privileges those texts which can, as Bate puts it, enable us to 'think fragility' (Bate, 1996, 447). Allied to an ethos of respect towards the natural world, this new critical paradigm has begun to generate its own counter-canon of literary texts which are seen to model a more ecologically sustainable mode of being and dwelling in the world than that which has predominated in the lived reality of the modern era.

REVALUING NATURE WRITING

Environmentalists, not unlike Gramscian Marxists, tend to be pessimists of the intellect and optimists of the heart. No matter how grim the statistics on the degradation of soil, air and water, on the loss of biodiversity, on global warming and the depletion of the ozone layer, on rising human population and consumption levels, we continue to wager on the possibility that the extraordinary beauty, diversity and fecundity of the earth can, in some measure, yet be saved, and that we might one day learn to live on this earth more equitably. Buoyed by this leap of faith, we continue to seek for sources of hope: places from which change for the better might be initiated. For environmentally committed literary critics and cultural theorists, attempting to reconcile their love for the more-than-human natural world with their professional engagement with works of human culture, this has meant that critique has often taken a back seat to recuperation. This recuperative impulse was already evident in Meeker, whose critique of tragedy and pastoral is conjoined with a revaluation of comedy and the picaresque. In the ecocriticism of the 1990s, the recuperative predominates even more strongly over the critical. Here it is important to note that in the US especially, ecocriticism to a considerable extent grew out of the study of that hitherto highly marginalized genre, nature writing. Among those who founded the Association for the Study of Literature and the Environment (ASLE) at the 1992 annual meeting of the Western Literature Association, several key players were scholars of nature writing, including ASLE's first president, Scott Slovic, and Cheryl Glotfelty, editor of the first ecocriticism reader and co-founder of *The American Nature Writing Newsletter*, which later became the *ASLE Newsletter*.[8] Nature writing figures prominently in ASLE's official mission, 'to promote the exchange of ideas and information pertaining to literature that considers the relationship between human beings and the natural world', and to encourage 'new nature writing, traditional and innovative scholarly approaches to environmental literature, and interdisciplinary environmental research' (cit. Glotfelty, 1996, xviii).

This revaluation of nature writing, or, somewhat more broadly, 'environmental literature', constitutes the third way in which ecocriticism recasts the canon. According to the checklist provided by Lawrence Buell (1995, 7–8), an environmentally oriented work should display the following characteristics:

1. *The nonhuman environment is present not merely as a framing device but as a presence that begins to suggest that human history is implicated in natural history. [. . .]*
2. *The human interest is not understood to be the only legitimate interest. [. . .]*
3. *Human accountability to the environment is part of the text's ethical framework. [. . .]*
4. *Some sense of the environment as a process rather than as a constant or a given is at least implicit in the text. [. . .]*

While some of these characteristics might be found in particular works in a variety of genres, including prose fiction, lyric poetry and drama, Buell argues that the kind of literature that most consistently manifests most or all of his ecological desiderata is non-fictional nature writing. Buell's landmark study of this neglected genre is centred on the work of Thoreau, especially his classic text *Walden* (1854). Thoreau is the only author of environmental non-fiction to have been admitted to the canon of American literature. Buell nonetheless redefines Thoreau's canonicity by reconnecting the 'order of the text' with the 'order of the body' (Buell, 1995, 373): that is, by restoring flesh-and-blood readers and writers as agents in the world, while nonetheless recognizing that 'perforce they must operate and cooperate within the realm of textuality as a limit condition of their exchange' (Buell, 1995, 384). In order to do this, Buell argues that it is necessary to consider not only the literary and scholarly reception of an author, but also their place in popular imagination and the lived practices that they modelled and inspired. In the case of Thoreau, this includes not only the (increasingly touristic) pilgrimage to Walden, but also countless practical endeavours to find ways of living in closer communion with the natural world. Buell's reading of Thoreau and his reception is not entirely uncritical. However, he concludes by affirming that, 'Thoreau's importance as an environmental saint lies in being remembered, in the affectionate simplicity of public mythmaking, as helping to make the space of nature ethically resonant' (Buell, 1995, 394).

Although Buell, like all ecocritics, is concerned to develop a form of criticism that will ultimately lead us back to the world beyond the page, he is also alert to the ways in which all writing and reading is sustained by a dense mesh of intertexts. Thus he includes a fascinating appendix to his study in which he reconsiders the intertextuality of *Walden* in relation to the many forms of environmental non-fiction that were popular during Thoreau's time: literary almanacs, homilies celebrating the divine in nature, literary regionalism, the picturesque, natural history writing and travel writing. Although some canonical texts are included here, such as Emerson's *Nature* (1836), Buell's inventory highlights the importance of a great number of other texts, which have generally not been valued as literature, from Charles Darwin's *Journal of Researches [. . .] during the Voyage of HMS Beagle* (1839) to Susan Fenimore Cooper's *Rural Hours* (1850). Environmental non-fiction, in Buell's analysis, turns out to be even more 'heteroglossic', in Bakhtin's terms, than the novel.[9] Moreover, Buell's reconsideration of *Walden*'s many-tongued intertexts implies also a revaluation of later environmental non-fiction, such as that of Mary Austin, John Muir, Aldo Leopold, Edward Abbey, Annie Dillard, Terry Tempest Williams and Barry Lopez.

RETURNING TO ROMANTICISM

While much ecocriticism remains devoted to this counter-canon of environmental non-fiction, the revaluation of nature writing has also generated a new perspective on many canonical texts and traditions, including romantic pastoral. This tradition forms another crucial strand in the intertextual mesh of Thoreau's writing. As we have seen, pastoral comes off very badly in Meeker's *Comedy of Survival*, as indeed it tends to in most leftist criticism, especially of the New Historicist variety.[10] It was nonetheless a leading British Marxist critic, Raymond Williams, who initiated the left–green recuperation of romantic pastoral. In his highly nuanced account of the changing fortunes and perceptions of the country and the city from 1973, Williams demonstrates that pastoral is potentially far more than an expression of conservative nostalgia for a lost agrarian past. Thus he begins by observing that pastoral, which first emerged in Hellenistic Greek literature, may well have originated not in the escapist fantasies of an urban elite, but rather in the singing competitions of peasant communities themselves (Williams, 1985, 14). Latin, and to an even greater extent Renaissance and Augustan, pastoral writing did nonetheless undoubtedly tend towards forms of idealization, which elided the realities of rural life from the perspective of the labouring poor. In the 'green language' of romantic neopastoral, however, above all that of early Wordsworth and his younger contemporary John Clare, himself a rural labourer by birth, Williams finds an important locus of resistance to the increasing commodification and degradation of the land, which was then occurring in many parts of England and which is now worldwide. 'The song of the land,' Williams concludes, 'the song of rural labour, the song of delight in the many forms of life with which we all share our physical world, is too important and too moving to be tamely given up, in an embittered betrayal, to the confident enemies of all significant and actual independence and renewal' (Williams, 1985, 271).

Unfortunately, Williams's moving plea for a red-green revaluation of romantic pastoral was largely ignored by Marxist critics in the following decades. Williams's lead has nonetheless been followed by some ecocritics, including the eminent British literary scholar, Jonathan Bate.[11] In his 1991 monograph on Wordsworth, programmatically entitled *Romantic Ecology*, Bate reaffirms the value of romantic pastoral as nature writing. In so doing, he endorses what is probably the dominant non-academic reading of Wordsworth against the New Critical and deconstructionist claim that what Romanticism really valorizes is not nature, but the human imagination and human language. Arguing also against the New Historicist counter-claim that the ideological function of romantic imagination and pastoral was to disguise the exploitative nature of contemporary social relations, Bate repositions Wordsworth in a tradition of environmental consciousness, according to which human well-being is understood to be coordinate with the ecological health of the land. Thus understood, Romantic nature poetry stands in an ambivalent position to earlier pastoral writing, functioning simultaneously as continuation and critique. As Terry Gifford (1999) has argued, romantic poetry is perhaps more accurately termed 'post-pastoral', or even, notably in the case of Blake, 'anti-pastoral'.[12]

The importance of romanticism is explored further by Bate in *The Song of the Earth* (2000). Here, Bate extends his discussion of romantic ecology to a consideration of texts which are less obviously congenial to a sympathetic ecocritical reading, such as Byron's ludic writing of the body in *Don Juan* (1823). In his discussion of a range of later texts, from T. H. Hudson's *Green Mansions* (1904) to the work of the contemporary Australian poet Les Murray, Bate also demonstrates the continuing resonance of romantic 'ecopoetics'. Other ecocritics too have recognized in the romantic tradition a valuable point of departure for rethinking our relations with the earth. Karl Kroeber, for example, acclaimed Wordsworth's 'Home at Grasmere' as a model of 'ecological holiness' as early as 1974, and romanticism also provides the focus for his major work on *Ecological Literary Criticism* (1994). Historians of ecological thought have drawn attention also to the significance of romantic 'natural philosophy' and natural science in the emergence of a post-mechanistic, proto-evolutionary view of nature as a dynamic, autopoietic, unity-in-diversity.[13] And yet the romantic legacy too is a mixed one. Romantic thought undoubtedly overcame the Cartesian dualism of mind and matter by positing human consciousness and creativity as a manifestation of potentials inherent in nature. However, this very naturalization of mind can lend itself to a celebration of *techne* at the expense of *physis*, as in the image of the 'good mine' in Shelley's *Queen Mab* (1813), which embodies a symbiosis of mind and matter that, in Timothy Morton's reading, ultimately confirms the 'omnipotence of mind' (Morton, 1994, 418). Clearly, romantic holism does not always undo the hierarchies embedded in the oppositions that it reconciles. Nor is the romantic affirmation of *physis* in less technologically transformed landscapes entirely unproblematic either. It might be argued that the romantic aestheticization of nature has functioned historically not so much as a potential locus of *resistance* to its industrial exploitation, but rather as *compensation* for it. Under the Modern Constitution, it has been all too easy to move between the consumption of nature as raw material for economic production during the working week, to the consumption of nature as sublime or beautiful on Sundays. Moreover, even within the romantic celebration of natural beauty or sublimity, there is sometimes a transcendental strain, whereby the ultimate source of meaning and value is projected out of this world into a heavenly beyond, the true home for which many a romantic soul, in accordance with centuries of Christian teaching, continues to long.

To draw attention to these problematic elements is not to negate the value of the ecocritical return to romanticism. On the contrary, to the extent that elements of techno-utopianism, compensatory nature consumption and transcendental escapism are still very much with us, such a reconsideration becomes all the more important. On closer analysis, it might appear that in some respects at least, romanticism is part of the problem of modernity. In other respects, however, it could indeed represent a road not taken, to which we might now return in seeking to make our way forward into an alternative (post)modernity. As Greg Garrard has observed, 'we are fast depleting our limited indigenous resources of hope here in the West, and should therefore accept the Romantic offering of sympathy with and confidence in nature' (Garrard, 1998, 129).

RECONNECTING THE SOCIAL AND THE ECOLOGICAL

The romantic affirmation of the ties binding human well-being to a flourishing natural environment finds its critical counterpart in the recognition that 'ecological exploitation is always coordinate with social exploitation' (Bate, 2000, 48). This is the point of departure for much recent ecocriticism, which incorporates a concern with questions of gender, 'race' and class. This kind of eco-social critique is not entirely new. It is, for example, foreshadowed by Rousseau in his 'Discourse on the Origins of Inequality among Men' (1754). Paying close attention to Rousseau's voluminous footnotes to the work of Buffon and other eighteenth-century naturalists, Bate has reinterpreted this text as an early 'green history of the world' (Bate, 2000, 42). According to Rousseau, the progress of civilization in the domination of nature had been achieved at the price of increased social inequality, alienation and military conflict. This analysis is akin to what the German social theorists Theodor Adorno and Max Horkheimer would later term the 'dialectic of enlightenment' ([1944] 1979). By the time when they were writing as Jewish Marxist exiles from Nazi Germany during the Second World War, this dialectic had, they believed, generated a whole new order of barbarism right in the midst of the technologically most advanced civilization in world history.

While Adorno and Horkheimer were primarily concerned with domination on the basis of 'race' and class, they also pointed to certain connections between the domination of women and that of the natural world. The 'marriage of Mind and Nature', which Francis Bacon hoped would be effected by the new science and technology, was, they observed, always patriarchal (Adorno and Horkheimer, 1979, 4). This had implications for women as well as for non-human nature. Because of their close symbolic and to some extent also practical association with nature, namely through the kinds of labour they have traditionally performed, women have been cast either as 'primitive' and potentially 'monstrous', hence part of that nature that was to be mastered by rational man, or as an alluring embodiment of that nature to which rational man simultaneously longs to return. Such connections between the domination of women and nature have been explored more recently in far greater depth and detail by ecofeminist philosophers, historians, sociologists and critics.[14] The first major work of ecologically oriented feminist literary criticism was Annette Kolodny's *The Lay of the Land* from 1975. Here, Kolodny examines the metaphorization of the land as feminine in North American literature. In particular, she draws attention to the conflict between phallic and foetal attitudes towards the feminized landscape, whereby the impulse to penetrate and master the country as a whole has oscillated uneasily with a desire to preserve certain places perceived at once as 'virginal' and 'maternal'. Such privileged places are imaged as sites of (typically masculine) regeneration. This ambivalence, Kolodny suggests, might have its origins in universal aspects of the human psyche, but it is also overdetermined by certain geographical, social and cultural contingencies. The metaphoric feminization of the land is likely to have rather different consequences depending on the place and perception of women in society. In the patriarchal context of North America following white settlement, it has in Kolodny's view contributed to the development of land-use practices that are both contradictory and ultimately unsustainable. The nature and implications of the patriarchal association of women and nature in the work of both men and women writers in America has been explored further by other ecofeminist critics, most notably Louise Westling in *The Green Breast of the New World* (1996).[15] As Westling notes with reference to the work of Donna Haraway, this association has also had implications for the perception and treatment of indigenous peoples (Westling, 1996, 151). Here, ecofeminist and postcolonial concerns intersect.[16]

Another aspect of the exploration of interconnections between nature, gender, 'race' and class, also exemplified by Westling's work, is the consideration of the extent to which those who stand in a different relation to nature from elite males on account of their occupation, social position or cultural traditions might have valuable alternative understandings of the nature–culture complex. This consideration drives much ecocritical work focusing on environmental literature by women, Afro-American, Indian and Chicano authors. None of these heterogeneous groups, it should be emphasized, constitutes a locus of pure difference: all live, to a greater or lesser extent, in more than one world, participating in some aspects of the dominant culture, while nonetheless also having access to certain alternative understandings and practices. Some recent writers perceive this inhabitation of multiple traditions as at once alienating and liberating. One such writer is Gloria Anzaldúa, a 'border woman', who, as she puts it in the Preface to her autobiographical work, *Borderlands/La Frontera* 'grew up between two cultures, the Mexican (with a heavy Indian influence) and the Anglo (as a member of a colonized people in our own territory)' (1987, Preface).[17] As a lesbian ecofeminist Chicana, Anzaldúa is further distanced from the patriarchal and heterosexist elements of the various traditions she inherits. On the other hand, she is also able to draw inspiration from some other aspects of these traditions. Thus, for example, Anzaldúa reappropriates the Toltec Indian earth goddess, Coatlicue, as a model of female divinity and divine immanence, while simultaneously embracing western discourses of personal and collective self-determination. Hybridity is also manifest in *Borderlands* on the level of the written language Anzaldúa uses, which shifts continuously between English, Tex-Mex, northern Mexican dialect, Castilian Spanish and Nahuatl. From an ecocritical perspective, what is particularly valuable in Anzaldúa's work is her interrogation of the patriarchal, capitalist and racist values that have contributed to the ecological destruction of the Rio Grande Valley and the impoverishment of its inhabitants. As Terrell Dixon observes: 'By voicing the damage that the dominant culture visits on those whom it marginalizes', Chicano and Chicana writing such as Anzaldúa's, 'resists those national narratives that privilege metastasizing suburbs and environmentally debilitating consumption, and it emphasizes the lack of environmental justice in them' (1999, 1094). Dixon is among those ecocritics who believe that it is now necessary to turn our ecocritical attention 'from wide open spaces to metropolitan spaces' (Bennett, 2001).[18] If, as is widely anticipated, ever more people come to live in cities in the new millennium, social ecocriticism with an urban focus is also likely to be a growth area in the years to come.

REGROUNDING LANGUAGE

Although, as we have seen, ecocriticism often incorporates questions of social justice, it nonetheless differs from other forms of political critique in one important respect: namely, as a form of advocacy for an other, which is felt to be unable to speak for itself. If, as Gayatri Spivak (1988) has argued, the human subaltern cannot always be heard without the mediation of more privileged supporters, how much more so is this true of the subordinated non-human? This is not to say, however, that nature is entirely silent. Nor, despite all our best efforts at domination, is it truly subordinate (as we are forcefully reminded by every earthquake, volcanic eruption, passing comet and the sheer unpredictability of the weather). The perception that nature has indeed been enslaved is perhaps most readily arrived at by people inhabiting relatively gentle regions with the benefit of air-conditioning, electricity and clean water on tap. Similarly, the view that nature is silent might well say more about our refusal to hear than about nature's inability to communicate. Certainly, this view is not shared within animistic cultures, where, as Christopher Manes observes, human language takes its place alongside, and in communication with, 'the language of birds, the wind, earthworms, wolves, and waterfalls – a world of autonomous speakers whose interests (especially for hunter-gatherer peoples) one ignores at one's peril' (Manes, 1996, 15). In a very different discourse and context, contemporary biologists also testify to the abundance of signifying systems in the natural world. These range from the biological information system of the genetic code itself, through the largely involuntary production of a huge variety of indexical signs by all species of plants and animals, to the possibly intentional deployment of apparently conventional signs by many birds and mammals. More generally, whole ecosystems might be said to be sustained by complex networks of communication and exchange between species and non-biological elements of their environment. As Robert S. Corrington has observed, 'The human process actualises semiotic processes that it did not make and that it did not shape. Our cultural codes, no matter how sophisticated and multi-valued, are what they are by riding on the back of this self-recording nature' (Corrington, 1994, ix).

If, for us, nature has nonetheless fallen silent, this is perhaps because we inhabit an increasingly humanized world as heirs to a cultural tradition within which 'the status of being a speaking subject is jealously guarded as an exclusively human prerogative' (Manes, 1996, 15). This tendency to restrict language to the human sphere might be related to the rise of literacy, whereby language becomes tied to the exclusively human practice of writing. A further shift occurs with the invention of alphabetical writing, when the textual signifier looses all iconic connection to the signified. David Abram has argued that it is above all at this moment that human language and culture appears to emancipate itself from the natural world (Abram, 1997, 102). This liberation is nonetheless to a large extent illusory. Not only is our capacity to speak, write and create culture predicated upon the vastly more ancient and complex signifying systems of non-human nature. The particular languages that we use to communicate in speech and writing themselves bear the trace of the natural environments in which they evolved. 'Language', as Gary Snyder puts it, 'goes two ways' (Snyder, 1995, 174). This can most readily be seen on the level of lexicon. Take, for example, the many words for 'snow' in Inuit languages. This is often cited by semioticians as exemplifying the way language shapes perception. To the ecocritic, however, it also exemplifies the way in which language is shaped by environment. For these verbal distinctions would not have been created in the first place if the well-being and possibly survival of the speakers did not depend upon their ability to recognize the corresponding differences in their snowy environment. Thus, although the relationship between spoken and written signifiers and their signifieds might be arbitrary, the distinctions that they signify are not, or at least not entirely. Nor is the relationship between signifier and signified always arbitrary, as we are reminded by the existence of many onomatopoeic words in most, if not all, natural languages. Some writing systems, too, are mimetic of the world to which they refer through the use of pictographic elements. As Abram points out, even the alphabet, in its original Hebrew form, manifested residually iconic elements, and required the participation of the embodied subject in order for its vowels to be formed through the breath of speech (Abram, 1996, 240–3). Many uses of language also manifest a two-way movement between world and word. In the oral traditions of indigenous peoples, for example, the world created verbally through story, song and ritual, comprises a mnemonic of the physical world in which the speaking community dwells, encoding important messages about how to survive in the land with respect for its wider animal, vegetable, mineral and spiritual community (Abram, 1996, 154–79).[19] Arguably, even the most highly intertextual and imaginative works of modern science fiction ultimately derive their imagery from terrestrial experience of a more-than-human world. Thus, as Jim Cheney puts it, if it's 'language all the way down', then it is also 'world all the way up' (Cheney, 1994, 171).

Jonathan Bate develops a further argument that a specifically literary use of language can reconnect us to the natural world in the final chapter of *The Song of the Earth*. Taking his cue from Heidegger, Bate privileges metrical writing, which, he suggests, 'answers to nature's own rhythms' (Bate, 2000, 76). In a world where nature has been reduced to what Heidegger, in his 'Essay Concerning Technology' (1953) terms 'standing reserve', poetry becomes all the more important in recalling and sustaining a non-instrumental relationship to the world. Poetry, in this view, does not name things in order to make them available for use, but rather in order to disclose their being in language (Bate, 2000, 258). Poetry thus becomes a 'refuge for nature, for the letting be of Being' (Bate, 2000, 264). It does not necessarily do this by explicitly defending nature's 'rights'. The best ecopoetry, in Bate's view, is not overtly political, let alone propagandistic. Rather, poetry becomes 'ecopoietic' simply (or not so simply) through its disclosure within the realm of *logos* of the earth as our *oikos*, or dwelling place. It is in this sense that poetry might be said to be 'the place where we save the earth' (Bate, 2000, 283).

Yet, there remains a certain tension between *logos* and *oikos*, the world of the word and the earth which sustains it, but from which it also departs. The poet *qua* poet, as Bate observes, dwells in the *logos*, rather than in any earthly place (Bate, 2000, 149). Following Heidegger, Bate seeks to protect the *logos* of poetry from the machinations of technological reason. Poetic 'presencing', which discloses nature without 'challenging' it, is said to be opposed to technological 'enframing', which makes 'everything part of a system, thus obliterating the unconcealed being-there of particular things' (Bate, 2000, 255). According to Hegel, however, this is precisely what we do whenever we use language. The particularity of the thing, as he rather drastically puts it in the *Jena System Programme* of 1803/4, is 'annihilated' whenever we subsume it under a designation, the signifying capacity of which is determined by a logic not its own, namely that of the linguistic system (Hegel, 1975, 20). From this perspective, language is itself a system of enframing. Moreover, the specifically poetic use of language to speak of nature is not always innocent of instrumentalizing tendencies, especially if it is oriented primarily towards the elevation of the human soul. This does not mean that we should abandon poetry. But it does mean that we need to be cautious about what we can expect of literary language. Bate himself expresses an important reservation in acknowledging that what is disclosed in poetry is not Being in its fullness, nor even the singular being of particular entities, but only the trace of an experience, which is itself evanescent and always already conditioned to some extent by cultural constructs (Bate, 2000, 281).

While it is important to relocate human language within the wider signifying systems of the more-than-human natural word, it is also necessary to recall that there is more to this world than can ever be disclosed within the frame of human language. We fall back into hubris if we follow Heidegger in claiming that 'only the word grants being to a thing' (Heidegger, 1979, 164; my translation). Other entities in the natural world have their own systems of signification and can get along quite happily without the imposition of human designations. It is rather we who need language, and our own merely human language at that, in order to share understandings about the world as we see it. More specifically, as our world becomes ever more ecologically impoverished and technologically manipulated, we need writers and artists who can draw our attention to the beauty, complexity and potential fragility of the earth, mediating the 'voices' of non-human others, whose being and meaning we can never fully comprehend, and, perhaps, inviting us to join in their heteroglossic song.[20] From this perspective, we need a practice of reading which, in recalling the absence rather than the presence of that which is named in the text, inspires us, in Yves Bonnefoy's words, to 'lift our eyes from the page' (1990). 'It is not within the poet's scope to reestablish presence', Bonnefoy argues, but he or she 'can recall that presence is a possible experience, and he can stir up the need for it, keep open the path that leads to it' (Bonnefoy, 1990, 801). With reference to a sonnet by Mallarmé, Bonnefoy asks: 'How can we read about "forgotten woods" over which "somber winter" passes without going into woods that are our own, where we can either find or lose ourselves?' (Bonnefoy, 1990, 806). To this we might add, if the natural world around us is endangered, how can we read a poetic evocation of another's experience of it, without wanting to restore it as a possible locus of our own experience, since the poem itself cannot do so? Read in this way, ecopoetry may well become a factor in our efforts to 'save the earth', not only through our creative and critical writing, but perhaps in more directly political and practical ways as well.

NOTES TOWARDS A READING OF
WORDSWORTH'S HOME AT GRASMERE

Wordsworth's paean to his Lakeland dwelling-place was to be the first part of the first book of a long philosophical poem entitled *The Recluse*, of which *The Prelude* was the introduction. To his great regret, Wordsworth never completed

The Recluse, and although his major autobiographical poem *The Prelude* was published posthumously in 1850, *Home at Grasmere* only reached the public gaze in 1888, in a 'thin green volume of fifty-six pages bearing no editor's name' (Darlington, 1977, 32). Most critics were initially unenthusiastic about this new addition to Wordsworth's by now increasingly popular and highly regarded published works.[21] Subsequently, however, *Home at Grasmere* has come to be seen as standing 'securely on its own as Wordsworth's triumphant manifesto', as Beth Darlington affirms in introducing her edition of the work (Darlington, 1977, 32). From a contemporary ecocritical perspective, moreover, the choice of green for the cover of the first edition appears inspired. For, as Karl Kroeber recognized back in 1974, this is an exemplary work of ecopoetry (see also Bate, 1991, 102–3).

Until 1888, 'Home at Grasmere' existed in two main versions, one completed in 1806 (Ms. B) and the other in 1832 (Ms. D), in the form of two closely written, home-made notebooks without covers.[22] In view of Wordsworth's sparing use of writing materials and the frugality of his household as a whole, the ecological cost of the initial production of this text (if not its subsequent publication, republication and distribution) appears to have been slight.[23] What qualifies *Home at Grasmere* as a work of environmental literature is nonetheless to be found primarily on the semantic level of the text, whereby Wordsworth explicitly remembers and indeed honours the wider ecological conditions of possibility for his work. The non-human environment certainly figures here as far more than a framing device for the exploration of narrowly human concerns. For the primary purpose of this poem is to render an account of how Wordsworth's life as a poet was enabled by the rural 'retreat' (147), 'this small Abiding-place of many Men' (146), 'the calmest, fairest spot of earth' (73), which he had made his home. Grasmere is nonetheless not presented as a place of delight for the poet (and other human inhabitants) alone. It is celebrated rather as a place where all manner of life, human and otherwise, might flourish, a place which seems even to take pleasure in itself:

> Dear Valley, having in thy face a smile
> Though peaceful, full of gladness. Thou art pleased,
> Pleased with thy crags and woody steeps, thy Lake,
> Its one green Island and its winding shores,
> The multitude of little rocky hills,
> Thy Church and Cottages of mountain stone –
>
> (116–21)

As Wordsworth's reference to the church and cottages reminds us, by the time the poet and his sister Dorothy moved to Grasmere in 1800, the Lake District had long been a cultural landscape, shaped by thousands of years of human habitation. Its potentially treacherous mountain peaks, wooded hillsides, fast-flowing streams and deep lakes were nonetheless perceived by Wordsworth and his contemporaries as retaining something of the wild. Whereas other parts of northern England were caught in the first throes of industrialization, the Lake District was still overwhelmingly rural. Here, as elsewhere in Britain, the enclosure of formerly common land and the shift to a somewhat more intensive and commercialized form of agriculture were beginning to have an impact on the farming community. Among the 'untutored Shepherds' (428) who tended their small flocks on the hills and dales around Grasmere, Wordsworth could nonetheless still find evidence of a way of life and mode of relationship to the land that he knew to be endangered. It is perhaps in part precisely in the face of the changes that were underway elsewhere, and soon to encroach here too, that Wordsworth constructs Grasmere as a 'shelter' (113) and 'last retreat' (147). What Wordsworth appears to value especially about Grasmere, beyond his enjoyment of its lake, wooded hills, green vales and craggy peaks, is the extent to which it embodies the possibility of a reciprocal relationship between humanity and the earth. The 'Cottages of mountain stone' exemplify this reciprocity in that they signal an ethos of respect for that which is given by nature. The local culture of Grasmere is thus seen as having arisen from a process of accommodation to the natural environment of this particular bioregion, which had in turn been moulded by millennia of human habitation.

Wordsworth's Grasmere, however, is no pastoral idyll such as that projected by the idealizing poets of the Augustan age.[24] Although his first experience of the place as a 'roving School-boy' (2), recalled in the third person in the opening stanzas, was positively blissful, nature was not always kind here, as he and Dorothy discovered when they first moved to Grasmere in the middle of an especially harsh winter.[25] Wordsworth's Lakelanders are no 'noble savages' either: 'ribaldry, impiety, or wrath' (344) are not unknown to them, and their lives are shown to be often hard, fraught with personal suffering and economic hardship. This is nonetheless in Wordsworth's assessment still a place where most people can live in relative freedom and modest self-sufficiency,[26] as well as in 'true Community, a genuine frame/Of many into one incorporate' (615–16). Significantly, this is represented as an open community, welcoming strangers, such as Wordsworth himself, 'come from whereso'er you will' (148). It is, moreover, a more than human community, comprising 'a multitude/Human and brute, possessors undisturbed of this Recess, their legislative Hall,/Their Temple, and their glorious Dwelling-place' (621–4). Among the denizens of this wider community, Wordsworth focuses especially on the wild birds that frequent the shores of the lake and dwell in the woods and mountains. Within his more immediate community, he also recalls individual domestic animals, such as 'the small grey horse that bears/The paralytic Man' (505–6) and 'The famous Sheep-dog, first in all the Vale' (510). Moreover, Wordsworth emphasizes that he and his 'happy Band' (663) of family and friends were not alone in their affection for the more than human dimensions of their dwelling-place. Although he acknowledges that the local farming community had a more practical relationship to the land than his own household, whose source of income came from elsewhere, he nonetheless insists that 'not a tree/Sprinkles these little pastures, but the same/ Hath furnished matter for a thought, per-chance/For some one serves as a friend' (441–4).

Wordsworth was himself something of a 'reinhabitant', seeking to develop a sense of belonging in a world that was increasingly characterized by dislocation and alienation.[27] Among the rural inhabitants of Grasmere he nonetheless encountered an older sense of place, incorporating an appreciation of the land as something far more than resource and commodity. Here, the land was still a storied place, traversed by pathways both literal and figurative, and studded with sites of narrative significance; here, the land could still be experienced as a 'nourishing terrain', sustaining its inhabitants both physically and spiritually.[28] Grasmere was thus in Wordsworth's assessment a 'holy place' (277), where it was still possible to live in wholeness: in relationship, that is, with one's fellow men and women, with a richly varied natural world, and with the divine.

Home at Grasmere concludes with Wordsworth's famous poetic mission statement, which was published separately in 1850 as a 'Prospectus' to *The Prelude*. Here he proclaims that his great poetic work was to be a 'spousal verse', celebrating the marriage 'in love and holy passion' of 'the discerning intellect of Man' with 'this goodly universe' (805–10). In this context, the significance of *Home at Grasmere* lies perhaps in its demonstration of how the 'marriage' of the human mind and the more-than-human natural world needs to emerge from an embodied experience in and of place. This poem is thus itself a 'spousal verse', celebrating the marriage of the poet with the place that modelled for him the partnership of humanity and nature, of which he proposed to write in his work.

It is tempting to conclude here. And yet there remains a problem which no contemporary ecocritical reading of this poem should overlook: namely the extent to which taking refuge in 'Grasmere', as it is recalled by Wordsworth in this poem, is for us, if not necessarily for him, to retreat from the pressing issues of the contemporary world in nostalgic reminiscence of a world that we have lost, one that perhaps never even existed in quite the way that it is represented here. Ironically, Grasmere has itself in the meantime been transformed, not least by the growth of tourism, inspired in part by such a nostalgic urge and fuelled, ironically, by Wordsworth's own work.[29] Wordsworth himself nonetheless also provides an indication of how such unproductive nostalgia might be avoided: namely when he calls upon his readers to attend to and value what is good in earthly existence, here and now, 'Dismissing therefore all Arcadian dreams/All golden fancies of the Golden Age,/ The bright array of shadowy thoughts from times/ That were before all time, or are to be/Ere time expire' (625–9). If, for contemporary readers, most of whom live under the 'black sky' (603) of the city, 'by the vast Metropolis immured' (597), Wordsworth's *Home at Grasmere* has itself become an Arcadian dream, then we must endeavour to read it differently: not as a lost idyll, but as embodying an ethos of ecosocial relationship that is more relevant today than ever. *Home at Grasmere* cannot return us to Wordsworth's world. Read ecocritically, it might nonetheless inspire us in the 'greening' of those many and varied places, however urban, where we actually live today, and where we might yet learn to dwell equitably and sustainably in the future.

QUESTIONS FOR FURTHER CONSIDERATION

1. With reference to Buell's third criterion for environmental writing, consider to what extent and how *Home at Grasmere* incorporates an ethos of accountability to the natural environment.
2. With reference to Buell's fourth criterion, consider to what extent the environment is represented as a process, rather than a constant, in this text.
3. The metaphor of the 'marriage' of mind and nature that Wordsworth invokes here was also used by Francis Bacon as a model for science and technology. How does Wordsworth's conception of this 'marriage' differ from Bacon's? Does it seem to be any less patriarchal?
4. What role do class and gender play in Wordsworth's representation of Grasmere?
5. In the final section of *Home at Grasmere* that became the Prospectus to *The Prelude*, Wordsworth affirms the superiority of natural beauty, 'a living Presence of the earth', over artefacts made by humans (795–8). *The Prelude*, however, concludes with the assertion that 'the mind of man becomes/A thousand times more beautiful than the earth' (Wordsworth, 1971, lines 446–8).[30] How would you account for the apparent contradiction between these two statements?
6. In what ways do you think that your response to *Home at Grasmere* is influenced by the ecological and social context in which you yourself live, the place(s) in which you are (or are not) 'at home'?

ANNOTATED BIBLIOGRAPHY

Bate, Jonathan. *The Song of the Earth*. Cambridge, MA: Harvard University Press, 2000. This important book by one of Britain's pre-eminent ecocritics constitutes a sustained reflection on the enduring value of written works of the creative imagination in an era of growing disconnection from, and devastation of, the earth. Beginning with a consideration of the present popularity of Austen and Hardy, Bate proceeds to engage ecocritically with a wide range of literary and philosophical texts, primarily in the romantic tradition, but including also Ovid and Shakespeare, as well as contemporary poets from Australia, America and the West Indies. Bate's hermeneutic is informed by social and environmental history, the sciences of evolutionary biology, ecology and 'chaos theory', German critical theory and phenomenology. It is above all to Heidegger that he owes the lineaments of what he here terms *'ecopoesis'*. This is an eloquent and compelling call to attend to the 'song of the earth', while not forgetting also the wrongs of history.

Buell, Lawrence. *The Environmental Imagination: Thoreau, Nature Writing, and the Formation of American Culture*. Cambridge, MA: Cambridge University Press, 1995. This is probably the most significant work so far published on non-fictional nature writing, which remains a major focus of much ecocritical research, especially in the US. Although Buell's discussion centres on Thoreau's *Walden*, the importance of this book extends well beyond Thoreau scholarship. For in the process of rereading Thoreau, and Thoreau's contribution to the formation of American culture, from an ecological perspective, Buell provides some valuable theoretical and methodological pointers for 'green' literary studies more generally. As Buell notes, 'putting literature under the sign of the natural environment requires some major readjustments in the way serious late twentieth-century readers of literature are taught to read' (144). His book outlines some of the new kinds of questions and approaches that are necessitated within literary studies by the search for more ecocentric ways of imagining our relationship to the earth.

Coupe, Lawrence (ed.). *The Green Studies Reader. From Romanticism to Ecocriticism.* London and New York: Routledge, 2000. This is the second ecocriticism reader, and the first to be published in Britain. It is particularly valuable in that it embeds contemporary ecocritical research and reflection in a longer history of thinking about the relationship between nature and culture from romanticism through to the critique of modernity by twentieth-century writers and philosophers, such as D. H. Lawrence, Adorno and Horkheimer, and Heidegger. The second section on 'Green Theory' provides the basis for a more philosophically reflected ecocriticism by including work by critical theorists such as Kate Soper, Donna Haraway and Lyotard, while the final section provides a good range of examples of practical ecocriticism, including work on popular as well as canonical texts. Coupe's general introduction and introductions to each of the sections provide an excellent guide to the key questions motivating green theory and criticism today.

Glotfelty, Cheryl and Harold Fromm (eds). *The Ecocriticism Reader: Landmarks in Literary Ecology.* Athens, GA: University of Georgia Press, 1996. This is the first general reader in ecocriticism, and remains an excellent point of departure for new-comers to the field. Cheryl Glotfelty's introduction is invaluable in providing a background to the emergence of ecocriticism and an outline of its concerns. As well as including a range of essays from the late 1980s and early 1990s, Glotfelty and Fromm reprint a number of important earlier essays, such as those of Lynn White, William Rueckert, SueEllen Campbell and Joseph Meeker. Unlike Coupe's reader, this has a predominantly North American orientation, and includes contributions by the Native American writers Paula Gunn Allen and Leslie Marmon Silko.

Westling, Louise. *The Green Breast of the New World: Landscape, Gender and American Fiction.* Athens, GA: University of Georgia Press, 1996. Building upon the work of Annette Kolodny, Westling's book makes a major contribution to the flourishing area of feminist ecocriticism. Although her focus, like Buell's, is North American, Westling addresses questions that are of central concern to feminist ecocriticism generally, above all in relation to the highly gendered nature of most cultural constructions of land. Westling follows Max Oelschlaeger (1991) in con-textualizing her readings of nineteenth- and twentieth-century literature in a 'deep history' of changing understandings of nature from prehistoric times through to the present. Westling discusses in depth variations on the trope of land-as-woman in the work of women as well as men writers, focusing on the examples of Emerson, Thoreau, Willa Cather, Hemingway, Faulkner and Eudora Welty. In the final chapter, she also considers the work of Native American writer Louise Erdrich, arguing that if we are going to find new ways of imagining our place on earth, we might need to look outside the dominant European American cultural traditions of the West.

Williams, Raymond. *The Country and the City* [1973]. London: Hogarth Press, 1985. This highly nuanced study of the changing fortunes and perceptions of the countryside and the city by the pre-eminent British Marxist critic of the 1960s and 1970s is today widely valued as a precursor of ecocriticism. Inspired in part by his own experience of growing up in rural Wales and by his resultant dissatisfaction with the urbanist bias of much Marxist thought, Williams here seeks to recuperate the 'song of the land, the song of rural labour, the song of delight in the many forms of life with which we all share our physical world' (271) for a progressive left-green criticism and politics. His revaluation of the 'green language' of Wordsworth and Clare in particular has provided ecocritics such as Bate with an invaluable point of departure for their own more explicitly ecological reconsideration of the legacy of romanticism.

SUPPLEMENTARY BIBLIOGRAPHY

Abram, David. *The Spell of the Sensuous: Perception and Language in a More-than-Human World*. New York: Vintage, 1997.

Abrams, M. H. *Natural Supernaturalism: Tradition and Revolution in Romantic Literature*. New York: Norton, 1973.

Adorno, Theodor and Max Horkheimer. *Dialectic of Enlightenment* [1944], trans. John Cumming. London and New York: Verso, 1979.

Anzaldúa, Gloria. *Borderlands/La Frontera: The New Mestiza*. San Francisco, CA: Aunt Lute, 1987.

Armbruster, Carla and Kathleen Wallace (eds). *Beyond Nature Writing*. Charlottesville, VA: University of Virginia Press, 2000.

Bacon, Francis. *Novum Organum* [1620]. In *Works*, vol. 4, eds James Spedding, Robert Leslie Ellis, and Douglas Devon Heath. London: Longmans Green, 1870.

Bakhtin, M. M. *The Dialogic Imagination: Four Essays by M. M. Bakhtin*, ed. Michael Holquist, trans. Caryl Emerson and M. Holquist. Austin, TX: University of Texas Press, 1981.

Bate, Jonathan. *Romantic Ecology: Wordsworth and the Environmental Tradition*. London and New York: Routledge, 1991.

Bate, Jonathan (ed.). *Green Romanticism*, special issue of *Studies in Romanticism*, 35, 3, Fall 1996.

Bate, Jonathan. 'Living with the Weather'. In *Green Romanticism*, special issue of *Studies in Romanticism*, 35, 3, Fall 1996, 431–48.

Benjamin, Walter. *Illuminations* [1955], ed. and intro. Hannah Arendt, trans. Harry Zohn. London: Fontana, 1973.

Bennett, Michael. 'From Wide Open Spaces to Metropolitan Spaces', *ISLE*, 8, 1, Winter 2001, 31–52.

Bennett, Michael and David Teague (eds). *The Nature of Cities: Ecocriticism and Urban Environments*. Tucson, AZ: University of Arizona Press, 1999.

Bicknell, Peter (ed.). *The Illustrated Wordsworth's Guide to the Lakes*, foreword Alan G. Hill. Exeter: Webb & Bower, 1984.

Boisseau, Michelle. 'Parchment'. In *Poetry*, CLXXV, 3, January 2000, 177. The poem is reprinted by permission of the editor of *Poetry* and with the consent of the author.

Bonnefoy, Yves. 'Lifting our Eyes from the Page', *Critical Inquiry*, 16, Summer 1990, 794–806.

Branch, Michael, Rochelle Johnson, Daniel Peterson and Scott Slovic (eds). *Reading the Earth: New Directions in the Study of Literature and the Environment*. Moscow: University of Idaho Press, 1998.

Campbell, SueEllen. 'The Land and Language of Desire: Where Deep Ecology and Poststructuralism Meet' [1989]. In Glotfelty and Fromm (1996, 124–36).

Carson, Rachel, *Silent Spring* [1962]. London: Penguin, 1982.

Cheney, Jim. 'Nature/Theory/Difference. Ecofeminism and the Reconstruction of Environmental Ethics'. In *Ecological Feminism*, ed. Karen Warren. London and New York: Routledge, 1994, 158–78.

Corrington, Robert S. *Ecstatic Naturalism: Signs of the World*. Bloomington, IN: Indiana University Press, 1994.

Darlington, Beth, Introduction and Appendices to *Home at Grasmere. Part First, Book First of 'The Recluse' by William Wordsworth*. Ithaca, NY: Cornell University Press, 1977.

Dixon, Terrell. Contribution to 'Special Forum on Literatures of the Environment', *PMLA*, 114, 5, October 1999, 1093–4.

Dixon, Terrell (ed.). *City Wilds: Essays and Stories about Urban Nature*. Athens, GA: University of Georgia Press, 2001.

Easlea, Brian. *Liberation and the Aims of Science*. London: Chatto & Windus, 1973.

Elder, John. *Imagining the Earth: Poetry and the Vision of Nature*. Urbana and Chicago, IL: University of Illinois Press, 1985.

Gaard, Greta and Patrick Murphy (eds). *Ecofeminist Literary Criticism: Theory, Interpretation, and Pedagogy*. Champaign, IL: University of Illinois Press, 1998.

Garrard, Greg. 'The Romantics' View of Nature'. In *Spirit of the Environment. Religion, Value and Environmental Concern*, eds David E. Cooper and Joy A. Palmer. London: Routledge, 1998, 113–30.

Gifford, Terry. *Green Voices: Understanding Contemporary Nature Poetry*. Manchester: Manchester University Press, 1995.

Gifford, Terry. *Pastoral*. London and New York: Routledge, 1999.

Harrison, Robert Pogue. *Forests: The Shadow of Civilization*. Chicago, IL: University of Chicago Press, 1992.

Hegel, G. W. F. *Jenaer Systementwürfe I*, eds K. Düsing and H. Kimmerle. In Hegel, *Gesammelte Werke*, V. 6. Hamburg: Felix Meiner, 1975.

Heidegger, Martin. *Unterwegs zur Sprache*, 6th edn. Pfüllingen: Noske, 1979.

Heidegger, Martin. 'The Question Concerning Technology' [1953], trans. William Lovitt. In Heidegger, *Basic Writings*, ed. David Farrell Krell. San Francisco, CA: HarperSanFrancisco, 1993, 311–41.

Kerridge, Richard and Niel Sammells (eds). *Writing the Environment: Ecocriticism and Literature*. London and New York: Zed Books, 1998.

Kerridge, Richard. 'Introduction', in Kerridge and Sammells (1998, 1–9).

Kerridge, Richard. 'Small rooms and the Ecosystem: Environmentalism and De Lillo's White Noise' [1998b]. In Kerridge and Sammells (1998, 182–95).

Kolodny, Annette. *The Lay of the Land*. Chapel Hill, NC: University of Carolina Press, 1975.

Kroeber, Karl. '"Home at Grasmere": Ecological Holiness', *PMLA*, 89, 1, January 1974, 132–41.

Kroeber, Karl. *Ecological Literary Criticism: Romantic Imagining and the Biology of Mind*. New York: Columbia University Press, 1994.

Latour, Bruno. *We Have Never Been Modern*, trans. Catherine Porter. Cambridge, MA: Harvard University Press, 1993.

Leiss, William. *The Domination of Nature*. New York: Brazillier, 1972.

Leopold, Aldo. 'The Land Ethic' [1949]. In *Environmental Philosophy. From Animal Rights to Radical Ecology*, eds Michael E. Zimmerman et al. New York: Prentice Hall, 1998, 87–100.

Liu, Alan. *Wordsworth: The Sense of History*. Stanford, CA: Stanford University Press, 1989.

Lussier, Mark. *Romantic Dynamics: The Poetics of Physicality*. New York: St Martin's Press, 1999.

McGann, Jerome. *The Romantic Ideology: A Critical Investigation*. Chicago, IL: Chicago University Press, 1983.

Manes, Christopher. 'Nature and Silence'. In Glotfelty and Fromm (1996, 15–29).

Marshall, Peter. *Nature's Web. Rethinking Our Place on Earth*. New York: Paragon Books, 1994.

Meeker, Joseph. *The Comedy of Survival: Studies in Literary Ecology*. New York: Scribner's, 1972.

Mellor, Mary. *Feminism and Ecology*. Cambridge: Polity, 1997.

Merchant, Carolyn. *The Death of Nature: Women, Ecology and the Scientific Revolution*. San Francisco, CA: Harper & Row, 1980.

Merchant, Carolyn. *Ecological Revolutions. Nature, Gender and Science in New England*. Chapel Hill, NC: University of Carolina Press, 1989.

Merchant, Carolyn. 'Eve: Nature and Narrative'. In *Earthcare. Women and the Environment*. London and New York: Routledge, 1995, 27–56.

Merleau-Ponty, Maurice. *Phenomenology of Perception*, trans. Colin Smith. London: Routledge & Kegan Paul, 1962.

Mies, Maria and Vandana Shiva. *Ecofeminism*. London: Zed Books, 1993.

Morton, Timothy. *Shelley and the Revolution in Taste: The Body and the Natural World*. Cambridge: Cambridge University Press, 1994.

Murphy, Patrick. *Literature, Nature, and Other: Ecofeminist Critiques*. Albany, NY: State University of New York Press, 1995.

Naess, Arne. 'The Shallow and the Deep, Long-Range Ecology Movement: A Summary'. In *The Deep Ecology Movement: An Introductory Anthology*, eds Alan Drengson and Yuichi Inoue. Berkeley, CA: North Atlantic Books, 1995, 3–10.

Nichols, Ashton. 'The Anxiety of Species: Toward a Romantic Natural History'. *Romantic Circles*, 28, 1997: http://www.dickinson.edu/-nicholsa/Romnat/anxiety.htm (accessed 21 February 2001).

Oelschlaeger, Max. *The Idea of Wilderness: From Prehistory to the Age of Ecology*. New Haven, CT: Yale University Press, 1991.

Plumwood, Val. *Feminism and the Mastery of Nature*. London and New York: Routledge, 1993.

Rigby, Kate. 'Freeing the Phenomena: Goethean Science and the Blindness of Faust', *ISLE*, 7, 2, Summer 2000, 25–42.

Rose, Deborah Bird. *Nourishing Terrains: Australian Aboriginal Views of Landscape and Wilderness*. Canberra: Australian Heritage Commission, 1996.

Rothenberg, David. 'No World but in Things: The Poetry of Arne Naess's Concrete Contents'. In *Beneath the Surface: Critical Essays in the Philosophy of Deep Ecology*, eds Eric Katz, Andrew Light and David Rothenberg. Cambridge, MA: MIT Press, 2000, 151–67.

Rueckert, William. 'Literature and Ecology: An Experiment in Ecocriticism' [1978]. In Glotfelty and Fromm (1996, 105–23).

Salleh, Ariel. *Ecofeminism as Politics: Nature, Marx and the Postmodern*. London: Zed Books, 1997.

Scigaj, Leonard. *Sustainable Poetry: Four American Ecopoets*. Lexington, KY: University Press of Kentucky, 1999.

Slovic, Scott. *Seeking Awareness in American Nature Writing: Henry Thoreau, Annie Dillard, Edward Abbey, Wendell Berry, Barry Lopez*. Salt Lake City, UT: University of Utah Press, 1992.

Slovic, Scott. Contribution to 'Special Forum on Literatures of the Environment', *PMLA*, 114, 5, October 1999, 1102–3.

Snyder, Gary. *A Place in Space: Ethics, Aesthetics and Watersheds*. Washington, DC: Counterpoint, 1995.

Soper, Kate. *What is Nature?* London: Blackwell, 1995.

'Special Forum on Literatures of the Environment', *PMLA*, 114, 5, October 1999, 1089–104.

Spivak, Gayatri Chakravorty. 'Can the Subaltern Speak?' In *Marxism and the Interpretation of Culture*. London: Macmillan, 1988, 271–313.

Thomas, Keith. *Man and the Natural World*. New York: Pantheon, 1983.

White, Lynn. 'The Historical Roots of our Ecologic Crisis' [1967]. In Glotfelty and Fromm (1996, 3–14).

Williams, Raymond. *Keywords: A Vocabulary of Culture and Society*, rev. edn. London: Fontana, 1983.

Wordsworth, William. *The Prelude – A Parallel Text*, ed. J. C. Maxwell. Harmondsworth: Penguin, 1971.

Wordsworth, William. *Home at Grasmere. Part First, Book First of 'The Recluse' by William Wordsworth*, ed. and intro. Beth Darlington. Ithaca, NY: Cornell University Press, 1977.

Žižek, Slavoj. *Looking Awry: An Introduction to Jacques Lacan through Popular Culture*. Cambridge, MA: MIT Press, 1991.

NOTES

1. Shelley's participation in this 'revolution in taste' is explored by Timothy Morton (1994).
2. See in particular Meeker (1972), Kolodny (1975), and Rueckert (1996). Originally published in 1978, Rueckert's article includes the coinage 'ecocriticism'.
3. See, for example, the 'Special Forum on Literatures of the Environment' in *PMLA*, 114, 5, October 1999.
4. On the relationship between poststructuralism and ecophilosophy, see Soper (1995). The first ecocritic to seek a point of connection between poststructuralism and Deep Ecology was SueEllen Campbell in an article from 1989 (Campbell, 1996). See also Cheney (1994).
5. The following edited collections give a sense of the scope and diversity of contemporary ecocritical work: Glotfelty and Fromm (1996), Kerridge and Sammells (1998), Branch et al. (1998), Armbruster and Wallace (2000) and Coupe (2000).
6. In his *Novum Organum*, for example, Bacon proposed that through the arts and sciences, humanity could 'recover that right over nature which belongs to it by divine bequest', and should endeavour 'to establish and extend the power and dominion of the human race itself over the [entire] earth' (Bacon, 1870, 114–15).
7. In addition to Merchant (1980), see also the earlier studies of Leiss (1972) and Easlea (1973).
8. In 1995 Scott Slovic also took over from Patrick Murphy as the editor of the main ecocriticism journal, *Interdisciplinary Studies in Literature and Environment* (*ISLE*).
9. The term 'heteroglossia' was used by the Russian literary theorist Mikhail Bakhtin to describe the many voices that vie with one another in the form of the novel, and, more generally, the inevitably contextual and intertextual nature of meaning (Bakhtin, 1981, 259–422 and 428). See also Murphy (1995), for an ecofeminist deployment of Bakhtinian dialogics.
10. See, for example, McGann (1983) and Liu (1989), and Bate's critique of the New Historicist take on Wordsworth (Bate, 1991, 1–6).
11. It should also be noted that a segment from Williams's chapter on romanticism from *The Country and the City* is included in Laurence Coupe's *Green Studies Reader* (2000, 50–8).
12. For an extended ecocritical treatment of Blake, see Lussier (1999).
13. For example, Marshall (1994) devotes three chapters to romanticism in his history of environmental thought. On romantic natural history, see also Ashton Nichols (1997) and my own article on Goethean science (Rigby, 2000).
14. On ecofeminist philosophy, see, for example Plumwood (1993). For a historical perspective, see Merchant (1980 and 1989). On ecofeminist social and political theory, see Mies and Shiva (1993), Mellor (1997) and Salleh (1997).
15. On feminist ecocriticism, see also Murphy (1995) and Gaard and Murphy (1998).
16. See also Merchant (1995).
17. Further discussion of Anzaldúa is to be found in Chapter 3 in this volume by Hedrick and King.
18. See also Bennett and Teague (1999) and Dixon (2001).
19. Abram's ecophilosophy is based, in part, on his reading of the phenomenology of Merleau-Ponty, whose work is of considerable interest to ecocritics because of his emphasis on corporeality and the 'flesh of the world'. See Merleau-Ponty (1962). For an ecocritical deployment of Merleau-Ponty's phenomenology, see, for example, Scigaj (1999).
20. An ecopoetics of 'joining in' rather than 'speaking for' has been proposed by David Rothenberg (2000), who is himself a musician who delights in playing along with the diverse and unpredictable sounds of the more-than-human world.

21. See Darlington (1977, 460–2). Darlington nonetheless praises the insight of one critic, William Minto, who in a review of 1889 ranks *Home at Grasmere* as among the finest of Wordsworth's works.
22. This discussion follows Ms. D in the Cornell edition (1977); references to the text are given according to line numbers.
23. It should nonetheless be recalled that the material cost of production was also borne by Wordsworth's long-suffering wife Mary, who transcribed all of Ms. D and a substantial part of Ms. B. Wordsworth's devoted sister Dorothy also transcribed part of the latter, as did William himself.
24. Wordsworth differentiates his depictions of the Lake District from earlier pastoral writing in his allusion to 'The idle breath of softest pipe attuned/To pastoral fancies' (406–6).
25. It is very striking that Wordsworth follows his celebration of Grasmere as a place of 'Perfect Contentment, Unity entire' (151) with the sobering words, 'Bleak season was it, turbulent and bleak,/When hitherward we journeyed, side by side' (152–3). This first bleak winter is subsequently construed as a test of their resolve to settle there (182).
26. Wordsworth reassures us that, 'Labour here preserves/His rosy face, a Servant only here/Of the fire-side or of the open field,/A Freeman, therefore sound and unimpaired;/That extreme penury is here unknown,/And cold and hunger's abject wretchedness,/Mortal to body and the heaven-born mind; That they who want are not too great a weight/For those who can relieve' (359–67). Marxist critics might rightly object that Wordsworth is glossing over the existence of certain forms of social domination and exploitation here. However, it would doubtless be a category error to expect a detailed sociological analysis from what is essentially a song of praise.
27. On reinhabitation, see, for example, Elder (1985, 40–74).
28. I take this phrase from the title of anthropologist Deborah Bird Rose's book *Nourishing Terrains* (1996).
29. In addition to his many poetic works celebrating life in the Lake District, Wordsworth also wrote an extremely popular *Guide through the District of the Lakes* (1835; Bicknell, 1984). Wordsworth was nonetheless very concerned about the likely impact of mass tourism, which he feared would be encouraged by the projected construction of a railway linking the Lake District to the growing urban centre of Liverpool. See his letters to the *Morning Post* (1844) in Bicknell (1984, 185–98). For an ecocritical discussion of the *Guide* and Wordsworth's objections to the railway, see Bate (1991, 41–52).
30. This quote comes from the version of 1805–6 (Wordsworth, 1971).

CHAPTER 8

SPATIAL CRITICISM: CRITICAL GEOGRAPHY, SPACE, PLACE AND TEXTUALITY

Phillip E. Wegner

> All the world's a stage,
> And all the men and women merely players.
> They have their exits and their entrances,
> And one man in his time plays many parts,
> His acts being seven ages.
> *As You Like It* (II. vii. ll.139–43)

These celebrated lines from William Shakespeare's *As You Like It* powerfully illustrate some of the dominant assumptions about space and spatiality that come to prevail in the histories of western modernity: space is seen as an empty container, of very little interest in and of itself, within which unfolds the real drama, that of history and human passions. Michel Foucault similarly notes in an often cited 1976 interview the 'devaluation of space' that had prevailed for 'generations of intellectuals': 'Space was treated as the dead, the fixed, the undialectical, the immobile. Time, on the contrary, was richness, fecundity, life, dialectic.' Foucault goes on to argue:

> For all those who confuse history with the old schemas of evolution, living continuity, organic development, the progress of consciousness or the project of existence, the use of spatial terms seems to have an air of an anti-history. If one started to talk in terms of space that meant one was hostile to time. (Foucault, 1980, 70)

The Australian historian Paul Carter, even more directly echoing Shakespeare's lines, describes the dominant narrative mode of what he calls modernity's 'imperial history' as one 'which reduces space to a stage, that pays attention to events unfolding in time alone . . . Rather than focus on the *intentional* world of historical individuals, the world of active, spatial choices, empirical history of this kind has as its focus facts which, in a sense, come after the event' (Carter, 1987, xvi).

This privileging of temporality and history over space has its literary analogue in a critical tradition that, especially beginning in the latter part of the nineteenth century with writers like Henry James, celebrates the portrayal of the complex psychology of characters as the highest achievement of narrative art. Characters are fundamentally temporal constructs that unfold in a space, or 'setting', which, once established, seems to remain constant. Space is thus once again treated as the 'stage' upon which the drama of character development unfolds, and setting in such a tradition is viewed as distinctly secondary in importance to character. Moreover, in the increasing interiorization that occurs in certain strands of modernist fiction – which, in turn, have a marked influence on how we read earlier literary works as well – any concern with setting or space outside that of the monadic consciousness seems to all but vanish. This occurs in a moment that, as the geographer Edward Soja points out in his ground-breaking study, *Postmodern Geographies: The Reassertion of Space in Critical Social Theory* (1989), not coincidentally also saw the subordination of the spatial problematic in social theory (31–5).

It is precisely these presuppositions that have been increasingly called into question over the last twenty-five years by an emerging interdisciplinary formation centred on the problematics of 'space', 'place' and 'cultural geography'. Contributors to this vast and multiform research project might be numbered to include, among others, social theorists and historians like Arjun Appadurai, Carter, Michel de Certeau, Mike Davis, Foucault, Anthony Giddens, Henri Lefebvre and Saskia Sassen; geographers Derek Gregory, David Harvey, Doreen Massey, Neil Smith, Soja and Yi-Fu Tuan; architects Rem Koolhaas, Manfredo Tafuri and Bernard Tschumi; anthropologists James Clifford, Allen Feldman and Paul Rabinow; philosophers Edward S. Casey, Giles Deleuze, Jacques Derrida and Elisabeth Grosz; art critics Victor Burgin and T. J. Clark; and literary and cultural critics, bell hooks, Fredric Jameson, Caren Kaplan, Louis Marin, Meaghan Morris, Kristin Ross, Edward Said and Raymond Williams. There has also been a return to work of earlier thinkers who each in their own way took up what were in their own time unfashionable spatial questions: this would include the discussions of embodiment, 'world', enframement, and dwelling in Martin Heidegger's *Being and Time* and other later essays; the explorations of the relationships between northern and southern Italy in a moment of dramatic social and cultural modernization found in Antonio Gramsci's *Prison Notebooks*; the lyrical spatial phenomenology of Gaston Bachelard's *The Poetics of Space*; the detailed analysis of an array of the novelistic 'chronotopes', 'the intrinsic connectedness of temporal and spatial relationships that are artistically expressed in literature', offered by Mikhail M.

Bakhtin (1981, 84); and the stunning mappings of the spaces and cultural flows of nineteenth-century Paris found in Walter Benjamin's fragmentary and incomplete *Passagen-werk (Arcades Project)*.

What links the diverse projects of these various thinkers together is a common challenge to the Enlightenment and Cartesian notion of space as an objective homogeneous extension (*res extensa*), distinct from the subject (*res cogitans*), and the Kantian concept of space as an empty container in which human activities unfold. Against such presuppositions, the work of these diverse thinkers show in a stunning variety of ways how space itself is both a *production*, shaped through a diverse range of social processes and human interventions, and a *force* that, in turn, influences, directs and delimits possibilities of action and ways of human being in the world. Western modernity, as Soja emphasizes, is thus to be reconceived as both a historical *and* a geographical-spatial project, a continuous dissolution and reorganization of the environments, including our bodies, that we all inhabit.

This new attention to the productions of space has entered into literary studies from a number of different directions: from Marxism and critical theory, space being, as Soja and Harvey effectively demonstrate, already a central concern in much of Marx's own work; from colonial and postcolonial studies, which brought into focus the effects of European domination over space and the migrations and interactions of different cultures and populations; from feminism and gender studies, where the issues of the body, sexuality and the embodiment of the subject have long been of central importance; from popular culture and genre studies, where the specific practices of non-canonical cultural forms have been brought into sharper focus; and, as the list above suggests, from a rich and growing conversation with work being done in a broad range of other disciplines.

Two of the thinkers who have contributed the most to this revival of interest in the role of space in the projects of western modernity are the French social theorists, Henri Lefebvre and Michel Foucault. Lefebvre's major work of spatial theorization, *The Production of Space* (1974) – first translated into English in 1991 – has had a dramatic impact on work being done in a wide range of disciplines, ranging from urbanism, architecture, and social theory to literary and cultural studies. In his rich and brilliant example of a spatial dialectical thinking, Lefebvre definitively rejects the older 'representation' of space as 'a preexisting void, endowed with formal properties alone . . . a container waiting to be filled by a content – i.e. matter, or bodies' (1991, 170). Instead, he shows in great detail how the emergence and development of capitalist modernity occurs through a particular '(social) production of (social) space' – that is, a space that is fundamentally produced by and through human actions, and which is thus 'constituted neither by a collection of things or an aggregate of (sensory) data, nor by a void packed like a parcel with various contents, and . . . it is irreducible to a "form" imposed upon phenomena, upon things, upon physical materiality' (Lefebvre, 1991, 26–7). '(Social) space', Lefebvre maintains, 'is not a thing among other things, nor a product among other products: rather, it subsumes things produced, and encompasses their interrelationships in their coexistence and simultaneity – their (relative) order and/or (relative) disorder' (1991, 73). For Lefebvre, such a space is a deeply historical one, its moments of apparent stability short-lived and contingent at best: indeed, Lefebvre suggests that one of the great temptations produced by the Enlightenment conceptualization of space as a static construct is that we think of it as a reified thing rather than as an open-ended, conflicted and contradictory *process*, a process in which we as agents continuously intervene.

Moreover, Lefebvre argues that such a space is itself never constituted as a singularity, as other traditions of spatial thought might suggest, such as those of structuralism and phenomenology with their respective focus on the subjective and objective dimensions of space. Instead, Lefebvre develops a 'concrete abstract' tripartite model of space that attempts at once to take account of and draw into a coherent ensemble these various other dimensions. Lefebvre argues that any socially produced historical space is constituted by a dialectically interwoven matrix of what he calls 'spatial practices', 'representations of space' and 'spaces of representation', each allied with a specific cognitive mode through which we 're-present' it to ourselves: respectively, the domains of the 'perceived', the 'conceived' and the 'lived' (1991, 33–46). The first of his three 'levels' of space pertains to the most abstract processes of social production, reproduction, cohesion and structuration, and hence bears a striking resemblance to the concerns of the various structuralisms whose 'perceptual' apparatus takes on the abstract conceptual systematicity of a science. The third set of terms refers, on the other hand, to the space of the embodied individual's cultural experience and the signs, images, forms and symbols that constitute it: it is this level of space that has been mapped so thoroughly by phenomenology, whose emphasis on the individual's 'lived' existential experience of space resonates with that found in this dimension of Lefebvre's work. The middle terms, those of the representations of space or the realm of the conceived, point towards what we more conventionally think as 'space' proper, mediating between and drawing all three of the levels together into a coherent ensemble. Of the social and cultural practices that constitute this middle dimension of space, Lefebvre writes, 'conceptualized space, the space of scientists, planners, urbanists, technocratic subdividers and social engineers, as of a certain type of artist with a scientific bent – all of whom identify what is lived and what is perceived with what is conceived' (1991, 38).

Thus, bringing together the very different projects of structural and phenomenological criticism, Lefebvre's work also offers a powerful rejoinder to the tangential textualization of the world, or what he calls the 'generalization of the concept of mental space', at play in certain strands of structuralist, semiotic and post-structuralist theory (1991, 3). Lefebvre links these theorizations to a growing predominance in modern times of the 'visual', which, he argues, 'has increasingly taken precedence over elements of thought and action deriving from other senses' (1991, 139). This in turn is connected to the increasingly global trend in the history of capitalism towards what Lefebvre names 'abstract space' – a homogeneity on the level of spatial practices and fragmentation and isolation on the level of representations of space, or 'lived' experience (1991, 285–91). This latter formulation also has had a marked impact on the development in the last twenty-five years of the theorization of 'postmodernism', especially in the work of thinkers such as Harvey and Fredric Jameson. And in another important recent refinement of Lefebvre's project, Neil Smith eloquently argues for the necessity, when reading any particular cultural phenomenon, of taking into account its simultaneous embeddedness in a number of different 'nested' spatial contexts: body, home, community, city, region, nation and globe. Smith notes, 'By setting boundaries, scale can be constructed as a means of constraint and exclusion, a means of imposing identity, but a politics of scale can also become a weapon of expansion and inclusion, a means of enlarging identity' (1993, 114).

While Lefebvre's work offers a powerful mechanism for thinking through the spatial dimensions of modern society and culture, Michel Foucault, especially in his central text of the mid-1970s, *Discipline and Punish: The Birth of the Prison* (1975), presents a meticulous genealogical history of the spatial transformations that give rise to our modern world. Foucault's text is written very much in the spirit of earlier critical histories of modernity such as those offered by Max Weber and Theodor Adorno; however, Foucault's great achievement is to give this narrative a distinctively spatial turn. Foucault opens his examination by focusing a heightened attention upon the body, and in particular 'the way in which the body itself is invested by power relations' (1977, 24). Foucault announces that 'Our society is one not of spectacle, but of surveillance', and throughout his text he meticulously reconstructs the genealogy of such a modern form of power (1977, 217).

In the moment of the Absolutist monarch, Foucault argues, the individual body becomes the subject of a highly public 'theatre' of punishment that is located in a specific ritualized space, still distant from everyday life. However, precisely because this system is such a public and spectacular one, it is deeply unstable, open to a dramatic reversal at the hands of those who are its intended subjects. (A wonderful example of such an older system of power, as well as its potential for transgressive, carnivalesque inversion, is brilliantly portrayed in the opening chapters of Walter Scott's *The Heart of Mid-Lothian*.) Thus, in place of this older logic of power there gradually emerges a new system in which every body finds itself located in 'a great enclosed, complex, and hierarchical structure', and subject to a continuous regime of surveillance and manipulation (1977, 115). A whole series of operations, which Foucault names 'discipline' – 'instruments, techniques, procedures, levels of application, targets' (1977, 215) – arise with the aim of producing 'normal' subjects as well as marking out a whole finely graduated realm of deviancies: 'Thus discipline produces subjected and practised bodies, "docile" bodies' (1977, 138).

The model and most complete realization of this new kind of machinery of power are to be found in Jeremy Bentham's ideal of prison architecture, the panopticon. Within this structure, the individual prisoner is placed in a state of permanent 'visibility', subject to the unseen gaze of authority. Never knowing when they are under observation, these subjects come to internalize the self-policing demanded of them. Crucially, Foucault maintains that

> the Panopticon must not be understood as a dream building: it is the diagram of a mechanism of power reduced to its ideal form; its functioning, abstracted from any obstacle, resistance or friction, must be represented as a pure architectural and optical system: it is in fact a figure of political technology that may and must be detached from any particular use.
>
> It is polyvalent in its applications; it serves to reform prisoners, but also to treat patients, to instruct schoolchildren, to confine the insane, to supervise workers, to put beggars and idlers to work. It is a type of location of bodies in space, of distribution of individuals in relation to one another, of hierarchical organization, of disposition of centres and channels of power, of definition of the instruments and modes of intervention of power, which can be implemented in hospitals, workshops, schools, prisons. (1977, 205)

'Is it surprising', Foucault later asks, 'that prisons resemble factories, schools, barracks, hospitals, which all resemble prisons?' (1977, 228) As such a technology gets generalized across the social space, it generates a veritable 'carceral network' which 'in its compact or disseminated forms, with its systems of insertion, distribution, surveillance, observation, has been the greatest support, in modern society, of the normalizing power' (1977, 304).

The influence of Foucault's work across a wide range of disciplines has been profound. In terms of literary scholarship, his influence has been especially evident in work in the so-called 'New Historicism', Foucault's model of the panopticon being one of the inspirations, for example, of Stephen Greenblatt's brilliant re-reading of Thomas More's *Utopia* in his book *Renaissance Self-Fashioning From More to Shakespeare* (1980). Similarly, the questions concerning the production of the body and subjectivity raised by Foucault have been developed in fascinating and important new ways by recent feminist theorists. Elizabeth Grosz, to take only one example, argues that while it is important to think of questions of subjectivity in corporeal rather than disembodied conscious terms, the investigation needs to move even further: 'It is not enough to reformulate the body in non-dualist and non-essentialist terms. It must also be reconceived in specifically *sexed* terms. Bodies are never simply *human* bodies or *social* bodies' (1995, 84). Finally, one of the most interesting extensions of Foucault's investigation of social space can be found in the US anthropologist Paul Rabinow's *French Modern: Norms and Forms of the Social Environment* (1989). This rich and wide-ranging genealogical history focuses upon how a diverse group of nineteenth-century intellectuals, working in a number of distinct fields, all came to understand the ways in which 'norms' – proper behaviours in, inhabitations of and movements through the world – are shaped by various spatial 'forms' – architectural, urbanistic, national and so forth. Emphasizing the deeply spatial nature of the revolutions of modernity, Rabinow investigates transformations in nineteenth-century architectural and urban practices, among a diverse range of linked fields, in order to trace out a developing programme for using 'the planned city as a regulator of modern society' (1989, 12).

While Rabinow diverges from Foucault in his greater willingness to consider the progressive possibilities of certain productions of modern spatiality, both thinkers acknowledge that if social and cultural spaces, including the body, are indeed the product of human actions, then there is the possibility of our reconstituting human spaces, and hence human being-in-the-world as well. Space then is conceived not only as the *site* of politics, conflict and struggle, but also the very thing being fought over. This approach too suggests a link between contemporary critical examinations of space and spatiality and the great transformative architectural and urban planning programmes developed by Ebenezer Howard, Tony Ganier, the Bauhaus, Le Corbusier, Frank Lloyd Wright and others in the moment of cultural modernism – a moment that also saw in the realm of the visual arts the great widespread challenge of perspectivalism that had dominated both Western art and thought from the Italian Renaissance onwards. Not surprisingly, a good deal of the contemporary projects for reconstructing social space also arise from within the discourses of architecture and urbanism: these include, for example, Rem Koolhaas's 'retroactive manifesto' for the unfulfilled project he labels Manhattanism (1994, 9–10), and Jacques Derrida's provocative collaborations with architect Peter Eisenman on spaces to be produced for Bernard Tschumi's innovative *Parc de la Villette* in Paris. Derrida has described the latter project as involving a deconstruction of some of the fundamental assumptions that have underwritten western architectural discourse and practice: 'for instance, the hegemony of the aesthetic, of beauty, the hegemony of usefulness, of functionality, of living, of dwelling'. However, this is only part of the project of a deconstructive architecture, and Derrida goes on to argue that, 'then you have to *reinscribe* those motifs within the work. You can't (or you shouldn't) simply dismiss those values of dwelling, functionality, beauty and so on. You have to construct, so to speak, a new space and a new form, to shape a new way of building in which those motifs or values are reinscribed, having meanwhile lost their external hegemony' (Papadakis et al., 1989, 73).

There also has been in recent years more and more attention given to the ways that diverse subaltern publics are able to 'divert and reappropriate' dominated spaces. Such lessons are to be found, for example, in Michel de Certeau's celebrated evocation of a transgressive 'walking in the city' effected by the very people who inhabit it (1984, 91–110); in Meaghan Morris's brilliant reading of the innovative spatial project to be discovered in the Australian 'documentary' film, *A Spire* (1998, 123–57); in Judith Butler's examination of the new communal spaces figured in the film *Paris is Burning* (1993, 121–40); and in Allan Feldman's stunning analysis of the 'radical deconstruction and reassemblage of the body' that occurs in the IRA Hunger Strike of 1981 (1991, 204). These practices are of 'great significance', Lefebvre notes, 'for they teach us much about the production of new spaces' (1991, 167); however, as Lefebvre goes on to note, and indeed as Derrida and many of these other thinkers also point out, such moves must be considered only opening gestures, 'which can call but a temporary halt to domination' (1991, 168). The real aim always remains the 'production' of new kinds of spaces.

The conceptual reorientations that Lefebvre, Foucault and these other thinkers offer also promise to transform literary and cultural analysis in a number of different ways. First, their work has helped to foster an increasing attention to the representation of space within literary and other cultural texts and to the ways that an attention to spatial questions transform how we think about literary history. Such a dual project is already evident in Raymond Williams's classic survey of modern British literature, *The Country and the City* (1973). Williams examines the changing 'structures of feeling' concerning the relationships between the 'city' and the 'country', as well as the transformations and expansions that occur in the very definition of each of these inseparable conceptual poles, as these are negotiated in the tradition of modern British literature, a tradition he traces from the country-house poems of the sixteenth century up through the global literatures of the present day. Williams argues for a special significance of the English experience in this narrative, 'in that one of the decisive transformations, in the relations between country and city, occurred there very early and with a thoroughness which is still in some ways unapproached' – he is referring here to the British industrial revolution (1973, 2). Williams is especially sensitive to the ways literary and cultural texts *reflect* changes in actual spatial practices, those initiated by these processes of modernization, and to these works' sensitivity and capacity to register changing sensibilities before they enter fully into explicit public discourse.

More recently, a similar kind of investigation continues in such groundbreaking works as Kristin Ross's *The Emergence of Social Space: Rimbaud and the Paris Commune* (1988), a study drawing directly upon Lefebvre's work and looking at the ways Arthur Rimbaud's poetry, as well as a host of other cultural productions, respond to and draw upon both the expansion of French imperial power and the revolutionary urban spatial possibilities illuminated in the short-lived 1871 Paris Commune; Edward Said's magisterial *Culture and Imperialism* (1993), a text that argues for the importance of a careful attention to the 'geographical notation, the theoretical mapping and charting of territory that underlies Western fiction, historical writing, and philosophical discourse' (1993, 58); and Franco Moretti's *Atlas of the European Novel, 1800–1900* (1998), an examination of the productions of fictional space that occur within

European novels of the nineteenth century, and of the circulation and distribution of various novelistic productions across the 'real' space of Europe and the globe.

At the same time, an attention to spatial concerns further calls into question the very constitution of the literary canon as it helps us to become more sensitive to the different kinds of work that are performed by various literary genres, modes and other forms of textuality. This kind of reorientation is perhaps nowhere more evident than in the wide-ranging intellectual project of the influential Marxist literary and cultural scholar Fredric Jameson. For example, in his landmark book, *The Political Unconscious* (1981), Jameson contrasts the different representational work performed by the modern novel and the older prose romance. The goal of the romance, Jameson shows us, is to spark in the reader a new awareness of what it means to be-in-the-world by highlighting the *'worldness of world'*, the specific constructedness of the geographies and environments such a reader always already inhabits (1981, 112). Thus, if the novel focuses on 'character', making us aware of and even contributing to the development of a modern centred subjectivity, the romance gives expression to the 'experience' of settings, worlds or spaces. Character, Jameson maintains, thus functions in the romance in a very different way than in the novel: in this older form it serves as a formal 'registering apparatus' whose movements during the course of the narrative action produce a traveller's itinerary of both the 'local intensities' and 'horizons' of the space that the narrative itself calls into being (1981, 112). Jameson uses this rethinking of the work of the romance as the basis for reading the particular narrative operations of texts ranging from the classical chivalric cycles to Stendhal's *The Red and the Black* and Emily Brontë's *Wuthering Heights*.

Jameson has explored similar spatial mapping operations in genres and works as diverse as the *noir* detective fiction of Raymond Chandler, More's *Utopia*, James Joyce's *Ulysses*, the 'national allegory' of Third World literature, the conspiracy film and the great modern form of the prose romance, what H. G. Wells first named 'scientific romance', and what we call today science fiction. In each case, Jameson maintains that we need to dispense with the grail of a singular universal set of criteria defining 'great literature', against which we can then evaluate all works, regardless of the time, place or situation of their production, and instead become more sensitive to the particular aims, practices and strategies of diverse works, genres and forms. Thus, for example, in his much discussed essay on Third World literature, Jameson argues that one of the most common contemporary critical errors is the reading of 'non-canonical forms of literature' in terms of the canon itself (by which he means here the forms and rhythms of a hegemonic European realism and modernism): not only is such an approach 'peculiarly self-defeating because it borrows the weapons of the adversary', it passes 'over in silence the radical difference' of these works (1986, 65). And in one of his numerous analyses of science fiction, Jameson suggests that works in this genre eschew the pleasures and demands of canonical forms of literature – those of complex psychological portraits of 'realistic' characters and 'well-formed plots' – and thereby free themselves for an operation of *spatial* imagining: 'the collective adventure accordingly becomes less that of a character (individual or collective) than that of a planet, a climate, a weather, and a system of landscapes – in short, a map. We thus need to explore the proposition that the distinctiveness of SF as a genre has less to do with time (history, past, future) than with space' (Jameson, 1987, 58).

This attention to the way various cultural texts 'map' space has also contributed to one of Jameson's most influential formulations, that of the political aesthetic practice he names, drawing upon the work of architectural historian Kevin Lynch, 'cognitive mapping'. Jameson first describes the practices of cognitive mapping in his widely influential essay on 'postmodernism', which he describes as 'the cultural logic of late capitalism'. One of the most significant aspects of the new cultural situation of postmodernism is, according to Jameson, 'the waning of our historicity, of our lived possibility of experiencing history in some active way'; conversely, our culture is one 'increasingly dominated by space and spatial logic' (1991, 21, 25). Indeed, while Jameson acknowledges, again following the lead of Lefebvre, that all social organizations are defined by distinctive productions of space, 'ours has been spatialized in a unique sense, such that space is for us an existential and cultural dominant, a thematized and foregrounded feature or structural principle standing in striking contrast to its relatively subordinate and secondary (though no doubt no less symptomatic) role in earlier modes of production' (1991, 365). Jameson's periodizing description of postmodernism thus also enables us to account for the sudden renewal in the early 1970s of interest in questions of space and spatiality (it's worth noting here that the texts of Williams, Lefebvre, Foucault and de Certeau discussed above all appear within a few years of one another): for this is the moment, Jameson argues, when postmodern emerges as a new 'cultural dominant' within the western industrial nations. These theorizations of space then themselves become both symptomatic of and important preliminary efforts to navigate the terrain of this new cultural situation.

However, mutations in space on all its levels have created difficulties for us as individual and collective subjects. 'We do not yet possess the perceptual equipment' to navigate and position ourselves within this increasingly urbanized and global social and cultural space, our cognitive 'organs' having been developed in an earlier historical situation (1991, 38). In order to help us overcome this lag, Jameson issues a call for a new kind of 'cognitive and pedagogical' cultural practice, one which 'will necessarily have to raise spatial issues as its fundamental organizing concern' (1991, 50–1). It is this aesthetic practice which Jameson names cognitive mapping: 'a pedagogical political culture which seeks to endow the individual subject with some heightened sense of its place in the global system' (1991, 54). Thus, occupying a place similar to Lefebvre's 'conceived' space, the *practice* of cognitive mapping – which, it should be stressed, is never to be confused with some impossible total cognitive 'map' – provides a way of connecting our lived experiences of the present to the abstract systematic theorizations we have of this new global cultural and social network. On this basis, Jameson investigates the way an incredibly rich variety of cultural practices – ranging from the science fiction novels of Philip K. Dick, popular films such as *Dog Day Afternoon, Something Wild* and *Blue Velvet*, the installation art of Robert Gober and the architecture of Frank Gehry – engage in incomplete forms of or stand as allegories for cognitive mapping. For example, in his discussion of Gehry's much analysed home in southern California, Jameson argues that 'the very concept of space here demonstrates its supremely mediatory function, in the way in which its aesthetic formulation begins at once to entail cognitive consequences on the one hand and sociopolitical consequences on the other . . . The problem, then, which the Gehry house tries to think is the relationship between that abstract knowledge and conviction or belief about the superstate and the existential daily life of people in their traditional rooms and tract houses' (1991, 104, 128).

As the above descriptions suggest, Jameson's model of cognitive mapping represents an attempt to develop the tools required to 'think' a new kind of *global* cultural and social reality, as well as our place within it, a project he then makes explicit in his film study, *The Geo Political Aesthetic: Cinema and Space in the World System* (1992). In this book, Jameson notes that such an emerging global space

> may henceforth be thought to be at least one of the fundamental allego-
> rical referents or levels of all seemingly abstract philosophical thought: so
> that a fundamental hypothesis would pose the principle that all thinking
> today, is *also*, whatever else it is, an attempt to think the world system as
> such. All the more true will this be for narrative figurations, whose very
> structure encourages a soaking up of whatever ideas in the air are left and
> a fantasy-solution to all anxieties that rush to fill our current vacuum.
> (1992, 3–4)

In this way, the increased attention to questions of space and spatiality more generally converges with the burgeoning interest in the issue of 'globalization'. David Harvey has recently suggested that while the attention now given to globalization does indeed put the issues of space and cultural geography on centre stage, we need to recognize that any concept like 'globalization' is always already a deeply ideological one, occluding the particular agency and interests involved in such a process of spatial 'reterritorialization' – to deploy the concept first developed in Giles Deleuze and Félix Guattari's great work of spatial thinking, *Capitalism and Schizophrenia* (1972 and 1987) – while also poten-tially performing the same pedagogical role as its temporal twin, the 'end of history', teaching us to think of it as a baleful and inexorable, almost natural, process of evolution towards a world of universal commodification and cultural homogenization. Harvey thus proposes that we shift our language from 'globalization' to 'uneven geographical development' (2000, 68), thereby laying emphasis on the fact that our present moment is witness to a rearticulation on a new spatial scale of the contradictory logics of capitalist modernization, the latest in what is in fact an unbroken historical series of 'spatial fixes' and reterritorializations.

An attention to the historical spatial dimensions of globalization will similarly transform how we think about literary history and contemporary cultural practices. In many ways, this has already long been the case in much of the work in postcolonial literary studies. In *Culture and Imperialism*, for example, Said critiques Williams's earlier *The Country and the City* for its narrowly national focus. In contrast, Said argues that there is no 'British' national culture that can be understood independent of the nation's large far-flung imperial networks and spheres of influence and investment, and this is the case from a much earlier moment than Williams and others would grant. Thus, any discussion of modern national literature must be attentive to the ways the works composing it respond to and negotiate its global spatial context, a practice Said names 'contrapunctual reading': 'In practical terms . . . it means reading a text with an understanding of what is involved when an author shows, for instance, that a colonial sugar plantation is seen as important to the process of maintaining a particular style of life in England . . . The point is that contrapunctual reading must take account of both processes, that of imperialism and that of resistance to it' (1993, 66).

In terms of our own historical situation, Jameson points out that cultural forms such as the Hollywood film should be understood as 'not merely a name for a business that makes money but also for a fundamental late-capitalist cultural revolution, in which old ways of life are broken up and new ones set in place' (1998, 63). Meaghan Morris similarly notes that the emergence of 'theory' itself is linked to the current production of new kinds of global spaces: 'what we call "theory" does the work of fabricating an address to the topics deemed inherently interesting in a given transnational space. Within such a space, theory *is* the work of extracting a cosmopolitan point from the most parochially constructed or ephemeral "events"' (1998, 6). And finally, Franco Moretti has issued a call for a new kind of 'world literature' studies, one that eschews the demands of the canonical close reading, and instead attempts to map the intersections and connections between the trends in a wide variety of national and cultural traditions. All of these theorizations emphasize the necessity for any mapping of the global space to move beyond the canonical opposition of high and low, or the spatial one of core and periphery, and instead produce a new multi-perspectival view of literature and cultural activities, exchanges and flows. Only in this way, they all suggest, can we gain a richer sense of the complexity and originality of the global spaces we inhabit today.

NOTES TOWARDS A READING OF JOSEPH CONRAD'S *LORD JIM*

Of course, an awareness of the gradual development of this new kind of global cultural, social and economic space is already evident in literary works produced much earlier in the last century. This is very much the case, for example, in the great turn-of-the-century novels written by Joseph Conrad, *Heart of Darkness* (1899), *Lord Jim* (1900) and *Nostromo* (1904). In order to give some sense of how a literary criticism oriented towards spatial concerns might enable us to read familiar texts in new ways, I would like to take a brief look at the work many now consider to be Conrad's masterpiece, *Lord Jim*. First published at the very high point of British imperial power, this narrative represents one of the first attempts to 'think' or, to use Jameson's phrase, to 'cognitively map' an emerging global reality. A good deal of the brilliance of Conrad's novel then lies in the ways it accomplishes this task on the levels of both content and literary form.

Lord Jim is divided into two distinct parts. The first centres on the story of the steamship, *Patna*, and the revelation of Jim's 'failure' while serving as first mate aboard it: when the *Patna* threatens to sink and take down with it all of its 400 passengers, Jim, along with the other crew members, 'jumps' ship. The great irony of this event (and Conrad is one of the great masters of modern irony) lies in the fact that Jim sees himself as somehow distinct from and superior to these, and indeed all other, men: 'The quality of these men did not matter; he rubbed shoulders with them, but they could not touch him; he shared the air they breathed, but he was different' (61). Raised on a tradition of 'light holiday literature' – romantic tales not unlike those that led to the undoing of Jim's great predecessor in modern literature, Don Quixote – Jim constructs an image of himself as 'an example of devotion to duty, and as unflinching as a hero in a book' (47). Put to the test, however, his self-image collapses: Jim, we learn, is, to take one of the central repeated motifs of the novel, really 'one of us' – an imperfect and fallible human being. The central ethical question the novel raises concerns whether Jim himself ever learns this lesson: he attempts to 'escape' the truth of his experience, first wandering from port to port across the great expanse of the south seas. Then, in the second part of the novel, he apparently succeeds in leaving 'his earthly failings behind him' as he becomes the ruler of the fictional Sumatran island community of Patusan (204). In this latter place, he does seem to redeem himself, as he now willingly accepts death as the consequence of his later errors in judgement: in this way, he confirms his commitment to a 'shadowy ideal of conduct' (351).

Every reader who encounters this novel for the first time is struck by the difficulties raised by Conrad's mode of presentation and style in the work's opening section: from the book's first pages, Conrad continuously manipulates chronology, multiplies points of view, deploys impressionistic techniques, and uses devices such as what Ian Watt names 'delayed decoding', the presentation of an effect while withholding, sometimes for many pages, its cause. All of these strategies and devices exemplify Conrad's deeply experimental modernist sensibility: his dissatisfaction with the older 'realist' practices of representation, his critical 'estrangement' of them, to use the term developed by the Russian

Formalist critic, Viktor Schklovsky, and his attempt to produce new and more 'effective' aesthetic forms.

The first question this form raises concerns why such a dissatisfaction with the older ways of doing things – a dissatisfaction clearly not limited to Conrad alone – arises when and where it does. The conventional answer is that through these means, Conrad, and writers like him, can more 'accurately' reveal the essential 'truths' of human psychology, epistemology and ethics. Of course, such an answer is deeply teleological and even anti-historical, suggesting a singular linear development of literary practice as it moves towards some ultimate perfection of form.

Moreover, and even more importantly for our concerns here, such an answer occludes the deeply spatial orientation of this particular novel. This focus is already made explicit by the novel's third paragraph. Here, Conrad describes Jim's efforts to escape the 'fact' of what he had done while a mate on board the *Patna* (while deferring the revelation of what that act in fact was):

> When the fact broke through the incognitio he would leave suddenly the seaport where he happened to be at the time and go to another – generally farther east. He kept to seaports because he was a seaman in exile from the sea, and had Ability in the abstract, which is good for no other work but that of a water-clerk. He retreated in good order toward the rising sun, and the fact followed him casually but inevitably. Thus in the course of years he was known successively in Bombay, in Calcutta, in Rangoon, in Penang, in Batavia – and in each of these halting-places was just Jim the water-clerk. Afterwards, when his keen perception of the Intolerable drove him away for good from seaports and white men, even into the virgin forest, the Malays of the jungle village, where he had elected to conceal his deplorable faculty, added a word to the monosyllable of his incognitio. They called him Tuan Jim: as one might say – Lord Jim. (46)

As this passage so beautifully indicates, the very progression of the plot will involve a movement through a succession of spaces. The very choice of verbs here – 'leave', 'go to', 'retreated', 'drove' – all suggest a dynamic restless motion forward. And in so doing, the plot's unfolding will generate for the reader a veritable map of the space it covers. Indeed, we might take Jim's 'story' as no more than, to use another concept of the Russian Formalists, 'the motivation of the device', the excuse to pursue this project of spatial mapping.

One of the most striking aspects of this first section for the spatially oriented reader is the immense scope of the space in which Jim's adventures unfold: 'To the common mind he became known as a rolling stone, because this was the funniest part: he did after a time become perfectly known, and even notorious, within the circle of his wanderings (which had a diameter of, say, three thousand miles), in the same way as an eccentric character is known to a whole country-side' (187). Our narrator, Marlow, too travels across an immense amount of space as he collects different elements of Jim's story. The comparison Conrad makes in this passage is instructive for another reason: it suggests Conrad's recognition of the fairly recent *expansion* of the *scale* of space that human beings inhabit, and within which their tales must now unfold. The very fact that Jim's story becomes 'known' across such a tremendous space also points towards the development of transportation and communication technologies that enable this kind of knowledge and information to circulate across such space as readily as did older tales across the local space of the countryside. Moreover, despite its immense scope, Conrad suggests that such a space is in fact a closed one: Jim cannot escape the knowledge of his actions, and at the end of Chapter 13, in a kind of internal climax, we get this terrible image of Jim: 'He was running. Absolutely running, with nowhere to go to. And he was not yet four-and-twenty' (157).

This awareness of the tremendously expanded spatial scope of the narrative action thus offers us a way to construct an alternative account of the reasons for Conrad's difficult experimental form. Mikhail Bakhtin shows in great detail how the formal strategies and context of the modern realist novel, in the form of what he calls its 'second stylistic trend', serve as a way of bringing into focus the space of the modern nation-state: central to such a practice is the chronotope of the road, linking together diverse spaces and producing a place of encounter for the various publics making up what Benedict Anderson calls the 'imagined community' of the nation (Bakhtin, 1981, 243–4). If these strategies emerge as a way of grasping a particular kind of enclosed space, then Conrad's – and indeed all of the great modernist writers' – dissatisfaction with them may now be understood as their implicit recognition of the insufficiency of these older practices for 'representing' a newly expanded and unified space. Conrad's 'experiments' thus participate in a great multinational effort aimed at developing the representational tools that might be adequate for making sense not only of the scale but the complexity of this kind of global space – a space in which we as individuals must learn to navigate.

And yet, interestingly enough, Conrad abandons these experimental strategies in the novel's second part, wherein he describes Jim's adventures in the imaginary community of Patusan. Here the narrative becomes much more conventionally linear, and even deploys many of the plot devices associated with the 'light holiday literature', the popular prose romances, which Jim had consumed to such a deleterious effect while a youth. Conrad himself acknowledges this shift at a number of places: when Jim is provided with a talismanic ring by one of the community's inhabitants, he tells Marlow, 'It's like something you read of in books' – but really only in the kinds of books that Jim himself reads (215). And later, Conrad writes, 'But do you notice how, three hundred miles *beyond* the end of telegraph cables and mail-boat lines, the haggard utilitarian lies of our civilization wither and die, to be replaced by pure exercises of imagination, that have the futility, often the charm, and sometimes the deep hidden truthfulness of works of art? *Romance* had singled Jim for its own – and that was the true part of the story, which otherwise was all wrong' (251; emphasis added).

Many critics, following the lead of F. R. Leavis, find this second section to be markedly inferior to the first. Of course, such an evaluation once again imposes a single set of criteria – criteria established in a large part by the novel's first part – against which all literary and representational practices are to be evaluated. There is a tremendous circularity in such an approach: finally, are we saying anything more than that the first part of the book does what it does better than the second part does what the first part does? As I suggested above, a spatial criticism is much more sensitive to the *differences* between different kinds of literary practices. Thus, we need to consider the possibility that Conrad's *decision* to shift form indicates not a slackening of literary energy, but rather signals that the very aims of the novelistic mapping have changed as well.

Interestingly in this regard, Conrad makes it clear to his readers, as evident in the passage cited above, that upon entering Patusan Jim has also entered into a very different kind of space. Indeed, Marlow's first reference to the place takes the form of a question: 'I don't suppose any of you have ever heard of Patusan? . . . It does not matter; there's many a heavenly body in the lot crowding upon us of a night that mankind had never heard of, it being outside the sphere of its activities and of no earthly importance to anybody but to the astronomers who are paid to talk learnedly about its composition, weight, path' (203). And later, Marlow will describe the village as 'one of the lost, forgotten, unknown places of the earth' (281). Of course, to describe Patusan as 'outside the sphere' of 'mankind's' activities, and as a 'lost, forgotten, unknown' place is in fact to *locate* it very precisely in relationship to the closed world illustrated in the novel's first part: Patusan remains, for the moment at least, 'beyond the end of telegraph cables and mail-boat lines', the communication and transportation network that serves to suture together the space in which Jim's failure and subsequent wanderings take place. Such a place is, of course, the 'world' space produced by European imperial and economic expansion. The fact that Patusan has only been 'forgotten' by Europe, and is not truly 'unknown' to it, is emphasized at the beginning of Chapter 22, where we learn that 'the seventeenth-century traders went there for pepper, because the passion for pepper seemed to burn like a flame of love in the breast of Dutch and English adventures about the time of James the First' (209). The story Conrad tells us in the rest of the novel concerns Europe's 'remembering' of this place, and the consequences that follow from such an act of recovery.

Here then we have our answer to why Conrad decided to shift his prose form in the second part of the novel: in so doing, he reinforces the sense of the exteriority of this older space to that then being produced by European economic and political power. The tenuous thread linking these two worlds is the figure of Marlow's friend, the adventurer-turned-trader, Stein. Once a figure of romance himself (tales of his youthful adventures are related to us in Chapter 20, and Marlow describes his earlier life as one rich 'in all the exalted elements of romance' (202)), and now very much ensnared in the 'haggard utilitarian lies' of European economic calculation, Stein recognizes Jim's in-ability to fit within the modern world – 'I understand very well. He is romantic' (199). It is Stein then who enables Jim to kick free of the 'earth', the dramatically expanded 'old world' of European power, and 'leap' into the 'new' frontier landscape of Patusan. Here, the 'rules' that order the closed world of empire no longer hold; and, in such a space, Jim-the-failure has the chance to realize his romantic image of himself as Jim-the-hero – that is, as Lord Jim.

And yet, ultimately, this heroic project fails; as Marlow succinctly puts it, 'He had retreated from one world, for a small matter of an impulsive jump, and now the other, the work of his own hands, had fallen in ruins upon his head' (345). A group of men, led by the demonic Gentleman Brown, arrive from Jim's previous 'world' – 'These were the emissaries with whom the world he had renounced was pursing his retreat' (328) – and instigate a series of events that culminate in the murder of Jim's friend, Dain Waris, and Jim's submission of himself for summary execution at the hands of Dain's father (350–1).

However, crucially, Conrad makes it clear that it is Jim's very activities in Patusan that guarantee the eventual arrival of these kinds of men. That is, Jim unwittingly becomes the very tool of his own destruction. Dain Waris is first described by Marlow as a 'being' who possesses the gift of being able to 'open to the Western eye, so often concerned with mere surfaces, the hidden possibilities of races and lands over which hangs the mystery of unrecorded ages' (236). It will be Jim himself then who will tap into this hidden potential, as he begins a project of spatial modernization in the land: 'The ground rose gently, the few big trees had been felled, the undergrowth had been cut down and the grass fired. He had a mind to try a coffee-plantation there. The big hill, rearing its double summit coal-black in the clear yellow glow of the rising moon, seemed to cast its shadow upon the ground prepared for that experiment. He was going to try ever so many experiments' (280). These activities have the effect of inserting Patusan at once into the space and history of European imperial power. The great irony here is that Patusan can serve as a 'retreat' for Jim only as long as it remains 'separate' from the European sphere of influence; and yet, the very activities that Jim performs guarantee that this spatial autonomy will very quickly come to an end. Indeed, the choice of a coffee-plantation for Jim's primary 'experiment' is not accidental: for coffee is a trade export crop, one whose production cannot sustain the community independent from the larger global networks of ex-change (in other words, you can't eat coffee). Thus, the arrival of Gentleman Brown and his men simply accelerates a process that Jim himself had already begun.

The real brilliance of Conrad's decision to switch his prose form in the novel's second part now finally becomes clear. In this latter part of the book, Conrad provides a devastating allegory of the process of what has been called 'informal' British imperial expansion, the ways that what appear to be local spatial transformations in fact reinscribe, often unintentionally, these spaces within a larger network of global economic circulation. The motivations behind these activities are, Conrad also suggests, similarly 'informal' – the very desire for 'adventure' and 'heroism' so much a part of Jim's make-up, and inculcated in him by the reading of popular romances. The realization of the romance plot, Conrad meticulously demonstrates, in effect destroys the world, the spaces 'outside' the stable and closed networks of European power, where romance might still be possible. Conrad's story then is one of the closure of the imperial frontier, the apparently irrevocable process of reconstructing the entire globe in Europe's image. And it is this world, the world their own actions inadvertently produce, which has no place for Jim, or his predecessor, Stein. Conrad signals this fact in the novel's bittersweet final lines: 'Stein has aged greatly of late. He feels it himself, and says often that he is "preparing to leave all this; preparing to leave . . ." while he waves his hands sadly at his butterflies' (352). If there will be any challenge to the terrible inevitability of this process of spatial incorporation, it is one Conrad cannot, from his location in time and space, see. We fortunately, might be able to see differently. And seeing differently is finally, the goal of the kinds of spatial criticism outlined above.

QUESTIONS FOR FURTHER CONSIDERATION

1. Most of what we currently value as the highest expressions of literary art are concerned with what Edward Soja calls Lefebvre's 'Thirdspace' – 'spaces of representation', or the lived. Discuss the impact of Lefebvre's tripartite schema of space on how we think about the work of different kinds of literary texts. Are there literary works that focus upon the other two levels of space? How does an attention to all three, as well as the more nuanced model of spatial scales outlined by Neil Smith, influence how we read literature and culture? What things suddenly come to our attention?

2. Mikhail Bakhtin maps out a range of traditional 'chronotopes' in the history of the novel, including the road, the parlour, the castle, the provincial town, and the threshold. In what ways have the situations of our world transformed these novelistic chronotopes? Have any new ones emerged? For example, does the electronic informational space produce new chronotopes for the novel? Discuss some examples.

3. Jameson's description of cognitive mapping offers a strategy both for the production and interpretation of various kinds of cultural practices. Discuss how a work of literature might be said to engage in forms of cognitive mapping. What are some of the criteria for its success? In what ways does this occur through form as well as explicit content? How does our attention to these operations transform how we think about literature and culture?

4. An attention to issues of space and spatiality promises to change not only how we read literature, but also what we read. What assumptions and expectations about literary value are revealed when we shift our

attention in some of the ways outlined above? How might we then read canonical texts in new ways? What are some of the marginalized forms and practices that become increasingly important? Why so?

5. A good deal of work in contemporary literary and critical theory and cultural studies brings into sharper focus questions of identity – class, race, gender, sexuality and so forth. In what ways do the questions of space supplement, intersect with and pose anew these vital concerns? What roles do space and spatial differences play in the production of identities? How does an attention to these differences shape how we think about bodies? How does the attention to space enable a different reading of the production of identity itself?

6. A literary criticism and cultural studies attentive to questions of space is not only interested in the ways cultural productions map and illuminate already existing spaces, but also in the contributions they might make to the vital political project of imagining, and then making, space anew. This project of spatial remaking ranges from the most abstract global level to that of our individual bodies, all spaces we all inhabit all of the time. Discuss the role that literary and other cultural texts play in such a spatial politics. How do they help us to imagine new kinds of space? What forms do this kind of work most effectively? What lessons do we learn? How might we then put these lessons into practice in our activities outside of the classroom?

ANNOTATED BIBLIOGRAPHY

Carter, Paul. *The Road to Botany Bay: An Essay in Spatial History*. London: Faber & Faber, 1987. One of the more interesting developments in the spatial turn in literary and critical theory and cultural studies has been the wealth of important contributions made by thinkers working in Australia. Carter is one of these, and this book has become something of a cult classic among historians and literary scholars. Carter is deeply influenced by the work of the French phenomenologists, and he demonstrates the indispensability of their work for any discussion of the production of space. He opens this book with a critique of what he calls 'imperial history', and argues for another mode, a new kind of 'spatial history' attentive to the ways linguistic and representational practices such as naming, cataloguing, mapping, and surveying literally produce a new kind of place, making European inhabitation of the continent possible. Carter begins his story with Captain Cook's voyages, and treats a rich variety of documents and texts, including log books, diaries, travel narratives, and grid surveys. Then in his brilliant final two chapters, he looks at, first, the counter-narratives produced by the European convicts, and then the radically different spatial histories inscribed on the landscape by the aboriginal peoples.

Foucault, Michel. *Discipline and Punish: The Birth of the Prison*, trans. Alan Sheridan. New York: Vintage, 1977. Foucault's brilliant narration of the history of modernity has influenced literary and cultural critics for nearly a quarter of a century. While very much in the spirit of earlier critical histories of modernity, Foucault's great achievement is to give this narrative a distinctively spatial turn. Foucault opens his examination by focusing attention upon the body, and 'the way in which the body itself is invested by power relations'. Foucault offers a meticulous genealogy of the development of the modern practices of surveillance and discipline, and shows how many modern institutions – including the prison, the barracks, the factory, the hospital and the school – work to produce the 'docile bodies' required for the efficient functioning of modern society. Foucault's opening description of the execution of a regicide still shocks many readers, while his analysis of Jeremy Bentham's panopticon as both the ideal and real manifestation of this new cultural logic remains a crucial starting point for any spatial consideration.

Harvey, David. *The Condition of Postmodernity*. Oxford: Basil Blackwell, 1989. The most accessible of the works written by perhaps the single most important geographer now contributing to the interdisciplinary project of spatial thought, this volume is less useful for its discussions of postmodern culture than for its brilliant description of the processes of spatial transformation that are central to the project of capitalist modernization. Harvey traces out in great detail the series of 'time-space compressions' that have occurred throughout this history, before looking at the particular spatial transformations that shape our world. Harvey also offers a wonderful introduction to work of the French Regulationist school of political economy, and their important work on the economic and social transformations that have occurred in the decades following the Second World War. Moreover, prefiguring the argument he will advance about globalization in *Spaces of Hope* (2000), Harvey argues that while the post-modern does represent a reorganization of capitalism, it does *not* signal any more fundamental change within its essential form.

Jameson, Fredric. *The Political Unconscious: Narrative as a Socially Symbolic Act*. Ithaca, NY: Cornell University Press, 1981. Although this work is not centrally a spatial study of literature, Jameson's important discussions of the romance form, and of Joseph Conrad's *Lord Jim* and *Nostromo* (on which I have drawn above), open up significant avenues in spatial thought. Moreover, this text offers one of the most sustained examples of the kind of interdisciplinary work that will be at the heart of the entire spatial turn in literary and cultural criticism.

Jameson, Fredric. *Postmodernism, or, The Cultural Logic of Late Capitalism*. Durham, NC: Duke University Press, 1991. A landmark work that both reprints essays that had become central touchstones in any discussion of contemporary culture – including the title essay that had originally appeared in *New Left Review* seven years earlier – and a number of new chapters. In this massive work, Jameson pursues two distinct projects. First, he offers a symptomology of various dimensions of a properly first-world, and particularly US (as well as a specifically class-based), experience of the postmodern. His list of its features are now quite familiar – the collapse of critical distance, the waning of affect, the weakening of historicity, the dissolution of the centred subject, the new centrality of the image, the inability to map our place in this new reality, and so forth. Jameson also emphasizes the original spatial dimensions of this new cultural experience, and the way these are registered in a rich variety of cultural productions. Jameson then issues a call for the development, in terms of the original situation of the postmodern, of a new 'pedagogical political culture' – the particular aesthetic practice of cognitive mapping. The rest of the book then moves between these two projects, analysing privileged symptomatic texts – for example, the experience of the space in the Bona-venture Hotel, nostalgia films, New Historicism, Paul De Man's deconstructive criti-cism, the fiction of Claude Simon, and the experimental video *AlienNATION* – to see what aspects of the postmodern condition they might illuminate for us, and exploring allegories of the cognitive mapping process – the 'thinking' we find in the architecture of Frank Gehry's house, 'allegorical encounter' films and Robert Gober's installations – for further lessons about what such a new political aesthetic might look like. Much of Jameson's subsequent work – including *The Geopolitical Aesthetic* (1992) and *The Seeds of Time* (1994) – build upon and enrich the discussions begun here.

Lefebvre, Henri. *The Production of Space,* trans. Donald Nicholson-Smith. Oxford: Blackwell, 1991. One of the single most important texts in the theorization of space, the influences of this work have begun to be felt in a wide range of disciplines. Lefebvre opens this work with a critical examination of the absence of questions of space in much of what was then contemporary French theory. He calls for a heightened attention to the '(social) production of (social) space'; develops his tripartite schematization (outlined in more detail above); traces out a vast social and cultural history of these transformations, beginning with the 'origins' of space in the initial cellular division between inside and outside; and outlines strategies for a political contestation of contemporary capitalist space. As original and daring in form as in conceptualization, developing a mode of what he names spatial dialectical thinking, Lefebvre's work can make for difficult reading for those who first enter into it; however, its rewards are immense.

Morris, Meaghan. *Too Soon, Too Late: History in Popular Culture*. Bloomington, IN: Indiana University Press, 1998. This volume brings together in a single collection some of the most influential essays of one of the most important cultural studies scholars working today. Morris, who like Carter is based in and writes primarily on Australia, deploys an analytical method grounded in feminism, semiotics, critical theory and history in order to offer insightful analyses of a rich variety of spatial practices and institutions – including motels, shopping malls and contemporary urban redevelopment projects. Morris argues for the necessity of at once being attentive to the local nuances and particular practices of each of these places, the ways they are used and appropriated by different people and groups, and their insertion in a larger global process of social and spatial change. Morris's great essay, 'Great Moments in Social Climbing', offers a stunning reading of both contemporary representations of redevelopment in the urban core of Sydney and the alternative spatial imaginaries produced in Chris Hilton's documentary film, *A Spire*, in order to move beyond many of the impasses plaguing current work in cultural studies.

Said, Edward. *Culture and Imperialism*. New York: Alfred A. Knopf, 1993. This work by one of the founding figures of postcolonial theory shows how the geopolitical and spatial practices of European imperialism become manifest in many of the most important works of European and British literature and culture, including Jane Austen's *Mansfield Park*, Rudyard Kipling's *Kim*, Giuseppi Verdi's operas and Albert Camus's *The Stranger*. Said argues for a greater attention to the 'geographical notation, the theoretical mapping and charting of territory that underlies Western fiction, historical writing, and philosophical discourse'. He shows how literary and cultural texts articulate many of the fundamental assumptions that underlie the imperial project, as well as the ways these continue on into our own present.

Soja, Edward. W. *Postmodern Geographies: The Reassertion of Space in Critical Social Theory*. New York: Verso, 1989. The first book in a trilogy that now includes *Thirdspace* (1996) and *Postmetropolis* (2000), Soja's work was a breakthrough text as it offered a careful and sustained argument for a 'reassertion of a critical spatial perspective in contemporary social theory and analysis'. He offers a marvellous history of the repression of spatial questions in social theory, before tracing its re-emergence in a wide range of social and critical work, including that of Foucault, Jameson and Lefebvre. (*Thirdspace* also presents one of the best introductions to Lefebvre's *The Production of Space*.) Soja then puts his insights to work in some powerful discussions of the struggle over the spatial productions of contemporary Los Angeles, work that should be read in conjuncture with Mike Davis's brilliant *City of Quartz* (1990) and *Ecology of Fear* (1998).

Williams, Raymond. *The Country and the City*. Oxford: Oxford University Press, 1973. A ground-breaking study that surveys modern British literature in terms of its changing representations of the 'city' and the 'country', and the relationships between these changing spaces. Williams shows how literature and cultural texts both reflect actual changes in spatial practices and serve as one of the first places where changing attitudes and assumptions, what Williams calls 'structures of feeling', are made manifest. Many of his particular readings are still brilliant and original, and this work remains an indispensable starting point for anyone interested in the way spatial questions transform how we read literature.

SUPPLEMENTARY BIBLIOGRAPHY

Anderson, Benedict. *Imagined Communities: Reflections on the Origin and Spread of Capitalism*. London: Verso, 1991.

Appadurai, Arjun. *Modernity at Large: Cultural Dimensions of Globalization*. Minneapolis, MN: University of Minnesota Press, 1996.

Ashcroft, Bill. *Post-Colonial Transformation*. London: Routledge, 2001.

Bachelard, Gaston. *The Poetics of Space*, trans. Maria Jolas. Boston, MA: Beacon Press, 1969.

Bakhtin, Mikhail M. *The Dialogic Imagination: Four Essays*, ed. and trans. Caryl Emerson and Michael Holquist. Austin, TX: University of Texas Press, 1981.

Benjamin, Walter. *The Arcades Project*, trans. Howard Eiland and Kevin McLaughlin. Cambridge, MA: Harvard University Press, 1999.

Buck-Morss, Susan. *The Dialectics of Seeing: Walter Benjamin and the Arcades Project*. Cambridge, MA: MIT Press, 1990.

Burgin, Victor. *In/Different Spaces: Place and Memory in Visual Culture*. Berkeley, CA: University of California Press, 1996.

Butler, Judith. 'Gender is Burning: Questions of Appropriation and Subversion'. In *Bodies That Matter: On the Discursive Limits of 'Sex'*. New York: Routledge, 1993, 121–40.

Casey, Edward S. *The Fate of Place: A Philosophical History*. Berkeley, CA: University of California Press, 1997.

Clifford, James, *Routes: Travel and Translation in the Late Twentieth Century*. Cambridge, MA: Harvard University Press, 1997.

Colomina, Beatriz (ed.). *Sexuality and Space*. Princeton, NJ: Princeton Papers on Architecture, 1992.

Conrad, Joseph. *Lord Jim*. London: Penguin Books, 1989.

Davis, Mike. *City of Quartz: Excavating the Future in Los Angeles*. London: Verso, 1990.

Davis, Mike. *Ecology of Fear: Los Angeles and the Imagination of Disaster*. New York: Henry Holt, 1998.

Davis, Mike. *Late Victorian Holocausts: El Niño Famines and the Making of the Third World*. London: Verso, 2000.

de Certeau, Michel. *The Practice of Everyday Life,* trans. Steven Randall. Berkeley, CA: University of California Press, 1984.

Deleuze, Gilles and Félix Guattari. *A Thousand Plateaus: Capitalism and Schizophrenia,* trans. Brian Massumi. Minneapolis, MN: University of Minnesota Press, 1987.

Derrida, Jacques and Peter Eisenman. *Chora L Works*, eds Jeffrey Kipnis and Thomas Lesser. New York: Monacelli Press, 1997.

Feldman, Allen. *Formations of Violence: The Narrative of the Body and Political Terror in Northern Ireland*. Chicago, IL: University of Chicago Press, 1991.

Foucault, Michel. 'Questions on Geography'. In *Power/Knowledge: Selected Interviews and Other Writings, 1972–1977*. New York: Pantheon Books, 1980. 63–77.

Gramsci, Antonio. *Selections from the Prison Notebooks*, eds and trans. Quintin Hoare and Geoffrey Nowell Smith. New York: International Publishers, 1971.

Greenblatt, Stephen. *Renaissance Self-Fashioning From More to Shakespeare*. Chicago, IL: University of Chicago Press, 1980.

Gregory, Derek. *Geographical Imaginations*. Oxford: Blackwell, 1994.

Grosz, Elizabeth. *Space, Time, and Perversion: Essays on the Politics of Bodies*. New York: Routledge, 1995.

Harvey, David. *The Urban Experience*. Baltimore, MD: Johns Hopkins University Press, 1989.

Harvey, David. *The Limits to Capital*, new edn. London: Verso, 1999.

Harvey, David. *Spaces of Hope*. Berkeley, CA: University of California Press, 2000.

Jameson, Fredric. 'On Raymond Chandler', *Southern Review*, 6, 1970, 624–50.

Jameson, Fredric. 'Third World Literature in the Era of Multinational Capitalism', *Social Text*, 15, 1986, 65–88.

Jameson, Fredric. 'Science Fiction as a Spatial Genre: Generic Discontinuities and the Problem of Figuration in Vonda McIntyre's *The Exile Waiting*', *Science Fiction Studies*, 14, 1987, 44–59.

Jameson, Fredric. 'The Space of Science Fiction: Narrative in A. E. Van Vogt', *Polygraph*, 2/3, 1989, 52–65.

Jameson, Fredric. *The Geopolitical Aesthetic: Cinema and Space in the World System*. Bloomington, IN: Indiana University Press, 1992.

Jameson, Fredric. 'The Synoptic Chandler'. In *Shades of Noir: A Reader*, ed. Joan Copjec. New York: Verso, 1993, 33–56.

Jameson, Fredric. *The Seeds of Time*. New York: Columbia University Press, 1994.

Jameson, Fredric. 'Notes on Globalization as a Philosophical Issue'. In *The Cultures of Globalization*, eds Fredric Jameson and Masao Miyoshi. Durham, NC: Duke University Press, 1998, 54–77.

Koolhaas, Rem. *Delirious New York: A Retroactive Manifesto for Manhattan*. New York: Monacelli Press, 1994.

Lefebvre, Henri. *Writings on Cities*, trans. and eds Eleonore Kofman and Elizabeth Lebas. Cambridge, MA: Blackwell, 1996.

Marin, Louis. *Utopics: The Semiological Play of Textual Spaces*, trans. Robert A. Vollrath. Atlantic Highlands, NJ: Humanities Press International, 1984.

Moretti, Franco. *Modern Epic: The World System from Goethe to García Márquez*. London: Verso, 1996.

Moretti, Franco. *Atlas of the European Novel, 1800–1900*. London: Verso, 1998.

Moretti, Franco. 'Conjectures on World Literature', *New Left Review* (II), 1, 2000, 54–68.

Papadakis, Andreas, Catherine Cooke and Andrew Benjamin (eds). *Deconstruction: Omnibus Volume*. New York: Rizzoli, 1989.

Rabinow, Paul. *French Modern: Norms and Forms the Social Environment*. Cambridge, MA: MIT Press, 1989.

Ross, Kristin. *The Emergence of Social Space: Rimbaud and the Paris Commune*. Minneapolis, MN: University of Minnesota Press, 1988.

Sennett, Richard. *Flesh and Stone: The Body and the City in Western Civilization*. New York: W. W. Norton, 1994.

Smith, Neil. 'Homeless/Global: Scaling Places'. In *Mapping the Futures: Local Cultures, Global Change*, eds Jon Bird et al. New York: Routledge, 1993, 87–119.

Soja, Edward. *Thirdspace: Journeys to Los Angeles and Other Real-and-Imagined Places*. Oxford: Blackwell, 1996.

Soja, Edward. *Postmetropolis: Critical Studies of Cities and Regions*. Oxford: Blackwell, 2000.

Tafuri, Manfredo. *Architecture and Utopia: Design and Capitalist Development*, trans. Barbara Luigia Penta. Cambridge, MA: MIT Press, 1976.

Tschumi, Bernard. *Architecture and Disjunction*. Cambridge, MA: MIT Press, 1996.

Tuan, Yi-Fu. *Space and Place: The Perspective of Experience*. Minneapolis, MN: University of Minnesota Press, 1977.

Wegner, Phillip E. *Imaginary Communities: Utopia, the Nation, and the Spatial Histories of Modernity*. Berkeley, CA: University of California Press, 2002.

CHAPTER 9

CYBERCRITICISM

Stacy Gillis

kubernetes (Greek): helmsman or pilot.

Data trash crawls out of the burned-out wreckage of the body splattered on the information superhighway, and begins the hard task of putting the pieces of the (electronic) body back together again . . . data trash is the (e-mail) mind of the twenty-first century. Data trash loves living at the violent edge . . . When surf's up on the Net, data trash puts on its electronic body and goes for a spin on the cyber-grid.

(Kroker and Weinstein, 1994, 158)

Cyberculture: cyberspace, technoculture, virtual communities, virtual realities, virtual identities, virtual space, cyborgs, cybernetics, cyberbodies, spectacles, simulations, simulacra and so forth. Cyberculture exists within the globally networked, computer-sustained, computer-accessed and/or computer-generated multidimensional virtual realities. Originally existing in the pages of science fiction, cybernetics – systems of control and communication in animals and machines – made cyberculture 'reality', although it exists only virtually. Cyberculture is a closing down of space and time, compressed by technological advances. In 1964, Marshall McLuhan noted the acceleration of community through the acceleration of technological development.

> After three thousand years of specialist intervention and of increasing specialism and alienation in the technological extensions of our bodies, our world has become compressional by dramatic reversal. As electrically contracted, the globe is no more than a village. Electric speed in bringing all social and political functions together in a sudden implosion has heightened human awareness of responsibility to an intense degree. It is this implosive factor that alters the position of Negro, the teen-ager, and

some other groups. They can no longer be *contained*, in the political sense of limited association. They are now *involved* in our lives, as we in theirs, thanks to the electric media. (McLuhan, 1964, 5; emphasis in original)

Although McLuhan was not specifically addressing the computer revolution, his 'global village' is a cybercultural one, predicated upon the cultural meaning of technology in the digital information age. This cybercultural village is in an embryonic stage, as is the school of cybercriticism that attempts to understand it. Cybercriticism is concerned with the technology/virtuality and the body, analyses of technology, the cultural readings of technological tools and virtual communities. As cyberculture changes, accelerated by the intensification of technological development, so too will cybercriticism.

COMPUTING HISTORY

Cyberspace. A consensual hallucination experienced daily by billions of legitimate operators . . . A graphic representation of data abstracted from the banks of every computer in the human system. Unthinkable complexity. Lines of light ranged in the nonspace of the mind, clusters and constellations of data. (Gibson 1991, 51).

As a 'space behind the computer' – a notion to which I shall return – cyberculture cannot be understood without being located within computer history. In 1833, the first technological arrangement that could be termed a computer was designed by Charles Babbage. Although this steam-powered programmable 'Analytical Engine' was never built, the promise of a machine that could perform some of the intellectual functions of humans marks the genesis of the computer of the twentieth century. Although computing machines, such as the Hollerith punchcard, had been used by the business and military worlds since the late 1890s, the first electronic computer was Colossus. Powered by vacuum tubes and programmed with punched paper tape, Colossus was developed by the British during the Second World War to decode the messages that had been encrypted by the German Enigma machines. Computers from Colossus onwards were not much more than variations of Babbage's design in that their purpose was to perform huge calculations correctly. The operation of these computers was accomplished through a process of setting up a program through the manipulation of switches and patches. The required expertise to run these machines, as well as their size, meant that there was no economic reason for the development of general software. The size alone ensured that a relationship between an individual and a computer – a crucial prerequisite of cyberculture – was difficult.

In 1964 only large mainframe computers existed, each with its own separate set of users. If you were lucky the computer was time-shared, but even then you could not get far away since the terminals were hard-wired to it or connected by local phone line. Moreover, if you wanted data

> from another computer, you moved it by tape and you could forget
> wanting software from another computer. (Roberts, 1988, 143)

The invention of the transistor in the 1950s and the use of integrated circuits in the 1960s allowed the size of the computer to decrease substantially, thus solving one problem. The development of general-use software was by large corporate companies. IBM had dominated the field in electromechanical office equipment and moved into computers, controlling 65 per cent of the market by 1965, thus determining the course of computer development. But although the computer had moved from Babbage's 'Analytical Machine' to an essential business tool by the end of the 1960s, it still retained an intellectual identity as a calculating machine.

This has changed dramatically in the last twenty years of the twentieth century. As early as 1960, one of the founders of artificial intelligence was looking to the day 'much less than twenty-five years' in the future when 'we shall have the technical capability of substituting machines for any and all human functions and organization,' including 'emotions, attitudes, and values' (Weizenbaum, 1976, 244). Although by the 1970s, the business computer was firmly established and some personal computers – such as the Apple, the Commodore and the TRS-80 – were on the market, the computer was still largely perceived as a calculating machine. Roszak draws attention to Elmer Rice's satire *The Adding Machine* (1923), in which the protagonist Mr Zero is an office clerk lost in a wasteland of filing cabinets (5). He is offered a hyper-adding machine in order to facilitate his work of compiling figures and reducing people to statistics. This notion of the computer – both in terms of what it could do and what it would do to its user – was common until the computer revolution of the 1980s. Heralded by the launch of the IBM Personal Computer in 1981 and the Apple Macintosh in 1984, the computer revolution was a successful marketing strategy that placed the personal computer in the home and opened up the possibilities of Simon's vision of the machine substituting for all human functions and organizations. The new computer of the 1980s' computer revolution was marketed as enabling human existence.

With the computer revolution came an exponential growth in software and hardware and, crucially, the development of the Internet. Even ten years ago, the Internet was relatively unknown. It had its origins in a computer network developed at the University of California at Los Angeles in 1969 by the Department of Defense's Advanced Research Projects Agency (ARPA). The network was constructed to guarantee military communications in the case of nuclear attack. On the ARPANet, data was broken down, sent over high-speed lines and reassembled. It was invulnerable to attack because if a portion of the network went down, traffic would be automatically rerouted. In 1983, ARPA-Net was divided into military and civilian networks. The civilian network was, at this point, still controlled by a single source – the US National Science Foundation. The NSF made the network available to all faculty and students at any member institutions and as more and more universities began connecting to the network, the civilian ARPANet transformed into a revolutionary global network that could not be controlled or contained from a discrete source. By 1990, ARPANet had, in fact, disappeared, absorbed by the internetworking of the Internet. The implosion of information, with the compression of time and space upon which communication on the Internet is predicated, reconfigured 'all operations, all information, all associations' (McLuhan, 1964, 12). The World Wide Web contains the immense series of networks, within the Internet, that are most commonly accessed by the average web user, seeking information or a product. This new cyberspace, a term coined by William Gibson in *Neuromancer* (1984), involves a new electronic geography of virtual communities and cybercultures.

CYBERPUNK

> I've seen things you people wouldn't believe. Attack ships on fire off the shoulder of Orion. I watched C-beams glitter in the dark near the Tannhauser gate. All those moments will be lost in time, like tears in rain. Time to die. (Batty to Deckard, *Blade Runner*)

Fears of computerized rationalization and computerized intelligence were common in post-Second World War science fiction. George Orwell's vision of the computer as an interactive observer in the service of a totalitarian state in *Nineteen Eighty-Four: A Novel* has been reworked in a number of narratives, including *Brazil* (Gilliam, 1984). An alternative form is the central computer that asserts control on its own, such as in *2001: A Space Odyssey* (Kubrick, 1968). The Orwellian Big Brother could, to some degree, be categorized as cyberpunk. But the sub-genre of science fiction that is cyberpunk is unique to the last twenty years of the twentieth century. The term first appeared in Bruce Bethke's short story 'Cyberpunk', which appeared in *Amazing Stories* (November 1983), and was a play on cybernetics, the study of communication and control systems, and punk, the musical movement of the late 1970s and early 1980s. Concerned with computerized rationalization and computerized intelligence, cyberpunk is neither technophiliac or technophobic although there is a tension between the military industrial monster that produces technology and the sensibility of the technically skilled individual trained for the world of high technology. In short, cyberpunk was a signal of new attitudes to new technologies and the fictive textual voice of cyberculture and cyberspace.

Gibson claims not to have invented the cyberpunk genre but his *Neuromancer* (1984) stands as the canonical cyberpunk novel. Cyberspace, in *Neuromancer*, is the 'consensual hallucination' that there is a 'space' behind the computer screen and connections are made within the matrix of computer networks. It exists in the world which is created when people log their nervous systems directly into the network, increasing the intimacy of mind and matrix.

Neuromancer employed the metaphors that embodied the experience of the information technology. When Gibson published his novel, the technology of virtual reality was being developed and ARPANet was expanding the possibilities of internetworking. In 1984, personal computers were beginning to appear on desks, computerized videogames were common and networks and mainframes were becoming accessible to universities and corporations. Computers were also becoming smaller and entering the domestic space in the form of televisions, wrist watches, calculators and so forth. However, there was an absence of vocabulary to describe these new technologies. Gibson's novel filled this gap, providing the terminology to describe the rapid technological change of the 1970s and 1980s. Moreover, it reached those who had been tantalized by George Lucas's vision in the *Star Wars* trilogy of humanity and technology bound together. Gibson's cyberspace metaphor allowed a fictive depiction of the electronic environments with which virtual reality programmers were experimenting but which themselves were forms of fiction. Indeed, the borrowing of a great number of terms from science fiction to describe the new auspices of information and technological existence can only underscore the extent to which this new referend is a simulation, no less real because it is fictional.

Cyberpunk fictions arranged major techno-corporations and governments in opposition to equally technologically outsider. Cyberpunk terms include:

- hacker: one who successfully breaks into computer systems/networks and can manipulate them for his/her own use;
- cracker: one whose attempts to break into computer systems/networks may not succeed but whose attempts will impact upon those systems;
- phreak: one who attempts to break into telephone systems;
- cypher-punk: one who attempts to break codes and to foil security systems;
- transhuman: one who attempts to exploit technology to increase life expectancy and human potential;
- extropian: transhumanists with an ardent interest in space colonization.

Literary cyberpunk has moved beyond Gibson, who remained highly ambivalent about his identification with the movement. Other cyberpunk novelists include Bruce Sterling, Pat Cadigan, John Shirley and Rudy Rucker. Gradually, however, cyberpunk has come to refer less to a sub-genre of science fiction than to the underside of new digital cultures – computer undergrounds, rave cultures, zine culture among them – that were emerging from the digital worlds of the Internet. In this way, the new cybercultures that cyberpunk had foretold were the demise of cyberpunk as a literary form.

TECHNOPOLY

[Technopoly is] the deification of technology, which means that culture seeks its authorization in technology, finds its satisfactions in technology, and takes its orders from technology. This requires the development of a new kind of social order, and of necessity leads to the rapid dissolution of much that is associated with traditional beliefs. (Postman, 1992, 71)

Such rapid technological change destabilized the perimeters between human and machine, space and time and self and other. The computer revolution of the 1980s presented one challenge to the Enlightenment's rational centred subject.

> Reason, which was supposed to legitimize the neo-pagan and emancipatory activities of Enlightenment, is now itself in need of legitimation. It can no longer assume the capacity for self-legitimation without assuming an exclusivity . . . It produces an administered society, not a rational society: reason is replaced by efficacy and by the aesthetic and formal vacuities of rational*ism* . . . Enlightenment reason is in fact a potent weapon in the production of social normativity, driving people towards a conformity with a dominant and centred 'norm' of behaviour. (Docherty, 1993, 13–14; emphasis in original)

Baudrillard argues that it is not reason (as the principle of reality) and the subject of reason which require legitimation in the late twentieth century but rather the Other of the real, which legitimizes cultural practices.

> So there is something more than that which is peculiar to our modern media images: if they fascinate us so much it is not because they are sites of the production of meaning and representation – this would not be new – it is on the contrary because they are sites of the *disappearance* of meaning and representation, sites in which we are caught quite apart from any judgement of reality, thus sites of a fatal strategy of denigration of the real and of the reality principle. (Baudrillard, 1987, 28; emphasis in original)

The freedoms promised by the Enlightenment were representations of an aesthetic, rather than a political, nature. If the representations of the subject of reason are called into question as a specific historical, cultural, racial, gendered and organic self by cyberculture, then the subject is left both without representation and with infinite representation, protected by the fluidity of cyberspace.

This fluidity of movement is made possible by hypertext. The giant calculating machines emerging from the Second World War and common in industry until the late 1960s had given the impression that, no matter how complicated the computations, what happened inside a computer could be mechanically unpacked and explained. Computer programming was a technical skill that, when performed correctly, followed the linear path of the traditional narrative. Such traditional notions of reading or assimilating information – linear, logical and hierarchical – have, since the computer revolution of the 1980s, been replaced by new methods of storing and retrieving information. The result is 'a body of work active not passive, a canon not frozen in perfection but volatile with contending human motive' (Lanham, 1993, 51). This change has been largely effected through the cyberconstruct of the World Wide Web and the expanding possibilities of hypertext. Not only has hypertext enabled the functioning of the World Wide Web but open-ended hypertext has subverted traditional notions of linear narratives and definitive readings. Landow and Delaney point out that 'so long as the text was married to a physical media, readers and writers took for granted three crucial attributes: that the text was *linear*, *bounded*, and *fixed*' (1991, 3; emphasis in original). Hypertext transcends these demands because it can be read non-sequentially. Such projects as Landow's *The Dickens Web* or the *Victorian Women Writers Project* (http://www.indiana.edu/~letrs/vwwp) exemplify this. The former, primarily an undergraduate study aid, puts into practice the hypertextual arguments that Landow advanced in *Hypertext* (see annotated bibliography). Much like electronic footnotes, hyperlinks make connections between items. The latter is a more diffuse project sustained by Indiana University, and a classic example of academic research, which may be difficult to publish finding a home on the Internet. What is crucial about the *Victorian Women Writer's Project* is that it is always being updated and its hyperlinks checked, so that it remains at the cutting edge of research, unlike a book which can quickly become critically moribund.

Moreover, hypertext allows arguments and connections to be made that are not possible on paper. 'The stepping-up speed from the mechanical to the instant electronic form reverses explosion into implosion. In our present electric age the imploding or contracting energies of our world now clash with the old expansionist and traditional patterns of organization' (McLuhan, 1964, 47). Certainly, hypertext, with its terminology of blocks, links and frames, resonates with such postmodern aesthetics as intertextuality, fragmentation and the decentred subject. Kristeva outlined a three-dimensional textual space of the intersection of the writing subject, the addressee and exterior texts.

> The word's status is thus defined horizontally (the word in the text belongs to both writing subject and addressee) as well as vertically (the word in the text is oriented towards an anterior or synchronic literary corpus) . . . each word (text) is an intersection of words (texts) where at least one other word (text) can be read. (Kristeva, 1986, 37)

Each text is informed by the other texts which the reader has read. On a technologically simplistic level, intertexuality is articulated by the footnotes that provide the sources for material to which the text is referring. Hypertext makes manifest Kristevean intertextuality in that hypertextual intertextuality is a mosaic of multiple texts, with the connections being made by the individual. The digital and archival abilities of hypertextual cyberspace have extended the virtual resources of the text into a unified mega-text, in which comprehension is the result of navigation as well as analysis. This is a far cry from the original 'Analytical Engine' that Babbage had designed, with a centralized structure and programmed rules, as a tool. If cybernetics was originally to do with calculation and linear logic, hypertext and new cyberspaces moved it towards simulation, navigation and interaction.

THE BODY AND TECHNOLOGY

> Knowledge is power! Do you suppose that little fragile form of yours – your primitive legs, your ludicrous arms and hands, your tiny, scarcely wrinkled brain – can *contain* all that power? Certainly not! Already your race is flying to pieces under the impact of your own expertise. The original human form is becoming obsolete. (Sterling, 1990, 25; emphasis in original)

The posthuman marks the end of the dissolution of the autonomous rational subject of humanism: the subject is decentred not only in relation to itself but also in relation to the world. Cyberspace situates the subject as multiple points on a map of virtual reality and cyberculture catches the 'subjectless' subject within a web of interactive networks, displacing autonomy. Technology has expanded and perfected the techniques of representing 'the real' to the extend that the ontological status of the real has been called into question on a grand scale.

> So it is with simulation, insofar as it is opposed to representation. The latter starts from the principle that the sign and the real are equivalent . . . Conversely, simulation starts from the *utopia* of this principle of equivalence, *from the radical negation of the sign as value*, from the sign as reversion and death sentence of every reference. Whereas representation tries to absorb simulation by interpreting it as false representation, simulation envelops the whole edifice of representation as itself a simulacrum. (Baudrillard, 1983, 11; emphasis in original)

Cyberspace undermines the symbolic distance between the metaphoric and the real, abandoning the latter by presenting an increasingly real simulation of a 'real' reality. Information loses its body in cyberspace.

The liberal humanist doctrine of possessive individualism – the freedom to dispose of property at will, including the property of the body – is lost in the webs of cyberspace. The movement from the human to the articulated posthuman, of which the cyborg is an example, is, in effect, a transition from order to chaos. Freud's notion of the uncanny can elaborate upon the relationship between human and machine. He remarks that the uncanny can entail 'manifestations of insanity, because these excite in the spectator the impression of automatic, mechanical processes at work behind the ordinary appearance of mental activity' (1955, 226). Certainly, the liberal humanist consanguinity of ideology and material embodiment is broken apart by the apparent random nature of cyberculture. The human/machine interface becomes a place in which traditional notions of subjectivity and embodiment are potentially abandoned. Despite attempts to sustain the notion of the liberal humanist subject, the late twentieth century has seen 'a new way of looking at human beings. Henceforth, humans were to be seen primarily as information-processing entities who are *essentially* similar to intelligent machines' (Hayles, 1999, 7; emphasis in original). In cyberculture, the self is multiple, fluid and constituted only via interaction with technology.

Our dependence on technology leads us to ask whether or not we are all cyborgs, a term first employed, with its present meaning of a transgressive mixture of biology and technology, by Donna Haraway in 'A Manifesto for Cyborgs: Science, Technology and Socialist Feminism in the 1980s' (1985) and 'The Biopolitics of Postmodern Bodies' (1988) (Haraway, 1991). As the boundaries between technology and nature undergo fundamental restructuring, partly as a result of the computer revolution, the analytical categories are made unreliable or redundant. 'Formed by technology at the same time that it creates technology, embodiment mediates between technology and discourse by creating new experiential frameworks that serve as boundary markers for the creation of corresponding discursive systems' (Hayles, 1999, 205). Cosmetic surgery and bodybuilding form part of the discourse of the cyborg, remodelling, removing and regenerating the body. The performance artist Stelarc is incorporated, literally, within a series of prosthetic devices that his body manipulates – or which manipulate him. His third arm is controlled using the muscles of his stomach but the erratic movements of one of his original arms is the result of an electric charge which he cannot control. Similarly, the performance artist Orlan has staged a series of performative cosmetic surgeries in which her likeness is transformed into Renaissance and post-Renaissance representations of female beauty. By breaking up and redeploying these art works – the forehead of da Vinci's *Mona Lisa*, the chin of Botticelli's *Venus*, the eyes of Grome's *Pysche*, the mouth of Boucher's *Europa* – Orlan's cyborgic body simulates beauty through a particularized relationship with technology. Films such as *Tetsuo* (Tsukamoto, 1988), *Terminator* (Cameron, 1984), *Robocop* (Verhoeven, 1987) and *Videodrome* (Cronenberg, 1983) combine human and machine in prosthetic extensions of the body as well as new flesh, whereas the simulation of the body in *Blade Runner* (Scott, 1982) and the *Terminator* films implies that the original may be a simulation. In cyberspace, the body is always cyborgic.

If the body is always cyborgic in cyberspace, then identity is openly simulated. Computer-cross-dressing is a standard feature of exchange on the Internet, most common in Multi-Use Dungeons or Domains (MUDs – a structured digital social experience, managed by a computer program and usually involving a loosely defined context) or chat rooms. Changing one's identity in a chat room or a MUD is a matter of simply editing one's description. Moreover, the user can have multiple identities of racial, cultural, gendered, sexed and economic difference. The decentring power of cyberspace has enabled the subject to disappear into the 'hyperreality' of digital reproductions and representation that 'bears no relation to any reality whatever: it is its own pure simulacrum' (Baudrillard, 1983, 11). Hyperreality, sustained by cyborg envy – a fascination with augmenting or disembodying technologies – is the new cyberculture. In the cybercultural relationship between the body and technology, identity does not exist.

THE CYBERCRITIC

Late twentieth-century machines have made thoroughly ambiguous the difference between natural and artificial, mind and body, self-developing and externally-designed, and many other distinctions that used to apply to organisms and machines. Our machines are disturbingly lively, and we ourselves frighteningly alert. (Haraway, 1991, 152)

If cyberculture is to be experienced rather than described, and identity does not exist in cyberspace, what, then, is cybercriticism? It could be argued that Mary Shelley's *Frankenstein* (1818) is a cybercritical piece, addressing the relationship of the body with technology. Certainly some science fiction from H. G. Wells onwards was concerned with depicting this relationship. But it was not until the artificial intelligence work after the Second World War that cybercriticism – that is, the theorizing of a radically new relationship between the body and technology (now understood primarily as information technology) – slowly emerged. If cybercriticism is based on the universal mediation of writing on a computer, then it can only exist in the latter half of the twentieth century. That said, there have been several identifiable strands of cybercriticism which have only recently begun to recognize one another. Those working in cybernetics did not have the theoretical apparatus with which to frame the practices about which they were writing. These early writings are often replete with cybernetic facts but not located within a larger argument. Those working in the humanities had the theoretical apparatus but were not able, until well after the computer revolution of the 1980s, to gain the hands-on knowledge required. For the most part, early cybercriticism in the humanities was largely constituted of hyper-textual teaching aids, similar to Landow's projects. Those working as journalists or novelists began to bring the two sides of cybercriticism together, as exemplified by cyberpunk fictions or the work of Mark Dery. But it was not until the World Wide Web became a pervasive and tangible presence in the mid-1990s that the field of 'cybercriticism' emerged in the academy, albeit never formally. It gradually crept into course syllabi and reading lists as more and more theorists and academics realized the inescapability of cyberspace. At present, it is concerned with the gendering of technoculture, with fears of the autonomous possibilities of technology, with cybernetic power conspiracies and with the relationship between the organic and the inorganic. In short, the cybercritic is one who is aware of and reads the decentralizing possibilities of this new cyberculture.

NOTES TOWARDS A READING OF *THE MATRIX*

Disneyland tells us that technology can give us more reality than nature can. (Eco, 1986, 44)

The Matrix (Wachowski Brothers, 1999) appeared at the end of a decade which had witnessed a phenomenal rise in computer usage in the West and the rapid explosion, even by twentieth-century standards of technological development, of the Internet into western life. *The Matrix* mediates the notion, within the narratorial strategies of the mainstream Hollywood film, that there is no possibility of (real) representation. With hackers, crackers, phreaks, cypherpunks (and machines that do very well at the transhuman level), the film also gathers together multiple strands of cyberpunk ideologies, 'producing' (as it is certainly not merely reproducing) the major ideologies that inform cyberpunk, such as the fear as well as the validation of technological development. Certainly, the mirrorshades and leather outfits favoured by Neo, Trinity and Morpheus provide a direct location within cyberpunk industry, as the street rebels with attitude. Moreover, Neo's Matrix incarnation – as Thomas Anderson – is a computer programmer working in a large corporation, similar to the bureaucratic Mr Zero, who is also aware of and researching the possibilities, through the Internet, of alternative virtualities. The film's major motif of enslavement is the summation of the human body to an electrical conduit. But the film narrativizes a notion of resistance through the same methods. In the breeding grounds, the human body exists as a plugging-in, as a battery. When the hackers enter their training programme – the Construct – they are similarly plugged in. Reduction to information technology is the method of enslavement, but it is via telecommunication – their mobile phones – that the hackers terrorise. For all its reflexivity, cyberpunk is caught up in the individualization of marketing technology as consumer goods.

The Matrix theorizes an alternative body as a norm. If reality, in the film, exists 'only as part of a neural-interactive simulation that we call the Matrix' (Morpheus to Neo), then the film is intent on indicating that it is the 1999 reality and a 1999 notion of the body that is a simulation. It is extremely ambivalent about an alternative definition of the human body (that is no longer born but grown) provided by the auspices of present-day interaction with information technology. If we might define that body free from the Matrix as natural, the film firmly suggests that apprehending the body within notions of the natural/unnatural binary is obsolete. Neo requires rebuilding by Dozer and even Tank and Dozer, supposedly natural humans without holes, refer to themselves as 'homegrown'. These cyborgic provisonalities point up the gendered and racial subjectivities we assign information technology. When Neo is learning various martial arts, Tank salutes his endeavour by describing him as a machine. Agent Smith describes the human race as a disease, spreading like a virus, or a computer virus. Experience is defined as simply electronic signals interpreted by the brain. The film's only available definition of the human body is not racial or gendered but electrochemical. There is a fear here that the brain is a form of information technology – but it is not a computer – it is an internet. And the thing about an internet is that it does not actually exist – it cannot be measured because it is a series of connections. When Morpheus says to Neo 'welcome to the real world,' we could be encouraged to see the world escaped to as 'the real'. But the hackers of the *Nebuchadnezzer* are in their own mini-matrix, their own construct, and, given the uninhabitable real world, are as dependent upon technology as they were in the Matrix. Neo's escape is referred to by Cypher and Morpheus as a fantasy – as Oz and as Wonderland – rather than an escape from fantasy. The artificiality of both Matrix identities and hacker names also underscores the provisionality of subjectivity. The fluidity of cybercultural identities, with neural programs that can be added or deleted like games or computer files, foregrounds the impossibility of authentic selfhood or identity, whether within the Matrix, the Construct or our own cybercultures.

QUESTIONS FOR FURTHER CONSIDERATION

1. 'Because our cultural imagination aligns masculinity and rationality with technology and science, male gendered cyborgs fail to radically challenge the distinction between human and machine. Female cyborgs, on the other hand, are culturally coded as emotional, sexual, and often, naturally maternal' (Balsamo, 1988). Does the cyborg perpetuate gender stereotypes?
2. 'Various nonwhite, nonmale subjects may possess specific relations to the postmodern situation for which the cyborg is the appropriate myth' (Foster, 1993). Does cyberspace dehistoricize and departicularize the body?
3. 'All media are extensions of some human faculty – psychic or physical. The wheel . . . is an extension of the foot. The book is an extension of the eye . . . clothing, an extension of the skin' (McLuhan, 1964). Discuss in terms of cyberspace.
4. Is there a difference between the relationships machine technologies and information technologies have with the body?
5. What is the gender of information technology in *The Matrix*?
6. If the Hollywood mainstream in the 1980s and 1990s produced a wealth of multi-cultural buddy movies, how is *The Matrix* intent on producing, locating and negotiating race within information technology?
7. Is information technology represented as a democratizing force in *The Matrix*?
8. 'Cyberspace. A consensual hallucination experienced daily by billions of legitimate operators' (Gibson, 1984). With reference both to *The Matrix* and cyberculture, do terms such as 'consensual' and 'legitimate' have any relevance or meaning?

ANNOTATED BIBLIOGRAPHY

Bell, David and Barbara Kennedy. *The Cybercultures Reader*. New York and London: Routledge, 2000. The companion volume to Bell's *An Introduction to Cyberculture* (2001), this collection provides an accessible yet rigorous guide to the major forms, practices and meanings of cyberculture and the ways in which new technologies are reshaping cultural forms and practices. The collection contains key interdisciplinary writings in the field of cyberculture, including pieces by Arthur Kroker, Andrew Ross, Vivian Sobchak and Michael Weinstein. An effective balance is struck between such influential pieces as Haraway's Cyborg Manifesto and a range of less well-known and more recent pieces. A strong introduction and an extensive bibliography frame topics such as cybersubcultures, cyberfeminisms, cybersexualities, cyberbodies and posthumanism. Issues covered include theoretical approaches to cyberculture, representations in fiction and on film, the development of distinct cybercultures and feminist and queer approaches within cyberculture. This is an essential piece of reading for students interested in cyberculture.

Dery, Mark. *Escape Velocity: Cyberculture at the end of the Century*. London: Hodder & Stoughton, 1996. Taking as its premise that the computer revolution has given rise to a digital underground, the members of which are using technology in ways never intended, this is a provocative analysis of the wired revolution, engaging in a studious discussion of the subcultures that make up cyberculture: cyberdelia, cyberpunk, cybersex, cybernetic body art and cyborging. A successful mixture of journalese and rigorous scholarship, Dery writes with authority, using such theorists as Bataille, Foucault and Baudrillard to situate cyberculture within postmodernity while providing the lay reader with an informative and animated tour of cyberculture.

Landow, George. *Hypertext: The Convergence of Contemporary Critical Theory and Technology*. Baltimore, MD: Johns Hopkins University Press, 1992; *Hypertext in Hypertext*. Baltimore, MD: Johns Hopkins University Press, 1993. In the 1992 version, Landow – the creator of several hypertexts, including the award-winning Dickens Web – predicted how hypertext would impact upon traditional notions of reading, writing, textuality, literature and pedagogy. He argued that hypertext embodies elements of the postmodern aesthetic, with its multivocality, intertextuality and decentred narration. The relationship between critical theory and the (then) latest advances in computer software is explored in order to delineate the possible effect technology could have on scholarship. In hypermedia, Landow saw a strikingly literal embodiment of many major points of critical theory, particularly Derrida's idea of 'decentring' and the Barthesian readerly versus writerly text. The argument and theory are admirably presented but the book fails precisely because it remains a book and not a hypertext. In 1993, the book was released in hypertext, thus providing an electronic version of the original text. There are some problems with the hypertext environment (it is stand-alone and allows for little interaction from the reader) which, in part, contradict Landow's claim that hypertext allows readers to become writers. That aside, *Hypertext* was ground-breaking in both theory and design and serves both as a useful introduction to the possibilities of hypertext as well as acting as a moment in the history of cyberculture.

Penley, Constance and Andrew Ross (eds). *Technoculture*. Minneapolis, MN: University of Minnesota Press, 1991. Although this was the first collection of essays which attempted to locate the study of technology within a cultural studies perspective it has aged well and provides a snapshot of cybercultural theory before the Internet explosion of the mid-1990s. The collection carefully negotiates the fine line between locating technology as a tool for domination and exalting it as a moment of the postmodern sublime, while providing an assessment of the politics in the cultural practices of technology. It provides a model of what can be done in the dialogue between technology and the humanities. The collection includes essays on computer hacking and the technological underpinnings of rap as well an interview with Donna Haraway.

Wolmark, Jenny (ed.). *Cybersexualities: A Reader on Feminist Theory, Cyborgs and Cyberspace*. Edinburgh: Edinburgh University Press, 1999. The cyborg and cyberpunk have opened up new feminist readings about embodiment and identity in relation to technology and this anthology is the first of its kind to gather together essays debating these readings. The three sections – Technology, Embodiment and Cyberspace; Cybersubjects: Cyborgs and Cyberpunks; Cyborg Futures – address various moments and aspects of the human–technology interface. A strong introduction surveys the ways in which cyborg and cyberspace metaphors have been deployed in critical theory. The collection brings together key authors in feminist and cyber theory that demonstrate the wide range of contemporary critical work while challenging constructions of gender, race and class. Like *The Cybercultures Reader*, the essays in *Cybersexualities* range from classic pieces of cybercultural theory to less canonized pieces, all drawn together by the introductions to each section.

SUPPLEMENTARY BIBLIOGRAPHY

Aronowitz, Stanley, Michael Menser and Barbara Martinsons (eds). *Technoscience and Cyberculture: A Cultural Study*. New York and London: Routledge, 1996.

Balsamo, Anne. 'Reading Cyborgs Writing Feminism' [1988]. *Cybersexualities: A Reader on Feminist Theory, Cyborgs and Cyberspace*, ed. Jenny Wolmark. Edinburgh: Edinburgh University Press, 1999, 145–56.

Barry, John. *Technobabble*. Cambridge, MA: MIT Press, 1991.

Baudrillard, Jean. *Simulation*, trans. Paul Foss et al. New York: Semiotext(e), 1983.

Baudrillard, Jean. *The Evil Demon of Images*, trans. Paul Foss et al. Sydney: Power Institute of Fine Arts, 1987.

Bell, David. *Introduction to Cyberculture*. New York and London: Routledge, 2001.

Bukatman, Scott. *Terminal Identity: The Virtual Subject in Postmodern Science Fiction*. Durham, NC: Duke University Press, 1993.

Calcutt, Andrew. *White Noise: An A–Z of the Contradictions of Cyberculture*. London: Palgrave, 1998.

Cavallaro, Dani. *Cyberpunk and Cyberculture: Science Fiction and the Work of William Gibson*. London: Athlone, 2000.

De Landa, Manuel. *War in the Age of Intelligent Machines*. New York: Zone Books, 1991.

Dery, Mark (ed.). *Flame Wars: The Discourse of Cyberculture*. Durham, NC: Duke University Press, 1995.

Docherty, Thomas. 'Introduction'. In *Postmodernism: A Reader*. New York and London: Harvester Wheatsheaf, 1993, 1–31.

Eco, Umberto. *Travels in Hyperreality*. Orlando, FL: Harcourt Brace Jovanovich, 1986.

Featherstone, Mike and Roger Burrows (eds). *Cyberspace/Cyberbodies/Cyberpunk*. Thousand Oaks, CA: Sage, 1996.

Foster, Thomas. 'Meat Puppets or Robopaths? Cyberpunk and the Question of Embodiment' [1993]. *Cybersexualities: A Reader on Feminist Theory, Cyborgs and Cyberspace*, ed. Jenny Wolmark. Edinburgh: Edinburgh University Press, 1999, 208–29.

Freud, Sigmund. 'The Uncanny'. In *The Complete Psychological Works of Sigmund Freud. Volume XVII (1917–1919)*, ed. James Strachey, trans. James Strachey. London: Hogarth, 1955, 221–52.

Gaggi, Silvio. *From Text to Hypertext: Decentering the Subject in Fiction, Film, the Visual Arts and Electronic Media*. Philadelphia, PA: University of Pennsylvania Press, 1997.

Gibson, Stephanie. *The Emerging Cyberculture: Literacy, Paradigm and Paradox*. Geskill, NJ: Hampton Press, 1999.

Gibson, William. *Neuromancer*. New York: Ace Books, 1984.

Haraway, Donna. *Simians, Cyborgs, and Women: The Reinvention of Nature*. New York and London: Routledge, 1991.

Hawthorne, Susan and Renate Klein. *Cyberfeminism: Connectivity, Critique and Creativity*. Melbourne: Spinifex Press, 2000.

Hayles, Katherine. *How We Became Posthuman: Virtual Bodies in Cybernetics, Literature, and Informatics*. Chicago: University of Chicago Press, 1999.

Herman, Andrew and Thomas Swiss. *The World Wide Web and Contemporary Cultural Theory: Magic, Metaphor, Power*. New York and London: Routledge, 2000.

Kristeva, Julia. 'Word, Dialogue and Reader'. In *The Kristeva Reader*, ed. Toril Moi. New York: Columbia University Press, 1986, 35–61.

Kroker, Arthur and Michael Weinsten. *Data Trash: The Theory of the Virtual Class*. New York: St Martin's Press, 1994.

Kroker, Arthur and Marilouise Kroker (eds). *Digital Delerium*. New York: St Martin's Press, 1997.

Landow, George (ed.). *Hyper/Text/Theory*. Baltimore, MD: Johns Hopkins University Press, 1995.

Landow, George and Paul Delany (eds). *Hypermedia and Literary Studies*. Cambridge, MA: MIT Press, 1991.

Lanham, Richard. *The Electronic Word: Democracy, Technology and the Arts*. Chicago, IL: University of Chicago Press, 1993.

McLuhan, Marshall. *Understanding Media: The Extensions of Man*. London: Routledge & Kegan Paul, 1964.

Postman, Neil. *Technopoly: The Surrender of Culture to Technology*. New York: Alfred A. Knopf, 1992.

Roberts, Lawrence. 'The ARPANET and Computer Networks'. In *A History of Personal Workstations*, ed. Adele Goldberg. New York: ACM Press, 1988, 143–67.

Rochlin, Gene. *Trapped in the Net: The Unanticipated Consequences of Computerization*. Princeton, NJ: Princeton University Press, 1997.

Roszak, Theodore. *The Cult of Information: The Folklore of Computers and the True Art of Thinking*. Cambridge: Lutterworth Press, 1986.

Rushoff, Douglas. *Cyberia: Life in the Trenches of Hyperspace*. New York: Harper, 1994.

Shenk, David. *Data Smog: Surviving the Information Glut*. San Francisco, CA: HarperEdge, 1997.

Sterling, Bruce. *Crystal Express*. New York: Ace Books, 1990.

Tofts, Darren and Murrray McKeich. *Memory Trade: A Prehistory of Cyberculture*. North Ryde, NSW: 21.C/Interface, 1997.

Weizenbaum, Joseph. *Computer Power and Human Reason: From Judgement to Calculation*. San Francisco, CA: W. H. Freeman, 1976.

FILMOGRAPHY

Blade Runner. Dir. Ridley Scott. Prod. The Ladd Company. Starring Harrison Ford, Sean Young and Rutger Hauer. USA, 1982. 117 minutes. Colour.

Brazil. Dir. Terry Gilliam. Prod. Universal Pictures/Embassy International Pictures. Starring Jonathon Pryce, Robert De Niro and Katherine Helmond. UK, 1985. 142 minutes. Colour.

The Matrix. Dir. Andy and Larry Wachowski. Prod. Village Roadshow/Silver Pictures/Groucho II Film Partnership. Starring Keanu Reeves, Laurence Fishburne and Carrie-Anne Moss. USA, 1999. 136 minutes. Colour.

Star Wars: Episode IV, A New Hope. Dir. George Lucas. Prod. Lucasfilm Ltd. Starring Mark Hamill, Harrison Ford and Carrie Fisher. USA, 1977. 121 minutes. Colour.

CRITICAL VOICES

CHAPTER

10

DELEUZEAN CRITICISM

Claire Colebrook

Above all else, Gilles Deleuze was a philosopher. His works always insisted on the power of philosophy to question and transform life. But Deleuze also thought that philosophy could only be truly transformative if it encountered other powers, such as the powers of art, cinema, literature and science (Deleuze and Guattari, 1994).

Before looking at how we might 'translate' Deleuze's philosophy into literary theory it is necessary to consider just what the concept of 'literary theory' presupposes about the relation between philosophy and literature. 'Theory' is derived from the ancient Greek 'theoria' – a mode of elevated looking that intuits the stable truths behind the flux of appearances. Theoria is therefore connected with the privileging of *being* – or what remains the same and knowable – over *becoming*. Following the French philosopher Henri Bergson (1859–1941), Deleuze argued that it is theoretical knowledge that fixes and spatializes the temporal flow of life. For practical purposes we do not attend to the fluxes of difference that make up the real. Instead, we perceive a world of determined and stable beings. Deleuze's own work has insisted that we need to take philosophy and all thinking beyond the narrow viewpoint of conceptual knowledge. Philosophy, from Plato onwards, has been *theoretical* because it intuits or sees the truth of *what is*; it is elevated above the flux of perceptions to discern those truths and forms that make perception possible. In this respect, most philosophy has been committed to *transcendence*, or what lies outside experience and remains the same. Indeed, philosophy has always formed its *transcendental* or grounding questions on the basis of some *transcendent* or external being. The relation, and difference, between transcendent and transcendental is crucial in Deleuze's philosophy. We may have experiences within the world – of this or that *transcendent* or external object – but philosophy reflects upon how we see or know anything at all. Philosophy, from Plato to

UNIVERSITY COLLEGE WINCHESTER
LIBRARY

Deleuze, has affirmed its *transcendental* potential: rather than being concerned with any given or *transcendent* thing, it asks how the experience or being of things, in general, is possible. This is transcendental questioning, which does not begin from any already given term within the world but asks how anything like a world, experience or being could exist at all. Whatever transcendent events we perceive within the world, we can always adopt a transcendental viewpoint: how are such events possible?

That identity not be first, that it exist as a principle but as a second principle, as a principle *become*; that it revolve around the Different: such would be the nature of a Copernican revolution which opens up the possibility of difference having its own concept, rather than being maintained under the domination of a concept in general already understood as identical (Deleuze, 1994, 40–1).

According to Deleuze, western thought has more often than not failed to ask properly transcendental questions. We usually begin from some transcendent term, or 'plane of transcendence'; we presuppose the mind of man, or matter or the perceiving human eye. To think transcendentally requires, Deleuze insists, a commitment to immanence. This is a refusal to explain life by some outside or transcendent plane; it is to think the power of life on its own terms, without subordinating life to an already existing image (Deleuze and Guattari, 1987, 499). A truly transcendental viewpoint does not accept that the world that we experience at a day-to-day level is the truth or whole of life. In order to arrive at the very life of things we need to go beyond any single or specific event and ask how events, differences and 'singularities' are possible.

Literary theory has tended to expose the practice of traditional literary criticism to these sorts of transcendental considerations. How is meaning or reading in general possible? With literary theory we do not just read or interpret a text as though its meaning were simply something 'there', or transcendent, waiting to be discovered. *Theory* demands that we account for *how* we read or see a text, how we generate the meanings that we do. It demands that we reflect upon our practices and our point of view as readers and interpreters. Once we recognize the possibility of theory – that we always approach the text from some point of view – then we also admit that any interpretation that claims *not* to have a theory is merely blind to the decisions and assumptions it must make in order to read. Given this claim of theory in general – that reading is always a decision in relation to a text – what sort of theory does Deleuze offer? To begin with we can note that Deleuze tries to overcome the idea of a theoretical viewpoint, and this also includes the concepts of meaning and interpretation. Far from *deciding* what a text means from some separate point of view of judgement, and far from making sense of a text, Deleuze's own practice of reading was one of *encounter*: what does this text *do* to thinking? And sense, for Deleuze, is not something a reading uncovers. We do not see text or hear sounds and then shuffle through our memory bank to match it to some meaning. Sense is not something we consciously decide upon, interpret or intuit through a theory. Sense is a virtual plane or whole opened up by a text that confronts us or does violence to our presuppositions.

We can read a sentimental novel or attend a performance of a Romantic opera and find ourselves moved to tears or have our heart rate elevated by anticipation and desire for narrative resolution; we are not interpreting this work – finding some signification behind its signs. The work offers itself as a whole world of affects and senses: a sense of love, loss, cliché or even cloying sentimentality. It is not that we *feel* love or are in love, but we experience the *sense* of love. Now for Deleuze this means that the point of view of the separate and disengaged subject of theory, the subject who decides upon or interprets, does not go far enough in asking the transcendental question. Before there are subjects who perceive and form theories Deleuze insists on the impersonal domain of sense: on affects of love, for example, that are felt as such, without being the love *of* this or that person for this or that beloved. This is why art – as the creation of affects – is so crucial for Deleuze's philosophy of immanence. For it is only if we move beyond theory and the judging and interpretive point of view to those senses and affects that invade us and produce us that we will arrive at thinking life itself, and not any of its organizing or transcendent terms.

Many philosophers of Deleuze's generation, particularly Jacques Derrida and Michel Foucault, questioned the status of philosophy as transcendental. Philosophy could not be some pure theory separated from the particular events and texts of this world. Philosophy had its own textual conditions (its use of metaphors, figures, syntactical idiosyncrasies and embedded norms) along with specific historical conditions, such as what constitutes a legitimate question for any epoch. On the one hand, then, the twentieth century saw an emphasis on theory: on reflecting upon the conditions and decisions that form philosophy and judgement. For Derrida this meant looking at textual conditions or the way syntax and language determined decisions. For Foucault this meant looking at the historical a priori, or all the ways in which thinking was determined by the 'unthought', including spatial, technical and material conditions. For Deleuze, by contrast, far from abandoning the possibility of a philosophy capable of thinking the very genesis of life, Deleuze insisted that we should not collapse transcendental questions – questions about life *as such* – into worldly questions. Philosophy for Deleuze is not just another form of writing or textuality; it has a power to think beyond any actual or given differences. Where Deleuze differs from many of his contemporaries is his insistence on the force and essence of philosophy and its difference from the force and essence of literature. This has two important consequences.

First, Deleuze insists in general on a philosophy of transcendental empiricism. It may be that any philosophical text will have elements of the literary about it, but this does not mean we cannot intuit essentially philosophical tendencies. An essence for Deleuze is not some isolated and unchanging thing, such as the supposed essence of 'human nature'. An essence is a capacity, tendency or power to become. The essence of philosophy does not lie 'in', say, the works of

Plato; it is a power to produce philosophical problems, both in the actual texts of the past, and the potential texts of the future. Philosophy and literature differ in their powers or potentials. A novel may have passages of philosophical reflection but what makes it a novel or an instance of literature is its specifically artistic power: its power to create sensations and affects beyond the reader's own world. I read a novel such as Charles Dickens's *Bleak House* and perceive a sense of disorder, futility, stultification and hopelessness, a sense that is conveyed through images of mud, slime, delay and obstruction. Literature has this power to release sense from specific persons and situations and give us a general affect.

Philosophy, also, has its own power which can be discerned or intuited even if all the texts of actual philosophy are mixed with scientific and literary elements. It is the power to create concepts. Such concepts do not label things. Rather, creating a philosophical concept entails thinking beyond things to the forces or tendencies that make things possible. A concept does not label an event within the world; it allows us to think of the world in a new way. The concept of 'desire' in psychoanalysis, for example, does not generalize or label a collection of things *within the world*. It is desire that produces bodies, passions, perceptions, images, histories, fantasies and human societies (Deleuze and Guattari, 1983, 30). Deleuze's philosophy of desire is *transcendental* because it refuses to reduce life to any of its already existing manifestations. It strives to think the hidden or virtual potential of life, above and beyond any living thing. Philosophy is the tendency to create concepts that allow us to think this virtual life.

Second, a transcendental approach does not end with the power of philosophy. Life, according to Deleuze, can express or become through different and divergent tendencies; indeed, it may well be impossible to combine the perceptions of science, art and philosophy into one coherent world. Literature or art are specific tendencies and should not be seen as the stylistic expression of scientific or philosophical ideas. Whereas philosophy is the power of producing concepts (enabling us to think the whole of life), and science is the power of producing functions (allowing us to form practical observations and laws that organize life), art produces affects and percepts. We will look at this in far more detail below, but to do so we need to add more concepts to Deleuze's project of transcendental philosophy: the concepts of univocity, empiricism and immanence.

Concepts, Deleuze argues, are never isolated entities. A concept allows thought to move around and create, but it can do so only by producing a 'plane': a series of interconnected moves that allow us to ask meaningful questions. How could we have the philosophical concept of 'mind', for example, without the connected concepts of logic, knowledge, certainty, thoughts and individuals? And all these concepts presuppose a certain drama or image of thought (Deleuze, 1994, xx), such as a philosopher alone in her study asking what is really true. For Deleuze, recognizing these planes or unstated presuppositions and images means exploring the sense within which we move and think. Sense is neither stated nor represented, but it has to be there as a medium in order to state or represent. We could not have the concept of mind without the assumption that it makes *sense* to ask certain questions. We have the concept of mind in response to certain problems. If I ask, 'How do I know the experiences I have are real?' then this can only make *sense* if we assume a mind disengaged from a world, a subject set over against experience. Before there can be decisions about truth or falsity there has to be this milieu of sense. This attention to sense gives us a transcendental method, for as we ask more and more questions and create further problems we free ourselves from dogma and opinion and begin to *think*. No concept makes sense without some presupposed plane; these are not personal presuppositions, for there has to be some milieu of sense before there can even be the concept of the person.

Deleuze's own concepts of univocity, empiricism and immanence are created across the plane of his own philosophy, although he also tried to create multiple planes and even co-authored a work called *A Thousand Plateaus*, which was not a coherent thesis so much as the creation of diverging problems. Univocity is a commitment to *one* being with no outside or external viewpoint (Deleuze, 1994, 35). Western thought has tended to be *equivocal*, dividing being into two hierarchized substances, such as mind and matter, reality and illusion, creator and created, actual life and virtual life, or subject and being. For Deleuze equivocity *cannot* make sense. To say that something *is* is to admit its existence or being. If I say that something *is* an illusion, a fiction, an error or even an evil, then I already acknowledge its force and its reality. For Deleuze there is one being that includes ideas, matter, the future, difference, the past, stories, representations, particles and concepts. And if perceptions are themselves real then it also makes no sense to see them as images or copies *of* the real. The real itself is just the totality of possible perceptions and events, with the totality being necessarily open to further difference and perception. This is univocal being, with no substance being elevated above, or given priority to, any other: 'Univocity of being thus also signifies equality of being. Univocal Being is one and the same time nomadic distribution and crowned anarchy' (Deleuze, 1994, 37). Minds are not pictures of reality, nor is reality a projection of mind; mind and matter are different expressions of the one life.

Univocity therefore leads to immanence. Western thought has been enslaved to transcendence: the idea that there is some outside or external world to be known, the idea that being simply *is,* or that it transcends us and that we somehow have to break through images and becoming in order to get to the real and transcendent world. (Deleuze and Guattari, 'Transcendence: a Specifically European Disease', 1987, 18). Against this, Deleuze insists on immanence. There is not a transcendent real world outside or beyond images and perceptions. Being *is* perception. This does not mean that being is a mental event or something inside our heads. If we thought this then we would still be grounding the world on some privileged external point – such as the mind, brain or human perception. To say that being *is* perception is to say that life as such is imaging and perceiving: sound waves, light waves, genetic mutations, nucleic acids and proteins, computer errors and viruses all 'perceive' each other in the dynamic whole that is life. The human brain is one point of perception among others, with the peculiar capacity to form a concept or idea of this whole imaging process. There is, for Deleuze, just one immanent life, an open whole precisely because there is no single point, no transcendent outside, that can act as the ground or viewpoint for any other. Each event in life perceives its own world, and there are as many worlds as there are potential for perception: plant worlds, animal worlds, fictional worlds, the worlds of the microscope and other machines.

Univocity and immanence, in turn, connect with empiricism. Empiricism is opposed to idealism. Idealism insists that any world or experienced thing is known *as* something and is therefore determined and made possible by the idea we have of it. Deleuze's empiricism argues the contrary. It is not that there is a mind, language or culture that constructs or determines a world. Mind, ideas and languages are effects and creations of life (Deleuze, 1994, xx). This argument is explored most imaginatively in two of the books Deleuze co-authored with Félix Guattari: *Anti-Oedipus* and *A Thousand Plateaus*. Mind and language are described here as effects of a general and inhuman desire. Life begins as an 'intense germinal influx' – an open whole of becoming, creation and interaction (Deleuze and Guattari, 1983, 164). We need to get rid of the idea of pre-human life as an undifferentiated chaos (Deleuze, 1988b, 103). For Deleuze and Guattari the pre-human is intensively diverse, mobile and creative of differences far too rich for any single human eye or language.

From the pre-human complex of flows, relative points of stability gradually form, such as tribes or territories. These blocks of assembled bodies create further marks and differences, such as scarring, tattooing and body-painting, which organize and code the genetic differences or the germinal influx. Once these territories become relatively stable it is possible for one body or mark to organize the whole; one body *deterritorializes* to become a leader or author of the assemblage. This body that leaps outside the territory can, through even further force and desire, construct an image of law or separate power: the king's body is the sign of a divine right not reducible to the material body. This gives life a virtual centre or governing origin. Deleuze and Guattari's main point is that such a virtual body that enslaves life is actually created from desire and the imagination, from perception and excess: it is by taking more than the other bodies, and by *not* producing, that the royal body becomes law. When, in modernity, we overthrow such divine origins and assert the rights of 'man' or the 'subject' we have merely taken one point of transcendent illusion and substituted another. We are still subjected to transcendence: the illusion that there is some image within life – the subject – that is the point of explanation for life in general, 'the ultimate private and subjugated territoriality of European man' (Deleuze and Guattari, 1983, 102).

The task of literary theory, therefore, should be the destruction of this subjection to transcendence. This requires two moves. First, there is no such thing as theory. There is no privileged point or origin from which life might be judged. There are theoretical concepts and tendencies, but if these become 'a' theory then they lose their power to theorize: to think beyond already given images. Instead of trying to step outside the whole of life to establish a point of theory and reflection we need to create concepts – such as Deleuze's concept of desire – that enable us to think of life as an infinitely complicated, inhuman, differing and open whole. Second, instead of thinking of language as a 'signifier' used by the subject (or culture) to represent and determine the world, we need to see language as a flow of signs alongside other signs, signs which themselves are effective and productive without being *meaningful*. Instead of interpreting a text by asking what it means or wants to say – as though the text were a way of getting to the world – we need to see what a text does as an event of becoming, as itself a 'world'.

STYLE

The usual understanding of style is tied up with traditional and, for Deleuze, debilitating metaphysical notions of transcendence, equivocity, subjectivism and representation. If we imagine that there simply *is* a transcendent or external world that is then represented, then we will imagine style as some type of secondary ornament or overlay. There would be being and then its various styles of existence, or the representation of being supplemented by stylistic differences. Good thinking would supposedly represent the world with as little difference as possible. The model of truth would be the universal proposition that can and must be agreed upon by all subjects: propositions in accord with a purely formal logic free of stylistic content. On this picture, style would be in danger of distorting truth and the straightforward presentation of the world. To understand style in this way is to see difference as negative. It is as though there is a self-same world that could be represented through this or that different style. The differences of style would then be grounded on some prior sameness.

Such an understanding of style also commits us to subjectivism. There would be an original point or ground – the subject – which forms the basis for various differentiating statements. Bear in mind that the 'subject' refers to the 'I' who speaks, the subject of the sentence that can then be predicated, and to the ultimate ground – the subject of discussion. Deleuze wants to think style independently of all these senses: a style freed from a subject's point of view, a mode of writing that does not use the subject/predicate form of the proposition, and a mode of thinking that does not refer difference and variation back to some prior ground. The subject is that which precedes or stands outside various acts of predication, difference and style. The act and event of style is thereby subordinated to what it creates. This concept of the subject also ties in with equivocity: we imagine an actual world of being or material substance, and then a world of representation. Such a metaphysics for Deleuze is not only in error – for it makes no sense to posit a 'real' world *behind* thoughts, style and representation. Thinking, styles and images are themselves fully real and part of life, not supplements added onto life. 'Becoming produces nothing other than itself. We fall into a false alternative if we say that you either imitate or you are. What is real is the becoming itself, the block of becoming, not the supposedly fixed terms through which that becoming passes' (Deleuze and Guattari, 1987, 238).

The metaphysics of equivocity, which separates being from its stylistic differences, is also *reactive*. It enslaves the active creation and becoming of life to one of its created terms. A certain style of speech and existence produces the concept of the subject, and we then imagine that the subject preceded and grounded becoming and creation. But any such transcendent ground or external point from which we might judge life is, Deleuze insists, itself an event in the differential flow of life.

The standard notion of point of view – that there is a subject who speaks and predicates an outside world or who lies behind perceptions – needs to be supplanted by an *immanent* understanding of style. If there are just perceptions and differences, without preceding subjects, then we can imagine a world of interacting variations rather than fixed beings and relations. 'What is called a style can be the most natural thing in the world; it is nothing other than the procedure of continuous variation . . . Because a style is not an individual psychological creation but an assemblage of enunciation, it unavoidably produces a language within a language' (Deleuze and Guattari, 1987, 97). Here, style is not an ornament or affect used by subjects to express their point of view. Style is the difference of life itself from which subjects are effected: 'man' is the creation of certain styles of speech, action, anticipation and social connection. Animals have their own style: becoming-animal. We can imagine human life abandoning the concept of the subject and creating in other ways, such as becoming-woman: 'Language must devote itself to reaching these feminine, animal, molecular detours, and every detour is a becoming-mortal . . . Syntax is the set of necessary detours that are created in each case to reveal the life in things' (Deleuze, 1997, 2). Life as a whole is nothing more than stylistic variation, a potential to create ever more differences and perceptions. For each style of becoming can cross with other styles to create even further differences. A cat is a style of becoming-animal – a collection of moves, habits, preferences, capacities and potentials – including the potential to create styles in other styles of life. If a cat's perceptions and world are perceived by a poet then we might have a literature that no longer speaks with the voice of man. When T. S. Eliot (1888–1965) wrote *Old Possum's Book of Practical Cats* (1939) he did not describe or list propositions about cats, nor did he speak 'like' a cat. He allowed one style of life – human speech – to intersect with another – cat-life, and this produced a poetry that was certainly not 'about' the world so much as creative of a world.

Literary style, for Deleuze, is not a medium or vehicle that authors use to express ideas. Style is not a way of depicting life; style produces life and points of view:

> That is what style is, or rather the absence of style – asyntactic, agrammatical: the moment when language is no longer defined by what it says, even less by what makes it a signifying thing, but by what causes it to move, to flow, and to explode – desire. For literature is like schizophrenia: a process and not a goal, a production and not an expression. (Deleuze and Guattari, 1983, 133)

Free-indirect style, dominant in the literary modernism of the early twentieth century was a crucial manoeuvre in liberating style from the subject. In free-indirect style the text is neither in the first person – referred back to the expressing 'I' – nor in an omniscient third person who could oversee and speak objectively about characters and the world. Omniscient narration uses a language that would not be spoken by the characters themselves to describe their thoughts and actions. Much of the satire of Henry Fielding's *Tom Jones* is achieved by the narrator being able to view and describe all the motives and psychological depths that characters themselves might deny:

> The extremes of grief and joy have been remarked to produce very similar effects, and when either of these rushes on us by surprise, it is apt to create such a total perturbation and confusion that we are often thereby deprived of the use of all our faculties. It cannot therefore be wondered at that the unexpected sight of Mr. Jones should so strongly operate on the mind of Molly and should overwhelm her with such confusion that for some minutes she was unable to express the great raptures with which the reader will suppose she was affected on this occasion. (Fielding [1749], 1994, 190)

In so doing traditional omniscient narration creates a confident shared viewpoint between reader and narrator; we have satire because 'we' can see the motives behind actions and are thus able to discern the difference between the style the character presents and their actual intentions.

Free-indirect style, by contrast, employs the idiosyncrasies and verbal tics of a character in order to describe or speak about that character. *Simple* free-indirect style would therefore use a dialect to describe a character from a particular region, or it may even be quite subtle and express the values or inflections of the described character. In D. H. Lawrence's 'Jimmy and the Desperate Woman' the narrative voice moves seamlessly between words that would seem to be alien to the described character and near-exclamations that would be inwardly spoken by the character himself. The following sentences trace the very eye of the character, making their way through the description in the same way that an eye makes out and assesses details, with a 'yes' when something is identified.

> At last he came in sight of a glimmer. Apparently, there were dwellings.
> Yes, a new little street, with one street-lamp, and the houses all apparently

dark. He paused. Absolute desertion. Then three children. (Lawrence, 1950, 115)

This is not a narrator who has the plot and details spread out in advance from a single viewpoint. Instead of sentences and propositions grounded in observers there are detached perceptions: 'Absolute desertion'; 'Then three children'. It is impossible to say *who* is seeing or saying these 'percepts': the narration is just the list of the character's perceptions, but the character is presented, himself, as an assemblage of perceptions. Free-indirect style is located neither within the subject, nor above the subject in a describing narration; it is a style of writing that displays the production of selves and locations through perceptions and expressions:

> It is for this reason that indirect discourse, *especially free indirect discourse*, is of exemplary value: there are no clear, distinctive contours; what comes first is not an insertion of variously individuated statements, or an interlocking of different subjects of enunciation, but a collective assemblage resulting in the determination of relative subjectification proceedings, or assignations of individuality and their shifting distributions within discourse. Indirect discourse is not explained by the distinction between subjects; rather, it is the assemblage, as it freely appears in this discourse, that explains all the voices present within a single voice . . . (Deleuze and Guattari, 1987, 80)

Style, for Deleuze, is not what we use in order to speak; it is style that enables the creation of a 'we' and a shared mode of speech. For this reason, Deleuze writes of literature's production of a 'people to come': 'Health as literature, as writing, consists in inventing a people who are missing. It is the task of the fabulating function to invent a people . . . The ultimate aim of literature is to set free, in the delirium, this creation of a health or this invention of a people, that is, a possibility of life' (Deleuze, 1997, 4). There are not communities of speakers who share an identity and then speak; rather, through the production of styles relatively stable identities are created, but such creations are always open to future mutation and difference. Free-indirect style is important in this regard precisely because it shows the ways in which styles of speech are never fully or exhaustively owned by speakers. Speech and style bear their own force; to adopt a style of speech is to become in a certain way, to take part in a specific territory and to reinforce and reconfigure tendencies and habits:

> . . . for speaking is no less a movement than walking: the former goes beyond speech toward language, just as the latter goes beyond the organism to a body without organs . . . Creative stuttering is what makes language grow from the middle, like grass; it is what makes language a rhizome instead of a tree, what puts language in perpetual disequilibrium: *Ill Seen, Ill Said* (content and expression). Being well spoken has never been either the distinctive feature or the concern of great writers. (Deleuze, 1997, 111)

What free-indirect style then creates is the idea of a language freed from voice and subject: an 'it speaks', 'speaking' or 'to speak', rather than an 'I speak'. We can also note, here, a point about Deleuze's approach to history. If we see the power of modernist free-indirect style, this does not mean that we should try to re-create the very styles of modernism as *the* style most appropriate to Deleuzean criticism. Rather, if we see how modernism uses style to transform the concept of style – style is no longer spoken by the subject but creative of subjects – then we will be able to ask how we might repeat modernism's essence. Far from creating modernist works this would require reading the texts of today, or the past, with a sense of how style might work, what style might do – and not what style represents or reflects. How could other styles transform the very potential of style?

AFFECT

In *Anti-Oedipus* Deleuze and Guattari describe or imagine the 'intense germinal influx' or life as an inhuman swarm of differences: forces that attract and repel each other to produce points of relative stability, bodies or territories:

> In a word, the opposition of the forces of attraction and repulsion produces an open series of intensive elements, all of them positive, that are never an expression of the final equilibrium of a system, but consist, rather, of an unlimited number of stationary, metastable states through which a subject passes. (Deleuze and Guattari, 1983, 19)

Bodies, subjects or points of view are produced through the connection of intensities: the eye meets with light and in this attraction the eye becomes an organ of vision and the light waves become visible. For Deleuze, the world we know through relations – the world our eye sees, our ear hears, our mind imagines and our body feels – is the *actualization* of flows of difference. Light waves become visible when attracted by the eye, but the differences of light waves have other potentials – to be actualized as felt heat, just as sound waves can be visible for a bat who 'sees' through sonar. It is not that there are related points – eye and world – which *then* meet through affect. Rather, there are affects – sensibilities *to be* heard, seen or perceived – that produce the seeing eye, the thinking mind and the acting body: 'The mind begins by coldly and curiously regarding what the body does, it is first of all a witness; then it is affected, it becomes an impassioned witness, that is, it experiences for itself affects that are not simply affects of the body, but veritable *critical entities* that hover over the body and judge it' (Deleuze, 1997, 124).

Human life emerges from the intense germinal influx through the territorialization of affect. From a large range of affects – all the potential differences that the human body encounters – certain regularities are invested. The eye is drawn again and again to the same image, the mouth again and again to the same body part; this repetition *creates* difference. In repeating an affect, such as the eye re-finding an image, the image can become a sign, a symbol, a totem. The mouth that seeks the breast creates a relation between mother and child, a family, a culture. The repetition of affects produces distinct terms, with each term itself capable of further connections and creations. A tribe is formed by investing in the affect of a sound (a drumbeat). 'England' is formed by the investment in affects: the colours of the flag, the sounds of the national anthem, the continual quotation of phrases from Shakespeare. Such affects are not symbols *of Englishness*; Englishness is just the collection of bodies investing in certain repeated affects. Affects are those events of intersection prior to human thought. The eye that meets with light, the ear that hears, the body that starts or jumps from shock – all these are the affects from which we are formed.

Deleuze and Guattari define philosophy as the creation of concepts, concepts such as 'the intense germinal influx' or 'Being', which enable minds to think the virtual whole of life, virtual because such a whole could never be presented as an actual thing: '. . . the Whole is only virtual, dividing itself by being acted out. It cannot assemble its actual parts that remain external to each other: The Whole is never "given." And, in the actual, an irreducible pluralism reigns – as many worlds as living beings, all "closed" on themselves' (Deleuze, 1988b, 104).

Art, by contrast, creates affects and percepts. This is more than saying that art is affective (making us feel something), and it is more than saying that art is non-conceptual (presenting colours and sounds rather than meanings or ideas). Art may present colours we *perceive*, but it engages with *percepts* when it presents colour not just as an actual thing but as a potential or power for perception. A Rembrandt portrait is not just a dark canvas; we do not just see dark paint; we see what darkness can do. We can imagine a young painter seeing a Rembrandt who responded not by forging a painting (banal repetition) but by being provoked into taking darkness even further. Such repetition would respond to the percept: what is perceived is not just the actual and present – these dark shades – but an *Idea* of darkness, or what darkness might become: darkness as a virtual power *to differ*.

The problem, for Deleuze, that dominates common sense and everyday life, and that thereby leads to unthinking philosophy, is the lazy and undifferentiated attachment of concepts to affects and percepts. Green means go; darkness means negativity; 'man' is white; tartan, haggis and Burns are what it means to be Scottish. We no longer encounter affects – allowing ourselves to respond, become or question differences. We attach affects habitually to everyday concepts; we pass all too readily from affect to concept. For Deleuze this is the banality and rigidity of opinion, which underpins a society geared to 'communication' or the maximum circulation of information *without* ambiguity or distortion. Concepts are easily attached to affects: the 'foreigner' is a label for certain smells, sounds, gestures and rhythms. Similarly, certain affects are directly attached to concepts. Such attachments stop us from thinking. Deleuze and Guattari cite the example of the smell of cheese (Deleuze and Guattari, 1994, 146). The everyday man of opinion moves directly from affect – the nostrils recoiling at the smell – to concept: this cheese *is* disgusting or inedible. Common sense and opinion create a single, universal point of view of agreement, from which all affects are immediately recognized and judged:

> In every conversation the fate of philosophy is always at stake, and many philosophical discussions do not as such go beyond discussions of cheese, including the insults and the confrontation of worldviews. The philosophy of communication is exhausted in the search for a universal liberal opinion as consensus, in which we find again the cynical perceptions and affections of the capitalist himself. (Deleuze and Guattari, 1994, 146)

Art, by contrast, dehumanizes affect, liberating affects from everyday recognition (Deleuze and Guattari, 1987, 320). 'One' thinks that darkness means negativity, but art can create a canvas of darknesses taking the eye beyond a darkness that can be recognized as meaningful. Art carries affects to their 'nth' power; the eye feels a darkness beyond comprehension and habitual recognition. Often, the eye that views art, not only does not know what it is seeing, but also fails to know what *seeing is*: just how is one to view this? Poetry also does violence to the everyday language of opinion – the language that for the most part enables us not to think or see. By disengaging affect from concept, literature moves in two directions. The eye can see again. Language is no longer description, passing from what we see to what we say; language 'stutters' (Deleuze, 1997, 55). The words we say become noise or affect themselves in their difference from what is seen. The visible and articulable separate into two directions (Deleuze, 1988a). Words themselves become sound, noise, rhythm or stuttering; but in *not* seeing, designating or referring to the actual world, words can also open us up to the unseen, worlds beyond our present point of view:

> The work of art leaves the domain of representation in order to become 'experience', transcendental empiricism or the science of the sensible . . . Empiricism becomes truly transcendental, and aesthetics an apodictic discipline, only when we apprehend directly in the sensible that which can only be sensed, the very being *of* the sensible: difference, potential difference and difference in intensity as the reason behind qualitative diversity . . . The intense world of differences, in which we find the reason behind qualities and the being of the sensible, is precisely the object of a superior empiricism. This empiricism teaches us a strange 'reason', that of the multiple, chaos and difference (nomadic distributions, crowned anarchies). (Deleuze, 1994, 57)

NOTES TOWARDS A READING OF JAMES JOYCE'S *DUBLINERS*

Style

Free-indirect style presents language that is not so much owned by speakers as it is definitive of a certain locale or habitus. James Joyce's (1882–1941) *Dubliners* does not just describe the people of Dublin using verbal tics, although he does do this. (One character refers to a carriage with 'rheumatic wheels'.) *Dubliners* 'speaks' in the voice of newspapers, cheap novels and the hackneyed phrases owned by no one. These are phrases that circulate and *create* territories, without being intended from a single point. Think of the way bodies of football supporters are produced *as* a body through the chanting of rhythms, the wearing of colours and the assemblage of bodies. This is what Deleuze refers to as a collective assemblage created through investments in intensities and affects. The group does not precede and author the signs of identity; the signs do not refer back to a group; the group is the effect of a collection or assemblage of signs: '*Signs do not have objects as their direct referents*. They are states of bodies (affections) and variations of power (affects), each of which refers to the other. Signs refer to signs . . . Signs are effects: the effect of one body upon another in space, or affection; the effect of an affection or duration, or affect' (Deleuze, 1997, 141). The styles of *Dubliners* are not so much expressions of specific speakers as productions of a place or territory (a territory that would be *de*territorialized if it were then grounded on one single term, such as the 'Irish spirit'). Deterritorialization takes one body of the assemblage – such as the speaking voice – and uses it to explain the assemblage as a whole; this is what happens when the subject or a community is seen as the author and ground of signs, rather than as an effect of intensities. Joyce works against this tendency to produce a grounding Irish spirit; his stories present the affects and styles from which identities are retroactively assumed.

In 'A Painful Case' Mr Duffy has just read a newspaper report, contained in full in the story, of the death of a woman with whom he had been involved. The following passage is technically in the third person, but is expressive of Mr Duffy's moral outrage, employing his condemnatory tone and 'elevated' position. What Mr Duffy most objects to is not the death itself, so much as its description in a language which is devoid of moral judgement. The narrative voice that speaks is not just that of Mr Duffy; by adopting the viewpoint of consensus – 'Evidently' – it is a voice that confidently speaks for all such upright members of 'civilisation':

> The threadbare phrases, the inane expressions of sympathy, the cautious words of a reporter won over to conceal the details of a commonplace vulgar death attacked his stomach. Not merely had she degraded herself; she had degraded him. He saw the squalid tract of her vice, miserable and malodorous. His soul's companion! He thought of the hobbling wretches whom he had seen carrying cans and bottles to be filled by the barman. Just God, what an end! Evidently she had been unfit to live, without any strength of purpose, an easy prey to habits, one of the wrecks on which civilisation has been reared. (Joyce, 1995, 108)

It is often said that modernism is avowedly elitist and dismissive of the masses (Carey, 1992). This would certainly be the case if it criticized the voices of the city and populace through the creation of a higher and judging point of view. However, modernism's use of style frequently adopts the tone of bourgeois elitism and threatened narrow-mindedness, not to appeal to an existent 'we', but to signal the illusion and specificity of any supposed voice of man in general. T. S. Eliot, Ezra Pound and Virginia Woolf may not have been populists but the voice of parochial derision so often adopted in their works is by no means exhaustive of the narrative voice, a voice which is always interspersed with quotation, allusion and misread repetitions. To read in a Deleuzean manner is to reread: far from looking back at modernism's elitist intent we can see the necessary failure of any voice that imposes itself from on high. For, once expressed as style, manner and text the supposed universality or 'height' of voice is also contaminated by the depths: its emergence from sound, noise, received fragments and unthought inclusions. As Deleuze and Guattari argue in *Anti-Oedipus*, racism does not work by exclusion but by inclusion (Deleuze and Guattari, 1983, 85): assuming a voice of white, middle-class agreement and civilization as the voice of 'us' all.

Free-indirect style demonstrates that the man of reason is a specific style and manner of voice; the very citizen who would set himself above the inanity of the press and mindlessly circulating language is created through a no less repeatable style and manner: 'Just God, what an end!' Mr Duffy is the virtuous bourgeois soul who laments the fall of language into mere rhetoric and repetition. Free-indirect style, far from striving to find a point of origin and genesis *outside* style and repetition, adopts already-given styles – such as the moralism of Mr Duffy – to show how style produces and creates character.

Free-indirect style allows the thought of a difference that does not differentiate some prior sameness. There is no normal humanity or presupposed 'we' behind the dialects of *Dubliners*. The human is nothing more than its various stylistic differences. The concept of the human or the concept of some underlying subject or nature is destroyed through a style, such as free-indirect style, that affirms and multiplies differences rather than subordinating differences to some governing point of view.

Affect

There is a standard idea of realist fiction, where the voice of the text follows or views the scene and speaks what it sees. Joyce adopts this connection between viewing eye, speaking voice and organized affect in 'Ivy Day in the Committee Room' from *Dubliners*:

> A denuded room came into view and the fire lost all its cheerful colour. The walls of the room were bare except for a copy of an election address. In the middle of the room was a small table on which papers were heaped. (Joyce, 1995, 113)

The room itself bears the affect; the 'cheer' is not felt by any of the characters but is attributed to an object. The bare walls, heaped papers and waning fire given an affect of desolation, an affect that is not felt by any subject – neither narrator, nor reader, nor character. The redundant messages, discarded papers and unnoticed objects create an affect of emptiness, even though the characters speak vociferously and with a tone of conviction. Joyce presents an emptiness that will come to overtake the bodies in the room. By describing impersonal affects the voice of the story allows the characters' voices to appear as so much noise. The true power of literature lies in freeing affect from its organization by regular opinion. Great literature, for Deleuze, does not express who 'we' are, but produces new affects freed from subjective recognition: 'literature . . . exists only when it discovers beneath apparent persons the power of an impersonal – which is not a generality but a singularity at the highest point: a man, a woman, a breast, a stomach, a child . . . It is not the first two persons that function as the condition for literary enunciation; literature begins when a third person is born in us that strips us of the power to say "I"' (Deleuze, 1997, 3). This is precisely what Joyce's *Dubliners* goes on to do. It uses the descriptive affects of realism, where a world of sensations creates a general affect – a room of empty phrases, hopelessness and vacuity. After the description of the room, the characters of 'Ivy Day in the Committee Room' exchange their opinions – their ready-made phrases lining up candidates on one side or the other of politics. This is a politics of opinion – allegiances to single images such as the ivy-leaf lapel badge, and to the memory of Parnell. It is *paranoid* in Deleuze and Guattari's sense; it subjects itself to images and voices from outside, such as the spirit of Ireland: 'All paranoic deliriums stir up similar historical, geographical and racial masses' (Deleuze and Guattari, 1983, 89). But Joyce's description of the scene is *schizoid*; it pulls apart all the phrases, affects and images that create political groupings, all the ways in which these bodies form themselves *as* Irish through attachments to badges, phrases, remembered persons and anthems. 'If schizophrenia is the universal, the great artist is indeed the one who scales the schizophrenic wall and reaches the land of the unknown, where he no longer belongs to any time, any milieu, any school' (Deleuze and Guattari, 1983, 69). The whole point of this political scene as presented by Joyce is that the politics is not one of ideas or beliefs. The dialogue 'lists' perceptions and revulsions, commitments and prejudices as so many unthought and pre-personal attachments: desires that have become fixed through the repetition of banal phrases and anecdotes. Joyce is not analysing the beliefs or psyches of these characters so much as styles of speech that operate in compelled and automatic rhythms:

> 'What did I tell you, Mat?' said Mr Hynes. 'Tricky Dicky Tierney'.
> 'O, he was tricky as they make 'em, ' said Mr Henchy. 'He hasn't got those little pigs' eyes for nothing. Blast his soul! Couldn't he pay up like a man instead of: "O, now, Mr Henchy, I must speak to Mr Fanning . . . I've spent a lot of money"? Mean little schoolboy of hell! I suppose he forgets the time his little old father kept the hand-me-down shop in Mary's Lane'.
> 'But is that a fact?' asked Mr O'Connor. (Joyce, 1995, 116)

After the circulation of so much dialogue, so much language that flows in a habitual and near machine-like manner, the characters open bottles of stout by placing the bottle over the fire, allowing the gas to expand to produce a 'Pok!' The mere noise of speech becomes interspersed with the literal hot air from the bottles and a similarly compelled and automatic sound from the bottle. Joyce writes the noises of life, rather than speakers, into his stories.

According to Deleuze, we really begin to think when we ask of language, not 'what does it mean?' or 'who speaks?', but 'what does it do?' or 'how does it work?' (Deleuze and Guattari, 1983, 109). In *Dubliners* Joyce looks at the way meaningless affects create social groupings. We have to ask: would exhaustive footnotes that described the political context of this story make what the characters say any more meaningful? I doubt it. Joyce presents the voice of Ireland, his own language, as a foreign language (Deleuze, 1997, 113). Language seems to operate through and across these voices. The bodies in the room line up behind this or that opinion, this or that badge or poster; far from giving us a sense of character and distinct persons, we get the circulation of phrases that pass from point to point: Mr Henchy, Mr Hynes, Mr O'Connor. The story concludes with the recitation of a hymn to the remembered leader Parnell, a recitation that only briefly interrupts the further 'Pok!' of bottles and hot air, and the final recognitions of opinion:

> 'What do you think of that, Crofton?' cried Mr Henchy. 'Isn't that fine? what?'
> Mr Crofton said that it was a very fine piece of writing.

For Deleuze, politics is not about the exchange and recognition of opinions among persons. To really think politically we have to look at affects: all those investments that *create* personal positions and groupings. Joyce gives Dublin as a territory of affects: a style of speech, an investment in certain images, ceremonies, bodies (Parnell) and rhythms (from political anthems to religious services). Politics has less to do with competing ideas and beliefs and more to do with affect. Joyce's 'Ivy Day in the Committee Room' describes a political territory, but does so *micropolitically* – not referring to the ideas or meanings held by characters, but the formation of characters through the repetition of noises, gestures and symbols. Affective analysis, or diagnosis, pervades Joyce's writing.

> . . . the writer as such is not a patient but rather a physician, the physician of himself and of the world. The world is the set of symptoms whose illness merges with man. (Deleuze, 1997, 3)

Joyce both repeats the sounds that make up who we are – the rhythms of nationalism, the Church service and newspaper headlines – and creates and adds inhuman affects and pulsations: the 'Pok!' of hot air from bottles in *Dubliners*, the animal, machine and bodily noises of *Ulysses*, and the language of human speech in *Finnegans Wake* that mutates as it speaks, blurring the boundaries between textual accidents, human slips and idiosyncratic intentions. Such texts do not describe so much as create and open up worlds.

QUESTIONS FOR FURTHER CONSIDERATION

1. One of Deleuze's main objectives was to think *difference itself*, beyond the human point of view. For this reason he favoured literature that looked at machines, animals and all sorts of 'inhuman' desires. To what extent is such a project *utopian*? Would it be possible to achieve an inhuman viewpoint, or is this something writing can only work towards?

2. In his own time Deleuze argued that cinema, with its capacity to present images of time and becoming, provided new ways of thinking about art and philosophy. To what extent is recent fiction and art 'cinematic' – using images and sequences that are not tied to logical or unified order?

3. Deleuze argues that far too much emphasis was placed on metaphor and signification, or looking at what images and signs referred to. Instead, he suggested that we should look at the power and force of words and images themselves. Does this limit us only to very modern forms of art – such as modernism – or could we reread traditional works less for their meaning and more for their capacity to create affects?

4. Because of Deleuze's attack on the notions of representation and signification he is often criticized for being a *literal* philosopher: trying to think life itself rather than images of life. Deleuze's work is therefore out of step with a tendency of literary, social and political *theory* that stresses that we need to recognize and reflect upon our point of view rather than aim for a view from 'nowhere'. Do you think this criticism of Deleuze is valid?

5. In *What is Philosophy?* Deleuze and Guattari argued for distinct powers of literature, art and philosophy. No text may be purely artistic but we can discern distinctly artistic tendencies. Often, though, we read literature to demonstrate ideas and concepts. Is it possible to read with a view to distinct tendencies in literature? Could we, for example, read Virginia Woolf's *Mrs Dalloway* for its feminist philosophy on the one hand, and its affects or impersonal styles on the other?

ANNOTATED BIBLIOGRAPHY

Deleuze, Gilles. *Dialogues with Clare Parnet*, trans. Hugh Tomlinson and Barbara Habberjam. New York: Zone Books, 1987. Because this is a series of interviews it provides a way of approaching Deleuze through relatively straightforward language.
Deleuze, Gilles. *Difference and Repetition*, trans. Paul Patton. New York: Columbia University Press, 1994. This is arguably Deleuze's most important work, but also one of his most difficult. The third chapter includes his criticism of common sense and his affirmation of difference.

Deleuze, Gilles. *Essays: Critical and Clinical*, trans. Daniel W. Smith and Michael A. Greco. Minneapolis, MN: University of Minnesota Press, 1997. A series of essays primarily focused on literature and therefore particularly useful for literary studies.
Deleuze, Gilles and Félix Guattari. *Anti-Oedipus: Capitalism and Schizophrenia*, trans. Robert Hurley, Mark Seem and Helen R. Lane. London: Athlone, 1983. Until recently this was Deleuze's most influential work. It is an attempt to think beyond capitalism and enslaved desire and concludes with an introduction to 'schizoanalysis'.
Deleuze, Gilles and Félix Guattari (1994), *What is Philosophy?*, trans. Hugh Tomlinson and Graham Burchill. London: Verso, 1994. A late work in which Deleuze and Guattari define the distinct powers of philosophy, art and science.

SUPPLEMENTARY BIBLIOGRAPHY

Carey, John. *The Intellectuals and the Masses: Pride and Prejudice Among the Literary Intelligentsia: 1880–1939*. London: Faber & Faber, 1992.
Deleuze, Gilles. *Kant's Critical Philosophy: The Doctrine of the Faculties*, trans. Hugh Tomlinson and Barbara Habberjam. London: Athlone, 1984.
Deleuze, Gilles. *Cinema 1: The Movement-Image*, trans. Hugh Tomlinson and Barbara Habberjam. Minneapolis, MN: University of Minnesota Press, 1986.
Deleuze, Gilles. *Foucault*, trans. Sean Hand. Minneapolis, MN: University of Minnesota Press, 1988a.
Deleuze, Gilles. *Bergsonism*, trans. Hugh Tomlinson and Barbara Habberjam. New York: Zone Books, 1988b.
Deleuze, Gilles. *Spinoza: Practical Philosophy*, trans. Robert Hurley. San Francisco, CA: City Light Books, 1988c.
Deleuze, Gilles. *Cinema 2: The Time-Image*, trans. Hugh Tomlinson and Robert Galeta. Minneapolis, MN: University of Minnesota Press, 1989a.
Deleuze, Gilles. *Masochism: Coldness and Cruelty*, trans. J. McNeil. New York: Zone Books, 1989b.
Deleuze, Gilles. *The Logic of Sense*, trans. Mark Lester, ed. Constantin V. Boundas. New York: Columbia University Press, 1990.
Deleuze, Gilles. *Empiricism and Subjectivity: An Essay on Hume's Theory of Human Nature*, trans. Constantin V. Boundas. New York: Columbia, 1991.
Deleuze, Gilles. *Expressionism in Philosophy*, trans. M. Joughin. New York: Zone Books, 1992.
Deleuze, Gilles. *The Fold: Leibniz and the Baroque*, trans. Tom Conley. London: Athlone Press, 1993.
Deleuze, Gilles. *Negotiations 1972–1990*, trans. Martin Joughin. New York: Columbia University Press, 1995.
Deleuze, Gilles. 'Bergson's Concept of Difference', trans. Melissa MacMahon. In *The New Bergson*, ed. John Mullarkey. Manchester: Manchester University Press, 1999, 42–65.
Deleuze, Gilles. *Proust and Signs*, trans. Richard Howard. London: Athlone, 2000.
Deleuze, Gilles and Félix Guattari. *A Thousand Plateaus: Capitalism and Schizophrenia*, trans. Brian Massumi. Minneapolis, MN: University of Minnesota Press, 1987.
Deleuze, Gilles and Félix Guattari. *Kafka: Toward a Minor Literature*, trans. Dana Polan. Minneapolis, MN: University of Minnesota Press, 1986.
Eliot, T. S. *Old Possum's Book of Practical Cats*. London: Faber & Faber, 1939.
Fielding, Henry. *The History of Tom Jones*. Harmondsworth: Penguin, 1994.
Joyce, James. *Dubliners*, ed. Andrew Goodwyn. Cambridge: Cambridge University Press, 1995.
Lawrence, D. H. *The Woman Who Rode Away and Other Stories*. Harmondsworth: Penguin, 1950.

CHAPTER

11

LEVINAS AND CRITICISM: ETHICS *IN* THE IMPOSSIBILITY OF CRITICISM

Frederick Young

It is true that Ethics, in Levinas's sense, is an Ethics without law and without concept, which maintains its non-violent purity only before being determined as concepts and laws. This is not an objection: let us not forget that Levinas does not seek to propose laws or moral rules, does not seek to determine *a* morality, but rather the essence of the ethical relation in general. But as this determination does not offer itself as a *theory* of Ethics, in question, then, is an Ethics of Ethics . . . A coherence which breaks down the coherence of the discourse against coherence – the infinite concept, hidden within the protest against the concept.

Jacques Derrida, 'Violence and Metaphysics'

INTRODUCTION

Why write about a philosopher in an introduction to different approaches to the practice and theory of literary criticism? What can Emmanuel Levinas, whose ethical project goes not only against the grain of classical rhetoric, aesthetics and literary criticism, but also against the whole enterprise of philosophy itself, offer a student of criticism? In other words, what relevance does Levinas have for us? Levinas's contribution to Continental philosophy is the revitalization of the question of ethics and, more importantly, the rethinking of ethics not as a branch of philosophy (or ontology[1]) but as something that is prior to and unworks philosophy's totalizing practice. Levinas's ethics radically differs from ethics or morality as understood as a discipline within philosophy. Whereas philosophy attempts to speak for the Other,[2] to give the Other voice and meaning to what it doesn't understand, to perform the violence of speaking for the Other, Levinas's project is to refigure ethics as an interruption of the very practice of philosophy.

What can his work tell us about the nature and project of literary criticism? Because of Levinas's particular view of ethics, he would regard literary criticism, understood as pre-set principles which could then be applied to a literary text, as functioning similarly to philosophy, which by means of imposing a methodology, or code, attempts to speak *for* the Other. In this way, both philosophy and literary criticism are a discourse of the Same, that which does not respect difference or the possibility of encountering the Other. In other words, literary criticism imposes meaning on a work of literature, just as philosophy imposes meaning on that which eludes it. In literary criticism and philosophy, the *example* functions as a mimetic or representational relation. This process only reflects its own meaning, and by attempting to speak for the other, only reflects itself – the mimetology of self-reflexivity. For Levinas, ethics is always a problem of relation, and, I will argue, of unworking any form of mimesis or representation.

For Levinas, the project of philosophy as a process of totalization must itself be interrupted, and he does this through a radical rethinking of the question of ethics, no longer understood as a branch of philosophy, as systematic or codifiable doctrine, that *ought* to be applied to specific experiences or situations, but rather as a performative operation that exceeds, or perhaps interrupts, philosophy's grip. In other words, ethics for Levinas is prior to philosophy (the history of metaphysics, of ontology) and, then, before any philosophy of ethics. Thus, Jacques Derrida calls it an 'Ethics of Ethics', an ethics that does not follow the rule of representation or the example. For instance, there can be no example of an ethical action applied to a specific situation since there is no prior code of ethics to fall back upon. That is, ethics is a matter of relation with the Other and therefore before meaning itself. This encounter with the Other (Autrui), what Levinas terms the 'face to face' is a performative relation prior to an ontological mediation; thus, in the 'face to face' encounter with the Other, no code of ethics is applicable. As Jill Robbins states in *Altered Reading*, 'For Levinas . . . ethics denotes not a set of moral precepts but a responsibility – at its most originary – that arises in the encounter with the face of another' (Robbins, 1999, 41). This 'encounter' with the 'face of another' is precisely what is at stake for Levinas.

This chapter attempts to shed light on some of Levinas's important concepts as well as some of his terminology. This is in no way meant to be a comprehensive commentary on Levinas's work. Rather, this chapter attempts to explore key concepts of his project relating to notions of performativity, ontology, art, rhetoric and deconstruction.[3] However, before addressing these crucial questions in greater detail, it is necessary to understand Levinas's ethical project and its relation to philosophy. At the risk of momentarily oversimplifying Levinas, he loosely shares a common thread with many twentieth-century continental philosophers, who, perhaps taking their cue from Nietzsche, unwork the very project of philosophy itself, which tries to speak for the other by imposing meaning on that which is foreign to it.[4]

In the section on ethics and ontology below I will explore what Levinas has in common with Heidegger as well as some of their crucial differences. Levinas's ethics shares with Heidegger's 'fundamental ontology' a need to work against philosophy, or metaphysics, to somehow get behind or before it. Although their respective projects differ greatly – and that their own works transformed throughout their lives is also of importance – the section on ethics and ontology will delve more into Heidegger and Levinas. The section on saying and said will address how these two terms function for Levinas's project as a means of understanding how both the performative and constative operate. In the section on rhetoric and art, I will look at Levinas's views on both art and classical rhetoric against the project and possibility of ethics because, for Levinas, both art and rhetoric are involved with representation and application of a set of rules. However, this is complicated when we consider his relationship with Maurice Blanchot and Jacques Derrida. I will also then complicate Levinas's views on art and rhetoric to explore how his definitions are informed by a Platonic inheritance and how Levinas's interruptive ethics are much closer to investigations of the 'literary' itself and an ethical performative. In this sense, Levinas's project, although certainly not identical, is similar to that of thinkers such as Philippe Lacoue-Labarthe, Maurice Blanchot, Jacques Derrida, Hélène Cixous and Paul de Man in that the representational or mimetic structures of philosophy, relation and method are brought into question.

RELATION: ETHICS AND ONTOLOGY

In order to understand Levinas's importance for a student of criticism, it is vital to understand his relationship to ontology. Ontology, the question of being, is both fundamental and foundational to philosophy. The various branches of philosophy, such as epistemology, ethics and aesthetics, are all predicated upon ontology. To really grasp what is at stake in Levinas's ethics and his challenge to philosophy, we have to consider Martin Heidegger's 'fundamental ontology' as articulated in *Being and Time*, in which he calls for the 'destruction' of ontology, beginning with Plato and culminating in Hegel. Heidegger radicalizes the problem of ontology as well as offers a critique of the Cartesian subject[5] by means of the 'equipmental structure', what Heidegger calls Dasein (literally being there), and Dasein is always already 'being-in-the-world'.[6] Hence, the experience of Dasein is prior to the subject–object duality of Descartes. Heidegger uses the word Dasein, literally 'being there', because he does not want to use the word 'subject', which falls into the notion of the subject/object split and is based upon an abstract notion of being, precisely what the tradition of philosophy embraces and what Heidegger seeks to avoid. For Heidegger, the history of philosophy is, in a sense, 'a history of a mistake' in which philosophers since Plato have misunderstood the question of the meaning of being by understanding it as an abstraction, an empty category which serves to classify knowledge. Heidegger attempts to 'get behind' philosophy, which he sees as ontological, and develop a 'transcendental fundamental ontology'. Thus Heidegger turns to the question of Dasein, being-in-the-world, which, for him, is prior to the object/subject split of Descartes. By means of articulating the structure of the world in which Dasein is being-in-the-world, Heidegger attempts to get out of traditional ontology and Cartesian duality.

While this is not the place to attempt to describe Heidegger's project, what concerns us is the problem that Heidegger's 'fundamental ontology'[7] presents for Levinas's ethics. Even though Heidegger tries to unwork a Cartesian relation by destroying Cartesian precepts, for Levinas, Heidegger still understands *relation* as being, and this is the problem because, for Levinas, he inadvertently falls back into ontology. Thus Heidegger's project with Dasein, while opening up a critique of Descartes and the history of philosophy, nonetheless reinscribes ontology because first and foremost the question of being, not of the Other, is Heidegger's main concern. As Critchley asserts in *The Ethics of Deconstruction*:

> Levinasian ethics bears a critical relation to the philosophical tradition. For Levinas, Western philosophy has most often been what he calls 'ontology', by which he means the attempt to comprehend the Being of what is, or beings (das Sein des Seienden) . . . the most recent example of which is Heidegger's fundamental ontology, in which the elaboration of the question of the meaning of Being presupposes *ab initio* a comprehension of Being. (Critchley, 1991, 5)

We can begin to see what is at stake in how to think the problem of relation, of the Other, without a mediation of being. In *Totality and Infinity* Levinas states, '*Being and Time* has argued perhaps but one sole thesis: Being is inseparable from the comprehension of Being (which unfolds as time); Being is already an appeal to subjectivity' (Levinas, 1969, 45). As long as Heidegger continues to emphasize being, he cannot get away from the subject. Thus Heidegger's project falls short of the radical relation of Levinas's ethics because Heidegger, for Levinas, still has not eliminated being as a relation, and Dasein itself falls into a strange subjectivity. There is no direct 'face'-to-'face' relation for Heidegger; despite his invaluable critique of ontology, he still reduces the relation between Dasein and Dasein as mediated by the question and problematic of being. The problem Heidegger's 'fundamental ontology' presents is that the tradition of philosophy is based upon abstraction, and while Heidegger attempts to get beyond philosophy, he still remains within being, which for Levinas misses the ethical. In *Totality and Infinity* Levinas states the problem explicitly:

> The primacy of ontology for Heidegger does not rest on the truism: 'to know an existant it is necessary to have comprehended the Being of existents.' To affirm the priority of Being over existents is to already decide the essence of philosophy; it is to subordinate the relation with someone,

who is an existant, (the ethical relation) to a relation with the Being of existents . . . (Levinas, 1969, 45)

Again, for Levinas, Heidegger 'affirms the priority of Being over existants' at the expense of an ethical relation between existants. In his commentary on Levinas, Adriaan Peperzak further emphasizes the crucial difference between Levinas and Heidegger:

> The supremacy of reason, by which the human subject, according to Plato, feels at home in understanding the world as a relations of ideas [forms], is replaced by another relation between Dasein and Being, but still Dasein stays shut up in its relation to the phosphorescent Anonymous enabling all beings to present themselves to it, without ever producing true alterity. The truth of Dasein is that the being which is 'always mine' is also a being for which its own being is the issue. (Peperzak, 1993, 53–4)

In other words, Heidegger replaces Plato's relation of ideas (the Forms) with another, or different, relation of Dasein being-with another Dasein, or of Dasein's relation to being. We can see Dasein is based upon Heidegger's 'fundamental ontology', which replaces Plato's traditional ontology. For Heidegger, being-in-the-world, which Dasein is always already in, is prior to Plato's notion of ontology, which bases being upon an abstraction. By extension, Descartes' subject, for Heidegger, is predicated on Platonic ontology. However, while Heidegger clearly radicalizes the problem of being for philosophy, he nonetheless fixates on a nostalgia for being.

Heidegger becomes vital for Levinas because *Being and Time* was the first real attempt to challenge the sovereignty of the Cartesian subject. Levinas's ethical project undoes the notion of being and how all relation, albeit Cartesian or Heideggerian, relies on ontology. Levinas attempts to unwork the very notion of relation as ontology. He regards his ethics and the 'face to face' as prior to Heidegger's ontology and the description of how Dasein relates to another Dasein as *mitsein*. What is at stake for a student of literary criticism is to see how, for Levinas, literary criticism, so long as it functions as a method of application, would necessarily *be* part and parcel of an ontological practice. In other words, any relation between a literary method and an *object* of study, such as a film or work of literature is mediated by ontology, or being. Thus, we can begin to see for Levinas how literary criticism is haunted by ontology. Levinas attempts a radical unworking of relation as being, which sets up the possibility of application; his ethics will involve an asymmetrical relation based on a performative ethics, which interrupts the mediation of relation based on being.

According to Levinas, however, ethics is not a branch of philosophy but rather the interruption of philosophy's attempt at totalization, to speak *for* the Other, or in relation to the Other as an *object* of study. Hence, ethics for Levinas is prior to philosophy or ontology: 'The establishing of the primacy of the ethical . . . a primacy upon which all other structures rest (and in particular all those which seem to put us primordially in contact with an impersonal sublimity, aesthetic or ontological), is one of the objectives of the present work' (Levinas, cit. Robbins, 1999, xxi). Thomas Wall, in *Radical Passivity*, also states that 'Ethics is beyond experience. It is beyond the experience of a subject and that of Dasein' (Wall, 1999, 38). Ethics is a relation, or perhaps really a non-relation, an excess of being that works against the relation of subject and object, which is central to philosophy, especially since Descartes and Hegel. Levinas's ethics cannot be codified; it is not a prescriptive set of maxims that one ought to live by. Rather, what's at stake is a matter of an asymmetrical and non-mimetic relation prior to ontology, in which one faces rather than speaks for the Other (Autrui), that can never be static or repeatable but is performative. The encounter with the Other interrupts the sovereignty of the subject/object relation of traditional ontology as well as *Befindlichkeit* (how Dasein always already finds itself in the world) of Dasein. It is a relation without relation, an excess, a performative operation that unworks the subject/object split. As Critchley states, 'In the language of transcendental philosophy, the face is the condition of possibility for ethics. For Levinas, then, the ethical relation – and ethics is simply and entirely the event of this relation – is one in which I am related to the face of the Other . . .' (Critchley, 1992, 5).

Thus, it is also crucial to understand how the notion of identity and the Same function not only for western philosophy, but for any of its derivative disciplines. For philosophy, everything under investigation is reduced to the Same. In other words, or putting words in for the other, philosophy collapses the relation between the Same and the Other into the Same. The relation is absorbed into mediation. What is at stake is how the relation (un)works in Levinas. Levinas introduces the figure of the face as a means of understanding the ethical. As Robbins states, 'the face is a collusion between world and that which exceeds world' (Robbins, 1999, 58).

Levinas's project in *Totality and Infinity* explores the ethical of the face of the Other, unmediated by being, in order to avoid the violent appropriation of ontology, the violence of speaking for the Other. The face does not represent anything for Levinas. Rather, it is a performative, or as Wall expresses it in *Radical Passivity*, ethics is 'an operation' (Wall, 1999, 35). Robbins quotes Levinas, who states, 'The relationship with the other . . . puts me into question, empties me of myself . . . The I loses its sovereign coincidence with itself, its identification, in which consciousness returned triumphantly to itself . . . The I is expelled from this rest' (Levinas, 1969, 350–3). Furthermore, as Robbins contends, 'For Levinas, ethics in the most general sense is the question of self-sufficiency, the interruption of self – described variously as an obligation, an imperative, an imposition, a responsibility – that arises in the encounter with the face of the other' (Robbins, 1999, 23).

According to Levinas, the face is a condition for the possibility of ethics (Critchley), an excess that cannot be contained or contextualized. In this sense, it is a performative; ethics opens up a relation (Robbins, 1999, 5–7). 'I don't think the infinity of Autrui, I face it; speak to it' (Robbins, 1999, 7). The relation to the other is not a relation in the sense of a mediation, even to call it a relation is tenuous; rather 'the other is . . . a surplus, radical asymmetry' (Robbins, 1999, 4). As Levinas remarks of this relation: 'The relation between the Other and me, which dawns forth in his expression, issues neither in number or concept. The Other remains infinitely transcendent, infinitely foreign; his face in which epiphany is produced and which appeals to me breaks with the world that can be common to us, whose virtualities are inscribed in our *nature* and absolute difference' (Levinas, 1969, 194). Levinas describes how the face resists sublation and containment:

> The face resists possession, resists my powers. In its epiphany, in expression, the sensible, still graspable, turns into total resistance to the grasp. This mutation can occur only by the opening of a new dimension. For the resistance to the grasp is not produced as an insurmountable resistance, like the hardness of the rock against which the effort of the hand comes to naught, like the remoteness of a star in the immensity of space. The expression the face introduces into the world does not defy the feebleness of my powers, but my ability for power. The face, still a thing among things, breaks through the form that nevertheless delimits it. This means concretely: the face speaks to me and thereby invites me to a relation incommensurate with a power exercised, be it enjoyment or knowledge. (Levinas, 1969, 197–8)

Significantly, although Levinas describes the face, it is not the face of a subject; it is important to realize that the face is not literal or empirical but rather interrupts the ontological relation. Precisely because it is not a subject, it interrupts the ontological grounding that constitutes subjectivity: 'The face is present in its refusal to be contained. In this sense it cannot be comprehended, that is encompassed. It is neither seen nor touched – for in visual or tactile sensation the identity of the I envelops the alterity of the object, which precisely becomes a context' (Levinas, 1969, 194). But what is crucial for Levinas is that the face is not a sign nor a representation of a subject; it is not semiotic – rather, as Critchley states, 'its possibility is the condition of ethics'. As Robbins puts it, 'For Levinas, to decode the face in the manner of other signs would be to reduce it violently, to turn it – horribly, into a mask, that is, not just a surface but something petrified and immobile' (1999, 60) To 'petrify' the face would be to ontologize it.

Because the face cannot *be* contained, it radically interrupts an ontological 'context'. The Other should not be understood as an object or another subject, nor a dialectical negation, because both must assume an ontology. Rather, the Other (Autrui), for Levinas radically breaks any relation mediated by being. The Other is in excess of being:

> The relation between the Other and me, which dawns forth in his expression, issues neither in number or concept. The Other remains

infinitely transcendent, infinitely foreign; his face in which epiphany is produced and which appeals to me breaks with the world that can be common to us, whose virtualities are inscribed in our *nature* and absolute difference. (Levinas, 1969, 194)

SAYING AND SAID

The crucial question here is how does Levinas's ethics perform the radical relation, or interruption, of ontology? To think about the difference between Levinas's 'face to face' and ontology is to think about the difference between the Saying and the Said. In the *Ethics of Deconstruction* Critchley states, 'Whereas *Totality and Infinity* writes about ethics, *Otherwise than Being* is the performative enactment of ethical writing' (Critchley, 1992, 8). Provisionally, we can note that Saying is performative, while the Said is constative. In other words, Saying is ethical while the Said is ontological. In his famous lectures, *How To Do Things With Words*, the Anglo-American philosopher of language J. L. Austin introduced the concept of performatives and constatives.[8] For Austin, a performative is, or rather, I should say, *does* the following:

> When I say before the registrar or altar, &c., 'I do', I am not reporting on a marriage: I am indulging in it. What are we to call a sentence or utterance of this type? I propose to call it a performative sentence or a performative utterance, or for short, 'a performative'. The term 'performative' will be used in a variety of cognate ways and constructions, much as the term 'imperative' is. The name is derived, of course, from 'perform', the usual verb with the noun 'action': it indicates that the issuing of the utterance is the performing of an action – it is not normally thought of as just saying something. (Austin, 1975, 7)

For Austin, a performative is not a statement of truth; it is not verifiable, but rather concerns solely the action. 'I do' speaks of the action of 'doing', not of whether that action is good or bad, true or false. In other words, the performative is not subject to the traditional representational conditions of truth.[9] In contrast to the performative, however, the constative can be verified. According to Austin, the constative, unlike the performative, is a statement of fact.

For Levinas, Saying or speech is the way to unwork the ontological reification of the subject to the Other: 'the Saying is the sheer radicality of human speaking, of the event of being in relation with the Other; it is the non-thematizable ethical residue . . . of language that escapes comprehension, interrupts philosophy, and is the very enactment of the ethical movement form the Same [of ontology] to the Other' (Critchley, 1992, 7). Thus, for Levinas, the Saying is a performative that cannot be reduced to a constative, to the calculative functions of truth and identity. The Saying is not descriptive. Levinas employs the term Said to describe the prepositional, or constative, function of philosophy/ontology. The Saying, unlike the Said, opens up an 'exposure to the other'.

The Saying opens up a relation[10] to the Other unmediated by being, the 'face to face.' In other words, the Saying is in excess of any mediation of being, nor can this performative *be* Said. The Said, in contrast, is constative and occurs when the Saying is reduced to meaning, wherein it is static, becomes codifiable and is brought back into philosophy, or the Same. Thus, 'the ethical movement from Same to Other' opens up a relation more primal and direct, always performative, which 'interrupts' the constative or ontological relation of philosophy. According to Levinas, the performativity of Saying exposes me to the Other, creating an opening to the Other that cannot be refused nor closed by philosophy. Critchley argues that 'The Saying is my exposure – corporeal, sensible – to the Other, my inability to refuse the Other's approach. It is a performative stating, proposing, or expressive position of myself facing the Other. It is a verbal or non-verbal ethical performance, whose essence cannot be caught in constative prepositions. It is a performative doing that cannot be reduced to a constative description' (Critchley, 1991, 7).

For Levinas, this performative operation of Saying occurs in the 'face to face', in which the Other is greeted without being reduced to the Same. It is important to understand that the 'face to face' is not just another figure in the history of western philosophy such as the subject/object split or Dasein being-with another Dasein. As Robbins asserts, 'The face is always on the move' (Robbins, 1999, 48). It is a performative, which opens up the relation to the Other. As Robbins states, 'the face is performative and not personified. It does not represent an actual face, but rather opens up the ethical relation with the Other.' While, on the other hand, 'the Said', as Robbins continues, 'is the linguistic equivalent of the economy of the Same. The Saying and the Said is a correlative relation (exceeding correlation) that marks the difference between a constative speech, oriented toward its addressee, interlocutionary and ethical, and a speech oriented toward the referent, more like a speaking *about* than a speaking *to* the other' (Robbins, 1999, 144). Again, we can see that the Saying is a performative that does not speak *about* the Other, as philosophy does, but rather, the Saying speaks *to* the Other, an absolutely crucial distinction for Levinas.

That stated, how is the Saying not reduced or brought back to the Said? And yet, is it possible to maintain the distinction between the Saying and the Said? Have I *said* too much about Levinas's performativity? Is not the Saying at risk of falling back into the Said as the performative is described or reinscribed back into philosophy? In other words, does not the Saying once described become Said? Does not the performative, once understood, return to the Same, the Said, philosophy? As Critchley notes, 'Given that philosophy speaks the language of the Said – that is, it consists of propositions and statements – The methodological problem that haunts every page of *Otherwise Than Being* is the following: How is the Saying, my exposure to the Other, to be Said or given a philosophical exposition without utterly betraying this Saying? How can one write the otherwise than Being in the language of Being . . . ?'[11] (Critchley, 1992, 164). We can now see the importance of Saying as a performative for

Levinas as well as how the Said as constative reifies the ontological relation that he attempts to unwork.

ON ART AND RHETORIC

Critical for students of criticism, Levinas views both aesthetics and classical rhetoric as antithetical to his ethical project. His conception of rhetoric and aesthetics goes back to the Platonic conception of art as a representation, or image, of a representation of truth, or being. For Levinas, art as an image, based on Plato's metaphor of the cave, is far removed from truth though still locked within ontological assumptions. Levinas regards rhetoric as a type of 'angling', or sophistry, designed to manipulate language and twist its meaning. In other words, rhetoric goes against the 'face to face' encounter with the Other and attempts to use language to convert the Other, which necessarily objectifies it. Therefore classical rhetoric, for Levinas, manipulates the Other and obfuscates the 'face to face' encounter. Hence, such conceptions of rhetoric and art would be incommensurable with Levinas's ethical project.

What appears problematic in Levinas's notion of art and rhetoric, however, is that he inherits this particular Platonic conception without applying the same critical rigour with which he otherwise is so careful to critique Plato and the ontological tradition of philosophy. In other words, both art and rhetoric are based on ontological presuppositions. Levinas's view and distrust of art and rhetoric has more to do with the question of ontology and how both art and rhetoric as branches of understanding miss the critical ethical relation. Levinas opposes an aesthetics that would represent, or speak for, the Other, as well as a rhetoric with a set of precepts deployed to manipulate the Other. In other words, art or rhetoric as a set of codes applied to a specific situation is no different, really, than morality or ethics as a branch of philosophy. Thus, any concept of art and rhetoric as well as literary criticism, which applies meaning to art, is necessarily 'incommensurable' with Levinas's ethics. As Jill Robbins states in *Altered Reading*:

> Any approach to the question of the relationship of Levinas's philosophy to literature has also to deal with the incommensurability between Levinas's ethics and the discourse of literary criticism. Literary criticism, whether it is conceived as the determination of a work's meaning or as an analysis of its formal structures, would be derivative upon Levinas's more originary question of the ethical, part of what Heidegger calls a regional ontology. Hence Levinas's philosophy cannot function as an extrinsic approach to the literary work of art, that is, it cannot give rise to an application. (Robbins, 1999, xx)

We can see how literary criticism, by attempting to interpret meaning and analyse form, is already inscribed for Levinas as ontological. Any effort to attribute meaning or to apply a method to a work of art attempts to speak for the Other. What now begins to emerge for Levinas, classical rhetoric as prescriptive obfuscates or, perhaps, abolishes the possibility of the ethical – an act of ontological violence. According to Levinas, as a system of static devices classical rhetoric could only offer a modality of 'angling', or appropriation, that reduces the relation to a mediation of being. Therefore, both art and rhetoric cannot escape ontology because they are ontology.

Does this then mean that Levinas has no interest in aesthetics or rhetoric? That his ethics is incommensurate with any project of criticism and therefore of no use or aid to the student of criticism? In *Altered Readings*, Jill Robbins suggests that what 'Levinas is really interested in is art in relation to ethics, interruption rather than ontology' (Robbins, 1999, 154). In other words, Levinas could only understand aesthetics and rhetoric as an ethical interruption, a performative, that unworks ontology. What becomes crucial, then, is to begin to think of art and rhetoric not as an ontological relation of the Same that would describe a constative condition, but rather as a performative that radically unworks and brings into question the ontology of relation. What is at stake for Levinas, I would argue, is the problem of how art and rhetoric are conceived traditionally as mimetic. Therefore, the task, in order to face the Other, is to interrupt mimesis.[12] In this sense, Levinas is quite interested in aesthetics and rhetoric but not as they are *conceived* in philosophy, rather as an 'interruption', as a performative that unworks the literary text as an *object* of study to which a method could apply or 'angle' meaning. What really is at stake for Levinas, and here he is quite close to Blanchot and Derrida,[13] is the very possibility of the literary, not as static but as something that, perhaps, unworks meaning.

NOTES TOWARDS A READING OF
ANDREY TARKOFSKY'S *THE SACRIFICE*

'The first thing to describe is the event, not your attribute to it.'

'The Sacrifice is a parable. The significant events it contains can be interpreted in more than one way.' (Andrey Tarkofsky, *Sculpting in Time*)

How is it possible to interpret a work of literature in light of Levinas's radicalization of ethics? Any attempt to *apply* a theory of Levinas to a work of literature, or film, risks reducing the ethical performative relation back into ontology, mimesis. Again, the question must be asked, what can Levinas offer a student of literary criticism, when literary criticism, as a domain of ontology, reduces the Other to the Same? In other words, any application of Levinas would fail before it began. The problem here is that of mimesis, of representation. Is it possible to approach a literary text without deploying a methodology, without representing Levinas?

In the last and infamous scene of Tarkofsky's *The Sacrifice*,[14] Alexander burns down his house, his books, and the map (a gift from the postman, Otto[15]). Alexander, an intellectual, sacrifices his house after WWIII begins – it remains unclear as to whether or not the war is actually taking place or if Alexander has just imagined it. Our question is, how do we read this sacrifice? Is the sacrifice something to bring about harmony? Is it to bring about an exchange – to sacrifice oneself in order to save others? In other words, does the one who sacrifices expect something in return? If so, then it would fall into the economy of mimesis because it would require something from the Other – an exchange. The event of the sacrifice would be reduced to a constative, the Said. The agreement in advance of the sacrifice would explain (away) the event, would close off the 'face to face' with the Other. Vital to our concern with the sacrifice is the (im)possibility of an event, the event of sacrifice. In other words, if we look at the event of the sacrifice as a performative, then understanding the event, applying meaning to it, becomes impossible.

In *Sculpting in Time*, Tarkofsky conveys his idea of sacrifice:

> What moved me was the theme of the harmony which is born only of sacrifice, the twofold dependence of love . . . I am interested in the character who is capable of sacrificing himself and his way of life – regardless of whether that sacrifice is made in the name of spiritual values, or for the sake of someone else, or of his own salvation, or of all these things together. Such behavior precludes, by its very nature, all of those selfish interests that make up a 'normal' rationale for action; it refutes the laws of a materialistic worldview. It is often absurd and unpractical. And yet – or indeed for that very reason – the man who acts in this way brings about fundamental changes in people's lives and in the course of history. The space he lives in becomes a rare, distinctive point of contrast to the empirical concepts of our experience, an area where reality – I would say – is all the more strongly present. (Tarkofsky, 1996, 217–18)

The question we have to ask is whether or not Alexander's sacrifice can be seen as harmonious. If the sacrifice is a gift in order to exchange oneself to prevent a greater disaster, such as the annihilation of the world, we must ask whether or not such an exchange is mimetic. Does a sacrifice, if understood as harmonious, really offer itself to the Other, or does it impose its own demands, in which case it would be the Said? I sacrifice myself in order that the Other accepts my demands. For Levinas, this form of sacrifice would obliterate the 'face to face' of the Other. Remember that the face to face makes no demands on the Other and interrupts any attempt to do so. Rather than opening up to the Other an unconditional gift, if such as thing is possible, sacrifice for the sake of harmony is mimetic – it is an exchange within the economy of the Same – the face is closed off from the self who sacrifices it*self*. The performative of the sacrifice is already inscribed as predetermined or stated by the self who sacrifices – this is ontological *par excellence*.

However, it is possible to read *The Sacrifice* against the grain of how Tarkofsky describes it in *Sculpting in Time*. I would argue that, rather than look at the event of the sacrifice as constative, as ontological, as Said, as speaking for the Other, it is vital to think of the sacrifice, the event itself, as a performative interruption and impossible to determine and assign it meaning. The performative Saying exceeds any agreement, contract or exchange; it does not attempt to get an 'angle' on the Other. The event of the burning house, of Alexander running away from the ambulance drivers, all of this is only the affect of the interruption of the event, the sacrifice, which we cannot experience. Remember that experience remains part and parcel of ontology and the subject, the 'I'. A cue to this unsettling event, to the performative or asymmetrical relation of the sacrifice, comes in the final scene. Alexander's son, the 'little man', is lying under the Japanese tree that he and his father planted at the beginning of the film. The ambulance carrying Alexander passes by the boy, and it is uncanny that this does not affect him. Throughout the film, the boy had not spoken because of a throat operation that took place outside of the film. The boy looks up at the sky as the camera begins to pan up the tree and breaks his silence: 'In the beginning was the Word . . . Why is that papa?' In *Sculpting in Time*, Tarkofsky sees addressing the father as perhaps Christian – as recalling Christ's sacrifice. Christ's sacrifice makes demands on the Other by calling on people to renounce their sins. Christ's sacrifice does not face the Other, but rather makes demands on the Other. But if we look at the sacrifice as performative, something that resists meaning, or exceeds or interrupts meaning, what Christ Said, then we can begin to see how the act of the sacrifice faces the Other without demand.

The 'little man's' constative statement, 'In the beginning was the Word', is out of place. It should have taken place before the disaster, the sacrifice, but rather is a strange affect displaced after the event; the beginning should precede the disaster. The boy's calmness, the uncanniness of his speech, indicates that something is out of joint. Any meaning or definitive explanation is off frame, outside of what is given. The constative grounding, or explanation of the meaning of the sacrifice, is displaced by the unknowable and undecidable, the performativity of the sacrifice. The sacrifice is not harmonious, or Said, but rather is performative, outside the demands of the self on the Other. Through performativity the sacrifice opens up the only possibility of the 'face to face' with the Other – there are no demands of the self in the (im)possibility of the disaster.[16] After the displaced constative, comes the boy's interrogative, 'Why is that papa?' Aside from the strangeness of the boy addressing his father by looking up at the sky just after his father passes by in the ambulance, the unanswered question itself fails to address the performativity of the event, of the sacrifice. The question, or what Heidegger calls the 'piety of the question',[17] comes after the displaced constative and cannot get to the performativity of the event because the question is ontological, it demands meaning, the Said. In other words, the sacrifice, read as performance, unworks the ontological basis of the question – thus, the sacrifice is an interruption, a Saying that opens up the 'face to face'. In this way the question can only address or explore the ontological nature and the essence of something knowable, of something that can be Said. The question never reaches the performativity of the event or sacrifice. In this sense, both the constative utterance and the question of the boy are displaced and cannot get at the event, the performativity of the sacrifice. In order to open up the 'face to face' with the Other, the sacrifice must unwork (interrupt) the demands of the self on the Other, the harmony of exchange.

QUESTIONS FOR FURTHER CONSIDERATION

1. Discuss how the problem of gender or race might be introduced into Levinas's ethics.
2. While Levinas's project clearly challenges traditional ethics, would you consider Levinas political? Explain.
3. Levinas's work is considered to be anti-humanist. He challenges the Enlightenment concept that 'man' is the center of the universe. Can you think of any way in which Levinas might fall back into humanism?
4. Discuss the relationship between the Saying (performative) and the Said (constative). Is it possible to have one without the other? How would you write about Saying without describing it, without falling back into the Said?
5. The film maker Jean-Luc Godard once remarked: 'Tracking shots are a question of ethics.' Discuss how *The Sacrifice* might be read in light of Levinas and Godard from a filmic standpoint, in other words in terms of cuts, composition, panning, long takes, what might be occurring off camera, etc.
6. Choose another scene from *The Sacrifice*, such as when Otto (the postman) gives Alexander a map as a gift. How do you think Levinas would understand such a scene?

ANNOTATED BIBLIOGRAPHY

Critchley, Simon. *The Ethics of Deconstruction: Derrida and Levinas*. West Lafayette, IN: Purdue University Press, 1999. Critchley lucidly explores and problematizes the complexities, the stakes, similarities and agons at work between Levinas's ethics and Derrida's deconstruction. In addition to developing the problematics between ethics and deconstruction, Critchley explores the relation between Derrida and Heidegger in order to elucidate the importance of the end and closure of philosophy – a key to understanding Levinas's ethics. The book ends with an explanation of the relationship between deconstruction, ethics and politics.

Irigaray, Luce. *An Ethics of Sexual Difference*, trans. Carolyn Burke and Gillian C. Gill. Ithaca, NY: Cornell University Press, 1993. Irigarary investigates the question of ethics in relation to sexual difference. Working from Lacan, Irigarary explores classical philosophical and contemporary texts, from Plato to Levinas. She also critically discusses the problems of ethics and sexual difference as they relate to dominant binaries such as self/other, masculine/feminine and subject/object.

Levinas, Emmanuel. *Totality and Infinity: an Essay on Exteriority*, trans. Alphonso Lingis. Pittsburgh, PA: Duquesne University Press, 1969. This is a major work by Levinas in which he offers a sustained critique of philosophy, transcendence and ontology. Levinas explicates how ethics is more primary than philosophy and ontology. This rigorous text works through the ideas of many important figures in philosophy such as Heidegger, Kant, Husserl and Descartes.

Levinas, Emmanuel. *Otherwise Than Being: or, Beyond Essence*, trans. Alphonso Lingis. Boston, MA: Marinus Nijhoff. Levinas takes up many similar concerns as in *Totality and Infinity*, but this later text also takes into account the linguistic turn of continental philosophy. As Simon Critchley points out, *Otherwise Than Being* attempts to perform some of the problems that ethics poses, while, on the other hand, *Totality and Infinity* can be seen as a constative description of how ethics performs.

Robbins, Jill. *Altered Reading: Levinas and Literature*. Chicago, IL: University of Chicago Press, 1999. Robbins explores many of Levinas's critical concepts such as the gift, the face and infinity. Such concepts are examined in the light of rhetorical and poststructuralist notions of reading, as well as the problem of the 'literary' and aesthetics.

Wall, Carl Thomas. *Radical Passivity: Levinas, Blanchot and Agamben*. State University of New York Press, 1999. This philosophical investigation discusses the notion of radical passivity as it pertains to Levinas, Agamben and Blanchot. Wall challenges the notion of passivity as understood by the classical concept of the subject. Agamben's notion of 'whatever', Levinas's ethics and Blanchot's disaster all suggest a radical way of problematizing the concept of passivity.

SUPPLEMENTARY BIBLIOGRAPHY

Assoun, Paul-Laurent. 'The Subject and the Other in Levinas and Lacan', trans. Dianah Jackson and Denise Merkle. In *Levinas and Lacan: The Missed Encounter*, ed. Sarah Harasym. Albany, NY: State University of New York Press, 1998, 79–101.

Austin, J. L. *How To Do Things With Words*, eds J. O. Urmson and Marina Sbisa. Cambridge, MA: Harvard University Press, 1975.

Bernasconi, Robert and Simon Critchley (eds). *Re-Reading Levinas*. Bloomington, IN: Indiana University Press, 1991.

Bernasconi, Robert. 'Deconstruction and the Possibility of Ethics'. In *Deconstruction and Philosophy: the Texts of Jacques Derrida*, ed. John Sallis. Chicago, IL: University of Chicago Press, 1987.

Blanchot Maurice. *The Space of Literature*, trans. Ann Smock. Lincoln, NE: University of Nebraska Press, 1982.

Blanchot, Maurice. *The Writing of the Disaster*, trans. Ann Smock. Lincoln, NE: University of Nebraska Press, 1986.

Butler, Judith. *Bodies That Matter: On the Discursive Limits of Sex*. New York: Routledge, 1993.

Champagne, Roland. *The Ethics of Reading According to Emmanuel Levinas*. Amsterdam: Rodopi, 1998.

Cixous, Hélène. *Readings: The Poetics of Blanchot, Joyce, Kafka, Lispector, and Tsvetayevea*. Minneaplois, MN: University of Minnesota Press, 1991.

Cornell, Drucilla. *Beyond Accommodation: Ethical Feminism, Deconstruction, and the Law*. Lanham, MD: Rowman & Littlefield, 1999.

Critchley, Simon. *The Ethics of Deconstruction: Derrida and Levinas*. West Lafayette, IN: Purdue University Press, 1999.

Derrida, Jacques. 'Violence and Metaphysics,' trans. Alan Bass. In *Writing and Difference*. Chicago, IL: University of Chicago Press, 1978.

Derrida, Jacques. 'Geschlecht: Sexual Difference, Ontological Difference'. *Research in Phenomenology*, 13, 1983, 65–83.

Derrida, Jacques. *The Postcard: From Socrates to Freud and Beyond*, trans. Alan Bass. Chicago, IL: University of Chicago Press, 1987

Derrida, Jacques.*Limited Inc.* Evanston, IL: Northwestern University Press, 1988.

Derrida, Jacques. *Of Spirit: Heidegger and the Question*, trans. Geoffery Bennington and Rachel Bowley. Chicago, IL: University of Chicago Press, 1989.

Derrida, Jacques. *The Gift of Death*, trans. David Wills. Chicago, IL: University of Chicago Press, 1995.

Derrida, Jacques. *Adieu to Emmanuel Levinas*, trans. Pascale-Anne Brault and Michael Naas. Stanford, CA: Stanford University Press, 1999.

Descartes, René. *Discourse on the Method; and, Meditations on First Philosophy*, ed. David Weissman, New Haven, CT: Yale University Press, 1996.

Dreyfus, Herbert. *Being-In-The-World: A Commentary on Heidegger's Being and Time, Division I*. Cambridge, MA, and London: Press, 1991.

Eaglestone, Robert. *Ethical Criticism: Reading after Levinas*. Edinburgh: Edinburgh University Press, 1998.

Gibson, Andrew. *Postmodernity, Ethics, and the Novel: From Leavis to Levinas*. London: Routledge, 1999.

Hegel, Georg Wilhem Friedrich. *Phenomenology of Spirit*, trans. A. V. Miller. Oxford: Oxford University Press, 1977.

Heidegger, Martin. *What Is Philosophy?*, trans. William Kluback and Jean T. Wilde. New York: Twayne Publishers, 1958.

Heidegger, Martin. 'On The Essence of Truth', trans. David Farrel Krell. IN *Basic Writings*. San Francisco, CA: Harper & Row, 1977.

Heidegger, Martin. *Being and Time*, trans. Joan Stambaugh. Albany, NY: State University of New York Press, 1996.

Lacoue-Labarthe, Philippe. *Typography: Mimesis, Philosophy, Politics*, ed. Christopher Fynsk. Cambridge, MA: Harvard University Press, 1989.

Levinas, Emmanuel. *Time and the Other*, trans. Richard Cohen. Pittsburgh, PA: Duquesne University Press, 1985.

Levinas, Emmanuel. 'The Trace of the Other', trans. Alphonso Lingis. In *Deconstruction in Context: Literature and Philosophy*, ed. Mark C. Taylor. Chicago, IL: University of Chicago Press, 1986, 345–59.

Levinas, Emmanuel. 'Philosophy and the Idea of Infinity'. In *Collected Philosophical Papers*, trans. Alphonso Lingis. Dordrecht: Martinus Nijhoff, 1987, 47–59.

Levinas, Emmanuel. *Basic Philosophical Writings*, ed. Adriaan T. Peperzak, Simon Critchley and Robert Bernasconi. Bloomington, IN: Indiana University Press, 1996.

Levinas, Emmanuel. 'Is Ontology Fundamental?', trans. Simon Critchley, Peter Atterton and Graham Noctor. In Levinas, *Basic Philosophical Writings*, 1996, 2–10.

Levinas, Emmanuel. 'Meaning and Sense', trans. Alphonso Lingis. In Levinas, *Basic Philosophical Writings*, 1996, 33–64.

Lyotard, Jean-François. *The Postmodern Condition: A Report on Knowledge*, trans. Geoffrey Bennington and Brian Massumi. Minneapolis, MN: University of Minnesota Press, 1984.

Miller, J. Hillis. *The Ethics of Reading: Kant, de Man, Eliot, Trollope, James, and Benjamin*. New York: Columbia University Press, 1987.

Norris, Christopher. *Truth and the Ethics of Criticism*. New York: St Martin's Press, 1994.

Peperzak, Adriaan. *To The Other: An Introduction to the Philosophy of Emmanuel Levinas*. West Lafayette, IN: Purdue University Press, 1993.

Robbins, Jill. *Altered Reading: Levinas and Literature*. Chicago, IL: University of Chicago Press, 1999.

Tarkofsky, Andrey. *Sculpting in Time: Reflection on the Cinema*. Austin, TX: University of Texas Press, 1986.

NOTES

1. Ontology is the study of being; it is considered to be the foundation of philosophy. Martin Heidegger, as we will see later in this chapter, complicates how ontology has been understood by philosophy since Plato.

2. The Other is an important notion in philosophy. The German philosopher Georg Wilhem Friedrich Hegel understood the Other as something to be overcome. For Hegel, the Other must be posited in order to be overcome. For those interested in the complexities of Hegel's dialectic, see the *Phenomenology of Spirit*. For many twentieth-century French philosophers such as Levinas, Maurice Blanchot and

Jacques Derrida, the Other is not something to be overcome, understood, but rather something more radical. The Other for many poststructuralists is something estranged or outside of understanding, beyond meaning.

3. For example, Levinas's relation to gender, religion and animality are not explored here but are quite important. See Critchley (1992) for a reading of Derrida on Levinas about the importance of gender. Levinas's ethics, like Heidegger's Dasein, does not fully work through the implications of gender. Regarding animality, Critchley discusses Derrida and Llewelyn's criticism: 'One might conclude . . . as Derrida has recently done, that Levinasian ethics has no way of experiencing responsibility towards plants, animals, and living things in general and that despite the novelty and originality of Levinas's analysis of ethical subjectivity, he ends up buttressing and perpetuating a very traditional humanism, that of Judaeo-Christian morality. This issue is very sensitively discussed by John Llewelyn when he explores the question "Who is the Other (Autrui)?" by asking whether animals – dogs in particular – can obligate humans to the same degree as other human beings . . .' (1992, 180).

4. Like Heidegger, Levinas is critical of philosophy. In the section on ontology, I will discuss some of the crucial differences between Heidegger and Levinas. Levinas, also like many poststructuralists such as Derrida, Lyotard, Nancy and Lacoue-Labarthe, is critical of the totalizing project of philosophy, especially as exemplified by Hegel. This thematic grouping of Levinas with Blanchot, Heidegger and many poststructuralists, is provisional and only meant to show the common thread they share against the totalizing discourse of philosophy which culminates in Hegel's dialectic. The various critical differences and productive agons between these thinkers is, of course, crucial.

5. In the *Meditations*, René Descartes' famous phrase 'Cogito ergo sum' (I think, therefore I am) begins modern philosophy. Descartes, out to prove God's existence in the *Meditations*, begins by doubting everything except that he exists while he is thinking. The 'I', or subject, becomes foundational for Descartes, and the material world, which includes the body, becomes a *res extentia*, split from the 'I', the thinking subject. This begins the modern problem of the subject/object split. The problem of the subject has haunted all philosophers since Descartes.

6. An excellent guide for those interested in reading Heidegger's *Being and Time*, see *Being In The World* by Herbert Dreyfus (1991). Dreyfus's book does an great job explicating the complexities of what Heidegger means by Dasein, equipmentality, and being-in-the-world.

7. See *Being and Time*, Division I for the articulation of Dasein and Division II for Dasein's relation to temporality.

8. For a detailed analysis of the performative and constative, see Austin's *How To Do Things With Words*. Also crucial is Jacques Derrida's *Limited Inc.* (1988), which offers a 'deconstructive' reading of Austin and his student John Searle. See also, Judith Butler's *Bodies That Matter* (1993), esp. the chapter 'Paris is Burning', to see how the problematic of gender enters into the performative discourse.

9. For a complication of truth as representational see Section 44 of *Being and Time*, as well as Heidegger's *On The Essence of Truth*.

10. Jill Robbins makes the point that 'The other is not a relation but a surplus radical asymmetry' (Robbins, 1999, 4). Thus Levinas's 'relation', unmediated or predicated by ontology, is a non-relation, asymmetrical.

11. For Critchley, the Saying and the Said are of two different temporal orders, and although there is no way to escape the Greek logos that our language is inherently ontological, nonetheless the modes of synchrony and diachrony of the Saying and Said differ. 'The Saying is a performative disruption of the Said that is instantly refuted by the language in which it appears' (Critchley, 164).

12. A crucial text which haunts and informs my own interest in mimesis is Lacoue-Labarthe's, *Typography: Mimesis, Philosophy, Politics* (1989).

13. The relationship between Derrida, Levinas and Blanchot is quite complex, and they do not have a united notion of the 'literary'.
14. While these notes deal with specific thematic concerns in the film, a productive and developed reading of the filmic qualities of Tarkofsky is crucial. Such a reading might begin with Godard's well-known comment, 'Tracking shots are a question of ethics.'
15. Another productive reading could explore both the gift and the postman. See Derrida's *The Postcard* (1987) and *Given Time* (1994).
16. For more on the disaster, see Blanchot's *The Writing of the Disaster* (1986).
17. For a rigorous complication of Heidegger's question, see Derrida's *Of Spirit: Heidegger and the Question* (1989).

MATERIALITY AND
THE IMMATERIAL

CHAPTER 12

SPECTRAL CRITICISM

David Punter

It would be difficult to claim that there is such a thing as a 'school' or even emerging tradition of 'spectral criticism'. Rather, what use of the term might seek to bring together would be a series of images and tendencies which have arisen within critical thinking over the last twenty or so years, from a diversity of sources, and which seem set to continue to exercise an appropriately ghostly influence over the critical activities of the next decades. If one were to go further back, the concerns of Maurice Blanchot with deaths and dubious returns of the literary voice, and with the ambiguous, liberating yet also menacing 'spaces' of literature, might figure as an (already inevitably occluded) 'originary' point.

We might think, for example, of Blanchot writing in 1955 about the act of reading and its inevitable encounter with what is dead, with what is not yet dead, and with what ineffably fails to declare its status in relation to death, resurrection and the phantom:

> What makes the 'miracle' of reading more singular still, and has perhaps something to say for the significance of magic in general, is that here the rock and the tomb, besides containing the corpse-like void that has to be revived, represent the presence, albeit a hidden presence, of what will be revealed. To roll away the rock, to dynamite it, is indeed a miraculous undertaking; but it is one we are constantly performing in everyday conversation; at every hour of the day we converse with this Lazarus – dead for three days, or since the beginning of time – who, under his finely woven winding cloth and sustained by the most refined conventions, answers us and talks to us in the privacy of our hearts. (Blanchot, 1982a, 253)

What Blanchot therefore points us to is, first, the unavoidability of considering reading under the heading of a dialogue with the dead; and second, the quotidian reality of this inscription of a phantomatic reality atop the bizarre illusion of normalcy which might otherwise attend the act of reading itself, epitomized as it might be in the construction and interpretation of the epitaph, the memorial to the dead. The figure of Lazarus here invoked will – perhaps inevitably – crop up again below.

This increasing realization that the act of reading is of an uncanny nature, that in it the type of 'converse' we practise is necessarily also 'perverse', that it cuts across while it supposes itself to succour any 'normal' rule of 'conversation', can be seen as one of the roots of the growing insistence on spectrality in criticism, a sense that any involvement with or in literature is inseparable from the phantom, the ghost, that the continuing survival and material reality of the book is itself the possible subject of scrutiny, anxiety, even fear. Andrew Bennett and Nicholas Royle, writing in 1999 in the second edition of their *Introduction to Literature, Criticism and Theory*, propose 'ghosts' (although they did not do so in the first, 1995 edition) as an essential *topos* of the critical:

> Ghosts are paradoxical since they are both fundamental to the human, fundamentally human, and a denial or disturbance of the human, the very being of the inhuman. We propose to devote this chapter, to dedicate it, to the living-dead, to the ghost(s) of literature. And we propose that this scandal of the ghost, its paradoxy, is embedded in the very thing that we call literature, endlessly inscribed in multiple and haunting ways, in novels, poems and plays. (Bennett and Royle, 1999)

This mention of the 'inhuman' perhaps serves to connect the possibility of a spectral criticism with other, better-known critical practices that seek to displace the overweening human subject; the word 'devote', however, with its associations of madness and obsession, indicates the mass of difficulty and resistance to interpretation that would need to be encountered in the process of practising a truly spectral criticism, the impossibility, as it were, of such a criticism ever emerging fully into the light of day. Spectral criticism, then, denotes not a programme or task to be fulfilled but rather a substrate of all dealings with text, an undecidable ground on which our reading occurs, a reinvocation of a terrorizing but desired communion with the dead.

In what ways, some would ask, could this address the concerns of a more 'materialistic' tendency in criticism? The answer might, perhaps, not be as simple as it appears. While the ghost, the phantom, might appear to be the most insubstantial of apparitions, one might also say that in this way it uncannily redoubles the mode of appearance of textuality itself, that it is 'materialistic criticism' which deals only in metaphor – for, after all, materialistic criticism is rarely concerned with the materials themselves, with the parchment, papyrus, paper that might be all that is left after the word has been erased, whereas these emptied substances, always awaiting the reality of their inscription, are precisely the substance of the spectral, which is never confident of the actuality it appears to perceive.

These roots of spectral criticism I would summarize as leading to a formulation of what I have referred to elsewhere as the 'law of the orphan' (Punter, 1998, 200–21). Whereas many other schools of criticism have looked at issues of tradition and influence, of authorization and paternity/maternity, of intertextuality and inheritance, spectral criticism finds itself instead seeing texts as paradoxical in their relation to the past, fundamentally unparented and 'unhouseled, disappointed, unaneled', to quote *Hamlet*; they speak to us indeed all the time of the past, but the voice they use is not authoritative, it is instead monitory, omenistic, it warns of dooms past and to come and above all it reiterates our own complaint of being not at home in the world, of being adrift, lost in a prior space that can never be re-created by any rolling away of the stone.

The most familiar pathway for these concerns – which are, at the end of the day, also political and social concerns – in the 1980s and 1990s was the rise of Gothic criticism, that is to say, the change in the fortunes of Gothic writing that accompanied the emergence of a criticism that looked at it with some seriousness but thus inevitably, some would say, became involved, infected with the multiple anomalies of the supernatural. Although to begin with one might say that such criticism involved a 'recapitulation', an attempted recovery of meaning from various textualities over the last two hundred years, one can also sense the emergence of a double problem that in the end led to a series of doubts about the very status of criticism. First, there is the vexed question of where, or indeed whether, 'Gothic' could be said to have 'begun', shading off as it always does into an imagined 'prior' that proves increasingly impossible of recapitulation. Second, there is an increasing recognition that the 'supernatural' material with which Gothic claims to deal itself comes to constitute an 'excess' around the space of criticism, an ongoing challenge to criticism itself as a branch of enlightenment.

> Gothic persists in eluding this notion of 'rule'. What haunts Gothic . . . is Gothic: a ghost haunted by another ghost, almost as eighteenth-century Gothic was haunted by Jacobean tragedy, and Jacobean tragedy by the horrors of Greek drama; and as all these textual manifestations are themselves further haunted by a world which comes prior to text yet which we can know only in and through text, a world of oral tradition, of more primal hauntings by word of mouth. (Punter, 1998, 14)

According to this vision of – or from – the Gothic, there would be no possibility for criticism to isolate a single text, a non-duplicitous textual act; instead criticism would only be able to realize itself by entering into the 'hall of absence', the clinic for chronic originary doubt. Like a ghost tied to, and doomed to return to, an already inscribed location, criticism itself would be doomed to haunt a site which can never be fully recaptured.

The way in which this 're-vision' of the Gothic has been taken into a wider field of critical speculation is well exemplified in the recent collection of essays, *Ghosts: Deconstruction, Psychoanalysis, History*, edited by Peter Buse and

Andrew Stott. This volume, Buse and Stott claim, argues 'that modern theory owes a debt to ghosts' (1999, 6), even if that debt is often unacknowledged. The word 'debt', reminding us as it does of work on Freud done by Samuel Weber and others, is significant in this context; but equally significant is the tripartite scheme into which the editors divide their chapters: 'Spectrality and Theory', 'Uncanny Fictions' and 'Spectral Culture'. All of these categories are, as we may see later, susceptible of further development: the second of them, as envisaged in this volume, is solidly on the terrain of the Gothic, with chapters on, for example, 'Spectres of Marx, Derrida and Gothic Fiction', the 'Mysteries and Domesticities of *Udolpho*' and 'The Postcolonial Ghost Story'.

Among the echoes called to mind here are those of the spectre and the uncanny, and these inevitably draw us close to the concerns of deconstruction and psychoanalysis respectively. There is, for example, an overarching question about the ambiguities of deconstruction, and especially about deconstruction's workings between textuality and politics. The emblematic text here is Derrida's *Specters of Marx*, which essays a 'different' version of history: not as linear development, but as the site of multiple hauntings. Speaking with the ghost of Hamlet's father – to which I shall return – in mind, Derrida suggests that

> . . . everything begins by the apparition of a specter. More precisely by the *waiting* for this apparition. The anticipation is at once impatient, anxious, and fascinated: this, the thing ('this thing') will end up coming. The *revenant* is going to come. (Derrida, 1994, 4)

Everything, then, begins in – and perhaps continues to reside in – an absence, a premonition of arrival which will never be fully removed or replaced. Thus – and here as the spur to an account of recent European history and the fate of communism – Derrida engages with the looping circularity of history, whereby there is, as in the Gothic, never an origin, or a never-origin, a state whereby the past refuses to be entirely occluded but remains to haunt the apparent site of enlightened new beginnings: in the beginning – apparently – is the apparition. History therefore cannot be written without ghosts, but the point goes further than this: the narratives of history must necessarily include ghosts – indeed they can include little else – but they will also be written *by* ghosts. History is a series of accounts of the dead, but it is also a series of accounts *by* the dead; the voices we overhear in our dealings with history are spectral without exception, they spectralize the possibility of knowledge.

This inevitably connects, through the notion of the uncanny, through the conflation of the homely and the unhomely, the familiar and the unfamiliar, with the older tradition of 'Freudian history', from which, as from the unconscious, nothing ever goes away. We need to have in mind, for example, the vision Freud offers of Rome in *Civilisation and its Discontents*; he offers it to us as a city which, as he remarks in a resonant phrase, is now 'taken by ruins'. But 'now' – perhaps, therefore in a different but equally problematic 'present' moment –

. . . let us, by a flight of imagination, suppose that Rome is not a human habitation but a psychical entity with a similarly long and copious past – an entity, that is to say, in which nothing that has once come into existence will have passed away and all the earlier phases of development continue to exist alongside the latest one. (Freud, XXI, 7)

According to this vision – although we might equally refer to it as a hallucination – 'in Rome the palaces of the Caesars and the Septizonium of Septimius Severus would still be rising to their old height on the Palatine', 'the castle of S. Angelo would still be carrying on its battlements the beautiful statues which graced it until the siege by the Goths', and so forth. In other words, according to a Freudian historiography, a history of the unconscious, nothing would ever have gone away. Clearly the mention of the Goths – as the ineffectual erasers of a prior memory that will never go away, as the sign of the hovering and recurring possibility symbolized by the 'dark ages' – is not accidental here; but neither is the tense of the verb, that repeating 'would' that characterizes spectral criticism, that comes helplessly to replace the 'is' that can no longer stand in the light of the endless returns of history: the rule, we might say, of the phantomatic hypothesis.

According to the development of this new historiography – which is at the same time a recrudescence of the concept of the 'ancient' – social life and its cultural textualities, however material they may appear, are constituted as much by absence as by presence, and the past takes the form of a series of apparitions that can be neither addressed nor banished. This, of course, has been the 'lesson' of psychoanalysis right from its own – deeply contested – origins; what, after all, was the status of linear history under the conditions of hypnosis and somnambulism within which psychoanalysis emerged? What, however, has been distinctive within the last two decades has been the insistence with which psychoanalysis has associated itself with the (Gothic) language of the crypt and the phantom. Emblematic here has been the work of Nicolas Abraham and Maria Torok, first in *The Wolf Man's Magic Word* and later in the essays collected in *The Shell and the Kernel*.

What this work principally points to is a psychic space different from the unconscious, a location that is not a location but whose existence is felt only as an insistent pressure from an otherwise absent or unattributable source. This 'crypt', according to Abraham and Torok, is the repository of the secrets of the past, it is the place where the memories of our parents and grandparents are buried, the site on which are stored all the stories which have been too painful, too embarrassing, too revealing to tell; it is in the crypt that the secrets of our own genesis may be buried, but we are ourselves unaware not only of its contents but of its existence or whereabouts, and even psychoanalysis, according to this theory, can exert only a limited influence over the crypt's role in psychic life, however much the psychoanalytic encounter seeks to replicate the conditions of an underlying dialogue with the dead.

This in turn, we might say, suggests new approaches to textuality, approaches based on a notion of the 'text instead', ways of reading 'through' the material text to a 'different absence'. The whole tenor of *The Wolf Man's Magic Word* is geared towards the exposure of a 'text that lies beneath the text' which haunts all words with its insistent pressure; Abraham and Torok's final reckoning with the Wolf Man – a reckoning which is itself, of course, really an engagement with the phantoms of Freud and of the Wolf Man himself – results in the excavation of a single word, but a word which, because of its 'magic' proclivities, takes on a phantomatic status, as though it has secretly controlled the Wolf Man's whole life from, as it were, behind his back.

We may choose to take issue with the simple act of banishment which concludes, but at the same time undercuts, the subtleties of Abraham and Torok's dealings with the subterranean and the absent, but it nonetheless follows from this that no word can be understood in terms of its own claim to status, its own referent; often the words we use, the words we read, can only be paradoxically understood as responses to prior signals, more originary forms, forms that remain incomprehensible in themselves. Within all of us, Abraham and Torok suggest, such a crypt exists, and we place over it a guard, emblem of the strength of our resistance to the arrival of the apparition, to the return of the undead, a 'cemetery guard'. Nevertheless:

> . . . sometimes in the dead of night, when libidinal fulfilments have their way, the ghost of the crypt comes back to haunt the cemetery guard, giving him strange and incomprehensible signals, making him perform bizarre acts, or subjecting him to unexpected sensations. (Abraham and Torok, 1994, 130)

A battle, then, between two phantomatic figures, one who seeks to remind and one who seeks the prevention of such dangerous rememoration; this is perhaps an encounter reminiscent of similar battles on the terrain of trauma. In so far as this might be so, it would therefore have to be realized that the critical act of isolating and interpreting takes place only within an encircling horizon of mistranslation, of uninterpretability: the words we read, like the words we utter, are themselves always responses, they are answers to questions we cannot perceive, they are attempts to solve problems we cannot imagine, they are mere residues of an entirely different, spectral struggle. What we experience of the dialogue presupposes a phantom 'on the other side', a side of the dialogue to which we can never gain access but which nevertheless ineluctably reconstructs itself within the very harmonics of the voice we think we hear.

We are here on a terrain of compulsion, much like the Gothic's compulsive, obsessive return to a prior terrain; we are in the place which is haunted, where we know a ghost to 'exist' but can nevertheless offer no explanation for the bizarre recurrences and effects of its apparition:

> The phantom's periodic and compulsive return lies beyond the scope of symptom-formation in the sense of a return of the repressed; it works like a ventriloquist, like a stranger within the subject's own mental topography. The imaginings issuing from the presence of a stranger have nothing to do with fantasy strictly speaking. They neither preserve a topographical status nor announce a shift in it. (Abraham and Torok, 1994, 173)

Like a stranger, like a 'foreign body' within the self, like a ventriloquist, calling into question the 'authenticity' of the words we speak even as we speak them, reminding us that 'our' words are always simultaneously the residues, the traces, of the words of others.

It would therefore follow that the ghost in the text cannot be experienced either as conserving the past or as ridding us of the past's hold: to suppose either would be to attempt to categorize the phantom within Enlightenment norms, to 'subject' the ghost to a logic that cannot recognize its existence (and thus remains inexplicably haunted by its own other). This would be the logic also explored by Julia Kristeva in her *Strangers to Ourselves*, where she explores the notion of foreignness in relation both to the external other and also to the other within ourselves; it would also lead us to a more extensive encounter with the 'foreign body', with the other within ourselves, always again implicit within Freudian theory but emerging with particular force in the criticism – and also in the literature – of the last two decades.

However, before proceeding down this line one would also want to consider the recent work of Jean Laplanche on otherness and its potential implications for textual study. Laplanche's main argument in his *Essays on Otherness* is against Jacques Lacan's famous – or notorious – claim that the unconscious is structured like a language, with the concomitant implication that the unconscious can be in some sense deconstructed according to a certain set of rules – the issues of metaphor and metonymy, condensation and displacement are central here – so as to yield meaning. The unconscious, according to Laplanche, is quite different from this, and this 'difference' is to be grasped only in terms of the 'message' and the enigma.

According to Laplanche, Lacan's account of the unconscious is hostage to an unexamined assumption of the primacy of language; thus anything he has to say is vitiated by his very act of saying it, his blindness to the possibility of alternative primacies, other origins, that might relegate the verbal – and thus the textual – to a different role in development, and one that is inevitably haunted by that which preceded it. This then would be the essence of haunting, that the very words in which we try to describe our experience come only as replacements, as – as we have already suggested – a 'text instead'.

> The messages which are the object of the first translations are not essentially verbal, nor are they 'intellectual'. They include in large part signifiers of affect, which can be either translated or repressed: a smile (in Leonardo), an angry gesture, a grimace of disgust, etc. These signifiers, if

they are repressed, will be designified, in the same way as are more 'intellectual' signifiers. The 'exclusion' of affect here is nothing but a general consequence of the exclusion of the signified. (Laplanche, 1999, 108)

All communication, according to Laplanche, is predicated on a radical incompleteness: the gesture, the represented affect, that the child perceives is not only incomprehensible to the child but, more importantly, it is incomprehensible to and unperceived by the parent, and can therefore only be transmitted as an enigma. The enigma is not at all the same as a problem, for a problem may have a solution; the enigma, as Laplanche sees it, is incapable of solution, for it is inexplicable even to its own apparent originator; it is a ghostly message which might appear in the form of a conundrum but which comes with no key with which to unlock the 'apparent secret' (a paradox, of course, in itself).

Thus, if we were to extend Laplanchean theory, we might say that all communication (and thus all textuality) is accompanied by a *different* communication, one that mysteriously takes place *between* crypts, one in which the word has no part to play except as a covering over a 'different' scenario. As we talk, ghosts behind our backs gesticulate and murmur to each other; as we turn to observe them, they vanish. What we think we understand is putatively rescued from the enigma; but in the beginning, as it were, is the sphinx. On this reading, the Oedipal myth would not have much to do with sexuality; it would hinge rather on the shared triumphalist myth that the sphinx's words can somehow be recapitulated, understood; it would be this logocentric error that sealed Oedipus' fate, his assumption – shared with the entire city of Thebes – that the existence of a riddle presupposes the existence of a solution.

Ghosts obey no such logic, and this in turn links with developments on the interface between the literary and the theological, where an emblematic text would be the proceedings, edited by Philippa Berry and Andrew Wernick under the title *The Shadow of Spirit: Postmodernism and Religion*, of a conference held in Cambridge in 1990 whose themes underlined the phantomatic status of text itself, the inevitable (at least within the western Christian tradition) pressure of 'spirit' (however that term may be conceived) upon materiality. '[A] darker, more obscure way of seeing and thinking – a perspective which is perhaps more appropriate to the twilight regions where philosophy now finds itself – appears gradually to be replacing our long-established visual drive to power and truth', Berry suggests in her introduction to the volume, thereby situating the concept of the shadow within the very 'oculocentric' rhetoric of enlightenment. She refers also to an 'in-between and shadowy intellectual region which we have inherited from Nietzsche and others', to the possibility expressed by Emmanuel Levinas of thinking the gods and the divine 'otherwise', to the 'nonabsent absence of the holy' (Berry and Wernick, 1992, 2, 4).

In these formulations – and in many others in the various essays in the volume – one cannot but hear the ambiguous presence of the spectral. Although

Berry and the other contributors wisely avoid essaying a definition of what the relation might be between the postmodern and this haunted condition, we may nonetheless extrapolate that the icy and knowing fracturings of the postmodern need also to be seen as a 'new' set of defences – defences which, as is always the way of defences, call our attention to precisely the material that they are apparently designed to repel. An important question might then be put: when we ask what the postmodern is doing, we need to break this question down and to look at it under two different (although inseparable) headings. First we need to ask what the postmodern is trying to protect us from; but second, what is it calling into being, 'calling up', invoking in its gestural language, under the guise of its status as 'cemetery guard'?

On these bases we might now move to formulate some hypotheses about spectral criticism. It depends, as we have seen, upon the 'law of the orphan', the assertion that no attempt to assert textual parentage can properly 'take', that neither paternity nor maternity can be known and that the provenance of the text will immediately take us into a shadowy realm that lies behind the word – and even behind the imagistic realm of the womb, gestation, the creative matrix. Its model would be the Gothic, the apparent return of a transmuted past – a past which, to be sure, we know full well to have little historical accuracy but which continues to inflect our dealings with that past and which will, in the end, grow monstrously so as to occlude the possibility of accuracy altogether, as memory itself selects its own moments, unconsciously and frequently with trauma as its only guide, to represent but simultaneously to defeat a past that cannot be rendered wholesale. Its fundamental trope would be the uncanny, the impossibility of discerning a clear disjunction between what is known and what is not known – we would be here on the terrain of what Christopher Bollas (1987) has memorably referred to as the 'unthought known', that body of 'knowledge' that is incapable of conscious recapitulation yet which forms the ground of our every action. Its characteristic form would not be language but the enigmatic 'message', the message seen as always shadowed by the incomprehensible, always containing within itself the *enigmatic* possibility that we are, as it were, looking at the wrong side of the paper (or at the paper before, or after, it has been temporarily inscribed). The text, therefore, would always be open to construal as the 'text instead', the wrong text, a ghostly alteration of a prior state of material being which is unsusceptible of recapture.

Interestingly, we can see a convergent development in theology itself with books such as *Reading Bibles, Writing Bodies: Identity and the Book*, edited by Timothy K. Beal and David M. Gunn (1997), which seek to recast the 'spiritual' concerns of the Bible in terms of the materiality of the word (the Word). Here a new field shows signs of coming into being, a field in which the term 'spirit' itself, with its phantomatic associations, becomes the heart of the problem. This western, Christian constellation itself, however, has been recently further offset or 'ghosted' by other concurrent developments in criticism. The most important instance here would be that of postcolonial criticism, which has repeatedly called attention to the spectral presence in postcolonial texts of past histories of violence, imperialism and exploitation as the principal ground on which a postcolonial writing must be constructed. According to these ideas, history is again conceived as a matter of ghosts, phantoms, haunted sites; thus, for example, terms like 'primitivism' and 'superstition' can be subjected to a reversal and seen less as 'natural' features of specific colonized cultures than as the outcroppings of primal encounters between cultures, encounters which have been repressed beneath the rewritings – or reroutings – of history but which nevertheless remain in the explosive crypts of defeated nations. An example here would be Michael Taussig's (1993) work on South American shamanism, which sets out to show that the powers of healing ascribed to the 'native' were effects more of the desire of the western invader to be 'healed' than of anything 'pre-existent' in a native culture itself; according to studies such as this, which turn the entire concept of 'anthropology' on its head, what is revealed by the western 'invasion' of other realms is a refracted, distorted image of the invader himself, a ghostly representation in which the will to dominate is shown in its true colours but where simultaneously the essential weakness, the terror that accompanies violence, stares back at us from the mirror, robed in death.

The most important provocation here would be towards a re-examination of the ways in which deconstruction and postcolonial criticism themselves relate as mutual phantoms. One way of approaching this terrain would be through a consideration of the 'foreign body'. According to Royle, the term '"foreign body" would name that which makes every identity, all language, perception and experience different from itself . . . there is a certain foreign body which works *over* our language, over what we say and read and write, and which corresponds . . . to a notion of what Derrida refers to as "the 'other of language"'; the other "which is beyond language and which summons language"' (Royle, 1995, 146). This, it seems to me, is approximately in accord with a general dialectic of the spectral. What one might, however, reply – or at least propose as a 'supplement' – in the postcolonial moment to such assertions might hinge on the conception of the 'foreign', on how such a category comes to be constituted, on what imagistic models one might be unconsciously relying on to provide an image of radical alterity.

One might also suggest that, although the phantomatic may be a function of language in general, it might *also* be a function of specific relations between and among languages, so that the issue of the speaking voice would never be reducible to a singularity but would instead be considered in terms of the 'foreigning' of the apparently natural, the inner sense of a language not our own – which again would have general implications in terms of the domination of the linguistic, but would also be brought to a head when considering what languages can be used in postcolonial situations, in situations where a certain violation, an imperialist robbery of authority, has always occurred and where the voices speaking at our shoulder, the ghosts of the past, are all too apparent, the 'apparitions' all too 'present'. Do all ghosts, we might ask, speak English?

The colonial and postcolonial scenes are, whatever our reply to that question (and in whatever language), populated by ghosts. Robert J. C. Young develops this point in an essay on – and addressed to – Derrida and in particular to Derrida's position as Algerian and as Jewish. He quotes Albert Memmi on this 'inarticulated' community:

> Their constant and very justifiable ambition is to escape from their colonised condition . . . To that end, they endeavour to resemble the coloniser in the frank hope that he may cease to consider them different from him. Hence their efforts to forget the past, to change collective habits, and their enthusiastic adoption of Western language, culture and customs. But if the coloniser does not always openly discourage these candidates to develop that resemblance, he never permits them to attain it either. Thus, they live in constant and painful ambiguity. (Young, 2000, 204–5)

One of the (haunting) references here, although it may not be explicit, is nonetheless pressing: it is to the crowd of shades on the banks of the Lethe, who indeed 'live in constant and painful ambiguity', although perhaps 'live' is too unambiguous a word. We might think, in the same vein, of the character in T. S. Eliot's *Little Gidding* who encounters 'the eyes of a familiar compound ghost/Both intimate and unidentifiable'. 'I was still the same', he protests in the face of this uncanny revelation:

> Knowing myself yet being someone other –
> And he a face still forming; yet the words sufficed
> To compel the recognition they preceded.
> And so, compliant to the common wind,
> Too strange to each other for misunderstanding,
> In concord at this intersection time
> Of meeting nowhere, no before and after,
> We trod the pavement in a dead patrol.
>   (Eliot, 1963, 217)

This, then, would be one image for the condition of the spectral: to recognize and yet not to recognize the other; to recognize a foreign body at the heart of the self; to be aware and yet to be unable fully to articulate the sense that one's very vocabulary, even perhaps one's gestures, have been formed by the other. There is, to put it in a different rhetoric, a mutual impossibility of banishment: the colonizer can no more remove his 'subject' from his sight than can the colonized lift the weight of imposition from his heart. Instead, there emerges a spectral logic in which the foreign body is loosed yet simultaneously tied in place, free – like a ghost – to roam the world, yet simultaneously shackled – like a ghost – to a particular place and time, the significance of which may only be revealed on the horizon of an unascertainable future.

This though, spectral criticism will go on to say, is inseparably the condition of both the postcolonial – considered as the defining mark of an age rather than of specific cultures – and the postmodern; for all representation, according to some arguments, now falls under the revealed but occluded sign of the phantom – a sign which now, it would seem, has come to occlude Jean Baudrillard's simplistic and commercially problematic late twentieth-century notion of the 'simulacrum'. Let us consider another example, another time, another medium. 'Early viewers of film', we are told by one critic, 'were amazed and moved by this miraculous gift dispensed by film, that of reanimating what had gone . . . Like Christ calling Lazarus, film seemed to bring back to life what had been irrevocably lost; it blurred uncannily the distinction between life and death' (Smith, 2000, 121). Lazarus again, the evidence which defies all evidence, the test of truth and faith which, if accepted, will plunge us into a universe of ghosts. The complete transcript, the irrefutable truth: film appeared to promise – promised like an apparition – the incontrovertible; yet simultaneously, as we are now increasingly seeing in the literally endless lying of videotape, it paved the way for the most powerful of all challenges to the integrity of the past, it allowed for the insertion of a radical, phantomatic doubt about 'the truth' which has now come to bear fruit in what we – perhaps temporarily – designate 'virtual reality'.

As we look now, with twentieth-first-century eyes, at these developments then there emerges an obvious connection with alterations in the notion of textuality itself, particularly in so far as it is now mediated through 'virtual reality' – although perhaps we would do better to see this simply as a different type of 'virtual reality', in series with all the other 'imaginary truths' that textuality has promised us down the ages. Examples here might be drawn from critical writing, but they also abound in the various 'cyber-genres', as practised by William Gibson,[1] Iain Banks and others, with their consequences for the notions of the 'enduring word'. The wholesale revision of the time and space of literature thus suggested would produce its own ghosts, the relics of a textuality already on the point of vanishing, beyond recall in the very moment of its emergence as the cyborg exerts a spectral influence over the domain of the literary.

In Gibson's emblematic *Neuromancer*, for example, the logic of the spectral prevails. Regardless of the demands of narrative, we need to negotiate the reality status of passages such as this:

> Directly overhead, along the nighted axis, the hologram sky glittered with fanciful constellations suggesting playing cards, the faces of dice, a top hat, a martini glass. The intersection of Desiderata and Jules Verne formed a kind of gulch, the balconied terraces of Freeside cliff dwellers rising gradually to the grassy tablelands of another casino complex. Case watched a drone microlight bank gracefully in an updraft at the green verge of an artificial mesa, lit for seconds by the soft glow of the invisible casino . . . He'd seen a wink of reflected neon off glass, either lenses or the turrets of lasers. (Gibson, 1994, 180)

The question would be, in what sense – or perhaps to what (altered) senses – are these scenes recognizable? But in this specific case, this could also readily resolve itself into a question of perspective: from what position are we looking, through what sorts of eyes – and what then is the self – or not-self – that lies behind these perceptions? The recognizability, such as it is, could lie in the scenario of the very rich, in the possibility that we are here simply looking at wealth and dominance through the eyes of a spectator who is himself – or herself, or itself – a foreign body, and that thus we can 'retranslate' these fragments into a recognizable societal whole. The alternative, however, might be well signalled by the notion of the 'intersection of Desiderata and Jules Verne', the question, as we might say, of the desired object that can nevertheless never be found, the source of the endless journey of Captain Nemo in the shadowy darknesses of the oceans, the suggestion that a ghost's eyes might be permanently, as it were, under water, open but only to blindness, or dazzled by possibilities that are too numerous, too fast, too instantly self-replicating, to permit any grasp on the 'cliff' of the virtually real.

Such a perception would always be, in some sense, ruined; it would take place only in a realm where the sight and the understanding had already been severed, the optical nerve cut off at the root. Ghosts, we might say, with large eyes, wide shut. And it would be on the note of the term 'ruin' that the notion of spectral criticism both returns us to its own origin in the Gothic ruins of the eighteenth century (and of the Dark Ages, and of Greece and Rome) and simultaneously gestures forward towards further developments: for what is the ruin?

All texts, perhaps, are ruins; that is to say, they are relics of the unrealized projects of their former selves. They have, as it were, already collapsed; none the more so than the literary masterpieces of the canon. When we come to read a text in the half-light of spectrality, we find ourselves approaching a ruin, an object of antiquarian delight and fear, the site of a potential reconstruction whose success will always elude us. Thus, we might say, spectral criticism offers a certain – and deeply uncertain – humility in the face of the text, a necessary opposition to the vaunted possibilities of accurate historical exhumation, a realization of the partiality of all our efforts. In this light, again, we might want to say that our efforts to focus on the text are all but destroyed before they have begun; this is not to say that spectral criticism has no discursive role to play, but rather the reverse: that the role it plays is the only possible one unless we are to succumb to the fantasy identifications that attend on our other attempts to inhabit the house of the dead.

Texts, therefore, are not themselves; they are something quite other, and it is only in (or with) this spirit that a text may be approached.

NOTES TOWARDS A READING OF FATHER(S) OF *HAMLET*'S GHOST

The reading of a 'canonical text' that I offer would ideally be a reading of *Hamlet*, and it would start from a question posed to me recently by a student at the end of a discussion of *Hamlet* and the uncanny. The question was: 'But is the ghost *real*?'

In pursuit of this question, although not of its answer, I would offer the following fragments of a reading – not of *Hamlet*, but of some of the locations where we might *find Hamlet* if, like ghosts, we were to be looking with other eyes. Freud, for example, reads *Hamlet* in *The Interpretation of Dreams*. Royle writes of *Hamlet* and of hearing and writing in *Telepathy and Literature*. There is no space here to look at these readings and writings, except to say that in both cases *Hamlet* clearly (or obscurely) *haunts* the texts within which it is further embodied. Jacques Lacan writes about *Hamlet*, and specifically about the duel; and Royle writes about Lacan writing about the duel . . .

Ned Lukacher writes about *Hamlet* in his book *Primal Scenes: Literature, Philosophy, Psychoanalysis* (1986). For example, he says of the murder of Claudius:

> The manner of the crime is in effect Shakespeare's own signature in the play, the inimitable mark of his originality. With the ear-poisoning, Shakespeare signs his text twice, once as the author on the title page and again, in a kind of antonomasia, by dismantling his proper name into the common nouns that compose it: ShakespEARE'. (Lukacher, 1986, 227)

Antonomasia: 'the substitution of an epithet or appellative, or the name of an office or dignity, for a person's proper name, as *the Iron Duke* for Wellington, *his Grace* for an archbishop. Also, conversely, the use of a proper name to express a general idea, as in calling an orator *a Cicero*, a wise judge *a Daniel*' (*OED*). Lukacher's comment might appear to us entirely spurious, in parallel with the four musketEARS, but this will not do away with the question implicitly posed, which is about how such (mis)hearings affect our view of the text. What do we hear? How can we hear the voices of the dead? Only, of course, by reconstructing them – but as we do that, what happens to the alternative voices, the 'texts instead', that we simultaneously banish?

A further question is also proposed here, which is the question, as it were, of the 'name-of-Hamlet'. For that name has already whispered to us over time – and the 'us' here does not only refer to a western, 'educated' public, but to a much wider sphere. It would, a spectral criticism would say, be impossible to approach *Hamlet* – or indeed Hamlet, for there is already a ghosting present in the relation between the names of the play and of the character – without having *already seen the play*, without having in the mind's eye an image of what the play is to be.

And Hamlet/*Hamlet* keep 'popping up' (like ventriloquists' puppets, like theatrical spectres) in Bennett and Royle, as ghosts do whether they are summoned or not. Let us take a further example:

Hamlet's life, for instance, might be described as a sort of *anagnorisis* 'block', a ghostly series of apparent but ineffective *anagnorises* starting with his exclamation 'O my prophetic soul!' on discovering the murderous truth about his father's death and realising that this is what he had imagined, deep in his 'prophetic soul'. (Bennett and Royle, 1999, 100)

From antonomasia to anagnorisis; we again have recourse to the dictionary, although to do so is only to have recourse to the ruins of the past, to that which appears to have survived the wreck of libraries otherwise destroyed. Anagnorisis, at any rate: 'recognition: the *dénouement* in a drama' (*OED*). Hamlet, it would appear, keeps on experiencing moments when he appears – to himself, and to 'us', whatever that might be – to know what is going on; but in fact he is merely erecting defences against the inevitable condition, namely, of not knowing what is going on, of being 'present', if at all, on a scene already indefinitely altered by his own appearance – or apparition.

Bennett and Royle also refer to *Hamlet* as 'arguably the greatest "ghost work" in English literature' (1999, 133). Perhaps, then, the condition in which we think we discover what is going on is the condition that provokes the ghost. This may well be so in a great deal of postcolonial writing; it is the assumption that (at last) 'we' have come into a position where, like the fantasy of the imperial conqueror, we can survey all we know and own, it is this assumption that produces the ghost that has hitherto lain, inert, unseen, in the landscape that we are now seeking to claim as our own. Even, for example, these Danish battlements; even these, we might come to see, contain within themselves secrets.

The notion of the secret is crucial here, as it is to Abraham and Torok's whole theory, elaborated as it is around – of course – *Hamlet*. What, after all, does Hamlet *know*? Perhaps more to the point, in what way, and at what level, does he know it? There are so many quotations from *Hamlet* that one could offer at this point (as at any other), but I am going to offer none of them. This is not to suggest that spectral criticism is inaccurate; it is rather to say that it thrives – inevitably – not on the originary voice but on the *echo*.

Let us consider one such: Lacan's use of the 'name of Hamlet' as the provocation for his coining of the term 'hommelette'. For Lacan, part of the pun here is the suggestion that the originary self is broken into pieces, smashed like an egg; another part is to belittle the vaunting ego, perhaps especially in its male form: 'little man'. But another part of the mix is Hamlet: and in his allusion to Hamlet, or rather in his reintroduction of Hamlet into a 'different' scenario, Lacan is suggesting to us that critical attempts to reconstruct a sense of wholeness from the shattered fragments of 'Hamlet' is merely another fantastic – or indeed, Polonius-like, sententious – attempt to create a healed, solvent self from the morass of shards.

Hamlet, on this reading, does not need ghosts; he is himself a ghost. According to Derrida, the relation between Hamlet the character and *Hamlet* the play is intricate, yet in the end simple, because both are ghosts, and the more especially so because of their canonization, their acceptance as 'masterpiece': 'a masterpiece always moves', Derrida says, 'by definition, in the manner of a ghost' (Derrida, 1994, 18). The notion of the masterpiece, therefore, is *necessarily* spectral; Bennett and Royle 'translate' this further when they say that 'the canon is always a spectral affair' (1999, 136). There is, therefore, nothing of the margin about the ghost; the phantom does not hover about outside the window waiting to be asked in. On the contrary, the phantom is already inhabiting the site whereon we wish to ground the major monuments and institutions of culture; there is no other ground, no space that can be cleared, no conveniently unoccupied plinth. It is not possible to rid *Hamlet* of the ghost; any more than it is possible to rid Hamlet of the murder, and memory, of his father; or of his impossible mourning; or of his sense of the enduring, unendurable presence of Claudius, the king who is, wretchedly, unforgivably, not a ghost.

Hamlet is a spectral drama; it is also one that reveals the spectral nature of the literary, the uncanny dealings literature has with the secret and its disclosure. Bennett and Royle again:

> The Ghost at once tells and does not tell. The Ghost keeps the secrets of its prison-house even as it evokes the effects of their disclosure. This is another way of talking about the enigma of literature: whether in the form of Shakespearean tragedy or a twentieth-century whodunnit, literature is about what cannot be told . . . (1999, 229)

Is the ghost, perhaps, a form of capital? If so, then this circulation of capital would be essentially secret. *Hamlet* tells us *of* secrets; it cannot, by definition, tell us secrets. It can say that there *is* a secret; but it cannot define or describe what this 'is' might mean – where the secret might be held, or buried, what its form might be, on what paper or papyrus or parchment it might be written, whether its writing has outlived the centuries, whether the secret might now be the ruin of a secret, or what might be indeed most secretive about a secret in ruins, or indeed whether the secret of the fascination of all ruins is that they might contain (display, or reveal, or conceal) secrets; a ghost might be considered to be an ectoplasmic embodiment of secretions. Or not, for all we know. Such is life on the battlements (or in the Gothic castle).

But Hamlet (and *Hamlet*) will not go away. Derrida's *Specters of Marx* begins with a discourse of ghosts and spectres, structured around the question of whether 'learning' (knowing the secret, or educating oneself to forget its troubling existence within the castle's crumbling walls) belongs to the past, the present or the future:

> If it – learning to live – remains to be done, it can happen only between life and death. Neither in life nor in death *alone*. What happens between two, and between all the 'two's' one likes, such as between life and death, can only *maintain itself* with some ghost, can only *talk with or about* some

ghost . . . So it would be necessary to learn spirits. Even and especially if this, the spectral, *is not* . . . The time of the 'learning to live', a time without tutelary present, would amount to this, to which the exordium is leading us: to learn to live *with* ghosts, in the upkeep, the conversation, the company, or the companionship, in the commerce without commerce of ghosts. (Derrida, 1994, xxviii)

So *Specters of Marx* 'begins' in some sense with the spectre, but is also *begins*, in at least three peritextual senses, with *Hamlet*.

Where, then, is *Hamlet* written, where might we gain access to it, where are its 'haunts', its familiar places? It is Derrida who coins the odd word 'hauntology', but it is also Derrida who, curiously, seeks to cut the 'scholarly' off from the threat of the living dead. 'A traditional scholar', he says, 'does not believe in ghosts – nor in all that could be called the virtual space of spectrality' (1994, 11). What, we might fairly ask, is Derrida himself haunted by here? For what he says is certainly not true of, for example, the English ghost story, in which *above all* it is true that scholars are haunted by ghosts, the ghosts indeed that their own antiquarian, 'ancient' interests conjure. Perhaps after all one has to suspect, even to realize, that there are national, cultural ghosts at work here, *working over* the texts, for the language Derrida is speaking here is French, it is inseparable from the Enlightenment, it is precisely vulnerable to succumbing to a haunted, echoic betrayal of all that his argument appears to mean to say.

English Hamlets, French Hamlets: let us move to a further location, not far from the battlements, where Hamlet may be found (for he can only be found in words), but let us leave this one (if somewhat transparently) unattributed – in the manner of ghosts:

> Blanchot does not name Shakespeare here, but I cannot hear 'since Marx', since Marx, without hearing, like Marx, 'since Shakespeare'.

One might ask, alongside the question of the 'proper name', what an 'improper' name might be. How proper, or otherwise, might it be, for example, to drag a name into a 'different' historical context – and what impact would this discernment of propriety have upon any critical endeavour, which is based at root on historical miscegenation, on the impropriety of commentary? Or one might ask: what does one *hear* despite what is named – what does one hear, for example, 'here' or, indeed, 'not here', in the name of Hamlet – what echoes, what resonances accompany the attempted propriety of the 'proper name'?

What I have tried to show here – or, at any rate, somewhere – is that according to the logic of spectral criticism there is no 'one object', 'one text', to be 'analysed'. I will conclude with a strange 'Shakespearean' quotation from Freud, the master of the uncanny whose textual legacy (deeply imbued as it is with *Hamlet*) shows us that he was, at all points, mastered *by* the uncanny:

> We do not think highly of the cultural level of an English country town in Shakespeare's time when we read that there was a big dung-heap in front

of his father's house in Stratford; we are indignant and call it 'barbarous' (which is the opposite of civilised) . . . (Freud, XXI, 30)

This is Freud in *Civilisation and its Discontents*, and it puts all manner of things into question. It questions, for example, what the spectral plural might be, who the ghostly companions might be in whose company we are willing (whether coerced or not) to own to the 'we'. It questions what a readership might be, who might be willing to listen to this story from another place and another time. It might also invite us to ask where the dung-heap ought, according to Freud's theories, really to be – is there something particularly wrong with it being in an 'unnatural' place, 'in front of his father's house'; would it have been better for Hamlet if the dung-heap of the past had been 'behind' his father's house – decently hidden from view, or at least in the right place according to a non-perverse order of bodily functions? And then we might also ask where the 'barbarous' might belong – in Freudian theory, for example; or in the Gothic; or is it the preserve of 'ghosts' that come from beyond the 'civilised'?

'Unhouseled, disappointed, unaneled' again; such criticism can never find a place to rest. But let us finally reconsider Freud's 'dung-heap', and a brief phrase from *Hamlet*. In Act III, scene iii, Rosencrantz speaks of the 'cess of majesty', and is usually taken to be primarily referring to the menacing cessation or death of a king, with whatever terrifying consequences. But in *Hamlet*, as in all other literary texts, words are haunted by other words. A cesspool is 'a small well or excavation made in the bottom of a drain, under a grating, to collect and retain the sand or gravel carried by a stream'; a cleansing device, in other words, that might 'cease' the polluting activities of nature; but thereby, of course, eventually associated with its own opposite ('the most offensive cesspool or drain'). None of this would in itself be of interest to a spectral criticism, or indeed to an inspector of the provenance of Freud's dung-heaps, with their weirdly paternal associations, except for a small, bracketed note in the *Oxford English Dictionary*, attributing the first usage of this meaning of 'cess' to the year 1583, eighteen years before *Hamlet*, and to none other than Shakespeare's echo, his ghost, the irrepressible claimant of his 'proper' name: Bacon. A truly spectral criticism would find much to work over there.

QUESTIONS FOR FURTHER CONSIDERATION

1. Is the ghost of Hamlet's father 'real'?
2. Is Hamlet 'real'?
3. Is *Hamlet* 'real'?
4. Where is Hamlet's ghost to be found?
5. What would a non-spectral text be like?

ANNOTATED BIBLIOGRAPHY

Abraham, Nicolas and Maria Torok. *The Wolf Man's Magic Word: A Cryptonymy*, trans. Nicholas Rand. Minneapolis, MN: University of Minnesota Press, 1986. It is in this text that Abraham and Torok develop their notions of the phantom, the secret and the crypt. In the course of doing this, they add a further dimension to the geography of the psyche, and they therefore challenge conventional notions of communication and of the possible transmission and reception of psychic truth. Although we still await a full translation of these insights into the realm of the literary, the (phantomatic) effects of their questioning of the possibilities of revelation and demystification are already being felt in the critical field.

Buse, Peter and Andrew Stott (eds). *Ghosts: Deconstruction: Psychoanalysis, History*. London: Macmillan, 1999. This is an uneven collection of essays, but its very range – from Marx and Engels and Benjamin, back to Horace Walpole, Ann Radcliffe and Sheridan LeFanu, and on to Derrida – makes it significant reading. A useful summary of late twentieth-century thinking on the spectral.

Derrida, Jacques. *Specters of Marx: The State of the Debt, the Work of Mourning, and the New International*, trans. Peggy Kamuf. New York and London: Routledge, 1994. It is odd, and significant, that Derrida here 'sets the scene' for so much 'spectral criticism' precisely on the central materialist terrain of Marxism and its fate. The important thing is that he thereby asserts that the spectral is not a retreat from the material, but rather a way of looking at the material in greater depth, and of dealing with the apparent certainties of linear history with greater subtlety.

Freud, Sigmund. 'The "Uncanny"', in *The Standard Edition of the Complete Psychological Works of Sigmund Freud*, eds J. Strachey et al., Vol. XVII. London: Hogarth Press and the Institute of Psycho-Analysis, 24 vols, 1953–74. This is the classic text on the uncanny, and needs to be read before any other attempt to understand spectral criticism. This is not, however, to say that it should be read uncritically; almost every line seems to explode with spectral implications, and there are particularly inexplicable passages about crocodiles and prostitutes which continue to invite spectral speculation.

Punter, David. *Gothic Pathologies: The Text, the Body and the Law*. London: Macmillan, 1998. This book contains chapters that address the uncanny, psychopathology and sublimity, but all from the perspective of a potential spectral criticism grounded in the ongoing complexities of Gothic writing (whatever that might have now come to be). Like most other books, it is in need of ghostly rewriting.

SUPPLEMENTARY BIBLIOGRAPHY

Abraham, Nicolas and Maria Torok. *The Shell and the Kernel: Renewals of Psychoanalysis*, trans. Nicholas Rand. Chicago, IL: Chicago University Press, 1994.

Attridge, Derek. 'Ghost Writing'. In *Deconstruction is/in America: A New Sense of the Political*, ed. Anselm Haverkamp. New York and London: New York University Press, 1995, 223–7.

Beal, Timothy K. and Neil M. Gunn. *Reading Bibles, Writing Bodies: Identity and the Book*. London and New York: Routledge, 1997.

Bennett, Andrew and Nicholas Royle. *An Introduction to Literature, Criticism and Theory*, 2nd edn. London: Prentice Hall Europe, 1999.

Berry, Philippa and Andrew Wernick (eds). *The Shadow of Spirit: Postmodernism and Religion*. London: Routledge, 1992.

Blanchot, Maurice. *The Space of Literature*, trans. Ann Smock. Lincoln, NE: University of Nebraska Press, 1982a.

Blanchot, Maurice. *The Sirens' Song*, ed. Gabriel Josipovici. Brighton: Harvester, 1982b.

Blanchot, Maurice. *The Infinite Conversation*, trans. Susan Hanson. Minneapolis and London: University of Minnesota Press, 1993.

Bollas, Christopher. *The Shadow of the Object: Psychoanalysis of the Unthought Known*. London: Free Association Books, 1987.

Castle, Terry. 'Phantasmagoria: Spectral Technology and the Metaphorics of Modern Reverie', *Critical Inquiry*, 15, 1988. Rpt. as 'Phantasmagoria and the Metaphorics of Modern Reverie'. In *The Female Thermometer: 18th-Century Culture and the Invention of the Uncanny*. New York: Oxford University Press, 1995, 140–67.

Cixous, Hélène. 'Fiction and its Phantoms: A Reading of Freud's *Das Unheimlich* (The "Uncanny")', trans. Robert Dennomé. *New Literary History*, 7, 3, 1976, 525–48.

Devereuz, George (ed.). *Psychoanalysis and the Occult*. London: Souvenir, 1974.

Freud, Sigmund. *Civilisation and its Discontents*. In *The Standard Edition of the Complete Psychological Works of Sigmund Freud*, eds J. Strachey et al., Vol. XXI. London: Hogarth Press and the Institute of Psycho-Analysis, 24 vols, 1953–74.

Eliot, T. S. *Collected Poems 1909–1962*. London: Faber & Faber, 1963.

Freud, Sigmund. *The Interpretation of Dreams*. In *The Standard Edition of the Complete Psychological Works of Sigmund Freud*, eds J. Strachey et al., Vols IV and V. London: Hogarth Press and the Institute of Psycho-Analysis, 24 vols, 1953–74.

Gibson, William. *Neuromancer*. London: Victor Gollancz, 1994.

Jones, Ernest. *On the Nightmare*. London: Hogarth Press, 1931 and 1949.

Kristeva, Julia. *Black Sun: Depression and Melancholia*, trans. Leon S. Roudiez. New York: Columbia University Press, 1987.

Kristeva, Julia. *Strangers to Ourselves*, trans. Leon S. Roudiez. New York: Harvester Wheatsheaf, 1991.

Lacan, Jacques. 'Desire and the Interpretation of Desire in *Hamlet*', ed. Jacques-Alain Miller, trans. James Hulbert, *Yale French Studies*, 55/56, 1977. Rpt. in *Literature and Psychoanalysis: The Question of Reading: Otherwise*, ed. Shoshana Felman. Baltimore, MD: Johns Hopkins University Press, 1981, 11–53.

Laplanche, Jean. *Essays on Otherness*, trans. John Fletcher. London: Routledge, 1999.

Lukacher, Ned. *Primal Scenes: Literature, Philosophy, Psychoanalysis*. Ithaca, NY: Cornell University Press, 1986.

O'Brien, Geoffrey. *The Phantom Empire*. New York and London: W. W. Norton, 1993.

Punter, David. *The Literature of Terror: A History of Gothic Fictions from 1760 to the Present Day*. London: Longman, 1980 (revised two-volume edition 1996).

Punter, David. *Writing the Passions*. London: Pearson, 2001.

Royle, Nicholas. *Telepathy and Literature: Essays on the Reading Mind*. Oxford: Blackwell, 1990.

Royle, Nicholas. *After Derrida*. Manchester: Manchester University Press, 1995.

Shakespeare, William. *Hamlet*. New York and London: Signet, 1963.

Smith, Robert. 'Deconstruction and Film'. In *Deconstructions: A User's Guide* ed. Nicholas Royle. London: Palgrave, 2000, 119–36.

Taussig, Michael. *Shamanism, Colonialism and the Wild Man: A Study in Terror and Healing*. Chicago, IL: University of Chicago Press, 1993.

Weber, Samuel. 'The Debts of Deconstruction and Other, Related Assumptions'. In *Taking Chances: Derrida, Psychoanalysis, and Literature*, eds Joseph H. Smith and William Kerrigan. Baltimore, MD: Johns Hopkins University Press, 1984, 33–65.

Young, Robert J. C. 'Deconstruction and the Postcolonial'. In *Deconstructions: A User's Guide*, ed. Nicholas Royle. London: Palgrave, 2000.

NOTE

1. With reference to William Gibson, see the chapter by Stacy Gillis in this collection, above, on cyberculture studies.

CHAPTER 13

(A)MATERIAL CRITICISM

Tom Cohen

1

One is always, tradition suggests, after 'materiality' – that is, not only in pursuit of a promised ground or ontology that is also worldly, associable with reference and the 'thing', historical process or analysis, a real, but temporally after (as the model of the hunt suggests too), as though the term were bound nonetheless to linguistic traces, to something anterior to figurative systems.

The chapter I propose will track a key path by which the term 'materiality' is put in play on the coming horizons by a hybridization of the Marxian with the deconstructive traditions. With this in mind, a brief review of continuing spells that the word 'materiality' holds over sociological and political criticism – and why that seems at an impasse. The Aristotelian *hule* – one *ur*-term for 'matter' (linked to the stuff of wood) – was itself made possible by a Platonic binary in which it had been sustained by opposition to variable others (mind/body, spirit/matter). It promised a non-human – which is to say, extra-linguistic – or mute real whose legacy would be heard in the dialectical appeal of classical Marxism, for which 'material' and economic processes mapped along abstract schemata (base/superstructure) might both interpret and execute a programmed narrative for the overcoming of capitalist models. Can the term be used as a tool of reading or literary analysis, however, in an era of so-called 'globalization' where, to use Avital Ronell's term (1989), 'switchboards' of teletechnicity disperse and reroute notions of fixed historical events and material facts, redirecting definitions of memory, the 'human', the 'event' and performance?

To mark a use of 'materiality' in the afterlife of this term, we might speak of a certain *(a)materiality* – a ghostly materiality, perhaps, that persists in the cancellation of past associations with or promises of the irreducible real. Yet it may be here that the appeal of this term, still, to critical and 'literary' reading may find resonance, rather than in the archival and 'dialectical materialist' traditions that have used this assertion of ground as an appeal to historical fact. Rather than asserting a referential real or economic processes as the ontological ground of reference, such (a)materiality might locate itself at the junctures between linguistic performance and historial events, anterior programmes and mnemotechnic projections, inscription and 'experience'.[1] After reviewing one direction that such a prospect leads, I will suggest possible ways in which such (a)materialist reading strategies – when applied to canonical works, in this case Faulkner and Hitchcock – might partake of an ongoing epistemo-political transformation in post-humanist critical culture.

The term 'materiality', it turns out, persists today with a lure tied to various epistemo-critical programmes (historicism, pragmatism, empiricism, etc.) and thus this rich and diverse set of critical traditions maintain the 'ideological' mystifications of a metaphysical model. To displace these, we might appeal to directions indicated by Walter Benjamin's trope of 'materialistic historiography', and to where that model demands a return to a conception of the material event bound to inscription, memory, temporality and political intervention. How is this complicated, or translated, by contact with the problem – proper to linguistic and literary studies to come – of the 'materiality' of inscriptions? The latter phrase comes from Paul de Man, who in this respect is a continuer of Benjamin's project – although directing the latter from metaphoric grandeur to the engineering involved in a close reading of, and intervention in, potential programmes which generate world-views and perception. The topic shifts from tracking 'ideology' to intervening within a historial programme.

BENJAMIN'S LEAP

Rather than name and guarantee unfettered access to a mute real, the 'materiality' of language and mnemonics complicates future horizons of this tradition irremediably – at once suspending and reinscribing it, transitionally, in and as a kind of (a)materiality. On the one hand, we may point to the brute material networks that sustain linguistic memory and programme perception (or hermeneutics), such as so-called 'material' signifiers – letters, sound, inscriptions. On the other, this reflexive turn seems to precede and itself produce various systems of reference, value or association. 'Materiality' would seem an effecting-effect produced within and by signifying networks already replete with mnemonic imperatives, hermeneutic assignations, tropes.[2] 'Materiality', as (a)materiality, enters the new century burdened by this ghostliness: as a term, it is retired with the classic metaphysical monuments, yet rather than disappear, it mutates, marks that absence, and appears re-engaged around a problem of interest to reading: how do we track an (a)material and mnemonic effect that precedes and programmes figurative systems, particularly if it itself is defined by the absence of metaphor, something prefigural, like the black-hole and facticity of an inscription?[3] What, in the critical and 'literary' reading practices of an era programmed less by the hegemony of the Book than teletechnicity and mnemotechnics more generally, might 'materiality' come to signify?[4] Why, more-over, must a reinscription of this term alter not only our conception of the 'literary', or the event, but temporality, signalling an intervention in how past and future might be structured or produced?

We may root this discussion – at the juncture between rethinking Marxian and linguistic problematics – in directions indicated by Walter Benjamin's work. In his 'Theses on History', for example, he introduces the trope of a 'materialistic historiography (*der materialistischen Geschichtsschreibung*)' (Benjamin, 1968, 262; 1961, 278) as one name for an engagement with historial networks that links linguistic performance – an intervention in reading and writing – to a redeploy-ment of Marxian and theological figures. His programme, which suspends linear historical narratives and condemns 'historicism' – a term encompassing various epistemological regimes that archive history and its 'facts' – as complicit with a 'fascist' current in political thought. He seems to envision a return to a conception of the material event bound to inscription, memory, temporality, and political intervention. This last is imperative, for Benjamin, by repeating the odd phrase 'materialistic historiography' rather than 'historical materialism', say, seems to invoke a type of writing of history (*graphy*), of the 'present(s)', multiply and mutually encased, that stands to reinscribe the past epistemo-critical programmes (politics, here, is conceived of also as an epistemological regime), alters the site where inscriptions are encountered as already installed. Benjamin not only dovetailed the thinking of philosophic concepts with a meditation on linguistic performance (or literature), but identifies a moment in this conjuncture where received 'history' in the form of mnemonic programmes may be performatively contested, interrupted, opened to recasting. As such, the 'materiality' appealed to would seem to be located not in the world's objects but in *mnemonic* constella-tions and representational regimes, which for Benjamin programme the senses (or 'sensoria'). Which is also to say programme models of reading, archivism, the legislations of reference. If history is not a string of occurrences that have been mythologized and recorded but is an effect produced (within a certain archive), what strategies for turning that system back on itself stand to performatively intervene at some seemingly pre-originary site where mnemonic regimes are installed or set – offering a break with them? 'Materialistic historiography' wants to name what Benjamin sweepingly opposes to 'historicism', in the same way that a *performative* reading or reinscription which would have the potential to rewire history stands opposed to the archival machines which store and legitimize an older regime's programmes ('humanism', or 'empiricism', or 'pragmatism', and so on). The material appears used to conjure what is prefigural, invoking the impasse of how matter is personified to begin with, how 'man' is positioned, the 'human' constructed, the living and the dead assigned in performative language:

> Materialistic historiography, on the other hand, is based on a constructive principle . . . Where thinking suddenly stops in a configuration pregnant with tensions, it gives that configuration a shock, by which it crystallizes

> into a monad. A historical materialist approaches a historical subject only where he encounters it as a monad. (1968, 262–3)

Monad, that is, as an irreducibly individual nexus or node of proactive historial networks, both anterior and still virtual. Because the 'past' is addressed as sheer anteriority, the '(a)material' trace is bound to where the past, *was*ness (in Faulkner), is also managed and produced. Benjamin's Marxian trope of 'materialistic historiography' weaves together the structure of mnemonic relations with an experience of, and intervention in, their networking – where the patterns for otherness, interpretation, temporality and so on would have been installed. Because such a project is aimed at a pragmatic intervention this '(a)materiality' may be said, in one idiom, to lie at a site or non-site of prefigural inscription. 'Materialistic histori*ography*' appears a virtual technique of historial intervention intended not only to counter the spell of historicism ('where historical materialism cuts through historicism' (255)), of received narratives of linear time as an empty 'continuum' ('telling the sequence of events like the beads of a rosary' (263)), but as what stands to alter anteriority ('the dead') by way of a certain caesura-effect, or 'standstill', in which pasts and futures offer themselves as *virtual*. Elsewhere in Benjamin, this project of an intervention that critically and performatively turns back on the archival machines to produce another set of possible futures might seem to be called *allegory*, even *cinema*, and *translation* at times – for which the term 'materialistic historiography' seems a final avatar.

PHANTOM BODIES

What is an inscription if one can only point to a brute fact of mnemotechnics, against which memory and 'experience' might appear programmed? Is there a body or a horde of anterior inscriptions by which this '(a)materiality' can be thought? The phrase 'materiality of inscription' derives from the late work of de Man (1996), at a point in his work in which a redefinition of the 'aesthetic' becomes a dominant theme. De Man may in this respect appear a continuer of Benjamin's project – as if redirecting the latter's metaphoric sweep to the sort of unglamorous micrological engineering Benjamin shied from. When Benjamin speaks of turning 'the symbolizing into the symbolized' (Benjamin, 1968, 8) he implies that (a)material linguistic traces have been raised into a movement of active reading, at a prospective site of reinscription. It is not accidental that de Man's 'materiality of inscription' – what Derrida interprets in 'The Typewriter Ribbon' as a 'materiality without matter' (Cohen et al., 2001, 277–360) – emerges in association with a rethinking of the category of the aesthetic itself, in which the latter term appears to shift from a zone of Schillerian 'play' to a site where signs are phenomenalized, the senses or perception (*aisthanumai*) programmed. Hence the translation here, where 'materiality' now indicates an irreducible trace in which the anchors of memory and the 'human' are deanthropomorphized, defaced. What has been called this other (a)materiality thus supposes linguistic networks that precede the historical form that the 'human' takes, repositioning the 'material' in an experience of the non-living as well. In this movement or process one might want to speak of a broader conceptual transformation, or *translation*, in which a certain (a)materiality is itself foregrounded – be it as networks of sound, the letter, inscription, agency and so on.[5] These micrological players, however, rather than constituting a new corporeality of the text, say, tend to dismember any notion of the body that does not acknowledge the term's phantasmal, semiotic, multiple, inscribed and deanthropomorphized implications, bodies traversed by technicities before which there would be no pure (phenomenological) perception or 'experience'. This non-site for the installation of inscriptions organizing any narrative of events might suggest the '(a)materiality' which everyone, all along, was after; but such would *appear* always, *also*, bound to the movement of a trace that is prehistorial and prefigural.

This '(a)materiality' problematizes certain humanist appropriations of the term (materiality) that have been reinvested in the *body*. Cultural studies has gone far in complicating this figure, which has involved studies of pain (Scarry 1985), different ways that bodies are marked and materialized as 'identities', and the priority of techno-bodies and machinal figures – of which Haraway's 'cyborg' is but an early, genderized variant. But to invest 'body' with the legacy of materiality, as though a reversal of Platonic binaries were at issue, has been to risk returning to the figure an aura of the whole, the organic, the sensible, the present and so on, the reinvestment of a metaphysical site for the real, not to mention falling back into one or other variant phenomenologies. A departure from this tradition, with its great variety of bodies, has been Judith Butler's work on gender performance, where, as in *Bodies That Matter* (1993), an altered figure of 'materiality' would be restituted conceptually. In *Gender Trouble* (1990), an appeal is made to how the body is 'inscribed', realized through marking systems or performed.[6] In *Bodies That Matter*, Butler remarks: 'to warn against an easy return to the *materiality* of the body or the materiality of sex . . . To return to matter requires that we return to matter as a *sign*' (1993, 49). For mutually contesting, colonializing and erasing networks of signification to be always already in play, 'body' must be configured as a site undefined outside of 'matter as a sign', and the question of matter converts into a 'materialization' of inscriptive, mnemotechnic effects, that is, the phenomenalization of '(a)material' signs.[7]

A work that takes up the Marxian legacy at a point of its recently declared death with the collapse of Soviet communism and the onset of global capitalism, Derrida's *Specters of Marx* draws implicitly on Benjamin's 'Theses' for inspiration – particularly in the recursive use of a 'messianism without the messianic', which echoes and unpacks Benjamin's phrase 'weak *Messianic* power' (Benjamin, 1968, 254).[8] Derrida's spectrality, for which any 'present' would be reconceived as a network of traces, identifies the prospective site of reinscription in the traffic of spectres. That site would be sought after or projected by Benjamin's text ('leap', 'shock', 'translation') and is linked to that Marxian motif most to be prized by his various heirs, the claim to historial intervention. For Derrida, 'Marx is one of the rare thinkers of the past to have taken seriously, at least in its principle, the originary indissociability of technics and language, and thus of tele-technics (for every language is a tele-technics)' (Derrida, 1994, 53). Such a spectralized 'materiality' in the absence of this last term involves a translational task that would presage a new politics 'to come' (including a politics of memory) in which these programmes or legacies are transposed into other models of the event, alterity, 'experience', economy, ethics and so on.[9]

Can the confluence of these vectors – the epistemological revolution surrounding the materiality of language and the interventionist critique of leftist thought – open new projects of reading, and specifically reading 'literary' works? The 'materialistic historiography' that Benjamin proffered is a proactive agenda that eschews historicist archivism. It implies a 'moment' of passage in which a radical desemanticization of received reference or hermeneutic systems accompanies a recalibration of perception as such – rather than deriving from 'material' facts the latter appears to occur as the phenomenalization of signifying regimes, a reversal of the position of the 'aesthetic' itself. The disjuncture or caesura that it would practise proposes to alter anteriority itself, in an instantiation of suspense or rupture within current trace-chains. If tropes in general bring to mind colour, the iridescence of the rainbow, the prefigural bears the contradiction of appearing to precede light itself, or to be the latter's technical base. Bringing the virtual blackness of a trace or mark which in effect precedes phenomenality into contact with mimetic reading models induces a 'translation' effect in the model of reading – the attempted installation of a prospective, 'new' reading contract, and with it a conception of historial agency.[10] It does so, at first, by turning to the long occluded elements of material labour, bearers of 'sense', slave agencies (marks, sound, inscription) within the mimetic or referential regime.[11] This is perhaps what de Man terms an 'epistemological critique of tropes': that is, repositioning reading outside of the humanist or Schillerian models of relapse – the 'human' being for de Man a by-product of this structural hermeneutic relapse before (or after) a material event (a mnemonic intervention in the archive). This passage, or translation, involves a supposed movement from a system of tropes to something else called the 'performative'.[12] Performative, for de Man, might be heard multiply, as implying the actual act of a historical event – which cannot be reversed – and performative in the positional sense of inhabiting the mutant facades and faces of so-called 'speech-acts'. Tracking (a)materiality leads to unstable sites, since rather than presenting us the referential ground, it tends to open onto the ways in which the archive is itself managed or produced: that is, the site of pre-recordings, Althusserian rituals, installed hermeneutic systems. Reading 'materially' within this problematic entails reading with – and against – inscriptions and models of inscriptions, tracking where this model begins to install another system of reference, agency, perception, temporality and so on. It examines where such has always been in place within the traditions of the Book that have shaped global memory and is aware that all of this takes place within a transformation underway towards the tele-technological archive, a broad re-imprinting of (a)material memory across cultural archives. In the process of this review, it becomes apparent that rethinking the (a)material in this way involves rewriting the entire category of the aesthetic itself, the site of imprinting from which the senses (and, hence, hermeneutic models) appear programmed historically.

READING (A)MATERIAL(LY)

Reading is here conceived of actively as one name for a site in which legacies are relayed, constellations of 'textual' events reconfigured, hermeneutic regimes reimprinted, or, alternately, where epistemo-linguistic ruptures occur in which reinscriptions become possible – a moment to which Benjamin will attach terms like 'shock' or 'caesura'. If there is a 'materiality' to which reading is directed, a moment in the experience of memory and sign systems that moves us from a mimetic to a performative model of the text as virtual or historial event, then it may impact the identity of 'literature' as an institution. Such a project seems itself, in part, to participate in a broader translation of textual legacies into the terms of technicity that are likely to dominate (again) coming hybridizations of science and once humanistic discourses.

How do we read 'materially', or (a)materially? How is such an approach – in which the borders of life and death, human and non-human, historial and hyperpolitical become porous – linked to the terms of technicity that are likely to dominate (again) coming hybridizations of science and once humanistic discourses? Let me only suggest one possible approach to this, which might demonstrate how two seeming extremes – the claim to intervention in history, and the agency of desemanticized traces – interface. The 'material' would at first retain its old associations: the lower order in a binary, the promise of what is, of *hule* or matter, appearing in a slave (again lower) position to a master.[13] What Benjamin's 'historiography' would indicate is that this direction cannot be engaged without the received orders of temporality and historial mapping becoming disarticulated. An approach to texts is summoned that might desire to be void of aura, or anthropomorphization, in which the 'human' is open to redefinition when traversed by the traces of its non-human (undead, material) others. The implication is that after 'materialism' is closed as a metaphysical-referential promise, one nonetheless draws closer to another sort of (a)materiality in which the divide between the 'human' domain delineated by the ejection of its specular non-human others or organizing dyads has been dismantled – the borders as if between human and animal, living and dead, past and to come – in the optioning of an altered (a)terrestriality that is traversed by these categories.

Which is why this (a)materiality swerves against the tendency of cultural studies to relapse in humanist, mimetic, descriptive terms in which received models of reference retain (historicist) dominance. We have suggested that if the term 'materiality' has a future for literary and cultural studies – if they are called that – in an (a)material sense that derives from a coalescence of deconstructive and Marxian discourse, such a trajectory leads into a rewriting of this historical archive in the process. It involves epistemo-political consequences and resistances. I will attempt, at this point, a short reading – or perhaps two – using canonical texts in this regard: Faulkner (*Go Down, Moses*) and/or Hitchcock (the first *Man Who Knew Too Much*). The former allows a brief encounter with the ideology of 'race', the latter with the metaphysical categories of the idea, the eye, visibility, knowing (Benjaminian 'cinema'). I will call this project, derived from the tradition of rethinking allegory (Benjamin, de Man), allographical. Such a project, I will suggest in conclusion, makes claims on how we address the (a)materiality of the human, the animal, temporality, the political, mnemotechnics, the sensorium, the aesthetic and so on – while relinquishing of the term 'materialist' in its ontological sense. In the two sketches offered, strategies of reading are suggested in which two different epistemo-political problems are addressed: that of the hermeneutic pursuit as a ritualized model (Faulkner), and that of the light and solar poetics as the ideology of cognition and visibility in the West (Hitchcock). If the first example disarticulates the premise of 'literature' as a received institution, the second undoes received models of temporalization before a principle of repetition at once formalized by the cinematic machine (one literalizing on celluloid the facticity of an inscription that precedes phenomenalization) and yet Nietzschean in its consequences.

2

Engaging in (a)materialist readings of canonical works can suggest a translation of sorts – as though from familiar referential reading models to others in which a mnemonic trace void of semantic depth emerges. Such a trace brings together two apparent functions: it remarks the 'material' dimension of language and ruptures merely symbolic or figurative networks. It's identification inevitably involves an *active* renetworking, even as such a trope of the material reflexively inverts the referential, grounding and historicizing associations the term was once heralded to invoke. As in Benjamin's theorization of 'cinema', such a (non)figure may also suggest a site beyond *aura* when the latter is heard or understood as a discourse of (human) personification. Hence (a)materialist reading leaves the humanism of classical hermeneutics and may be called alloanthropomorphic.

NOTES TOWARDS AN (A)MATERIALIST READING OF FAULKNER

The case of Faulkner is instructive, since the dominant Americanist interpretations issue from a grand territorial assertion: Faulkner's regionality and value as a representational author has long inscribed his reception and interpretation in a quasi-realist logic that seems, in turn, to sustain his value as a regionalist author, even as it contains the performative transgressions his work seems to gamble its import on. This is certainly the case with *Go Down, Moses* (Faulkner, 1973), a work generally cast as a work of decline, but also (if contradictorily) a return to nineteenth-century realist narrative – particularly in its treatment of race and black figures – from the 'modernist' stylistic experiments. That is, authorial decline corresponds to a supposed return to hermeneutic proprieties. What is interesting, here, is what is defended against by the hermeneutic guardians: a text where an (a)material trace and the history of racial justice collude in their opposition to a plantation-era hermeneutic that manages or had managed property, definition, time, the Book, race definition, family and so on.

Both assumptions are directly questioned by the title of what is neither given as a 'novel' (rather, an allochronic network of seven tales) nor a collection. Indeed, if anything, the segments probe the parameters of received history and the era of 'the Book'. The 'going down' of the Mosaic author is both 'Faulkner' and a *going under* of the Mosaic laws of reading (and we can hear a Nietzschean resonance to 'going down'). It is not accidental that the last and titular text, 'Go Down, Moses', speaks of a lawyer whose 'serious vocation was a twenty-two year old unfinished translation of the Old Testament *back* into classic Greek' (371) – that is, a translation from an authoritative originary language which was not one (English, Old Testament) back into a pre-originary, aesthetic language which, too, was never original. The vocation of the lawyer, from the position of the law, presupposes an endless translation into an infra-linguistic space – what Benjamin, in his essay on 'Translation', may have termed 'pure language', the pure (a)material traces out of which languages (if such are at all discrete or extant) are materialized, or figuration, memory, and so on spawned.

Among other things, such a *translation effect* suggests that the way we have understood reference – history, anteriority – to operate in Faulkner is passive and regressed. A supposed return to historical realism around the representation of blacks (starting with the ante-bellum economy of the old McCaslin twin brothers in the opening tale 'Was') coincides with a divestment of that as the product of a ritualized slave economy. Since the black, like the animal, does not participate in the language of the white fraternal order – in 'Was', as though sterile (twin males co-habitating), bound to a plantational fiction, he is utterly ritualized. Indeed, blackness moves through the work in a manner always also dethreading the referential regime of the white masters – and, perhaps, nowhere more than in 'Pantaloon in Black', where the titanic black labourer Rider's name seems to echo, unexpectedly, both *reader* and *writer*.[14] (If reading – and, for that matter, writing itself – marks the incessant rethinking, bureaucratization, and recalibration of anterior traces that event can suggest a non-site where referential and epistemo-critical programmes are either enforced or recast.) Like 'Moses' before the Jordan River, the work can seem to disown and dissolve the supposedly (pre- and post-)modernist writing project that bears Faulkner's signature, anticipating a different 'law' of reading to come which it cannot designate. Such an other law, which is announced in a sense in the book's title, does and does not arrive. The work seems to poise itself before (and after) this translation. It is, moreover, connected to a site where the once slave status is associated with a material order of signifying trace. The black corresponds not only with the prefigural status of the animal – as bearer (horse), ritual prey (fox, runaway slave) or object of the hermeneutic hunt (bear) – but with the (a)material traces of what is called 'earth', with spectrality, with the sterility of hermeneutic ritual, with a precession of narrative history, with the way that aural and scriptive signifiers are re-empowered, with a recalibration of non-linear time.

It is not accidental that 'Was' names, innocently enough, sheer anteriority. The ante-bellum setting records the sterile rituals of the hunt in the hands of the phantasmal old twins – referencing a preoriginarily absent patriarch ('Old Carothers') whose legacy, clearly, paralyses both. But this setting is not, as is thought, that of (a) historical fiction. Rather it mimes the commodity of that 'genre' – a frontier tale – to put into play a post-contemporary gamble (the performative moment of the work, in this way, always puts something, and itself, at risk). The opening 'hunt' for a released and retrieved fox mirrors the ritual pursuit and return of the escaped slave, Tomey's Turl (half-brother to the twins). This ritual seems that of a modernist hermeneutics, letting the slave term escape (the material trace) only to return it in a pre-programmed interpretive notion of *reference* and property – one that is repetitive, sterile, poised before a cataclysm (or civil war). The black, like the fox, partakes of this escaped, desemanticized order, much as blackness itself appears prefigural, inscriptive, at the worm-hole of a representation or plantation system of 'meaning'. 'Was' puts anteriority, the received regime of memory management (or reference), into crisis, even as the definition of 'was' itself lingers without referential transparency. That is, if 'Was' indicates a comic view of what was, the structure of wasness is in question; if 'Was' is a genre tale (say, frontier comedy), it also declares that genre – historical fiction, regional hermeneutics – as over, past, gone down. As *was*. The (a)materialist reading that opens this transition in Faulkner involves a desemanticization and reinscription of the narratives traversed (including that 'of' Faulkner's own production and reception). The tale brings an entire system close to or beyond the point of dissolution – at a poker game between Hubert Beauchamp and the dexterous Uncle Buddy – in which the entire alignment of white and black property is at stake together with the prospective union of the absurd belated couple (Uncle Buck, Sophonsiba Beauchamp) on which the possibility of a future, or even the book itself (Isaac), depends. The system moves to the place of translation and draws back – Uncle Bud appears to bluff effectively in the poker game in which past and future are at risk, Hubert retreats, Uncle Buddy for now returns to the plantation, having escaped Sophonsiba's trap (which, since the book's narrative is written, and Isaac is born, we might assume occurs in a later interspace or *elsewhere*). The plantation economy and its sterile rituals seem restored for the *twins* – themselves tropes for a dialectical history at aporia (Greek/Biblical, Aesthetic/Ideation, Inside/Outside, and so on).

The only mention of the name 'Moses' in the work occurs here, and it is assigned to a ludicrous old hunting dog capable of chasing a fox around the house. He is called 'old Moses', as though discreetly enough an entire Mosaic metaphysics were assigned this role of the hermeneutic set-up linked to sterile ritual returns of escaped slave figures:

> And when they got home just after daylight, this time Uncle Buddy (that is, Amodeus) never even had time to get breakfast started and the fox never even got out of the crate, because the dogs were right there in the room. Old Moses went right into the crate with the fox, so that both of them went right on through the back end of it. That is, the fox went through, because when Uncle Buddy opened the door to come in, old Moses was still wearing most of the crate around his neck until Uncle Buddy kicked it off of him . . . and they could hear the fox's claws when he went scrabbling up the lean-pole, onto the roof – *a fine race* while it lasted, but the tree was too quick. (28)

The tree now appears a technical term. When animals (or escaped slaves) are run down, they get trapped at the top of a tree. No exit. That is, the lower or material term (the material signifier as aural or scriptive trace) arrives at the referential site of the signified, is itself caught as referent, what Benjamin called 'to turn the symbolizing into the symbolized' as the predicate for allegorical transformation – the reinscription or reprogramming of perception, the past or the aporetic predicate for such a re-gambling (in which virtual futures, as well, are at risk). In the above passage we see another example of this assertion, for one cannot not hear an aural transposition in 'a fine (t)race', particularly one that here was 'too quick', too safe, too predictable. For 'race' must echo, somehow, so-called racial difference and its hierarchies or conceptual stability: the site of race difference (and the determination of the human master as the sterile white brotherhood's narrative machine) appears linked to, or generated by, a hermeneutic system of property and propriety, a machine of the hermeneutic hunt as pre-ordered ritual. This 'race' has aesthetic properties. It mimes a model of reading which is ritualized, with memory predicting the rigged repetition as play. It is ritual as a game at this point, 'too quick'. 'Race' operates at the top of the tree, caught in this exposed impasse – perforated with diverse referents that, also, are at a point of disappearance (like the plantation economy designated the pre-modernist, and perhaps modernist and even postmodernist reading model, all the same suddenly). It is an *aesthetically* determined term or concept too, understanding 'aesthetic' to retain the Greek traces having to do with perception or the programming of such. The mnemonic hunt on which the routines of an older reading model depended, 'old Moses', appear unprede-termined, traversed by marking systems that necessitate readings, other assig-nations of reference, other conceptions of 'literature', as (historical) institution, anteriority and so on. At stake in the outcome of this gambling in and with 'was', as a term, is nothing less than the model of history itself – as is clearer in 'The Bear' – and with that temporalization, the 'Americanist' hermeneutic template, the event of performative writing or reading. One can predict more readings of this sort in the twenty-first century which break with prescribed programmes of history, reference, 'reading', mnemonic management.

NOTES TOWARDS AN (A)MATERIALIST READING OF HITCHCOCK

An evacuation of solar poetics can be seen, and differently ascribed an (a)materialist import, in select cinematic writing – and certainly that oeuvre most aware of these issues, Hitchcock's. 'Solar poetics' can be heard as a general figure for the ersatz Platonic assumption of an origin of light, the sun, from which both the plenitude of sense and the transparency of the visible – ocularcentrism, on which much of so-called film theory depends – derive. An example would be the first *Man Who Knew Too Much* (1934). The narrative is filed as 'about' the kidnapping of a child to silence parents who have been passed the secret of an assassination attempt that could precipitate a world war (notes Agent G). That information is passed in a writing hidden in a razor referencing a temple of sun-worshippers in Wapping, with a sketch of a pyramid before a sunburst. It is read in an Alpine resort, at St Moritz, before a closed door in which the hotel police present a cacophony of language types (German, Italian, French, English). 'Knowing too much', which silences a certain subject in Hitchcock, as with too many movements of a writing to speak (a recurrent problematic that takes various forms and is inscribed in a Hamlet-referenced paradigm), may appear linked to a Babel of languages resolved to aural-signifiers, an English become alien, or as Hitchcock says to Truffaut, dialogue understood primarily as sound. In the so-called West, of course, *knowing* has always been linked to light, to the sun (or sun-worship) and to sight – the *eidos* being that which would be visible, the 'idea'.[15] But the pyramid suggests not a Greek but an Egyptian problematic – as of the hieroglyphic metaphors used in the early years of cinema to conjure to new media's (*ur*-scriptive) powers before the onset of sheer commercialism. If 'knowing' is linked to the pretext of transparent sight or vision, the apparent predicate of cinema (or cinema as a mimetic medium), it is put in question by this most theoretically invested of auteurs. Instead of the eye, reading, we witness interrupted reading, as in Hitchcock's cameo in his 'first' talkie, *Blackmail*. In that cipher-cameo Hitchcock is interrupted reading by a bullying boy on an Underground train – the clacking of tracks and lights in attendance (what makes the 'train', static in movement, a premier prefigural trope for the transport of cinema). Sound is generated from machinal intervals, sight from the interruption of 'light', intervaled with absence or blackness.

Thus the temple of sun-worshippers must be examined, even as it is the front for the assassins. For on the one hand, it names a duped contingent. The worshippers are like a cinematic audience from whom money is collected (tickets) in a ruse – they come for the light, the sun, but the whole is a front, and that for an assassination attempt (a certain Hitchcock is always to be identified with the plot of world disruption). Moreover, the figure of the sun returns us to the earlier marksmanship contest between Jill and Ramon (the would-be assassin), which involves clay pigeons, black disks traversing the sky and shot at. Numerous black suns – or the prefigural mark or simulacrum that undoes or precedes the solar fiction of originary light or unveiling. Shot at, another black sun returns, as if shooting this mark – which does not take place once and for all – triggers an assault on how time, anteriority, or the trace is managed. This hyperbolic or Hyperion-like subtext is registered in terms like 'jumper' and references to Spring, a 'knowing *too much*' that both is a knowledge of excess and the undoing of a (political) model of the senses, of knowing, of sight. As this black sun or black trace is released across Hitchcock – for it accords with the little black dog that ran out on the white snow to occasion the opening fall of the agent Louis-Bernard in the opening – it recurs in transformative chains. Clearly imbued with the power to infect any sound or marking system as an (a)material trace that (like an escaped slave) stands in excess of the referential order it nonetheless precedes, this prefigure recurs in these early films as a black trace, a dog, a cat, chocolate, excrement, black buttons or marbles, sheer sound (*Secret Agent*). Included in the pop-cultural catalogue Hitchcock wants at stake is 'western' cultural history and memory preceding the scriptive origin of writing in the Egyptian hieroglyph. Without going into the panoply of signature-effects in Hitchcock – modes or writing which expose and dissolve the mimetic fiction of photography itself (Hitchcock dismissed other films as pictures of people talking) – it is interesting that, at the end of *Blackmail*, the blackmailer Trac(e)y seems to precede the Egyptian wing of the British Museum (through which he is chased), to fall through a glass copula to the Universal Reading Room. In the same vein, Mr Memory in *The 39 Steps* will seem to reference Mnemosyne, the Hesiodic muse, reduced to a recording machine of mere 'facts' – inscriptions or the pretext of photographic images, mechanical and (a)material. In the first *Man Who Knew Too Much* (and, uniquely in Hitchcock, the work generated a remake, as if an endless series of such could not satisfy to import of the narrative), 'knowing' is also referenced to a look on various faces of people who, shot, will die imminently. In each case (Louis-Bernard, Nurse Agnes), the face does not cognize anything: this 'death' is not biological, it precedes the opposition life/death, nodding towards the spectral space of cinema whose logics will be targeted repeatedly (*Rebecca, Vertigo, Psycho, Family Plot*), the seance nature of the 'cinematic' event. In *To Catch a Thief*, this black cat will be allied with the theft of diamonds, sex, meaning, history and light itself, a neo-promethean post-historial impasse.

This prefigurative agent that reduces reference systems to a skein of traces places temporality in question, even as it does identity, sight or for that matter gender markings. It does so, moreover, through an interrogative alliance between language reduced to its (a)material elements and mnemonics, opening a site for the recalibration (or reinscription) of these. It assumes a parallel between the experience of cinema as an artificed memory and sensorium and the way that a 'consciousness' which is the effect of (a)material traces that are neither living nor dead operates.

CONCLUSIONS

In each of the above an element appears identified that, while excluded from the chains of figural meaning proper (the slave, the black sun), is marked, and reflexively modifies or vacates the assumed referential programme or grid – that 'Was' is *about* a frontier, that cinema relays mimetic facts. In raising the symbolizing or (a)material mark or phoneme to the level of the signified, the textual event reconfigures itself and the older territoriality of sense is rewired through that performative factor. Reading becomes micrological and, at the same time, stands to recast inherited models of history, knowledge, time, perception and memory in what de Man perhaps calls an opening 'epistemological critique of tropes'. No alteration, no intervention, without a recasting of the programmatic or mnemonic regime (or ritual). To call this the predicate of (a)material reading may be misleading if the term 'material' does not go through an equivalent translation where the term returns, if at all, to mark a space that would never be attached to the earlier concept of the term (hence what Derrida calls, in speaking of de Man, a 'materiality without matter'). A term that had guaranteed reference – going back to the Aristotelian *hule* – has shifted, by designating a supposed 'materiality of inscription' that precedes mnemonic programme. According to this mode of thinking, whatever would reinscribe the site of conceptual terms or global memory would have to pass through this non-site.

QUESTIONS FOR FURTHER CONSIDERATION

1. What sorts of 'materiality' can be referenced to language and how does that complicate, or displace, any transparent use of the term?
2. What sort of mnemonic agency does an appeal to a 'materiality of inscription' suggest, and how might texts be considered events?
3. Why does what is called '(a)material' here make its appearance with a suspension of affirmed referential objects, matter and so on – as if a desemanticizing moment attends this advent?
4. What, in the Faulkner and Hitchcock texts examined, might be the connection between the role of the escaped slave in the first and the black sun as a visual trace in the second?

ANNOTATED BIBLIOGRAPHY

Benjamin, Walter. *Illuminations*, trans. Harry Zohn. New York: Schocken, 1968. Collection of writings attempting to rethink figures like 'cinema', technology, 'translation' and aesthetic politics, concluding with the 'Theses on History', which, in lapidary fashion, attempts to present the project of 'materialistic historiography' as a practice of writing that does not represent history but performatively reconfigures its course, inscriptions, futures.

Butler, Judith. *Bodies That Matter: On the Discursive Limits of 'Sex'*. New York: Routledge, 1993. Butler refines here the agenda of *Gender Trouble*, which concluded with the assertion of 'gender' as a performative and allosemiotic event not preceded by an ontologically determined 'sex', by examining strategies in which the figure of the 'body' and 'materiality' might continue to operate in a post-metaphysical discourse.

de Man, Paul. *Aesthetic Ideology*, ed. and intro. Andrzej Warminski. Minneapolis, MN: University of Minnesota Press, 1996. Essays engaging the problem of 'aesthetic ideology', the manner in which traditional reading tends to perform a hermeneutic relapse from the actual textual occurrence – compelling an altered approach to categories of agency, cognition, the 'human' and history referenced to a 'materiality of inscription'.

Derrida, Jacques. *Specters of Marx: The State of the Debt, the Work of Mourning, and the New International*, trans. Peggy Kamuf, intro. Bernd Magnus and Stephen Cullenberg. New York: Routledge, 1994. Derrida's rereading of the Marxian legacy, through the figure of a 'messianism without the messianic', an attempt to reclaim the 'spirit' of Marx's concern for modes of intervention within a broader 'politics of memory' rooted in programmes and textual events.

Jameson, Fredric. *Postmodernism, or, The Cultural Logic of Late Capitalism*. Durham, NC: Duke University Press, 1991. A powerful and influential continuation of variant materialist strategies to engage the contradictions of late capitalism in panoramic investigations of cultural and critical studies under the rubric referenced as 'postmodernism'.

SUPPLEMENTARY BIBLIOGRAPHY

Althusser, Louis. *Lenin and Philosophy and Other Essays*, trans. B. Brewster. New York: Monthly Review, 1971.

Apter, Emily S. and William Pietz (eds). *Fetishism as Cultural Discourse*. Ithaca, NY: Cornell University Press, 1993.

Aristotle. *Metaphysics*, trans. Richard Hope. Ann Arbor, MI: University of Michigan Press, 1960.

Benjamin, Walter. *Illuminationen*. Frankfurt: Suhrkamp, 1961.

Benjamin, Walter. *Ursprung des deutschen Trauerspiels*. Frankfurt: Suhrkamp, 1963.

Benjamin, Walter. *The Origin of German Tragic Drama*, trans. J. Osborne. London: NLB, 1977.

Bergson, Henri. *Matter and Memory*. New York: Zone Books, 1988.

Bloch, Ernst et al. *Aesthetics and Politics*, trans. Harry Zohn. London: Verso, 1980.

Butler, Judith. *Gender Trouble*. New York: Routledge, 1990.

Cadava, Eduardo. *Words of Light: Theses on the Photography of History*. Princeton, NJ: Princeton University Press, 1997.

Cochran, Terry. *Twilight of the Literary: Figures of Thought in the Age of Print*. Cambridge, MA: Harvard University Press, 2001.

Cohen, Tom. *Ideology and Inscription: 'Cultural Studies' after Benjamin, de Man, and Bahktin*. Cambridge: Cambridge University Press, 1998.

Cohen, Tom and Barbara Cohen, J. Hillis Miller and Andrzej Warminski (eds). *Material Events: Paul de Man and the Afterlife of Theory*. Minneapolis, MN: University of Minneapolis, 2001.

Davis, Paul and John Gribbin. *The Matter Myth: Towards 21st Century Science*. Harmondsworth: Penguin, 1991.

de Man, Paul. *The Resistance to Theory*, foreword Wlad Godzich. Minneapolis, MN: University of Minnesota Press, 1986.

Derrida, Jacques. *On the Name*, ed. Thomas Dutoit, trans. David Wood, John P. Leavey Jr and Ian McLeod. Stanford, CA: Stanford University Press, 1995.

Ezell, Margaret, J. M. O'Keeffe and Katherine O'Brien (eds). *Cultural Artifacts and the Production of Meaning: The Page, the Image, and the Body*. Ann Arbor, MI: University of Michigan Press, 1994.

Faulkner, William. *Go Down, Moses*. Vintage: New York, 1973.
Haraway, Donna Jeanne. *Simians, Cyborgs, and Women: The Reinvention of Nature*. New York: Routledge, 1991.
Hennessy, Rosemary and Chrys Ingraham (eds). *Materialist Feminism: A Reader in Class, Difference, and Women's Lives*. New York: Routledge, 1997.
Irigaray, Luce. *This Sex Which Is Not One*, trans. Catherine Porter. Ithaca, NY: Cornell University Press, 1985.
Kittler, Friedrich A. *Literature, Media, Information Systems*. Amsterdam: G+B Arts International, 1997.
Marx, Karl and Friedrich Engels. *The German Ideology: Including Theses on Feuerbach and Introduction to the Critique of Political Economy*. Amherst, NY: Prometheus Books, 1998.
Miller, J. Hillis. *Black Holes*. Stanford, CA: Stanford University Press, 1999.
Montag, Warren. '"The Soul is the Prison of the Body": Althusser and Foucault, 1970–75'. *Yale French Studies*, 88, 1995, 53–77.
Moser, Paul K. and J. D. Trout (eds). *Contemporary Materialism: A Reader*. New York: Routledge, 1995.
Ronell, Avital. *The Telephone Book: Technology, Schizophrenia, Electric Speech*. Lincoln, NE: University of Nebraska Press, 1989.
Scarry, Elaine. *The Body in Pain: The Making and Unmaking of the World*. New York: Oxford University Press, 1985.
Spivak, Gayatri Chakravorty. *A Critique of Postcolonial Reason: Toward a History of the Vanishing Present*. Cambridge, MA: Harvard University Press, 1999.
Sprinker, Michael (ed.). *Ghostly Demarcations*. New York: Verso, 1999.
Truffaut, François. *Hitchcock*. New York: Simon & Schuster, 1967; rev. edn. 1984.
Voloshinov, V. N. *Marxism and the Philosophy of Language*, trans. I. R. Titunik and L. Matejka. New York: Seminar Press, 1973.
Weber, Samuel. *Mass Mediauras: Form, Technics, Media*. Stanford, CA: Stanford University Press, 1996.

NOTES

1. *Mnemotechnic* is here used to suggest the manner in which memory itself is connected entirely to systems of marks, traces, writing, archives or regimes that implicitly organize and programme not only sensation and reference but cultural truths, reference and so on. As a technic, something 'material' in the sense of being associable with exterior marking-systems, it is a site that can be addressed as open to disinscription and reinscription.
2. For one recent account of the 'material' basis for the transformation of an era of the Book into that of teletechnological media, see Terry Cochran, *Twilight of the Literary: Figures of Thought in the Age of Print* (2001).
3. Stuart Sim, in his contribution to this volume on 'Chaos Theory, Complexity Theory and Literary Criticism', references Davis and Gribbin's *The Matter Myth: Towards 21st Century Science*, to address the 'death of materialism' (1991, 2) and its impact on Marxist criticism: 'The death of materialism is not good news for Marxism, which still essentially adheres to a mechanistic world view, with broadly determinable patterns of cause and effect, and whatever undermines Marxist philosophy also undermines Marxist critical theory, the authority of which derives from the philosophy in the first instance' (3). The most traditional forms of 'materialist' analysis continue, in this genre, to be mounted as archivally significant political analyses, such as is the case for the linkage of 'Marxism' to feminism in Hennessy and Ingraham's collection, *Materialist Feminism: A Reader in Class, Difference, and Women's Lives* (1997).
4. For a recent account of one 'material' basis for the transformation of an era of the Book into that of teletechnological media, see Terry Cochran, *Twilight of the Literary: Figures of Thought in the Age of Print* (2001).

5. When Benjamin speaks in his essay on 'Translation' of turning 'the symbolizing into the symbolized' (Benjamin, 1968, 8), he implies that (a)material linguistic traces have been as if raised from the lower or servant position to a vortex of signification.

6. In *Gender Trouble*, Butler critiques Foucault's invocation of inscription, to single out conception that takes a 'body' for granted that precedes the field of cultural inscription, a Foucault who 'points to the constancy of cultural inscription as a "single drama" that acts on the body . . . By maintaining a body prior to its cultural inscription, Foucault appears to assume a materiality prior to signification and form' (1990, 128). Butler critiques Irigaray's appropriation of the Platonic *Khora* to bring the figure of matter together with its inherent pun on mater, or female figuration, in the same vein (1990, 46–8). For an inverse take on *Khora* from the *Timaeus*, where 'materiality' emerges as a figure for a site of preoriginary inscription, a matter that is no mater, or mother, see Jacques Derrida's *Khora* in *On the Name* (Derrida, 1995). For a valuable interpretation of Butler's contribution at this juncture, see the extended treatment of her work in this volume's chapter on 'Gender and Trans-gender Studies', by Sarah Gamble.

7. A precursor of this tradition coming out of or citing Marxian thought, in which the materiality of differential signs is expounded, would be Voloshinov's *Marxism and the Philosophy of Language* (1973) – where the term 'sign' is both evacuated (being without inside or out, signified or signifier as such) and returns as a tropological place-holder. The place of this work within the Bakhtinian authorship helps explain the possibility of reading Bakhtin as a proto-Benjaminian project.

8. This phrase invokes the destructuration of received temporal models when the structure of the promise (that does not arrive), essentially that of radical performativity, is deployed to rethink the problematic of the event. For a series of counter-statements, and discussions, surrounding Derrida's rereading of Marx see Michael Sprinker's collection, *Ghostly Demarcations* (1999).

9. How, Derrida asks in 'The Typewriter Ribbon', 'is one to reconcile with the machine a thinking of the event (the real, undeniable, inscribed, singular event, of an always essentially traumatic type' (Cohen et al., 2001, 336).

10. For one use of the figure 'black hole' as a trope for where the trace of the material may appear known through a representational implosion and absence, rather than a promised referent, see Hillis Miller's *Black Holes* (1999).

11. One may think of the 'materiality' of language in the manner that Benjamin conceives, in his 'Task of the Translator', of a 'pure language' or *reine Sprache*, an inter-space of all supposed 'mono' languages (Benjamin, 1968, 69–83). 'Pure language' would, then, be the opposite of idealized meaning, indeed void of 'meaning', evoking instead a materiality-effect of all traces and bearers of mnemonic effect, such as marks and sound and inscriptions.

12. The 'movement', or 'passage', is presented as from 'cognition' or figuration to 'the materiality of something that actually happens, that actually . . . occurs materially' (132). This movement as if away from figuration or systems of tropes occurs by way of what de Man terms an 'epistemological critique of tropes' (de Man, 1996, 133): that is, in 'Kant and Schiller', positioning a reading outside of the humanist or Schillerian models of relapse from a Kant whose 'materialism [is] much more radical than what can be conveyed by such terms as "realism" or "empiricism"' (133). This 'relapse' is 'a kind of reinscription of the performative in a tropological system of cognition again' (133). The 'human' for de Man is not a given but a phantom by-product of this structural hermeneutic relapse before (or after) a material event (a mnemonic intervention in the archive), hence reading by inscription continues to use the term 'material' to indicate the non-human, or a perspective from which 'there is, in a very radical sense, no such thing as the human' (de Man, 1986, 96).

13. Only now it would be foregrounded, raised to the order of a signified in a process in which the signified is not *represented* (if anything, the signifier or 'symbolizing' is dissolved along with the bi-partite Saussurean model of 'sign'). The logic of

'allegory' that Benjamin develops as another nomadic assault on this transformation of programmes must be understood as other than representational – that is, a movement that negates what it represents, alters its own archival reserve (itself), in a process initially destructive. As Benjamin puts it in the *Trauerspiel*: '(Allegory) means precisely the *non-existence* of what it (re)presents' [*Und zwar bedeutet es genau das Nichtsein dessen, was es vorstellt*] (1977, 233; 1963, 265).

14. A further unpacking of the title 'Pantaloon in Black' would focus on the pantaloons, leg-trousers, in which the echo of *panta* (all) is heard across a serial use of 'panting' in the text. This isolation of the syllable-word-sound panta migrates, too, into the *pensere* of thought (confirmed by Rider's final reported words: 'Ah just cant quit thinking' (159)) and the *phainesthai* of appearance, phantasm, phenomenalization. Such a reading might suggest that, within the pantomimetology of the text read as performative event (in 'Faulkner', in the canon and archive virtually, and so on), what the writing pursues is a reinscription of the laws of phenomenality parallel to the destruction of an entire history (of which the author, 'Faulkner', is also a product).

15. For an important reading of the technicity of 'light' and photography in a Benjaminian vein, see Eduardo Cadava, *Words of Light: Theses on the Photography of History* (1997).

NOTES ON CONTRIBUTORS

Tom Cohen, a philosophical critic of language, cinema and cultural politics, is the author of *Anti-Mimesis* and *Ideology and Inscription: 'Cultural Studies' after Benjamin, de Man and Bakhtin*, as well the editor of *Material Events: Paul de Man and the Afterlife of Theory* and *Jacques Derrida and the Humanities*. He is also the author of *Re-Marking Hitchcock* (Johns Hopkins, forthcoming) and *Hitchcock's Black Sun* (forthcoming).

Claire Colebrook teaches English literature at the University of Edinburgh. She is the author of *New Literary Histories*, *Ethics and Representation*, *Gilles Deleuze* and *Distant Voices: Irony in the Work of Philosophy*.

Sarah Gamble is Senior Lecturer in English at the University of Sunderland. She is the author of *Angela Carter: Writing from the Front Line* and editor of *The Routledge Companion to Feminism and Postfeminism* and *Angela Carter: A Reader's Guide to Essential Criticism*.

Stacy Gillis completed her PhD on 'Popular Modernisms and British Detective Fiction' at the University of Exeter, where she is currently a Research Fellow in Cyberculture.

Tace Hedrick is Assistant Professor of English and Women's Studies at the University of Florida, where she teaches US Latino/a and Chicana/o literature, feminist theory and women's studies courses. She has contributed articles to journals such as *Latin American Literary Review*, *Luso-Brazilian Review* and *Critique: Studies in Contemporary Fiction*, and has essays ranging from Latin American to US Latina subjects in collections such as *Footnotes: On Shoes* and *Primitivism and Identity in Latin America: Essays on Art, Literature, and Culture*. She is finishing her manuscript, entitled *Mestizo Modern: Race, Nation, and Identity in Frida Kahlo, Cesar Vallejo, Gabriela Mistral, and Diego Rivera*. Professor Hedrick's present work explores the reinvention of a sense of history in the Chicano and Latino civil rights movements of the 1960s and 1970s.

Debra Walker King is an Associate Professor of English at the University of Florida, where she teaches African-American literature, American literature and Womanist theory. She is the author of several essays and one book, *Deep Talk: Reading African American Literary Names*, and is contributing editor for a collection of essays, *Body Politics and the Fictional Double*. Her present work includes an in-depth study of African-Americans and the culture of pain.

Sudesh Mishra has taught at universities in Fiji, Australia and Scotland. The author of a number of books, including *Preparing Faces: Modernism and Indian Poetry in English* (criticism), *Tandava* (poetry) and *Ferringhi* (play), Sudesh currently lives in Suva. His most recent book is *Diaspora and the Difficult Art of Dying*.

David Punter has held Chairs at the Chinese University of Hong Kong and the University of Stirling, Scotland; he is now Professor of English at the University of Bristol. His published books include *The Literature of Terror; Romanticism and Ideology*, with David Aers and Jonathan Cook; *Blake, Hegel and Dialectic; The Hidden Script; Introduction to Contemporary Cultural Studies* (ed.); *William Blake: Selected Poetry and Prose* (ed.); *The Romantic Unconscious; William Blake: The New Casebook (ed.); Gothic Pathologies: Spectral Readings*, with Glennis Byron (ed.); *A Companion to the Gothic* (ed.); *Writing the Passions; Postcolonial Imaginings; Writing in the Twenty-First Century*.

Kate Rigby is a Senior Lecturer in German Studies and Comparative Literature at Monash University, Australia. She has published widely in the areas of German studies, feminist and ecofeminist thought, ecocriticism and ecospirituality. Her books include *Transgressions of the Feminine: Tragedy, Enlightenment and the Figure of Woman in Classical German Drama* and (with Silke Beinssen-Hesse) *Out of the Shadows: Contemporary German Feminist Theory*, and she is currently researching a monograph on romanticism, ecology and the poetics of place to be published by the University Press of Virginia. Together with Freya Mathews and Sharron Pfueller, she is co-editor of the journal *PAN (Philosophy Activism Nature)*.

Stuart Sim is Professor of English Studies at the University of Sunderland. He has published widely on recent critical and cultural theory, as well as on seventeenth- and eighteenth-century prose fiction. His most recent books are *Contemporary Continental Philosophy: The New Scepticism; Post-Marxism: An Intellectual History* and *Lyotard and the Inhuman*.

Phillip E. Wegner is an Associate Professor of English at the University of Florida, where he teaches modern literature, narrative, critical theory and cultural studies. His book, *Imaginary Communities: Utopia, the Nation and the Spatial Histories of Modernity*, has been recently published by the University of California Press. He is currently at work on a new project, looking at the responses to globalization in contemporary science fiction, sections of which have already appeared in the journals *Rethinking Marxism* and *The Comparatist*, and the volume, *World Bank Literature*.

Julian Wolfreys is an Associate Professor with the Department of English at the University of Florida. He is the author and editor of numerous books and articles, including, most recently, *Victorian Hauntings: Spectrality, Gothic, the Uncanny and Literature* and *Readings: Acts of Close Reading in Literary Theory*. His other books include: (with Jeremy Gibson) *Peter Ackroyd: The Ludic and Labyrinthine Text*; *Writing London: The Trace of the Urban Text from Blake to Dickens*; *The Rhetoric of Affirmative Resistances*; *Deconstruction•Derrida*; and *Being English: Narratives, Idioms, and Performances of National Identity from Coleridge to Trollope*.

Kenneth Womack is Assistant Professor of English at Penn State University's Altoona College, where he specializes in twentieth-century British literature. He serves as editor of *Interdisciplinary Literary Studies: A Journal of Criticism and Theory* and as co-editor of Oxford University Press's *Year's Work in English Studies*. He is the author and editor of several volumes, including (with Todd Davis) *Mapping the Ethical Turn: A Reader in Ethics, Culture, and Literary Theory* and *Postwar Academic Fiction: Satire, Ethics, Community*.

Frederick Young is a PhD candidate in English at the University of Florida specializing in Critical Theory and New Media. He is currently working on his dissertation, 'Diogenes, Perversion and Performance Art: The Surface Ethics of the New Media', and recently completed a fellowship as Artist-in-Residence at the Atlantic Center for the Arts.

INDEX

Readings

Acts of Close Reading in Literary Theory

Julian Wolfreys

May 2000   192pp   Pb   0 7486 1352 8   £16.95

"Julian Wolfreys writes like an accessible Derrida. His achievement in *Readings* is a remarkable illumination of the often impenetrable relation of reading to questions of responsibility, guilt, political choice, democracy, resistance and performativity. There are few critics who combine complexity and exposition with such ease, or who can weave such an efficient summary of contemporary debates on the ethics of reading into such a subtle performance of their own as Wolfreys."
Mark Currie, University of Westminster

"Somehow – I wish I knew how he did it – Julian Wolfreys manages to write on the most intricate and subtle topics with something approaching perfect lucidity. He is clear; he is funny; he is right. This gentle and brilliant exploration of what reading can mean and what it can do is conducted with the kind of assurance and ease one associates with Maria Callas, with Pele, with Groucho Marx: a great pro working with such lubricated grace it looks like play. I certainly have never learned so much from a book, nor had such a fine time doing it."
James R. Kincaid, Aerol Arnold Professor of English, University of Southern California

"I think that *Readings* is a very welcome and even urgent book. A fine pedagogical sense allows Wolfreys to represent clearly and elegantly rather obscure or difficult texts building slowly a critical mosaic through a collage of exemplary readings. Julian Wolfreys is a sharp and astute literary critic who remains aware that literature cannot be reduced to context, history, or philosophy."
Jean-Michel Rabaté, Department of English, University of Pennsylvania

Through a series of short essays, *Readings* traces the consideration given to the act of close reading in literary criticism and theory over the last thirty years.

Focusing on short passages from a number of critical works, including those by Barthes, Cixous, de Man, Derrida, Foucault, Kristeva, Lacan and J. Hillis Miller amongst others, the essays enact close readings of the trope of reading - its movements and performances in each of the passages in question - so as to offer a more detailed comprehension of the nature of reading, and the ways in which critical thinking has transformed our understanding of what it means to read.

Readings addresses in a lively and engaging manner the varying rhythms and articulations made possible through the careful tracing of the process of critical reading which literary theory has made available.

Order from
Marston Book Services, PO Box 269, Abingdon, Oxon OX14 4YN
Tel 01235 465500 • Fax 01235 465555
Email: direct.order@marston.co.uk

Visit our website www.eup.ed.ac.uk

All details correct at time of printing but subject to change without notice

Literary Theories
A Reader and Guide

Edited by **Julian Wolfreys**

June 1999 672pp
Hb 0 7486 1213 0 £52.50 • Pb 0 7486 1214 9 £16.95

Literary Theories: A Reader and Guide is the first reader and introductory guide in one volume. Bringing together theoretically orientated readings by leading exponents of literary theory with lucid introductions, the book offers the student reader a foundation textbook in literary theory. Divided into 12 sections covering structuralism, feminism, marxism, reader-response theory, psychoanalysis, deconstruction, post-structuralism, postmodernism, new historicism, postcolonialism, gay studies and queer theory, and cultural studies, *Literary Theories* introduces the reader to the most challenging and engaging aspects of critical studies in the humanities today. Each section contains several influential texts that provide discussion of theoretical positions and striking examples of close readings of various works of literature from a number of perspectives. The introductions introduce the theory in question, discuss its main currents, give cross-references to other theories, and contextualise the readings that follow. An indispensable aid to understanding theory, *Literary Theories* is a significant introduction to theoretical approaches to literature.

- Unique combination of an anthology of core texts and a thorough introductory guide.   Each of the 12 sections contains:
  - Several key texts
  - An accessible 5000 word introduction
- Texts selected for their coverage of themes (ie questions of language, genre, the nature of reading, race and gender) and authors (from Shakespeare to Virginia Woolf)
- Three bibliographies: an annotated bibliography introducing the reader to the arguments of influential texts in each field, a supplementary reading list and a list of works cited

"For those to whom this field of academic life is a vast mystery or for those to whom its writings are a way of life, this collection will be equally useful."
Contemporary Review

Order from
Marston Book Services, PO Box 269, Abingdon, Oxon OX14 4YN
Tel 01235 465500 • Fax 01235 465555
Email: direct.order@marston.co.uk

Visit our website www.eup.ed.ac.uk

All details correct at time of printing but subject to change without notice

Introducing Literary Theories
A Guide and Glossary

Julian Wolfreys

June 2001   336pp   Pb   0 7486 1483 4   £14.95

Introducing Literary Theories is an ideal introduction for those coming to literary theory for the first time. It provides an accessible introduction to the major theoretical approaches in chapters covering: Bakhtinian Criticism, Structuralism, Feminist Theory, Marxist Literary Theories, Reader-Response Theories, Psychoanalytic Criticism, Deconstruction, Poststructuralism, New Historicism, Cultural Materialism, Postcolonial Theory, Gay Studies/ Queer Theories, Cultural Studies and Postmodernism.

A table of contents arranged by theoretical method and a second arranged by key texts offer the reader alternative pathways through the volume and a general introduction, which traces the history and importance of literary theory, complete the introductory material. In each of the following chapters, the authors provide a clear presentation of the theory in question and notes towards a reading of a key text to help the student understand both the methodology and the practice of literary theory. The texts used for illustration include: *In Memoriam A. H. H.*, *Middlemarch*, *Mrs Dalloway*, *Paradise Lost*, *A Portrait of the Artist as a Young Man*, *Prospero's Books*, *The Swimming Pool Library* and *The Tempest*. Every chapter ends with a set of questions for further consideration, an annotated bibliography and a supplementary bibliography while a glossary of critical terms completes the book.

Derived and adapted from the successful foundation textbook, *Literary Theories: A Reader and Guide*, *Introducing Literary Theories* is a highly readable, self-contained and comprehensive guide that succeeds in making contemporary theory easily understandable.

Each chapter provides:
- An overview of the theory
- Notes towards readings of canonical literary texts
- Questions for further consideration
- An annotated bibliography
- A supplementary bibliography

Key Features
- Complex ideas are clearly explained
- A double table of contents provides different ways of navigating through the volume
- Coverage of the theories is balanced with analysis of key texts
- Questions at the end of each chapter direct the reader to consider further theoretical matters and to make theoretically informed readings of literary texts
- Includes full guidance about further reading
- Offers an ideal guide for students at all levels who are new to literary theory as well as general readers
- Provides a Glossary of critical terms for easy reference

Order from
**Marston Book Services, PO Box 269, Abingdon, Oxon OX14 4YN
Tel 01235 465500 • Fax 01235 465555
Email: direct.order@marston.co.uk**

Visit our website www.eup.ed.ac.uk

All details correct at time of printing but subject to change without notice

Key Concepts in Literary Theory

Julian Wolfreys, Ruth Robbins and Kenneth Womack

October 2001   224pp   Pb   0 7486 1519 9   £9.99

Key Concepts in Literary Theory provides the student of literature with clearly presented and authoritative definitions of some of the most significant and often difficult to grasp terms and concepts currently used in the study of literary theory. It brings together terms from many areas of literary theory, including cultural studies, psychoanalysis, poststructuralism, marxist and feminist literary studies, postcolonialism, and other areas of identity politics with which literary studies concerns itself.

In addition, the volume provides accessible discussions of the main areas of literary, critical and cultural study, supported by bibliographies and a chronology of major critics whose work has informed critical studies of literature today, also accompanied by bibliographies.

Features

- Provides clear definitions of 300 terms in literary theory and criticism
- Provides readers with a range of essential literary concepts and period terms, including 'irony', 'existentialism', 'symbolism' and 'modernism' and concentrates on literary criticism and theory, from 'aporia' and 'liminality' to 'phallocentrism' and 'simulacra'
- Reflects contemporary literary theory's rapidly changing terminology and looks to the future shape of literary theory in entries from 'technoscience' and 'cyberwar' to 'mnemotechnic' and 'digitality'
- Includes terms such as 'gender parody', 'cyborg' and 'masquerade' to show that literary theory has made connections with gender studies and with media and popular culture
- Provides two accompanying reference sections:
  - Areas of Literary, Critical and Cultural study, which provides definitions of the significant movements and critical approaches within twentieth-century critical study, from Archetypal Criticism to Textual Criticism, each of which is accompanied by a bibliography of suggested reading
  - A Chronology of Critics, which covers thinkers from Karl Marx to Judith Butler, each entry being accompanied by a brief bibliography

Key Concepts in Literary Theory is an indispensable reference work for anyone interested in the complexities of literary, critical and cultural theory.

Order from
Marston Book Services, PO Box 269, Abingdon, Oxon OX14 4YN
Tel 01235 465500 • Fax 01235 465555
Email: direct.order@marston.co.uk

Visit our website www.eup.ed.ac.uk

All details correct at time of printing but subject to change without notice